Secession and Security

A VOLUME IN THE SERIES

Cornell Studies in Security Affairs

Edited by Robert J. Art, Robert Jervis, and Stephen M. Walt

A list of titles in this series is available at cornellpress.cornell.edu.

Secession and Security

*Explaining State Strategy
against Separatists*

AHSAN I. BUTT

Cornell University Press

Ithaca and London

Cornell University Press gratefully acknowledges receipt of a
subvention from the Schar School of Policy and Government, George
Mason University, which aided in the publication of this book.

First published 2017 by Cornell University Press

Printed in the United States of America

Library of Congress Cataloging-in-Publication Data
Names: Butt, Ahsan I., 1983– author.
Title: Secession and security : explaining state strategy against
     separatists / Ahsan I. Butt.
Description: Ithaca : Cornell University Press, 2017. | Series: Cornell
     studies in security affairs | Includes bibliographical references
     and index.
Identifiers: LCCN 2017007187 (print) | LCCN 2017011382 (ebook) |
     ISBN 9781501713965 (epub/mobi) | ISBN 9781501713958 (pdf) |
     ISBN 9781501713941 (cloth : alk. paper)
Subjects: LCSH: Separatist movements—Case studies. | Secession—
     Case studies. | Internal security—Case studies.
Classification: LCC JC327 (ebook) | LCC JC327 .B87 2017 (print) |
     DDC 320.1/5—dc23
LC record available at https://lccn.loc.gov/2017007187

Cornell University Press strives to use environmentally responsible
suppliers and materials to the fullest extent possible in the publishing
of its books. Such materials include vegetable-based, low-VOC inks
and acid-free papers that are recycled, totally chlorine-free, or partly
composed of nonwood fibers. For further information, visit our
website at cornellpress.cornell.edu.

Contents

Illustrations

Tables

Figures

Maps

Acknowledgments

It may not look like it, but I have had a lot of help writing this book. In January 2009, I sat with two friends, Rose Kelanic and Lindsey O'Rourke, at the University of Chicago's business school cafeteria to discuss my ideas. I knew I wanted to focus on why states are so reluctant to cede territory to separatists, and I knew existing research was not satisfactory, but that was about all I knew. The prospect of outlining even a question, let alone an answer, was daunting. Over panini and chips, Lindsey piped up and said (something to the effect of): "Why don't you focus on how state repression is caused by the external threat of the movement?" Why don't I, indeed.

The eight years since have been devoted to sorting out how, why, and the extent to which state strategies against separatist movements are tied to security concerns. In those eight years, I have been fortunate to receive generous support from the Mellon Foundation, the American Council of Learned Societies, the United States Institute of Peace (USIP), and the Belfer Center for Science and International Affairs at the Harvard Kennedy School. It is difficult to write without adequate financial support, and these institutions ensured I had it.

While money was important, the people who helped me write this book were more so. At Chicago, I was fortunate to find people who challenged, cajoled, intimidated, and inspired me. John Mearsheimer was the father figure I could never satisfy (not alone there—just ask any Chicago student from the past thirty years), Paul Staniland the older cousin whom I wanted to emulate (good luck with that), and Duncan Snidal the friendly uncle from Canada (unsolicited advice for graduate students: have at least one good cop on your committee). I will never be able to repay their attention to me and my work, from reading chapters to socializing me in the ways of academia, from providing guidance to putting the fear of god—or the job market—in me. I do hope, however, that a copy of this book suffices as a token.

I was also lucky to be surrounded by brilliant and generous students at Chicago. Whether it was reading a draft before a workshop presentation, or drowning shame and humiliation at Jimmy's after such a presentation, I consider myself fortunate that my time at Chicago overlapped with Adam Dean, Gene Gerzhoy, Eric Hundman, Burak Kadercan, Morgan Kaplan, Rose Kelanic, Adam Levine-Weinberg, Chad Levinson, Sarah Parkinson, Negeen Pegahi, and Lindsey O'Rourke. They were great colleagues but even better friends. Finally, Kathy Anderson was a pillar not just for me but for all graduate students in the department—a source of information, guidance, strategy, and warmth.

Two separate sojourns at the Harvard Kennedy School, one in 2011–12 and another in 2014–15, helped me complete this book manuscript. At Harvard, I received valuable mentorship from Sean Lynn-Jones, Martin Malin, Steve Miller, and Stephen Walt, while Susan Lynch taught me the true meaning of administrative efficiency. I was also surrounded by some of the best and brightest in IR and security studies. I especially learned from, and enjoyed the company of, Aisha Ahmad, Michael Beckley, Sarah Bush, Jennifer Dixon, Trevor Findlay, Kelly Greenhill, Jennifer Keister, Peter Krause, Josh Shrifinson, and Melissa Willard-Foster.

Since arriving at George Mason University in 2012, I have received tremendous support from leaders in my academic unit, whether it was Priscilla Regan at the erstwhile Department of Public and International Affairs, or Ming Wan and Mark Rozell at the Schar School of Policy and Government. Each of them has done everything possible to help me conduct and disseminate research. My GMU colleagues such as Colin Dueck, Mike Hunzeker, Mark Katz, Greg Koblentz, and Ed Rhodes in IR, or Bassam Haddad, Mariely Lopez-Santana, Peter Mandaville, Eric McGlinchey, Robert McGrath, Matt Scherer, and Jennifer Victor from the school at large, have helped create a first-rate research environment and made me feel at home. I have also been fortunate to have the likes of Janice Cohen and other staff ensure that I am never *too* confused about administrative procedures.

Aside from those at Chicago, Harvard, and George Mason, several friends and colleagues kindly read drafts of chapters, offered critiques, and pointed ways forward. I am grateful for the time and attention of Christopher Clary, Arman Grigoryan, Umair Javed, Shashank Joshi, Sameer Lalwani, Janet Lewis, Farooq Nomani, Paul Poast, Shahid Saeed, and Niloufer Siddiqui. I owe an especially weighty debt to Robert Art, Kathleen Cunningham, Harris Mylonas, and Manny Teitelbaum, who attended my book workshop in the fall of 2014 and set me on the track I needed to be on; their fingerprints, I hope they can see, are all over this book. Audiences at the annual meetings of the American Political Science Association, the International Studies Association, and the Midwest Political Science Association, as well as seminars at Chicago, Harvard, Lehigh, MIT, Tufts, and USIP, played a crucial role in hammering my ideas into shape.

Research for this book led me to talk to and learn from many people, not just scholars in my field. I cannot possibly list each of my interviewees here, not least because some spoke off the record, but I want to underline how crucial each one of those conversations was, and how immensely grateful I am to all the journalists, analysts, students, academics, artists, politicians, party workers, ex-cops, ex-soldiers, bureaucrats, businessmen, diplomats, negotiators, and activists who made time to talk to me. Having my world-view and scholarship shaped by those infinitely more knowledgeable was one of the most rewarding experiences of writing this book. Alongside these interviews, my archival work in the periodicals room at the Library of Congress in Washington, DC, as well as the National Archives in College Park, Maryland, could not have been possible without the patience and kindness of the staff. I never felt more like a scholar than when I was at the LOC or the archives.

Transforming this book from an imperfect submission to a less-imperfect publication was entirely down to the tireless efforts of the reviewers and editors at Cornell University Press. I am especially grateful to the anonymous reviewers whose incisive and careful criticisms helped me deliver a significantly better scholarly product. I also consider myself very fortunate to have had the opportunity to work with Roger Haydon and experience firsthand his patience, aid, and responsiveness, while Karen Hwa's editorial attention left me both deeply impressed and soundly confident that my work was in good hands. As a first-time author, I could not have asked for a better team to work, or be affiliated, with.

Finally, this book simply would not have been possible without the love and support of my family. For as long as I can remember, Amma and Abba have emphasized the value of education. They gave me everything. Abid, my brother, and Maheen, my sister-in-law, are our family's rocks, regardless of how many waves crash into them. My wife, Insiya, is the strongest person I know. No matter how much, or how many times, I wanted to quit, she would not let me. She is my best friend and my whole world, and this book exists only because I had her to lean on for the entire time I wrote it.

And then there is my brother Asim. No one was prouder of me. He painted, he said, to create what it is he wanted to see, to fill an absence in the world. But what of the void he left? I dedicate this book to his memory, crushed that he will never read it.

Secession and Security

Introduction

Ins and Outs of Separatist War

On the night of March 25, 1971, thousands of soldiers fanned out in Dhaka and other population centers of East Pakistan, the Pakistan military intent on crushing the Bengali movement for independence. Operation Searchlight targeted political leaders, students and radicals, unarmed civilians, even women and children. Soldiers attacked universities, raided newspaper offices, and wiped out entire villages. The Pakistan military's brutal repression, designed to keep East Pakistan within the bounds of the state, accomplished precisely the opposite: a grinding nine-month civil war, resulting in the deaths of many hundreds of thousands and the birth of an independent Bangladesh.[1]

Just two decades later, the world witnessed a very different divorce. Slovaks in what was then Czechoslovakia began clamoring for their own state, making their preferences clear in the 1992 election. Rather than use force, however, Czech politicians and leaders politely stepped aside in the face of Slovak nationalism and negotiated the secession of the Slovak Republic without a single shot being fired.[2] In contrast to the extremely high levels of violence that characterize other separatist disputes, the dissolution of Czechoslovakia was almost bizarrely peaceful.

A puzzle then presents itself: why do some states resist independence-seeking movements with repression and violence—such as Sri Lanka in its northern Tamil areas and the Ottoman Empire in Armenia—while others respond with a metaphorical shrug of the shoulders and territorial concessions, seen in the Velvet Divorce of Czechoslovakia or the separation of Norway from Sweden early in the twentieth century? Moreover, why do we see variation *within* states as they calibrate their responses to various independence movements? For instance, why did the Indian state treat Kashmiri separatism more harshly than secessionism in Assam in the 1980s and 1990s, and why was it more violent in Punjab after 1987 than before?

Why deal with some secessionists with the proverbial pen, others with the all-too-literal gun? In this book, I explain states' particular strategies—chosen from a menu of options, ranging from negotiations and concessions, to policing and counterinsurgency, to large-scale violence and repression—when dealing with separatist movements.

I argue that the external security implications of a secessionist movement determine a state's strategy, guiding whether, and how much, it coerces separatists. The choice of coercion turns on the state's fear of future war, or lack thereof. Future war worries states because secession negatively alters the balance of power, with respect to both the secessionist ethnic group and existing state rivals. The ethnic group poses a greater threat to the state after secession than before because of the military, economic, demographic, and legal benefits of statehood. Meanwhile, existing states pose a greater threat after the redrawing of a state's borders because its loss of territory and population axiomatically mean it possesses less material power than before. These large and rapid power shifts set up a commitment problem: why risk graver threats tomorrow if the state is stronger today? As such, if a state fears future war, it will adopt coercion against the secessionists to foreclose the possibility of such threats. Conversely, sanguinity about the future is necessary for the state to consider peaceful concessions, including the granting of full independence. Whether a state coerces separatists, then, depends on whether it believes it will face future war, which in turn depends on two factors. With respect to the seceded ethnic group, the state concludes future war is likely if there is a deep identity division between the group and the central state. With respect to the existing rivals, the state assesses future war as likely if its regional neighborhood has a militarized history, marked by conflict and war.

If the state chooses coercion based on either of these "trip wires," the extent of third-party support for the secessionists determines how much violence the state employs, for both materialist and emotional reasons. Materially, external backing makes the rebel movement stronger, increasing the amount of violence required to defeat it. Emotionally, deep alliances with rivals of the state can lead to pathological violence, fueled by a sense of betrayal. External security, then, is key to understanding both whether, and how much, states coerce secessionists.

Why We Need a Theory of Secessionist Conflict

Most wars today are civil wars, and most civil wars are fought between central governments, on the one hand, and ethno-nationalist groups seeking autonomy or independence, on the other. In the last seven decades, there have been about twice as many nationalist civil wars (ninety-five) as interstate wars of any kind (forty-six),[3] leading to the conclusion that such wars are the "chief source of violence in the world today."[4] Indeed, between 1946 and 2005, the world saw, on average, over twenty-five such conflicts in any given year.[5]

Even within the general category of civil wars, separatist conflicts are deadliest.[6] The primary distinction between so-called ideological and secessionist civil wars is that the latter feature an ethnic and territorial component, in which borders are contested.[7] The central question fought over in ideological wars is: which groups are in power? The corresponding question in separatist wars is: which groups are in the state? Peacefully resolving either is a challenging task, but on average, separatist wars tend to last longer.[8] Additionally, they occur slightly more frequently than ideological civil wars.[9] The bottom line is that if scholars and analysts are interested in explaining conflict in international politics, they could do worse than begin with secessionist violence, "one of the central puzzles surrounding civil war,"[10] or indeed war more generally.

War, it goes without saying, is a complex and multifaceted phenomenon, and explaining its trajectory over time is a herculean task. The challenge in studying war—indeed in social science more generally—lies in drawing general lessons about a phenomenon that hinges on a series of contingent factors. We make grand pronouncements about the lessons of World War II, but would we understand the pitfalls of aggressive expansionism differently had Hitler simply obeyed his generals and advanced straight to Moscow upon reaching the Dvina and Dnieper rivers, rather than toward Ukraine and Leningrad? Alternatively, would we remember the Great War as exemplifying trench warfare had the Germans wheeled east rather than west of Paris in the early stages of the Schlieffen Plan's execution, exposing their flank to the French? The overarching point, one that luminaries from Sun Tzu to Clausewitz have noted, is that war is a brutally complex process, and theorizing about its dynamics is devilishly difficult. Consequently, one needs a simplifying approach, and the one I adopt in this book is to focus on the critical junctures in the process that is war.[11] Specifically, I pay special attention to how states respond to separatists at what I term "secessionist moments," when a group's secessionism is made explicit to the central state.

I define secessionism as demands by an ethno-nationalist group for either independence from, or significant regional autonomy within, a modern nation-state.[12] There are two main reasons we would want to cast our definitional net to catch both "full" secessionist as well as regional autonomist movements. First, movements often vacillate between demands for statehood and autonomy based on short-term tactical considerations.[13] Second, gaining significant autonomy, such as when a region has its own police and military forces, or independent economic policy-making power, often proves a very long step toward establishing statehood.[14] Thus state decision makers—and scholars analyzing them—should treat demands for independence as essentially synonymous with those for significant autonomy.

A secessionist moment is when an ethno-nationalist group's demands are expressed in no uncertain terms to the central government. Such secessionist moments can take the form, among others, of an ethnic or regionalist political party winning a landslide election victory; a massive rally, riot, or demonstration that compels fence-sitters to choose sides in favor of those demanding independence; or an assassination, murder, or kidnapping that unites the opposition. A secessionist moment, at bottom, is when an ethno-nationalist group's demands have crystallized into a widely held collective desire for significantly greater autonomy or independence. It forces the incumbent government to make a decision: how do we respond to this?

It is that decision which I investigate. The reason for this focus is that states themselves determine to a large extent—and certainly to a larger extent than the ethno-nationalists—whether a secessionist struggle will be peaceful, violent, or genocidal. About half (75/163, or 46 percent) of all secessionist movements lead to full-blown war.[15] In other situations, states use lighter forms of coercion. In yet others, they may not use force at all. The range of actions available to states, owing to their institutional, legal, political, and military power, is simply wider than it is for nonstate actors. This is not to say that the preferences, constraints, tactics, and goals of the secessionist group are unimportant.[16] Rather, I claim simply that how states respond initially at secessionist moments has great import for how those secessionist movements proceed. If they offer negotiations or concessions, there is little likelihood that the secessionists will escalate to more violence. If they respond with violence, odds are the secessionists will too, setting a spiral in motion. Even the category of "violence" is much too wide. States can use largely discriminate or largely indiscriminate tactics; they can use strategies that rely more on the military than the police or vice versa, each with its own set of implications for a conflict's trajectory. Thus we can learn a great deal about the outbreak and development of ethno-nationalist civil wars by understanding states' decision-making at these secessionist moments. And, in turn, we can learn a great deal about states' decision-making by examining the external security implications of the secessionist movement.

My argument that the international system exerts a tremendous pull on state strategy against secessionists rests on two core insights in international relations (IR). First, the international environment has systematic effects on states' domestic politics.[17] Second, and more directly, states mired in security rivalries worry a great deal about shifts in the balance of power.[18] Indeed, as I emphasize throughout this book, the mere potential for shifts in the future balance of power can cause war.[19]

4

This theory builds on the explosion in research on civil war in the last two decades in IR, comparative politics, and security studies. Generally speaking, civil war researchers exploring violence break down into three camps: those who focus on structural conditions, others who concentrate on rebels and insurgents, and yet others who examine the state, as I do. Each type of scholarship is crucial to understand the whole picture of violence in civil wars.

Structural arguments point to factors correlated with the incidence and dynamics of civil war. These studies identify the broad patterns of internal conflict, explaining which types of states and territories are most likely to experience such wars and why actors' incentives in such contexts often encourage them to use violence.[20] Scholars of rebels and insurgents, meanwhile, study why their use of violence may vary across time and space. For instance, some have argued that civil wars that feature opportunist fighters, motivated by the promise of a share of natural resources or significant state sponsorship, are more likely to see indiscriminate violence than those that are fought by more ideologically committed fighters, since the latter are better placed to practice internal discipline.[21] Others argue that the resources on offer are not singularly determinative; rather, the precise social-organizational context in which insurgents enjoy resource endowments determines their use of violence.[22] Still others examine how movements, organizations, and insurgencies can splinter and how such internal splits can generate violence.[23] Notably, even these scholars that focus on the rebel side of the civil war equation underline the importance of the state, particularly in the most gruesome conflicts.[24] For their part, scholars who focus on states offer different explanations for the circumstances under which states become intensely violent. Some point to state desperation and a lack of viable alternatives as factors that push states to victimize large numbers of people.[25] Others argue that states "see" certain spaces and peoples in particular ways that render some more prone to violence than others.[26] Yet others investigate the role democratic institutions play in curtailing repression against citizens.[27]

Within this broad area of civil war research, several scholars have attempted to theorize state response to secessionism, my central explanatory task in this book. This research, however, overwhelmingly focuses on domestic factors. One dominant school of thought explains the reaction(s) of states to ethno-nationalists with reference to the concepts of reputation, signaling, and deterrence.[28] Scholars from this school argue that by fighting hard against the ethno-nationalist group du jour, and therefore acquiring "hard" reputations, governments can deter future would-be nationalists from even trying to secede.[29] This theory expects ethnically heterogeneous states to fight harder than relatively homogenous—especially binational—states because the former's relative diversity implies a greater number of potential secessionists that need to be deterred.

While logical and a substantial first step in the systematic study of secessionist conflict, the reputation argument has three main flaws. First, the evidence in its favor is mixed; some large-n statistical results are more supportive of this argument than others.[30] Second, the reputation argument underpredicts violence in binational states. While the absence of "other" groups for the state to deter would lead theorists to expect exceedingly peaceful measures by the state, as seen in Canada's or Czechoslovakia's confrontations with secessionist minorities,[31] Sri Lanka and Israel are binational too. Third and most important, it struggles to explain internal variation in state response to secessionism because its independent variable—states' demographic profile—does not change but the outcome— peace versus violence—does. This is problematic because the vast majority (136/163, or 83 percent) of secessionist movements took place in a state experiencing multiple movements. Furthermore, of those 33 "multiple movement" states, 19 (58 percent) sometimes used violence and sometimes did not, leaving aside even finer distinctions within the category of "violence." Internal variation is a big slice of the separatist violence pie.[32]

More recent research has argued that the internal structure of states affects how they respond to self-determination movements. One view is that the number of "veto factions" within a state—those factions that can veto policy change—constrains which states can offer concessions to movements and which cannot. Because states are "consensus-building," concessions can occur only when all relevant factions agree on their advisability. Large numbers of veto players are likely to result in internal deadlock, leaving the state unable to offer concessions. But, interestingly, even low numbers of veto factions make states less likely to offer concessions. The argument forwarded is that a state with few veto factions is a less credible bargainer in the eyes of self-determination movements, and as a result, it foresees that such groups will not place any trust in concessions it offers. Therefore, it does not make any concessions in the first place.[33] Thus there is a proverbial sweet spot of veto factions—about five—where concessions from states are most likely.[34] In other situations, either the state cannot offer concessions, or believing that ethnic groups will not accept them as credible chooses not to do so.[35]

Though the focus on the internal politics and factionalization of states and movements is valuable and a significant advance in conflict studies, this analysis too ignores the role of geopolitics. More important, while the internal structures of self-determination groups assuredly are important determinants of the state opting for concessions or war,[36] the relationship between states' internal structures and their strategies seems murkier, both empirically and theoretically. Empirically, even scholars favoring this argument admit to the more limited effects of the internal structures of states relative to that of groups and concede that their qualitative evidence says little about the role of veto factions in contributing to state strategies.[37] This lack of evidence on the causal mechanisms connecting veto factions to outcomes is made more troubling by the logical problems in the theory connecting the two. While one can easily accept why large numbers of veto factions, and the attendant potential for internal deadlock, may make concessions more difficult,[38] it is difficult to see why a low number of veto factions is similarly damaging to the prospect of concessions.[39] Why would a unitary or centralized state hesitate to make an offer of concessions simply because a group might deem such an offer untrustworthy, a suspicion based on nothing more than the number of veto factions within the state?[40] What would be the cost of having such an offer rejected? Is it even reasonable to expect state leaders to make such fine-tuned calculations, whereby they choose to forego offers of concessions they would have otherwise made because they believe the movement, itself deciding between whether the state has three or five or eight veto factions, would deem such an offer incredible if the number falls below a certain threshold? As such, the claim that there exists a curvilinear relationship between the number of veto factions within a state and the likelihood that it offers concessions requires further substantiation.[41]

Finally, some scholars marry an emphasis on internal institutions to the reputation logic, tracing how the nature of a state's administrative boundaries determines its response to separatists. The claim is that states are liable to allow peaceful secession to regions that represent a "unique" administrative type. By contrast, territories that share administrative status with others could instigate a domino effect were they granted concessions; such secessionist regions thus see resistance from states.[42] While an important contribution to the debate on separatist violence, this argument's treatment of the breakup of colonial empires and modern nation-states as one and the same is problematic. Colonial powers may have split their empires into various units, such that France administered Algeria differently than West Africa, but countries in the modern era are more uniform in how they divide territory, with just one major administrative line creating either provinces, regions, states, or cantons. Since states do not generally create differentiated administrative boundaries as empires did, this argument is less applicable to modern separatist conflict than the independence struggles of native nationalists against colonial rule.[43]

While this literature makes valuable and telling contributions, then, it leaves out a huge factor: the external security ramifications of secession, and how they condition a state's behavior. More generally, recent civil war research has tended to ignore geopolitics, focusing instead on explaining the dynamics of violence in specific local contexts.[44] Such inattention is a mistake. Because security is the most important international goal of states,[45] we miss a great deal by ignoring the bigger picture. Secession dramatically alters the international balance of power facing the rump state in very negative ways, which cannot help but color state responses to separatists. Establishing a new border would imbue a possibly threatening ethnic group with the considerable material, social, and institutional power that accompanies statehood.[46] As evinced by the Ethiopia-Eritrea and Russia-Georgia wars in the last two decades, along with grave tension between neighbors such as Kosovo and Serbia or Sudan and South Sudan or Russia and Ukraine, war between a rump and a seceded state remains a distinct possibility. Additionally, losing substantial territory and population at a stroke considerably weakens a state relative to existing state rivals, who can act opportunistically against the weakened state. Rather than face these (threats of) war against strengthened rivals, the state is better off using coercion. Even the calibration of how much coercion to employ depends on an external factor, third-party support, since such backing makes rebels stronger on the battlefield and decision-makers and security forces more emotional. This typology of coercion—from policing to militarization to collective repression—brings nuance to the view held by most scholars that states merely choose between peaceful concessions and violent denials when dealing with separatists.

Incorporating the external environment in theoretical accounts of state strategy to secessionism also seems reasonable given the ample attention it has received in related inquiries, especially in recent research on nationalism, ethnic conflict, and the creation and destruction of state boundaries.[47] For instance, scholars have found that external conditions are crucial in explaining decisions to assimilate, accommodate, or exclude particular nations or ethnic groups from the political-social fabric of the state.[48] Additionally, research has shown that ethnic cleansing is especially likely when rival states, in an effort to bring about changes to the territorial status quo, form an alliance with an ethnic group on the territory they seek to win.[49] More generally, the international environment often determines how long and bloody a civil war will be.[50] This is especially true when it comes to the involvement of third parties, who upon deciding to intervene in a secessionist conflict,[51] irrevocably change the dynamics of such wars. Under such circumstances, the civil war becomes "nested" under an unstable regional or systemic conflict, making it more intractable.[52] Civil wars that feature third parties are longer, more intense, and less prone to negotiated settlements.[53] In part, this is because third-party support for rebels can affect the calculations of the ethno-nationalist groups and their leaders. Insurgents will become emboldened and radicalized if they perceive that, due to the interventions of outside powers, the balance of power between them and the central governments will shift. Scholars have shown that even the mere prospect of support can lead such groups to adopt more extreme demands.[54] Finally, the external environment also plays a significant role in the (re)drawing of borders on the map,[55] the precise outcome secessionists hope to accomplish. Secessionists' ultimate success in forming states often depends on international relations,[56] and such states do not become fully sovereign unless they are recognized by the international community as such—recognition which is contingent on great power politics.[57]

The importance of international factors allows us to gain greater insights on separatist conflicts both past and present. Consider the Israel-Palestine dispute (chapter 5), a diplomatic and security problem festering for decades. My argument sheds light on how a "liberal" democracy such as Israel can go to the lengths it does to deny statehood to the Palestinians. The hostility of its Arab state neighbors historically, combined with an essentializing of Palestinians that subsumes them under a larger "Arab" identity, means that Israel's decision makers forestall Palestinian statehood, using as much coercion as necessary to do so. Similarly underlining the significance of geopolitical forces, Sudan and Ethiopia supported violent separatism on each other's territory for decades, while the long-running Nagorno-Karabakh dispute is essentially an internal conflict in Azerbaijan wrapped within its interstate rivalry with Armenia.

In addition to clarifying such disputes, this book makes several empirical contributions. First, unlike domestic-variable arguments, the theory I present here is adept at explaining internal variation in states' treatment of ethnic nationalists. Why might a state such as Pakistan treat Bengalis differently from Baloch in their respective quests for independence, merely two years apart? Why would India employ more brutal, indiscriminate tactics in Kashmir than Assam despite facing secessionist movements in both states at the same time? My theory can also account for variation over time: why the Ottoman Empire would treat Armenian nationalists differently in 1915 than in 1908, or why Sikh separatism in Punjab provoked more violence after 1987 than in 1985. Such internal variation is of enormous consequence because most secessionist movements (83 percent) take place in states experiencing more than one such movement, and in turn, most of these "multiple movement" states treat certain groups differently from others. Arguments that center on, say, ethnic heterogeneity struggle to explain why a state with an unchanging demographic profile may behave differently at different times against different groups.

Second, the ability to explain cases of extremely violent separatist conflicts is a strength of my theory. Most of the thirty-three cases of "intense" separatist warfare involve some external component.[58] In Africa, both the Nigeria-Biafra and Ethiopia-Eritrea conflicts featured high levels of support from regional and global powers.[59] The Sudan–South Sudan war had strong external reverberations not just because of Ethiopia's intervention, but also because the seceded state and its former host are on the verge of outright war. The bloodiest separatist conflicts in South Asia—Indian

Kashmir, northern Sri Lanka, and East Pakistan—had significant geopolitical implications, as we shall see later in this book. Long, deadly fights between the Kurds and various states in the Middle East, but especially Iraq, Iran, and Turkey, have been marked by fears of external wrangling. My argument attempts to make sense of why separatist conflicts that have an external angle to them are prone to extremely high levels of violence.

Third, the role of geopolitics in civil conflict is not especially well captured by existing research, much of it characterized by large-n statistical studies based on a few popular datasets. For instance, the widely used PRIO Armed Conflict dataset considers civil wars "internationalized" only when a state fashions its troops in support of domestic rebels; it is impossible given these data to examine the effects of more limited support, such as financial or military aid. I bring a finer-grained and more nuanced understanding of how external support can affect states' decision-making.

Focusing on external security does not just benefit academic research of separatist war but can also serve as a useful guiding principle for policymakers interested in curtailing the death and destruction that such conflicts usually leave in their wake. Understanding the factors that cause some governments to address secessionist demands on the battlefield, as opposed to the negotiating table, is crucial to peace building. Such an understanding would allow interested parties to pursue strategies designed to keep the peace between ethnic groups in a state, and promote stability more generally. Although the international community is often reluctant to interfere in civil conflicts because of concerns about political and legal sovereignty,[60] my research suggests that the roots of fighting within borders often lie outside those borders. This implies that the international community can play a significant role in these conflicts by allaying the fears of states facing separatist movements and providing them with reassurance of their security.

For instance, the international community can make the shift in the balance of power attendant on secessionism more palatable to the rump state by providing defensive guarantees and pledging protection from its military rivals in the future. The international community could tie the promise of security guarantees to good behavior in its dealings with the minority, as part of an explicit quid pro quo. For instance, if the United States had promised Pakistan military aid and a security partnership in 1971, in return for a more measured and less violent policy against the Bengalis, we might never have witnessed the genocide. A contemporary example of such a policy would be American military support of Israel being made contingent on more concessions to the Palestinian independence movement, while providing explicit security guarantees to Israel against state threats, including those from Palestine. A further implication of my study is that as a secessionist conflict brews in a particular country, the international community must restrain the state's geopolitical rivals. These rivals must make explicit and credible guarantees that they will not join forces with the secessionists in any meaningful way, either today or in the near future. This will aid in placating the state and make it less fearful of "encirclement," which often drives the most vicious of responses. A present-day example of such an idealistic policy would be to pressure both India and Pakistan to cease material support for Baloch and Kashmiri separatists respectively.

The research presented here, then, is highly relevant to policymakers who wish to curtail civil violence. In a nutshell, I suggest that the international community must place front and center the motivations of central governments repressing secessionists. It also implies that, as with most conflicts, the time to contain the conflict is before it actually erupts: by guaranteeing the security of the state in the future, the international community can protect the victims of the state in the present. The overarching lesson is: third-party involvement would be most useful in separatist conflicts if it is (a) early, before hostilities have taken place; (b) made contingent, such that exhortations for better treatment of ethnic minorities go hand in hand with security (and possibly other) cooperation with the host state, and (c) aimed at dissuading support for the movement by global or regional rivals of the host state.

Research Design

In this book, I deal with secessionist movements in the twentieth century. I consider any movement as falling within the scope of my argument if it sought to escape the control of a larger state by establishing a state of its own or an autonomous region. There were 163 such movements after 1946, a start date chosen because most datasets on political violence have little reliability before that date. I ignore decolonization movements, which I believe should not be conflated with secessionist movements in modern nation-states. Any anticolonial movement that was geographically cut off from its target by a substantial body of water,[61] as was the case for African and Asian movements against British, French, Portuguese, and Dutch rule, was not considered. With geographic contiguity in mind, I include in the dataset the dissolution of the Soviet Union, which some scholars consider an "empire,"[62] and conduct a detailed examination of the Ottoman Empire's treatment of its Armenian minority (chapter 5).

METHODOLOGY

As social scientists have discussed, case-study research has many virtues, including greater confidence in the theory's internal validity, a greater attentiveness to causal mechanisms, a deeper and more detailed accounting of empirical variation, and appropriateness for questions for which data and information are incommensurable across a population of cases[63]— assuredly a characteristic of separatist conflicts, some of which are significantly more opaque than others. It is for these reasons that my primary method of empirical research is historical. Much of the literature on civil war and secessionist violence employs quantitative methods and large-n datasets. Such research is not especially adept at showing causal mechanisms at work. As mine is a theory of decision-making, it is imperative to get the causal mechanism right, and this can be done only with close historical examination of cases of secessionism.

I employ the "most-similar" method, by which a researcher studies a pair (or more) of cases which are similar in all respects except the variables of interest.[64] In general, this method results in greater confidence in the theory if, within the pairwise comparison, there is wide variation in the independent and dependent variables and all other dimensions are highly similar.[65] At times, scholars can divide a single longitudinal case into two subcases, a technique known as "before-after research design," as long as care is taken to ensure only one significant variable changes at the moment that divides the two periods.[66] Combining this most similar method with process-tracing allows us greater confidence in the theory.[67] Process tracing is a method by which the researcher zooms in on the causal mechanisms linking a hypothesized independent variable to an outcome. Causal mechanisms are the "meat" of any theoretical argument; they are the processes and intervening variables through which an explanatory variable exerts its influence over the outcome in question.[68] Though there are valid varieties of process-tracing, the one I employ in this book is that of "analytic explanation," whereby historical narratives are couched in explicit theoretical terms.[69] Throughout these narratives, I emphasize both where my argument is consistent with the evidence as well as where it is contradicted by it, pointing to the importance of elements outside my theoretical framework in a number of cases. After all, no one social scientific theory can explain all relevant aspects of major phenomena or events, and it is incumbent on careful researchers to be attentive to the importance of other variables and contingencies.

CASE SELECTION

I choose to focus primarily on states experiencing more than one secessionist movement, for two main reasons. The first is methodological: choosing multiple cases falling within one state, especially in narrowly circumscribed periods, gives us the best chance of fulfilling the conditions of "most-similar" research design outlined above, since structural factors such as state wealth, institutional structure, and geography are likely to be common across both movements. The second is substantive: a vast majority of secessionist movements take place in "multiple movement" states. An argument that can explain variation in response to secessionism in one state would be considered, all else equal, more powerful than those that suffer at the hands of the internal variation problem.

Choosing individual cases to study from my larger universe of 163 movements after 1946, as well notable pre–World War II movements, requires careful consideration. How is a particular case situated in the more general population? Is this case being used to infer a theory or test one? Is it establishing a theory's range or its antecedent conditions?[70]

To test my theory, I focus on South Asia. Specifically, I examine Pakistan's reactions to Bengali and Baloch demands for independence in the 1970s in chapter 3, and India's responses in Kashmir, Punjab, and Assam in the 1980s and 1990s in chapter 4. Theories of secessionist violence have mostly been built on the experience of the Balkans and the Caucasus.[71] South Asia, generally speaking, has escaped the attention of scholars dealing with secessionism. This is a strange omission given each major state in South Asia—India, Pakistan, Bangladesh, and Sri Lanka—has experienced secessionism, and in India and Pakistan's cases, multiple movements across both space and time. One should endeavor to choose "typical" or "representative" cases,[72] and given that both South Asian neighbors are ethnically heterogeneous developing countries that have experienced multiple movements, they fit the bill. Furthermore, methodologists encourage cases with within-case diversity, encompassing the full range of values of the independent and dependent variables.[73] South Asia displays this variation in my independent variable amply; certain separatist conflicts have an extremely relevant geopolitical component (Kashmir, East Pakistan), others less so (Balochistan, Punjab), and still others even less (Assam). As far as the dependent variable of state strategy is concerned, South Asia sees a wide range of state behavior,[74] sometimes within the same conflict. Finally, by circumscribing my investigation in one region in one era—each of the conflicts studied occurred between 1971 and 1991—I hold structural conditions such as levels of wealth, state development and capacity, institutional structure, and demography broadly constant, leading to a more rigorous identification of why states choose the policies they do against separatists.

Later in the book, I expand the case selection to include vastly different time periods, geographic locations, and types of state. This empirical section is devoted to establishing the argument's explanatory range. The wider the theory's applicability across space, time, and context, the more confident we can be in its mechanisms.

I begin in chapter 5 with variation across time in the Ottoman treatment of its Armenian population between 1908 and 1915, when the Young Turk regime went from accommodating the Armenians in 1908 to seeking their wholesale forcible removal from Ottoman territory during World War I, leading to genocide. As scholars have pointed out, "extreme" cases, or those where either or both of the independent and dependent variable are present in large quantities, have significant methodological value. It is precisely because these observations lie far from the median that they prove so instructive.[75] The Ottoman case displays the largest variation in the dependent variable in this book, with state strategy veering from the most peaceful, "negotiations and concessions," to the most violent, "collective repression." Second, because the Ottoman case was not one of a modern nation-state, as are most of the cases I consider in this book, but an empire in the midst of dissolution, its inclusion increases the breadth of the sample being tested.

Chapter 6 continues the theme of gauging the theory's explanatory power in vastly different situations so that we can be confident that the argument "travels." I begin with the interaction between Israel and Palestinian nationalists, focusing especially on the first intifada, for two main reasons. First, this dispute allows a direct comparison of my argument with its primary competitors, centering on reputation and institutions. As a binational state, one that is a wealthy, liberal democracy no less, Israel has no "other" ethnic communities than the Palestinians, and thus should be expected to not have any concerns about establishing a "tough" reputation to deter future independence movements. At the time of the Madrid and Oslo talks in the aftermath of the first intifada, Israel was led by a center-left government with the support of Arab parties in the Knesset. Consequently it should have had little need to resort to violence against Palestinians. My argument would predict the opposite, given Israel's security concerns with the prospect of an independent Palestine. That is, Israel is a "most-likely" case my competitors—a case which is predicted to result in a certain outcome, but does not[76]—made more significant by the fact that my theory makes the opposite, and correct, prediction in this case.

I then investigate the Velvet Divorce separating Czechs and Slovaks at the end of the Cold War and the dissolution of the Norway-Sweden union in 1905. Generally, social scientists are "concerned not only with cases where something 'happened,' but also with cases where something did not."[77] It is important that any theory of separatist conflict address one or both of these cases, since they, as two of a handful of completely peaceful secessions of the twentieth century, occupy the extreme ends of the spectrum, just as the Armenian and Bengali genocides do. Choosing extreme cases only because they are extreme may strike some as violating the social science tenet to "not choose on the dependent variable." However, qualitative scholars encourage choosing such extreme cases, as long as they are accompanied by cases that are more representative, because it allows for maximizing "variance on the dimension of interest."[78] Without an understanding of what factors led to relatively rare outcomes in these cases, it would be difficult to identify the necessary and sufficient conditions for peaceful separatism more generally.[79]

Finally, I investigate the U.S. Civil War, even though it technically lies outside the data universe of my argument: it neither took place in the twentieth century, nor was it, strictly speaking, a case of an ethnic group seeking independence. Nevertheless, the very fact that it does not fit the profile of the type of secessionist struggle I study makes it a useful litmus test: if my argument can account for elements of a dispute that lies outside its original scope conditions, we can gain even greater confidence in its explanatory power.

The overall sample, then, consists of three states that experienced separatism before World War II (the United States, Ottoman Empire, and Sweden) and four after (Pakistan, India, Czechoslovakia, and Israel). The cases feature each of authoritarian, democratic, monarchic, and imperial governance. Some are highly centralized states, others highly federalized. The geographic scope is similarly varied: I cover North America, Northern Europe, Eastern Europe, the Middle East, and South Asia. Most crucially, the sample contains each of the four major strategies I discuss, ranging from negotiations to limited war to genocide, leaving me with a great deal of material to test my argument.

Table 1 Explaining case selection

Goal	Case	Methodological value
Testing the theory	Pakistan	Variation in IV and DV across space (Bengal vs. Balochistan)
	India	Variation in IV and DV across space (Kashmir vs. Assam vs. Punjab) and across time (Punjab 1985 vs. post-1987)
Establishing explanatory range of the theory	Ottoman Empire	Large variation in IV and DV across time (Armenians in 1908 vs. 1914–15)
	Sweden-Norway	Extreme case
	Czechoslovakia	
	Israel-Palestine	"Most-likely" case for reputation argument
	U.S-Confederacy	Outside original scope conditions

DATA

The empirical material for this book is drawn from various sources, including more than 110 semistructured interviews I conducted in person with current and former political, diplomatic, and security officials; journalists and analysts; insurgents; and scholars and academics (or, for those interviewees in Europe, the Middle East, or South Asia, over the telephone or Skype). Additionally, I draw on tens of thousands of pages of diplomatic archives, primarily from American and British sources.[80] Daily newspaper archives, especially but not only of the *Assam Tribune*, *Chandigarh Tribune*, *Dawn*, *Kashmir Times*, and *Times of India*, also proved invaluable.[81] In addition to these sources, I used other primary and secondary material, such as memoirs, interviews to the press, internal government memoranda concerning secessionist conflicts, and detailed case studies in other disciplines such as history and sociology, and biographies.

An External Security Theory of Secessionist Conflict

When confronted by secessionists, a state can adopt a wide array of policies, from granting independence or major concessions, to resisting the nationalists' demands with varying levels of violence. For states, the decision of how to respond to separatists is based on external security considerations. At particular secessionist moments, central governments weigh the extent to which the group is an external threat, and that calculation of vulnerability determines the strategy the state adopts: the more threatened a state feels, the more violent it is.[1]

At bottom, what drives a state's decision-making is the large and immediate shift in the balance of power that would accompany a change in its borders. If a secessionist group were to succeed in creating a new state, it would significantly weaken the host state with respect to not one, but two potential external rivals. The first actor to greatly benefit vis-à-vis the former host state would be the secessionists. Formerly an ethnic group without a large polity, now one in control of a state, this actor would have greater capabilities to hurt the former host state, should it choose to do so. Second, successful secession would weaken the host state relative to its geopolitical rivals, since it would have lost significant territory and population, two crucial components of power.

When such large, rapid shifts in the balance of power are in the offing, states must be careful about accommodating secessionists. States should be especially wary of offering concessions to such groups if they foresee war with either the newly independent state or a geopolitical rival. Why allow the balance to shift unfavorably if one anticipates security threats in the future? The creation of a potentially hostile state, or war against an already-existing state rival emboldened by the host state's loss of territory and population, are eventualities the host state is unwilling to countenance. To prevent such challenges to its external security, the state will fight the secessionists.

The factors that influence whether a state decrees future war likely, either against the ethnic group seeking independence, or regional state rival(s), are crucial. There are two particularly noteworthy issues that affect this judgment. First, is the ethnic group's identity opposed to the state's national core? Second, how war prone is the state's regional neighborhood? A state is sanguine about the security implications of secessionism only when it lives in a peaceful neighborhood and its national identity is not opposed to the separatists'. Such an optimistic, "postsecurity" environment is a necessary condition for a state to consider a "negotiations and concessions" strategy. This strategy is aimed at satisfying, or satisficing, the ethnonationalists' demands. If it succeeds, this strategy maintains the territorial integrity of the state at the cost of decentralization of certain powers and privileges to the regional nationalists. Even the worst-case scenario under this strategy—the separatists' using piecemeal concessions to pave the way to independence—does not spell doom for the state, for it has little reason to fear the security consequences of a new neighbor. Either way, recourse to violence is deemed not necessary.

However, states are rarely confident enough about their future security for such generosity. More likely, in situations in which the state is either located in a relatively militarized part of the world, or it suffers a significant identity division with the separatists, it would consider the possibility of border changes in more urgent, sometimes-apocalyptic, terms and attempt to forestall it with violence. In other words, the prospect of future war is a sufficient condition for the state to use coercion.

Once a state turns to coercion, it calibrates just how much violence to employ based on how much support the separatists enjoy from its geopolitical rivals. For both materialist and emotional reasons, more external support results in more repressive strategies. First, the higher the threat of military defeat, the more brutal states generally get.[2] Third-party support, by transferring "technologies of rebellion," makes the movement a stronger fighting force, increasing the level of violence required to defeat it.[3] Second, external backing of the separatists by rivals of the state fuels emotional, pathological actions by both leaders and security forces, directed by a collective sense of betrayal. Third-party support pushes the state to climb the escalatory ladder, from what I term "policing" to "militarization" to "collective repression."

The bottom line is that as perceived external threats to the state increase, so does the weight of the state's response: more serious threats are dealt with more violently. The extent of the external threat, in turn, depends on the state's evaluation of future war, either against the seceded state or an existing rival, and the degree of third-party support for the secessionists.

Setting up the Theory

My argument examines state strategy at secessionist moments. Though interesting, I do not consider the causes of, and route to, the secessionist moment in the first place.[4] Rather, I focus on states' decision-making at the point at which an ethno-nationalist movement has made a demand or declaration of independence or significant autonomy. Such secessionist moments can take the form, among others, of an ethnic party winning an election; a massive rally, riot, or demonstration that compels fence-sitters to choose sides in favor of those demanding independence; or an assassination, murder, or kidnapping that unites the opposition. There may be some strategic bluffing at play regarding the movement's true aims[5]—groups that would be satisfied with mere autonomy sometimes demand secession to set a high initial price; groups that ultimately desire secession sometimes demand autonomy to hide their goals—but either way, the central state is forced to sit up and take notice of its dissatisfied ethnic minority. My theory is aimed at deconstructing the state's calculus at that precise moment.

To build the theory, I rely on three assumptions. First, I assume that actors are strategic and forward looking. This is a fairly common assumption made by social scientists, though it is not without its critics. At bottom, this assumption holds that all relevant actors possess a reservoir of information and beliefs from which they weigh costs and benefits in a crude but identifiable way to help decide on which course of action is most suitable. Actors are not necessarily reasonable, intelligent, or accurate in their understandings of the world, nor is it unlikely that "nonrationalist" feelings, such as racism and prejudice, interfere with their decision-making. Indeed, as we shall soon see, leaders often behave in response to visceral, emotional cues. I assert only that decision makers are strategic in their interactions with other individuals and groups, and seek to maximize net gains on behalf of whichever organization or state they represent.

Second, I assume that states are more powerful than substate actors. Because states can draw on the organizational, military, and economic capabilities that inhere in statehood, they can be characterized as being more powerful than minorities within their borders. "Small" can still beat "big"[6]—tactics, terrain, the balance of resolve, and the public support all matter a great deal in any armed conflict—but, prima facie, the state would have to be favored in such a fight. Indeed, it is precisely the greater capabilities that states possess that motivate minority groups to pay, at times, high costs to attain those capabilities.

Third, I treat states as "unitary" actors, a long-standing assumption in international relations (IR).[7] This assumption implies that when dealing with external threats, even when such threats happen to emanate from within their borders, states will act "as if" they are unified entities. This is not to suggest the level of internal discord on policies is precisely zero. At times, governments are intensely divided into camps advocating different proposals to the problem of a separatist movement. However, at highly politicized moments—the start of wars, after a major attack, a deadly riot, a landslide electoral victory by an ethnic party—most decision makers will "fall in line" and afford considerable leeway to top leaders. Even in democracies such as India, Israel, the United States, and Czechoslovakia, domestic opponents fall lockstep behind executives at such times, to say nothing of authoritarian states like Pakistan or the Ottoman Empire, where crucial decisions are highly localized to one or a few actors. Because violence, or its threat, is inherently polarizing,[8] secessionist moments force domestic groups and factions to choose between the state and the secessionists, with the result that these groups invariably opt for the former. Notwithstanding tactical disagreements and opportunistic criticism, major and genuine disagreements among government leaders during secessionist crises are rare—at least if evidence from South Asia to the Middle East to Europe is anything to go by.

More important, the unitary-actor assumption affords us analytical traction on the external environment. Allowing for all relevant factors to vary, as they assuredly do in the real world, makes for unwieldy theories. If one wants to examine how the external implications of separatism affect state strategy, it is advisable to simplify the domestic politics angle. For useful theory building, abstraction has to occur somewhere in the process—either domestic politics are assumed away and external relations analyzed (as I do), or vice versa (as others do).[9]

Secessionism as an External Threat

War between a state and the one it was carved out of is a distinct possibility after secession. Consider the case of Ethiopia. In April 1993, Eritreans voted overwhelmingly for independence in a referendum. Rather than standing in their way, the Ethiopian government, tired from decades of conflict, "welcomed" the prospect.[10] This bonhomie led to optimistic prognostications about the two countries' ability and desire to live in peace in the future.[11] Such optimism was misplaced. In 1998, Eritrea attacked its former host state over a border dispute, a "stab in the back" to its erstwhile allies.[12] The war was immensely costly, leading to the deaths of between 70,000 and 200,000 people in two years, making it one of the deadliest interstate wars in recent history.[13] In Ethiopia, it exacerbated economic, power, and food crises.[14] Analysts have concerns about a similar trajectory with respect to the world's newest state. After South Sudan was created via a referendum in which 99 percent of its residents voted for independence, tensions concerning territory and oil wealth have led to fears of full-blown war between the two neighbors.[15] Other regions exhibit similar traits: Kosovo and Serbia have an icy relationship; Russia fought a war against Georgia less than two decades after the latter's independence,[16] and recently invaded Ukraine.

Aside from conflicts against new neighbors, states also face the prospect of war against its geopolitical rivals, especially those in the region. If it experiences secession, the state would lose territory and population. Such losses may embolden existing rivals to take advantage of the weakened state. For instance, thanks to substantial losses of land and people after its defeat in the Balkan wars in 1912, the Ottoman Empire was less able to withstand the exigencies of international security competition, evinced by its capitulation to Russian demands for Armenian reform, summed up in its Mandelstam Plan (chapter 4).

The threat of such wars, either against the seceded state or existing rivals, casts a foreboding shadow under which states must respond to separatist movements. Against this backdrop, states have to make relatively quick decisions about strategy at secessionist moments. They know that in the rough-and-tumble system of international politics, where actors have offensive military capabilities and unknown intentions, and where states generally have nowhere to turn to when faced with crisis or peril, the price for not being adequately fearful of potential security threats can be prohibitive.[17]

Consequently, states tread very carefully when dealing with separatism, with their overarching goal to ensure that their future security is not compromised. Most of all, states wish to avoid policies that could sow their own demise. If a state considers secessionists' success problematic for its future security, it would do whatever necessary to forestall an adverse shift in the balance of power. Why grant concessions and allow potential threats, whether existing states or new neighbors, to become stronger? At bottom, this means that a state fearful of future security threats is better off using coercion, not accommodation, against secessionist movements. As a result, optimistic states will systematically treat secessionists better than fearful ones.

I elaborate on each leg of the theoretical argument below, beginning with the first step: why secession represents a significant shift in the balance of power.

SECESSION AND THE BALANCE OF POWER

In IR, power is generally understood as being based on material capabilities. These include a state's military forces, its wealth, the size and talent—measured by education standards, perhaps—of its population, and its position of technological advancement. One prominent study of IR theory states simply that power is "based on tangible assets."[18] Setting basic definitional issues aside, what is important for our purposes is that in the international system, states uniquely possess these material capabilities on an aggregate level.

Secession changes the balance of power between the ethno-nationalists and their former host state, making the latter more vulnerable to attack. The balance of power shifts because attaining a state magnifies the capabilities of any social group controlling it, mainly for three reasons.

First, control of a state generally leads to control of the organized means of violence within it. Charles Tilly has famously written on the relationship between state building and war making, a connection vital to understanding the processes at work here.[19] What he terms the "state's tendency to monopolize the concentrated means of coercion," is a key element of the shift in the balance of power.[20] After all, if winning a state translates into the presence of an organized military, and an organized military is an important marker of capabilities, then the creation of a new state has enormous implications for the power of a group controlling it. Often, one of the key proximate causes of an ethnic group seeking its own state is that it is systematically excluded from military recruitment more generally, and officer positions in particular, in the multinational state. This leaves the group vulnerable to intimidation and control by forces often hostile to it. Conversely, there are tremendous advantages, both with respect to internal and external rivals, to gaining greater representation in the armed forces of a state. If an ethnic group can essentially come to dominate a state's military, it can better direct coercion against opponents.

This switch—from being systematically excluded from a state's military to essentially running one's own—is crucial to understanding the shift in the balance of power between the host state and the ethno-nationalist group potentially forming its own state. Suddenly, the ethnic group can stand up to its former host state in ways that were simply impossible when it was marginalized as a stateless group. Even if the new state's military is weaker than that of the rump state, the difference in strength between the two actors is now one of degree, not one of kind.

The second component of the shift in the balance of power is economic. Within this category, there are two central elements: domestic economic policy and foreign economic policy. With respect to domestic policy, the ethno-nationalist group in control of a new state now faces incentives such that what's good for the group is good for the state, and vice versa. Previously, in the unified state, coalitional politics, racism, and intergroup rivalry could have resulted in the sidelining of a particular ethnic group from economic growth or, in a logically equivalent way, economic losses could have been more than proportionately suffered by the group in question. With their own state, such concerns are no longer valid. The ethnic group can freely use its state to extract resources from its population in the form of taxes as well as fashion certain economic policies such as industrialization, the construction of dams and irrigation canals, and targeted investment in certain sectors of the economy.[21]

This is not to suggest that intergroup rivalry vanishes with the creation of a new state—political scientists have shown that the salience of particular ethnic and political cleavages changes with the redrawing of institutional and geographical boundaries[22]—but the particular ethnic group as a whole is no longer in danger of being unfairly targeted with respect to economic gains and losses. Economic nationalism can now take over, in every sense of the term, increasing the group's economic power as a whole. Indeed, it is widely acknowledged that one of the central motivations for organizing the modern nation state is to maintain economic competitiveness in an era of industrialization.[23]

Related to this issue is foreign economic policy, particularly trade and membership in certain intergovernmental organizations (IGOs). As a canonical study on trade and power noted, "Among the economic determinants of power, foreign trade plays an important part."[24] Foreign trade, by directing resources to more efficient avenues of production and consumption, increases the military and economic capacities of states.[25] It is taken as a truism that states' goals with respect to trade policy in particular, and foreign economic policy in general, include most prominently the aim of increasing their aggregate power.[26] Trade can also be used strategically to manage relations with other states, giving birth to and cementing alliances.[27] Finally, membership in international organizations aids states in managing external relations and achieving their policy goals.[28] Such institutional membership is a legalistic symptom of a more general point, which is that membership in the comity of states is a "social" enterprise—similar to college fraternities, one can join only when those already on the inside acquiesce.[29] Once a group is recognized as a state, and welcomed into "the society of states,"[30] its social and institutional power increases.

Once again, the contrast between being a subnational ethnic group and an ethnic group controlling the state is readily apparent. When a group is relatively powerless within a state, it cannot strategically manage foreign economic relations for its benefit; such a luxury is left to the group that controls the state. The distributional consequences of foreign trade are often quite severe for marginalized groups, as agents of the state ensure that rival groups bear the brunt of the costs of trade, while their supporters garner the benefits.[31] And minority groups certainly cannot win membership into international organizations, most of which are open only to states or their recognized representatives. When an ethno-nationalist group wins its own state, however, it can then partake in these benefits in ways that were unlikely or impossible in the status quo *ex-ante*.

The third power-magnifying benefit of state formation relates to demographics. All else being equal, the larger the population of a state, the greater its power.[32] The most widely cited source of material capabilities, the National Material Capabilities Dataset, part of the Correlates of War project, includes in its composite score six elements of state power; two of the six are demographic variables (total population and urban population). A larger population base means that states can build bigger militaries, that they can put more people to work in both peacetime and during war, that they can have a wider tax base, and that their consumer markets are more attractive for investment and capital building.

When it comes to ethnic minorities, winning a state can be a significant game-changer in this regard. Assuming the presence of a coethnic diaspora in other parts of the region and the world at large, a state exclusively devoted to a particular ethnic group means that, all of a sudden, there is a home to go to. In other words, the new state will not be populated just by the group that fought for it, but by their ethnic brethren from various far-flung corners of the globe. An illustration of this principle is Israel's Law of Return, passed in the immediate aftermath of independence, which allows Jews worldwide, along with their progeny and spouses, to become citizens of Israel, regardless of national origin. Decision makers, we can be assured, are aware of the possibility of an immigration explosion in the new state, as evinced by Ottoman leader Enver Pasha's thoughts on the creation of an Armenian state in the early twentieth century:

> In my opinion this is a very big mistake. *If today in the Caucasus a small Armenia possessing a population of five to six hundred thousand and sufficient territory is formed, in the future this government, together with the Armenians that will come mainly from America and from elsewhere, will have a population of millions.* And in the east we will have another Bulgaria and it will be a worse enemy than Russia because all the Armenians' interests and ambitions are in our country. Consequently, in order to remove this danger, the formation of even the smallest Armenian government must be prevented.[33]

By changing the balance of population, so to speak, between an ethnic group and its former host state, the creation of a new state irrevocably changes the balance of power between the parties too. Cold, hard numbers matter a great deal.[34]

Secession, then, would lead to the ethno-nationalist group posing more of a threat to the rump state than it would as a minority group within a unified one, mainly because statehood would endow the group with military, economic, institutional, and demographic benefits. Admittedly, self-government entails both benefits and costs: managing territory and population can present a unique and new set of challenges to the separatists. After all, mobilizing a population and governing it require different political skill sets. For instance, when the Asom Gana Parishad, a party of Assamese ethno-nationalists, gained power in state elections in December 1985 after months of agitation and negotiations with central state, its record was poor; it included corruption, nepotism, and a lack of development (chapter 3).[35] Similarly, rather than usher a promised era of liberty and progress, Bangladesh's hard-won freedom from Pakistan (chapter 2) resulted in significant political instability—including a coup and the assassination of Awami League leader Sheikh Mujib-ur-Rahman, his entire family with the exception of two daughters then in West Germany, and his personal staff— less than four years after it achieved statehood. Today, only half a decade after they won independence, South Sudan's leaders find themselves in the midst of a brutal civil war that threatens mass famine.

Even accounting for such costs, however, the creation of a new state leaves the host state more vulnerable to the ethnic group, generally speaking. First, the costs of managing territory and population, important as they are, are circumscribed to group elites, unlike the benefits—such as the gains from trade, membership in international organizations and international society, and nondiscrimination in military and civil service—which are distributed to the population at large. Thus it is reasonable to suggest that groups overall benefit from secession. Certainly, ethnic groups around the world believe the benefits of statehood far outweigh the costs; if they did not, they would not demand independence at the rates they do (163 movements between 1945 and 2000).

Second, even if we concede the real-world existence of situations where independence can hurt the ethnic group's power, the host state cannot make decisions based on such best-case scenarios. States operate in the dog-eat-dog world of international politics, where the costs of being wrong about prospective security threats can be prohibitive.[36] It is thus reasonable for the state to be concerned with the ethnic group gaining the massive military, institutional, and demographic resources that accrue to all states in the system.

Third, and most important, border changes shift the balance of power not just between the host state and the seceding ethnic group, but also between the host state and its existing state rivals. That is, in addition to losing out relatively to the ethnic minority, the state will also find itself weaker vis-à-vis other states in the region and around the globe. After all, if power "represents nothing more than specific assets or material resources available to a state,"[37] it stands to reason that losing significant amounts of territory and population in one fell swoop disadvantages states with respect to their rivals (and even friends).

Widely used datasets and major scholarly works in IR highlight the role of population as an important component of power.[38] Because territory and population are important components of states' reservoir of material capabilities, losing them wholesale results in significant shifts in the balance of power between the state and its adversaries. Consider the extent to which India pressed its advantage after East and West Pakistan split in 1971. Between 1970 and 1972, the ratio of India's material capabilities to Pakistan's increased by almost 50 percent, from 4.6:1 to 6.7:1,[39] a major part of this shift resulting from Pakistan losing half its population. Losing territory is also a major setback. No state likes to relinquish its hold on land easily, and indeed, the bulk of conflicts in modern international history have been fought over territory.[40] States have attachment to territory for a variety of reasons,[41] most compellingly the strategic, economic, and resource value of that land.

The problem with losing significant territory and population is that such a process makes states much weaker, leaving them more vulnerable to opportunist regional rivals. Scholars of territorial disputes have found that states are more likely to challenge rivals—or "engage in higher levels of diplomatic and military pressure"—the more advantageous their relative power position.[42] Even if this empirical pattern was not a fact of international politics, decision makers tend to behave as if it is. Generally speaking, states are quite suspicious of others' intentions and are loathe to acquiesce to any decrease in their relative power, given the exigencies of interstate security competition.[43]

Even in the highly unlikely situation where independence hurts rather than helps the ethnic group's power, then, the host state will still find itself more vulnerable to existing states. The sum consequence of the prospective changes supported by the secessionists, therefore, is a large and rapid shift in the balance of power between the state and two sets of rivals: the ethnic nationalists and geopolitical adversaries. In turn, the potential of large and rapid shifts in the balance of power activate the commitment problem.

THE COMMITMENT PROBLEM AS A CAUSE FOR CONFLICT ESCALATION

IR scholars have long grappled with a seemingly simple yet intractable problem: why do states fight wars? After all, two actors with conflicting interests need not go to war over them.[44] Doing so might even be considered irrational on the surface, because the divisions of gains and losses that is reached after the war could, in theory, have been reached in peaceful bargaining before any fighting took place, thus saving both actors the high costs of conflict. To put it in concrete terms, instead of fighting a war over Alsace-Lorraine, Germany and France—as rational, forward-looking actors—could conceivably see how such a war would unfold and divide the territory based on their estimates, without doing any of the fighting. Under such a scenario, both would be better off than in the case where they fought a war to find the same division of spoils.

One of the problems with this view, however, is that there is no credibility of commitment. Even when both sides have gained in the sense of not fighting a war, one side will gain more than the other with respect to the actual division of what is being contested—some territory, policy, or whatever. In turn, this means that one side is more equipped to attack the other in the future based on those very gains, as well as other gains in capability that accrue over time, such as arms buildups or a rising population. The actor whose power trajectory shows a steeper upward slope has no credible way of committing to *not* attacking the other side in the future. More important, the more vulnerable actor knows all of this, and as a result, initiates conflict. Why risk (the threat of) war against a strengthened rival, the logic goes, when we have a better chance of success today?

This framework helps explain why a state would adopt coercion to deal with separatism. At the heart of the commitment problem, an inability to trust that a bargain will be adhered to, are potential large and rapid power shifts, exactly the situation that characterizes secessionism. A state fearful of border changes cannot afford concessions, for such a policy makes its worst-case scenarios more likely. If the state offers negotiated deals that fall short of full statehood, the ethno-nationalists may use the greater organizational resources attendant on decentralization and regional autonomy to press their case further in the future. As Grigoryan writes, "Concessions will only embolden [the minority] to make more demands or to attempt secession from a position improved by those very concessions."[45] This is because autonomy only reinforces and reaffirms the distinctiveness of ethno-nationalist identity, in part by encouraging the growth of regionalist parties who play an important role in mobilizing the population for conflict and secessionism.[46] Large-n studies corroborate this argument and show that federalism facilitates the formation of substate identities.[47] Agent-based computer models based on constructivist identity theory also demonstrate that power-sharing encourages larger identitarian movements.[48] Accommodation allows groups to aggregate proto-statelike resources, administratively, politically, economically, and socially, spoils that make states leery of negotiated concessions.

Of course, coercion against separatists is not a riskless strategy either. Harsh repression can increase ethnic groups' later determination to secede. India, for instance, has found itself unable to stamp out Kashmiris' desire for self-determination, in part precisely because of the brutal methods it has employed over the last three decades in that state (chapter 3). However, as I detail below, states need not escalate to high levels of repression absent significant third-party support. Lower levels of coercion, such as policing, generally do not have high material or reputational costs associated with them.

More important, the risk of domestic, regional, or global reputational loss is less worrisome for states than the risk of creating bigger security problems for itself. Because accommodationist policies only kick the secessionist can down the road, setting the stage for more powerful and organized claims in the future, only states unafraid of border changes can afford to try them. That is, a benign security prognosis is a necessary condition for a state to consider concessions such as significant autonomy or full independence. If, on the other hand, the state foresees the creation of the new state as geopolitically problematic in its future, it would behoove it to use force in the present, and nip the threat in the bud.[49] The fear of future war, in this view, is a sufficient condition for state coercion against separatists. The question then becomes: how does a state determine whether future war is likely?

INDEPENDENT VARIABLE I: PROBABILITY
OF FUTURE WAR

As the examples of Eritrea and Ethiopia, Georgia and Russia, Kosovo and
Serbia, and Sudan and South Sudan show, there exists a possibility of conflict between a state and an ethnic group that achieved independence.
Decision-makers must consider not just such possibilities, but also the likelihood of future war against existing states, who may be emboldened by
the host state's loss of territory and population. For instance, the Ottoman
Empire, having lost about half its land and people in the Balkan wars of
1912 (chapter 4), faced a resurgent Russia in World War I, and India and
Pakistan fought in the snowy heights of Kargil in 1999, a quarter-century
after the former helped dismember the latter (chapter 2).

In my theory, the fear of future war is a sufficient condition for the state
to coerce separatists. Its fear of future war against the seceded state turns
on whether the ethnic group's identity is opposed to the state's national
identity. Its fear of future war against existing states depends on the relative
war proneness of the region the state inhabits. The possibility of war against
either foe functions as a proverbial trip wire for the state's adoption of coercion: if either or both are "set off," the state will attempt to forestall independence with violence.

Future War and Depth of Identity Divisions. Nation-states seek to build
national myths that strengthen social ties among its citizens and between the
citizens and the state.[50] This is especially true in the postcolonial regions of
Asia and Africa, whose states became independent in an age in which ethnic
and national identities were largely accepted as the dominant mode of state
organization. Importantly, not all ethnic or national groups are equally likely
to be in control of such myth-making ventures. To the contrary, certain groups
are more likely to be in control of the state, and certain "national" ideologies
are more likely to be adopted.[51] In turn, certain ethnic or national groups
find themselves in more direct opposition to the state's chosen nationalistic
narrative, even in states that practice so-called civic nationalism.[52]

Where does the secessionist ethnic group's identity fall on this spectrum
with respect to the core? A national identity can be inclusive of, indifferent
to, or opposed to an ethnic group. If, for instance, a state defines its identity
as that of a white Christian nation, then for the purposes of both Northern
European Protestants and Western European Catholics, its nationalism is
inclusive. If a national identity is inclusive of an ethnic group, it is unlikely
that the group would consider seceding, and thus while a possible value for
this variable, it drops out of the analysis. The variable then becomes dichot-
omous: identity relations can be indifferent or opposed. For our purposes,
secessionists with mobilizing identities opposed to the state's national narrative are deemed dangerous in the future.

An indifferent identity relation occurs when the key national character dimension—language, religion, race, ethnicity, creed, and sect—is orthogonal to the one on whose basis the ethnic group is mobilizing. For instance, if a state defines its nationality along linguistic lines and an ethnic group secedes on the basis of a difference in religion, then that ethnic difference will be categorized as indifferent. On the other hand, if a state's national identity is organized along racial lines, and an ethnic group attempts secession based on its racial character, then that constitutes opposed identity relations. Of course, in the real world, issues concerning identity are not as clear cut as dispassionate scholars and analysts often imply, and peoples and states often subscribe to, and mobilize around, multiple, overlapping identities. That said, the job of the theoretician is to simplify. In this case, it seems reasonable to assert that one identity marker, above others, exerts a greater political force on individuals and groups, particularly at highly politicized times such as secessionist moments.

This is not to suggest that the nation-state's or the ethnic group's identity are fixed and unchanging. To the contrary, scholars of ethnic politics find that the precise identity cleavage around which groups mobilize is context and institution specific.[53] Voters in Zambia, for instance, might organize along tribal lines under single-party rule, but along linguistic lines in multi-party rule. Fighters in civil wars may be motivated by regionalist identity in one year and an ethnic one the next.[54] Even the state's national identity is contested and ever in flux: the ruling Young Turk regime in the early 1900s changed the composition of its national identity from "Ottoman" to "Turk" in less than half a decade (chapter 4). This had profound consequences for how Armenians were seen in the empire. What this means in concrete terms is that the identity-distance variable can vary across both space and time, even if we are considering just one ethnic group and one state.

What I attempt to capture with this concept of identity division is the ethnic group's likelihood to have so-called greedy motives in the future. IR scholars generally distinguish between "security-seeking" and "greedy" states. Both types can be expansionist, but aggression by "security-seekers," as the term suggests, is geared toward increasing the state's security by, say, increasing resources or advancing borders to a more defensible frontier. On the other hand, "greedy" states are expansionist for nonsecurity reasons, such as wealth, prestige, or ideological fervor.[55] In essence, greedy states are more difficult to placate than security seekers; they do not take yes for an answer. As I conceive of it, the identity division between the center and the ethno-nationalists is a measure of the latter's future desire to strike back at the state for purely nationalistic or "greedy" reasons. Because one of the central political roles of ethnic identity is to reduce uncertainty,[56] the precise content of relational ethnic identities can influence actors' assessments of the likelihood of war or peace resulting from secessionism.[57]

If the identity division between the ethnic group mainly in charge of the state and the independence-seeking minority group is *especially* frayed, then the state is likely to be wary of the minority group. While it is true almost by definition that the relationship between an ethnic group seeking independence from a state and the state itself is not warm, some rivalries are especially intense. Some are decades and even centuries old, others more recent. Some have featured violence at high levels relatively regularly, others sporadically or not at all. For example, despite Bohemia and Moravia being occupied by a Nazi Germany that enjoyed an alliance with an "independent" Slovakia for most of World War II, Czechs and Slovaks did not subject each other to extreme levels of violence the way, say, Croats and Serbs did.[58] Fifty years later, the divorce between Czechs and Slovaks was many orders of magnitude more peaceful than the one that took place in Yugoslavia. The more damaged a relationship is perceived to be at the secessionist moment, the more likely the state is to ascribe malicious intentions to the group.

At times, the ethno-nationalists may use costly signals to reassure the state, attempting to lower the state's estimation of the likelihood of future war and increasing its inclination to offer concessions. After all, what truly drives the central government's perceptions of future conflict are the ethnic group's intentions, which can, technically, become more known.[59] However, given that talk is cheap and that secession necessarily implies such a large and rapid power shift, seceding groups have to take extraordinary measures to signal benign intentions. Such measures can include the destruction of military capabilities by the seceding minority, as Norway did in 1905, when it destroyed its border forts to make it easier for Sweden to acquiesce to its independence (chapter 5). Even better in this regard would be direct transfers of military or security-related assets from the ethnic group to the seceding state: what could be a more reliable signal of a group's benign intentions than it helping its former host state potentially destroy it? For instance, during the time of the Velvet Divorce, the vast majority of the formerly united Czechoslovakia's military capabilities were diverted to the Czech half, which made Slovak secessionism more acceptable (chapter 5). But even such assurances do not guarantee kind treatment from the state. The Palestinian national movement gave in to Israeli insistence, as far back as the Oslo agreements of the mid-1990s, that an independent Palestine should be demilitarized (chapter 5). Yet this concession has brought the Palestinians no closer to statehood; the reservoirs of distrust and suspicion between Israel and its neighbors run too deep for such a promise to assuage Israel of its future security. Generally, the prospect of a new state on one's borders spells trouble for one's security, and cases such as Czechoslovakia or Sweden-Norway tend to be exceptional. As Secretary of State William Seward asserted in the run-up to the American Civil War, "The new Confederacy . . . must, like any other new state, seek to expand itself northward, westward, and southward. What part of this continent or of the adjacent islands would be expected to remain in peace?"[60]

Future War and Existing States: Regional War Proneness. In addition to concerns about future war against the seceded state, a state must also consider the potential for war against an existing state, emboldened by the host state's loss of territory and population. Will border changes imperil its prospects in war too gravely? The state's assessment of the probability of future war against rivals turns on its prior experience with interstate war in its neighborhood, since this has implications for the constraints against war in its region.

Although war is a systemic phenomenon, certain subsystems appear better at avoiding it than others. For instance, South Asian states are twice as likely to threaten or use violence against one another relative to South American states, and Western Europe is half as war prone as the Middle East.[61] Just as it is for human beings, so it is for states: certain neighborhoods are worse to live in than others. And the type of neighborhood a state lives in conditions its view of the world—particularly the threats it faces.

States that live in "bad" neighborhoods, in which rivals regularly target one another militarily, would deem future war with existing rivals likely. Such states live under more permissive norms insofar as the use of force is concerned, and as such, they are likely to be on guard about the prospect of border changes and the attendant loss in relative power. A comparable state in a peaceful neighborhood, conversely, is likely to be unruffled by such an eventuality. For instance, both Israel and Canada are wealthy, liberal democracies dealing with a sole nationalist challenge—Palestinians in the former, Quebecois in the latter—but they differ in one crucial respect: the peacefulness of their neighborhoods. As Israeli insiders put it, "Six wars, numerous major confrontations, and ongoing violence, from low-level terrorism to massive rocket attacks, have been basic features of Israel's external environment. A sense of nearly unremitting Arab enmity prevails, of a conflict of unlimited hostility and objectives . . . national security issues in Israel are commonly addressed in existential terms."[62] As such, all else equal, we would expect Israel to be more afraid of the security implications of a new Arab state in the Middle East, even if such a state would be drastically weaker than it, than Canada would be with the creation of a French-speaking one in North America. Consequently, we would expect Israel to put up a stiffer fight against Palestinian independence than Canada against Quebecois separatism.

The bottom line is that states consider future war to be unlikely only under a relatively narrow set of conditions, and the rarity of these conditions explains why most separatist movements result in coercive state responses. After all, a necessary condition for the state to consider a peaceful strategy is that it must not fear future war. For this condition to obtain, the secessionists must mobilize around an identity that does not threaten the host state's dominant conception of itself, since this would assure it that the seceded state's independent guns will not be turned toward it, and the state must live in a peaceful neighborhood, since this would assure it that it will not be exploited by opportunist state rivals. These relatively rare conditions translate to an optimistic, postsecurity environment for the state, where border changes are not seen in urgent or apocalyptic terms, enabling the possibility of peaceful concessions in its dealings with separatists. Consistent with this expectation, it bears noting that during the latter half of the twentieth century, separatism failed to incite even low-level conflict mainly in those regions where interstate war is not a serious possibility—such as Western Europe and the Pacific.[63] Much more commonly, however, the power shift that inheres in secession leaves the state too afraid to try peaceful negotiations. The fear of future war, against either the separatists or an existing rival, is a sufficient condition for the state to decide on coercion. Such coercive strategies result in a stronger correlation between secessionism and the outbreak of war in regions such as the Middle East, South Asia,[64] Southeast Asia, the Balkans and Caucasus,[65] and sub-Saharan Africa.[66] As much as a state may balk at paying the material and reputational costs associated with such a strategy, such costs pale in comparison to those associated with facing interstate war against relatively strengthened rivals.

Table 2 Probability of future war

		Identity distance	
		Indifferent	Opposed
Regional dynamics	Peaceful	Future war unlikely	Future war likely
	War prone	Future war likely	Future war likely

INDEPENDENT VARIABLE II: THIRD-PARTY SUPPORT

Once a state has made an assessment that it must use coercion against secessionists because they represent an external threat, it faces the decision of how much force to employ. "Coercion," after all, can mean any number of things, from beatings to widespread torture, from localized violence to genocide. How far states will up the repressive ante depends on the precise level of external threat the separatists represent, which depends on whether, and the degree to which, they enjoy third-party support.

Third-party support shortens a state's time horizons. A geopolitical rival helping the ethnic group secede is not just an external security problem for the future, but one very much for the present. States do not generally take kindly to their rivals' attempts to destroy their territorial integrity, from within or without. The level of third-party support influences the strength of the secessionists by transferring the "technologies of rebellion";[67] higher levels of support mean the threat is to be taken more seriously, which in turn translates to a heavier hand by the state.[68] Third-party support also adds an emotional dimension to separatist conflict and can fuel pathological levels of violence if delivered at significant levels.

Secessionists as a Fifth Column. Classical statements on external support for separatist minorities focused on irredentism,[69] or the desire to incorporate a neighbor's secessionist region into one's own state. Such goals, however, constitute the extreme end of the spectrum when it comes to the strategic aims of third parties.[70] More commonly, they are motivated by less grandiose aims, such as the destabilization or "mere" dismemberment of the host state to favorably shift the balance of power. Support to the secessionist minority can also be spurred by an ethnic affinity with the movement or domestic calculations,[71] or a combination of these. Supporting a secessionist group from afar is often the best of both worlds for geopolitical rivals: their costs of engagement are significantly lower, they can retain plausible deniability, they are not seen as the aggressor by the court of global public opinion—which could invite verbal rebukes, or worse—and they trap the host state in a difficult conflict being conducted on its own soil. This was precisely the situation India found itself in during Pakistan's civil war in 1971, when its Border Security Forces trained and equipped the Mukti Bahini across the border, bleeding Pakistan at reasonably low cost before its eventual dismemberment (chapter 2).

States worry a great deal about so-called fifth-columns,[72] especially during times of war. There are two main factors about third-party support to separatists that makes states escalate: it enables stronger movements, and it encourages emotional decisions and behavior by leaders and security forces.

The first effect of third-party support is that outside help represents material support, which means a change in capabilities by the secessionists: the more help the nationalists have, the stronger they are, and the more violence is needed to defeat them. Civil war researchers have demonstrated how external backing results in the transfer of the "technologies of rebellion" that allow challengers to fight the state.[73] Within IR, it is a truism that states get increasingly violent the more desperate they get.[74] Outside support increases the capabilities of the challenging group and narrows the possibility of the state winning. A state is thus likely to respond to external sponsorship with high levels of violence to curtail the threat. Additionally, the more material support an outside power provides, the higher is its resolve, at least as perceived by the central government. Given increasing levels of outside support, the central government is forced to conclude that the outside power is in for the long haul, and that high levels of violence will be required to deal with the threat. Lower levels of support, by contrast, smack of context-specific opportunism, and while no state is likely be pleased that one of its ethnic groups is receiving support, it is less likely to deem low levels of third-party cooperation threatening to the state's survival.

The second factor about outside support that affects the state's strategy is decidedly nonmaterialist. Researchers exhort us against sidelining emotions when studying conflict, noting that "although the bloodless conventions of social science make it simpler for academics to sweep such messy emotions aside when building their theories, those who visit the [affected] region find it impossible to explain what they find without reference to emotions."[75] Ethnic separatists soliciting and receiving external support, especially from the host state's rivals, represents an emotional betrayal to the central state. It is one thing to divorce, another thing entirely to divorce as a result of an affair with a spouse's sworn enemy. Though states are not people, they often behave as such.[76] Indeed, emotions produced and consumed by groups, such as governments, are often more powerful than those of the individual level.[77] Emotions trigger action, because "emotional judgments are quicker and stronger than cognitive judgments" and because they "heighten the saliency of a particular concern."[78] During times of ethnic tensions, three emotions in particular—resentment, fear, and hatred—are said to catalyze violence.[79]

There is no doubting the importance of these emotions, but the process of secessionism leads to a distinct emotion, as-yet unconsidered by ethnic violence research: betrayal. According to scholars, the notion of betrayal connotes "a voluntary violation of mutually known pivotal expectations of the trustor by the trusted party, which has the potential to threaten the well-being of the trustor."[80] In essence, Ego is badly let down by Alter, contravening its expectations about the latter. Politically, the structural conditions that give rise to this emotion involve an antecedent institutional arrangement being threatened by either an active or passive contributor of that arrangement. For instance, many nation-states in Asia and Africa gained independence from their erstwhile colonial rulers through nationalist movements, which saw alliances between varied ethnic, linguistic, or religious groups. The nation-state, in this case, is the institutional arrangement. When this state's borders and existence are threatened by one of the very groups that fought for it, the core governing group feels betrayed. For example, when the Bengali Muslim population of undivided India went from fighting for an independent Pakistan in the 1940s to campaigning for an independent Bangladesh a quarter century later, it greatly angered Pakistani nationalists (chapter 2). Crucially, this baseline level of betrayal is significantly exacerbated by an alliance between the ethnic group and an external patron. From the perspective of the core group, it is bad enough that an in-group wishes to become an out-group, it is another thing entirely for this group to elicit the support of a rival. Irrespective of whether such an alliance is prompted solely by realpolitik, identity-based concerns, or some mix of the two, if an ethnic group partners with outside rivals, it fuels a betrayal that can result in almost pathological or genocidal violence (chapters 2 and 4). When groups become perceived as collectively traitorous, both leaders and security forces become thirstier for gruesome punishment. Put simply, hell hath no fury like a state betrayed by its own.

The relevance of these two aspects of third-party support—the separatists' material capabilities increasing and the state feeling betrayed—depends on the state's perceptions of how much help the ethnic group enjoys. At most times, these perceptions will be fairly consonant with the objective level of support provided. After all, states generally devote an enormous amount of resources to matters of security and intelligence, and should be able to accurately gauge both the source and extent of support reasonably clearly. More important, while third-party support operations are meant to be covert, designed to conceal the identity of the sponsor, they are rarely clandestine—those operations whose execution itself is meant to be secret. By its very nature, external sponsorship of rebels is hard to keep under wraps, and as such, states on the receiving end of it tend to well-informed of its nature and intensity. Nevertheless, in some cases, states do get it wrong. Such miscalculations of third-party support can be the joint product of bureaucratic friction and racism or essentialism.[81] A state may believe that at ethnic group is "in bed with the enemy" based on nothing more than ascriptive characteristics of that group and the enemy in question, with its internal politics precluding self-correction. For example, the Pakistani military leadership wrongly believed the Bengali movement for independence was operating hand-in-glove with the Indian state in March 1971, despite a number of local officials, even those hailing from West Pakistan, informing them otherwise (chapter 2). In such situations of misperception, the state will behave "as if" third-party support existed even when it did not.

Aside from these genuine misperceptions, states may make accusations of external sponsorship against rebellious groups that they know to be false, either to discredit the group or build support for the government. Indira Gandhi's government, to cite one of many examples, claimed that Khalistani separatists were backed by Pakistan years before they actually were (chapter 3). Sometimes governments go further still and seek to "frame" groups for receiving external backing, as when Zulfiqar Bhutto concocted an "interception" of arms ostensibly traveling from Iraq to Baloch rebels (chapter 2). Such episodes, however, do not present insurmountable problems for the researcher interested in uncovering the "true" perceptions of governments at secessionist moments. This is because "fake" accusations of third-party support are quite transparently contrived, especially in hindsight. The insights and opinions of neutral observers, especially, contained in diplomatic archives or contemporary news reports, can help disentangle those situations in which the state genuinely perceives third-party support from those in which it is engaged in propaganda. As we shall see in the empirical chapters, when a state *actually* believes a group is enjoying third-party support it behaves very differently to when it merely alleges such support for domestic gain.

Levels of Third-Party Support. A state's level of coercion is calibrated to its perception of third-party support, which can be broken down into three types, each representing an escalation in the level of threat, and betrayal, that the state faces. The most elementary level of support is "limited": this includes situations in which third parties provide verbal, financial, or sanctuary support to the secessionists. A state can provide verbal or diplomatic support to secessionists and be considered offering limited support for the purposes of my theory mainly because in international politics, as in many other walks of life, talk is cheap. Mere verbal support does not aid secessionists. Though there are rare occasions on which governments take even verbal support from outsiders to secessionists quite seriously because of what it supposedly portends—Abraham Lincoln and other American leaders, for example, were extremely sensitive to British rhetoric that signaled their backing of the Confederacy (chapter 5)—generally speaking, diplomatic and political support does not weigh heavily on states' calculations to use force.

Financial aid, meanwhile, assuredly makes it more difficult to defeat the rebels, and signals the third party's preferences about the outcome of bargaining between the ethnic group and its government. It must be noted, however, that delivering financial aid to rebels can be a challenging task, for reasons ranging from a lack of social and institutional connections to rebels and field commanders, to legalistic countermeasures taken by the host state, such as freezing accounts and wire transfers. Consequently, financial aid is often delivered only in limited doses. More generally, principal-agent problems abound—those on the ground have different incentives and preferences than foreign financiers, and often the latter group will not enjoy reasonable levels of oversight over the usage of the aid once it is delivered. Additionally, financial aid does not change the composition of the resource-palette that rebels enjoy, it only enlarges it. Thus it is not a "game-changer" in terms of the types of support a third party can give, unlike, say, direct military aid of equipment that rebels currently do not possess.

The strongest form of "limited" support is a physical sanctuary across an international border. Sanctuaries are more important than financial aid because states are much more qualified and capable of regulating activity and governing people within their borders than without. Scholars have noted that "state boundaries are perhaps the most fundamental international institutions in the modern state system" and *the primary function of international boundaries is to demarcate legal or de facto lines of military control and political jurisdiction.* The military and police forces of one state have no authority in another state, and crossing borders with such forces is seen as an act of aggression."[82] States are less able to target and monitor the activities of rebels if they take place across sovereign boundaries owing to the difficulties of pursuit and international norms for territorial integrity.[83] However, sanctuaries are purely a defensive "weapon." A group's hold on a sanctuary would enable it to escape state action under most circumstances, but it would almost never, by itself, lead to more destructive capabilities against the state or its coercive apparatus. Rather, it is only when cross-border bases are combined with recruiting, training, or the provision of supplies that they assume real potency.[84] For these reasons, I consider a sanctuary an important type of third-party support, to be sure, but not capable of tipping the balance in any meaningful way—unless complemented with more serious forms of third-party support.

I call the second level "moderate" third-party support, which includes military aid, in the form in the form of equipment, supplies, and/or training. Military aid accomplishes significantly more than financial aid when it comes to aiding the political prospects of the secessionists' demands. It can considerably improve the battlefield capabilities of rebels, since states have access to arms in much greater numbers, and in much greater variety, than substate groups. Often foreign benefactors will supply rebels with crucial technology aimed at upturning the balance of power.[85] The famous—and perhaps overstated—case of the Afghan mujahideen employing U.S.-supplied Stinger missiles to defeat the Soviets serves as an exemplar of this phenomenon. Additionally, rebel or militant organizations fighting on behalf of secessionists are often poorly trained or organized hastily as situations on the ground can change rapidly, causing them to be ill-prepared for armed conflict with a state's regimented forces. Military aid and training from outsiders can close that gap appreciably and fairly quickly. It took approximately ten weeks, for instance, for Indian Border Security Forces to train and equip Mukti Bahini fighters in their quest to win independence from the Pakistani state in 1971 (chapter 2).

Finally, the highest form of support a third-party state can give is to fight alongside secessionists in a conflict with the host state. Once this level of support is reached, then the two parties' behavior, as opposed to simply their interests, becomes consonant. States fighting secessionists joined by third-party states are often unable to distinguish between the two as a practical matter. If states offer "high" levels of support to secessionists, then for all intents and purposes the state is fighting an interstate war on its soil against an alliance composed of both internal and external rivals. This type of support was seen in Russia's support of Armenian nationalists in World War I. In such situations, we can expect the state to escalate viciously, using pathological levels of violence to reflect both the hard task of winning an interstate war as well as the perceived betrayal of the state by the ethnic group.

External Security and State Strategy against Separatists

To sum up the basic framework, states have two related concerns about the external security implications of any secessionist movement. First, is future war likely, either against the newly independent state or an existing regional rival? This assessment depends on whether the ethnic group's identity is directly opposed to the state's core, as well as the war proneness of the regional neighborhood. If the state foresees a geopolitical problem with the creation of a new state, it behooves it to use coercion in the present, so that the threat may be nipped in the bud. The fear of future war, in other words, is a sufficient condition for the state's adoption of coercion against separatists. Under these circumstances, the state must make a second calculation: how much third-party support do the secessionists currently enjoy? The existence and level of outside support will shorten the state's time horizons, bring external security concerns forward from the future to the present, and compel it to use escalating violence to deal with the threat.

A state can face, broadly speaking, four possibilities when confronted with a secessionist movement. The movement can be externally unthreatening, or if it is an external threat, it can be tied to either limited, moderate, or high third-party support. These possibilities correspond to four basic strategies a state can employ regarding separatists: negotiations and concessions, policing, militarization, and collective repression.

If the movement does not represent an external security threat because its identity division with the core is relatively muted and the state is sanguine about its regional environment, then the state is open to being peaceful in its response. Not being threatened with future war is a necessary condition for the state to use a "negotiations and concessions" strategy. This strategy entails the state meeting representatives from the ethno-nationalists, whether they are drawn from political parties or rebel organizations. The state may not necessarily offer concessions immediately, but the use of violence on any meaningful scale is ruled out. The state could offer a bargain short of complete independence to satisfy, or satisfice, the minority—primarily because no state likes losing territory—but if such a bargain is not acceptable to the minority, the state will not attempt to use force or violence to convince the ethnic group otherwise. The state essentially adopts an attitude that connotes: we would like you to stay, but if you still choose to leave, we will not stop you.

To that end, the state may offer concessions to convince the minority it is better off staying in the unified state than going its own way. Such concessions can include greater political autonomy; more economic aid from the center (if the ethnic group is disadvantaged) or allowing a higher proportion of tax revenue to stay in the region (if the ethnic group is advantaged); more control over its culture; and so on. Some concessions concern just one issue, such as policy concerning the language of instruction in schools; others are more multifaceted, such as decentralist changes in the state's administrative structure; some concessions transfer real governing power to the group or region, others not.[86] The bottom line is that bargaining takes place in smoke-filled rooms, not on the smoky ruins of the battlefield. These situations, seen only in states in comfortable, optimistic, postsecurity environments, result in either autonomy where the minority finds the concessions at least momentarily acceptable (as in Quebec and Scotland), or full-blown independence where it does not (as in Slovakia).

When the state perceives a likelihood of future war, by contrast, it is impelled to use coercion. If there is limited third-party support for the secessionists, then it will adopt the moderately violent strategy of policing. This strategy includes the use of the state's armed apparatus, but not to any great extent. The state may imprison or even physically beat separatist leaders, harass political parties at their headquarters, forbid large meetings and protest rallies, or shut down radio, television, or other media access the secessionists may enjoy. It is a coercive strategy but one with a relatively light footprint; one should not expect substantial casualties under policing. The state may also use concessions to isolate the moderate elements of the movement from the more radical[87]—the absence of significant third-party support renders the threat muted enough for the state to offer concessions as a tactical, if not strategic, measure. However, outright secession or anything even close, such as significant transfers of power, will be completely off the table. As a strategy, policing ensures that the movement does not gather momentum toward independence, already ruled out by the state fearful of the future, while keeping levels of violence at relatively acceptable levels. The major difference between policing and negotiations is that the state is not prepared to give up on territory without a semblance of a fight. However, unlike in situations where there is major outside support, the threat is relatively manageable. Because states prefer to keep violence at relatively moderate levels to avoid the potential of sowing deep resentment, they do not escalate to high levels of repression. Examples of policing include India's strategy in Assam between 1987 and 1990 (chapter 3) or the Israeli response to the first intifada (chapter 5).

Once a group starts receiving moderate support from outside powers, especially if it is in the form of military aid, the equation changes. Now the level of threat the state faces increases appreciably, mainly because the palette of resources the nationalists enjoy becomes more dangerous. This causes the state to up the repressive ante, both to deal with the threat as an aggregation of material capabilities but also to send a message that fifth columns are not tolerated. In such a situation, the state would practice militarization, using state forces and violence against training camps and population centers. The escalation to militarization is a safe indicator that the state is fighting a civil war. Militarization entails the use of the state's military and paramilitary forces, but largely against violent or militant organizations or those suspected of directly aiding rebels. This is not to suggest that states practicing militarization always use perfectly legal or ethical policy instruments; torture and enforced disappearances would be consistent with militarization. For this to be the case, however, such policies must be practiced on a relatively limited scale, and not be pursued as a matter of official or quasi-official state policy. Militarization is often seen in so-called simmering conflicts,[88] where the state strikes sporadically against purely military targets and then retreats, at least in a military sense. Typical cases of militarization include Pakistani policy in Balochistan in the mid-1970s (chapter 2) and India in Punjab after 1987 (chapter 3).

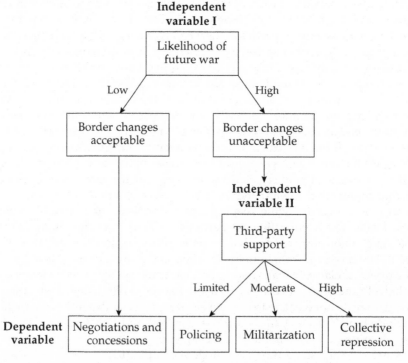

Figure 1. State decision-making when confronted by separatists

Finally, if the ethnic group enjoys high levels of external support, then the state would respond with collective repression. This is the harshest strategy a state can adopt. This policy includes the use of indiscriminate violence, including massacres against civilians; heavy-handed punishment, such as the burning of entire villages, forced migrations, and ethnic cleansing, as seen in the Bengali (chapter 2) or Armenian (chapter 4) genocides; and draconian legal instruments, such as emergency laws that grant the state the authority to imprison enemies of the state for long periods of time with no due process, as witnessed in India's conduct in Kashmir (chapter 3). Though genocide is not a necessary outcome of such a policy, huge numbers of deaths—in the tens or hundreds of thousands—can be common if the state chooses collective repression. This strategy demonstrates the state's lethality and sheer capability for inflicting widespread violence and pain. When states adopt collective repression, they are usually cited for vast human rights abuses and leave devastation and destruction in their wake. The severity of the external threat is what compels states to escalate to this strategy. First, for materialist reasons, the ethnic group becomes essentially as powerful as the external patron, given it is literally fighting alongside it. In such a situation, a state cannot hold anything back. Second, this situation sees the starkest consequences of a logic of betrayal, with the central government intent on revenge and sending a message. Angry leaders usually pave the way for angry militaries and paramilitaries, with the result that the violence on the ground is often pathological and indiscriminate. Figure 1 graphically represents the theoretical argument I proffer here.

Pakistan's Genocide in Bengal and Limited War in Balochistan, 1971–1977

States behave differently against different secessionists, I suggest, because state strategy against separatist movements is determined by the degree to which they are an external security threat. Can my theory account for the variation in response by the Pakistani state to two movements for independence in the 1970s? While Pakistan was assuredly coercive against both movements examined here, East Pakistan saw "collective repression" and Balochistan "militarization."

Acquiescing to a loss of territory was simply out of the question for a state like Pakistan in the 1970s, whether in Bengal or Balochistan. Pakistan was born an exceptionally weak state,[1] especially relative to its larger and more powerful neighbor. The country covered a quarter of undivided India's landmass but had only one-tenth its industrial base and one-sixth of its financial assets.[2] Conflict over Kashmir immediately after independence, the unequal division of British-India's assets and water at partition,[3] and a massive refugee crisis in the first months of statehood exacerbated its sense of "inferiority and insecurity" over its "precarious geopolitical situation."[4] In turn, this unfavorable security environment facilitated the outsized role of defense and foreign policy issues within the country. Most important, the Pakistani army and establishment was convinced that India would always threaten its security, and even existence as a state, with successive leaderships believing, in Liaquat Ali Khan's words, that India had never "wholeheartedly accepted" partition.[5]

It should not surprise us, then, that successive Pakistani leaders couched their reluctance for provincial autonomy in terms of the strength and prospects for survival of the state. In the ruling establishment's collective mind, Pakistan's security environment required a strong center,[6] and indeed, the emergence of the national security state was encouraged by the establishment's perception of the lack of loyalty to the state among various ethnic groups.[7] In his warning that some wanted to destroy Pakistan, Ayub Khan argued that "I have always told you that Pakistan's salvation lay in

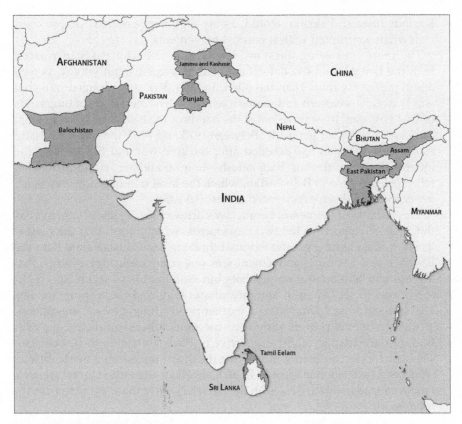

Map 1. Separatism in South Asia

a strong center."[8] Zulfiqar Ali Bhutto commented that the idea of autonomy was "a ridiculous one for a country that wants to count for something in the world."[9] Zia-ul-Haq confessed that he found the concept of
autonomy unfathomable: "I simply cannot understand this type of thinking. We want to build a strong country, a unified country." Scholars argue
that "whatever their background, Pakistani leaders have consistently seen
expressions of provincial feeling as a threat to the Pakistani state," especially when such movements are married to foreign enemies.[10] Between
1947 and the 1970s, when the two major secessionist conflicts under study
took place, Pakistan lost (or at least, failed to win) two wars against India.
Its neighborhood was dangerous—by one measure, the most militarized in
the world.[11] Given that most of its strategic decision-making was undertaken against the backdrop of the Indian threat, the idea of acquiescing
to border changes was anathema. Pakistan's environment was nothing
close to the optimistic, postsecurity context within which concessions are

feasible. Instead, Pakistan would, as my argument predicts, choose coercion when confronted with separatist movements.

The more interesting question, however, is not why Pakistan coerced both the Bengali and the Baloch national movements, but why it coerced one significantly more than the other. In 1971, Pakistan plunged into civil war between its eastern and western wings; at least hundreds of thousands of East Pakistani lives were lost at the hands of the Pakistani army, in what can plainly be called genocide. Between 1973 and 1977, the rump Pakistani state—East Pakistan had seceded after the civil war and had become the independent country of Bangladesh—fought another ethno-nationalist rebellion, this time in Balochistan, where the level of repression was much lower than had been experienced in East Pakistan.

This variation in violence, I argue, was driven by differences in perceived third-party support for the two movements, which meant that the Bengalis were considered a greater external threat to the Pakistan state than the Baloch were. The latter movement was one composed primarily of tribal leaders and left-leaning nationalists but was unable to secure the backing of the Soviet Union in any meaningful way, and aside from "moderate" support from Afghanistan, a weaker power, fought alone. In addition, global or regional powers supported the state rather than the rebels, with Iran, in particular, strongly supportive of Pakistani action in Balochistan. These factors in confluence meant that the threat represented by the Baloch rebels was deemed manageable. In turn, the relatively muted threat allowed Pakistani leadership to deal with the Baloch issue without using maximum repression.

By contrast, the Bengalis of East Pakistan were perceived by the central government as well as soldiers to be supported politically, militarily, financially, and diplomatically by India, a historical and significantly more powerful rival of Pakistan. This perception of "high" third-party support, especially at the outset of the crisis, was a product of cultural and religious essentialism. Pakistan's founding nationalism, encapsulated in the so-called two-nation theory, encouraged a suspicion of Bengalis of being more Indian than Pakistani. This purported relationship between India and East Pakistan was the emotional trigger behind the heavy, gruesome, and disproportionate use of force in quelling Bengali discontent. Additionally, actual—as opposed to merely alleged or perceived—Indian military support to the Mukti Bahini from May 1971 onward ensured a tougher fight for the Pakistani army in the postmonsoon phase of the conflict, and consequently more violence. That is, both effects of high third-party support, emotional and materialist, were operative in East Pakistan.

Figure 2 summarizes my theory's application to Pakistan in the 1970s.

As I detail later in the chapter, rival explanations do not explain the observed variation as well as my argument does. In the case of explanations grounded in mid-range IR theories—such as the reputation argument

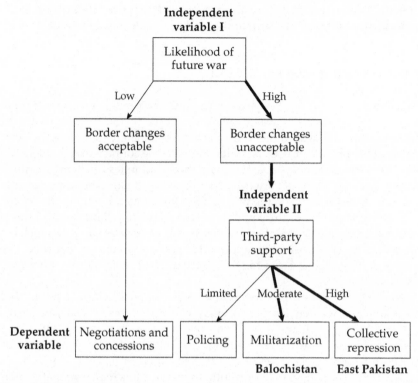

Figure 2. Variation in Pakistan's responses to secessionism in the 1970s

for fighting secessionists, or the veto-player argument for concessions—the case is either at odds with their predictions, or the causal mechanisms they identify were not operative. Meanwhile, explanations peculiar to the Pakistan case—such as the argument that blames pathological racism for the genocide in East Pakistan—do not adequately address the variation observed; they can explain why one war was very violent, but not why one war was significantly more violent than the other.

Juxtaposing the Bengal and Baloch secessionist conflicts has several benefits. First, there is significant variation in the independent and dependent variables in the two cases, which is useful for theory testing.[12] Second, by choosing a pair of conflicts in one country so close to one another temporally, I hold structural conditions broadly constant, allowing me to isolate the effects of variation in external security implications.[13] Third, no other study that I know of has compared these conflicts, even though they took place for similar reasons in one country in one relatively circumscribed time period; there is thus a pure empirical payoff. Fourth, scholars are encouraged to tackle puzzles that are of "intrinsic importance," episodes that drastically altered both history and a people's fate.[14] It is safe to say that the genocide that marked the birth of Bangladesh meets this criterion.

Pakistan Divided Between West and East

Pakistan's civil war, fought between the country's military and their conationals in East Pakistan was a quarter century in the making, with the antecedents of the war found in the period immediately following the overthrow of British rule in 1947. At independence, the country was divided into West and East Pakistan, separated by a thousand miles of enemy territory. It soon became obvious, however, that the vast Indian landscape was not the only division between the two wings. Questions concerning the official or national language of the country, as well as the legal and political rights of Bengalis, became contentious issues, and the consistency with which the West Pakistani establishment ignored Bengali aspirations led to a collective view that they had replaced the British colonial administration with a West Pakistani one.[15]

Tensions initially erupted over language. The East Pakistani public and its politicians wanted Bangla to enjoy coequal status with Urdu as the national language. Liaquat Ali Khan rejected the idea, saying, "It is necessary for a nation to have one language and that language can only be Urdu and no other language."[16] East Pakistanis, 56 percent of Pakistan's population, were asked to learn another language less than a year after purportedly ridding themselves of colonial masters.[17] The following month, the founder of the nation and its first governor general, Mohammad Ali Jinnah, decided to visit Dhaka, in response to language protests,[18] where he summarily dismissed Bengalis' language and their demands.[19] And while the center finally relented in 1954, the language issue remained only one of many concerns Bengalis had, including political, bureaucratic, military, and economic disenfranchisement.

Politically, there were two salient questions. First, what was to be the relationship between the provinces and the center? Bengalis would have liked Pakistan to be a loose federation, while the West Pakistani establishment preferred a more tightly bound centralist state. Second, what was the constitutional relationship amongst the provinces themselves? As things stood shortly after independence, East Pakistan demographically outmatched the provinces of West Pakistan—Punjab, Sindh, NWFP, and Balochistan. To counter East Pakistan's strength in numbers, the West Pakistani elite established the One Unit scheme in 1955, which claimed that the eastern and western parts of Pakistan each constituted a "unit," in effect, combining the demographic and political strength of the four western provinces. Even aside from One Unit, representation in parliament did not fairly reflect the demographics of the provinces.[20]

It was a similar story within the civil services and military. Bengalis were poorly represented in the bureaucracy, which tended to be dominated by Punjabis and Urdu-speaking Mohajirs from Sindh, and made up just 1 percent of the three armed forces. By the late 1960s, the situation was only marginally better, as Bengalis made up 5 percent of the officers and 7 percent of the other ranks in the military. Military doctrine and defense planning too was unfair toward the Bengalis. Because of the Pakistan military's belief that the "defense of the East lay in the West," the majority of the armed forces were to be stationed in the West. If India chose to attack East Pakistan, the military would respond by attacking India's western borders. Essentially, East Pakistan was left defenseless.[21] Sure enough, in the 1965 war that began in Kashmir, India invaded East Pakistan. The bare defenses stationed in East Pakistan—one relatively weak division, fifteen Sabre jets, and no communication with the Western wing[22]—were a stark notice of the prioritization afforded to Bengali security by the military establishment.

Finally, issues of economic inequality abounded. The economic disparity between the two wings, already appreciable at independence, became more acute through the 1950s and 1960s, to the point where per capita income in the west was 61 percent higher than that in the east. There were also significant transfers of wealth, as the state exploited the export earnings from jute, which was one of East Pakistan's primary revenue streams. Moreover, much of East Pakistan's industrial strength was actually in the hands of West Pakistani elites and businessmen; by the beginning of the 1970s, six non-Bengalis controlled more than 40 percent of East Pakistan's industrial assets.[23]

THE DECEMBER ELECTIONS AND THEIR AFTERMATH

This was the setting, then, of the 1970 elections. The elections were supposed to represent a peaceful transfer of power from Yahya Khan's military regime to civilian authorities. Instead, the polls marked the beginning of the end and set rolling a process that ultimately led to the creation of Bangladesh and the dismemberment of Pakistan.

There were three actors that drove events during and after the elections. The first was the Pakistani military, in control of the country since 1958 through two dictators, Ayub Khan and Yahya Khan (no relation), and generally suspicious of politicians, their ability to govern, and their competence. The second was the Pakistan People's Party, or the PPP, headed by Zulfiqar Ali Bhutto, a fast-rising party that shocked many observers with their excellent showing in the elections. The third was the Awami League, centered in East Pakistan and led by Mujib-ur-Rahman, a collection of disparate actors bound by an unwavering belief in greater autonomy for East Pakistan—captured by Mujib's famous Six-Points platform[24]—and a general anti–West Pakistan view, born out of two decades of exploitation.[25] The elections saw 162 National Assembly seats contested from East Pakistan and 138 from the west, for a total of 300. The Awami League swept the polls in the East, winning 160 out of its 162 seats and an overall majority in the National Assembly. In West Pakistan, the PPP dominated, winning 84 seats.[26] But the results were never allowed to speak for themselves by the military and Bhutto, who denied Mujib and the Awami League their rightful place as leaders of Pakistan.[27]

Throughout early 1971, the three principals—Yahya, Bhutto, and Mujib—met in various permutations to find a mutually acceptable agreement on questions concerning the National Assembly and constitution, to little avail. Notably, the first meeting was between the two men from the west, with Bhutto paying a visit to Yahya in late December, terming the meeting "very useful and constructive."[28] Yahya and Mujib then met in Dhaka on January 11 and 12, after which Mujib claimed he was "satisfied," and Yahya publicly said that "Sheikh Mujibur Rehman is going to be the future Prime Minister of the country."[29] On January 16, Yahya visited Bhutto in Larkana. It was after this meeting that Yahya first explicitly drew a public equivalence between Bhutto's and Mujib's positions, noting that "both are the major national leaders and they must cooperate."[30] Bhutto and Mujib then met with their aides on January 26, 27, and 28 "apparently without any agreement on the principles on which the country's future constitution should be framed."[31]

Mujib legitimately reasoned that since his party had won the elections fair and square, the National Assembly should be convened and allowed to formulate a constitution on the basis of his Six Points, for which the Awami League won an overwhelming mandate.[32] The problem was mainly Bhutto, who was bent on power, and treated himself and the PPP as Mujib's and the Awami League's equal. For Bhutto, his party represented the West while the Awami League represented the East,[33] even though the election results clearly placed the Awami League in a more advantageous position.[34] Bhutto believed that legally the majority party could form a constitution, but ominously warned that doing so without "the necessary consensus" would spell trouble for the country and its people.[35] Bhutto sought to portray the Awami League as ill-fitting as a representative of the entire country, arguing that it was exclusively an East Pakistani entity, his thinking perfectly encapsulated by his phrase that "a majority alone doesn't count in national politics."[36] He also claimed in a speech to PPP supporters that "we respect the majority . . . [but] . . . both Punjab and Sindh are centers of power. We may or may not form a government at the Center but the keys of the Punjab Assembly chambers are in my pocket [in addition to] the keys of the Sindh Assembly." He warned both Mujib and Yahya that "if the People's Party does not support it, no government will be able to work, nor will the constitution be framed."[37] Bhutto used his contacts within the upper echelons of the military, such as General Pirzada, a friend to both Bhutto and Yahya, to ensure that Bhutto had the president's ear before others.[38] His stance severely complicated what should have been a relatively simple transfer of power to civilian authorities.[39]

Matters soon came to a head. The most pressing area of disagreement became the date at which the National Assembly was to convene. Mujib wanted it to meet by mid-February; Bhutto, playing for time, wanted it to meet at the end of March. Yahya chose March 3 as a compromise.[40] While it was Mujib that should have been more aggrieved by Yahya's delay, it was Bhutto that fired the more loaded and damaging rhetorical salvo. In a speech on February 28, he helped create conditions under which it would be impossible to transfer power to the Awami League, threatening to "break the legs" of anyone from his party who dared to go to Dhaka for the first meeting of the National Assembly. Those that did choose to go, Bhutto warned, should proceed on a "one-way ticket," as they would be welcome back neither to the PPP nor to West Pakistan.[41] Yahya then decided to indefinitely postpone convening the assemblies without informing Mujib.[42]

Events soon began to spiral out of control. Dozens of people were killed in riots in East Pakistan.[43] In response to the assembly delay, Mujib announced a six-day strike to begin on March 3, promised that "you will see history made if the conspirators fail to come to their senses," and was particularly critical of Bhutto for "always acting in the most irresponsible manner."[44]

FINAL NEGOTIATIONS, THEIR FAILURE,
AND OPERATION SEARCHLIGHT

There were three key developments in March 1971 relevant to our story. The first was Yahya's too-little, too-late announcement of a date for the convention of the National Assembly. In a speech on March 6, amidst social and political unrest in East Pakistan, and surprised by the reaction to his earlier decision to indefinitely postpone the convention of the National Assembly, Yahya announced that it would meet on March 25. After years of promises unfulfilled, however, Yahya's latest claim simply lacked credibility.[45] As a response to Yahya, Mujib's speech on March 7 broadcast on Radio Dhaka was contradictory at times; he escalated his rhetoric from autonomy to something greater—"The struggle this time is the struggle for freedom; the struggle this time is the struggle for Independence"—but also left open the possibility for a negotiated settlement to be found with the words "before we go to the Assembly, our demands have to be conceded."[46] At the very least we can confidently state that Mujib and the Awami League were showing increasing signs of willingness to not be held in check by the politicking of the West Pakistani establishment and had grown more assertive.

The second important point was the final, futile efforts of the three principals to reach a negotiated solution in Dhaka. Yahya was determined to find a solution that had the "full endorsement of all major political leaders."[47] In Bhutto's words, "President Yahya Khan told me that he had made it clear to Mujibur Rahman that his concurrence to the proposal would be subject primarily to my agreement."[48] Perversely, by handing Bhutto veto-power, Yahya further incentivized him to act as a spoiler. Mujib was insistent that four conditions be met: the lifting of Martial Law, the withdrawal of military personnel in East Pakistan back to the barracks, an inquiry into the dozens of deaths that had occurred in antiriot policing in East Pakistan in early March, and the transfer of power to the provinces.[49] As late as March 23, it appeared that steady if strained progress was being made, before Yahya called off the talks. The failure of the talks hammered the final nail in the coffin of a political solution to the crisis.

The third noteworthy event was the violent crackdown by the military in East Pakistan, marking the beginning of the civil war that eventually ruptured Pakistan and halved its population. Given the loss of the government's central authority that he was witness to in Dhaka, along with misguided elements within his coterie of advisers counseling toughness, Yahya decided to order military action.[50] In his announcement banning the Awami League, outlawing all political activity, and censorship of the press, Yahya said that

> I should have taken action against Sheikh Mujibur Rahman and his collaborators weeks ago but I had to try my utmost to handle the situation in such a manner as not to jeopardise my plan of peaceful transfer of power . . . we have left no stone unturned. But he has failed to respond in any constructive manner; on the other hand he and his followers kept on flouting the authority of the Government even during my presence in Dacca . . . his obstinacy, obduracy and absolute refusal to talk sense can lead to but one conclusion—the man and his party are enemies of Pakistan and they want East Pakistan to break away completely from the country. He has attacked the solidarity and integrity of this country. This crime will not go unpunished. We will not allow some power-hungry and unpatriotic people to destroy this country and play with the destiny of 120 million people.[51]

Yahya closed by noting that he had ordered the army "to do their duty and fully restore the authority of the Government." The result was Operation Searchlight. The object of the operation was to restore central control over East Pakistan, to arrest Mujib and other top Awami League leaders, disarm Bengali military units—such as the East Pakistan Rifles—and police, and neutralize radical and student organizations.[52]

Operation Searchlight entailed extremely high levels of repression. The orders were to treat the Awami League, its supporters, and sympathizers as rebels. Any resistance was to be met with death.[53] The general officer commanding the operation, Major General Khadim Hussain Raja said that "I will muster all I can—tanks, artillery, and machine guns—to kill all the traitors and, if necessary, raze Dacca to the ground. There will be no one to rule; there will be nothing to rule."[54] The Pakistani military lived up to those words. On the first night of the conflict, troops entered Dhaka University and student hostels, killing hundreds, and filling mass graves. There was widespread violence in the form of rapes, murders, and massacres of entire villages—including women and children.[55] Intellectuals and journalists were targeted, as were Bengali Hindus. A Pakistani general later noted that some elements of the army went "berserk" as they sprayed bullets at random and destroyed whole villages at a time.[56] General Tikka Khan, a commanding general in the theater, was later nicknamed the "Butcher of Bengal." A senior officer in the military noted that any Bengali thought to be a rebel or member of the Awami League was to be "sent to Bangladesh"—a euphemistic phrase referring to execution without trial.[57] The total number of casualties that the Pakistan military inflicted on its citizens in the East is still debated; Mujib said it was more than 3 million while Tikka Khan placed it at 34,000. We can reasonably deduce that it was at least an order of magnitude above Tikka Khan's estimate, and probably at least 1 million, a genocidal figure when one considers the war lasted less than nine months. Simply put, the Pakistani military and its leaders chose to practice what I call "collective repression" in East Pakistan, the highest level of violence possible. Why, we must ask, was such extreme violence used?

THE EXTERNAL THREAT AND ITS ROLE IN VIOLENCE

India and its relationship with Pakistan was a central factor in the genocidal response the Pakistani state fashioned in East Pakistan. The Bengali nationalist movement was perceived to enjoy high levels of support from India because of West Pakistani leaders' and soldiers' racist views of Bengali identity, rooted in the country's foundational "two-nation theory." The two-nation theory's reification and ossification of the supposed civilizational differences between "Hindu India" and "Muslim Pakistan" would have vicious consequences on the ground in East Pakistan, especially for Bengali Hindus. Additionally, Indian covert support to the Mukti Bahini in the summer of 1971 made Pakistani counterinsurgency more challenging, and consequently more violent. That is, high third-party support had both emotional and materialist consequences on Pakistani strategy.

Conflating Bengali Nationalists, Hindus, and the Indian State. From the beginning of the crisis, the West Pakistani establishment dismissed Bengali aspirations as an Indian ruse to destroy Pakistan.[58] Importantly, such sentiments were not the product of post-hoc rationalization of the army's brutality; rather, the belief of Bengali-Indian collusion was widely accepted at the time. Indeed, the idea of a plot by India and Bengalis generally, and

Mujib and the Awami League specifically, to damage Pakistan's interests was an idea popular in the West for decades.[59] In 1971, this general unease with Mujib and the Awami League's intentions and faith in the Pakistani nation manifested in thinking that the Bengali uprising was the joint production of "a few [East Pakistani] miscreants" and Indian subversion, the entire episode characterized as "India's Trojan horse."[60]

It was certainly true that Mujib and the Awami League evinced a friendlier outlook toward India than the West Pakistani establishment. In a triumphant rally in Dhaka shortly after the elections, he stressed his desire to see disputes with India resolved peacefully.[61] One British diplomat stationed in New Delhi noted in February 1971 that "for the first time at least since 1965 a political leader has emerged in Pakistan who holds out the promise" of warming relations with India, mainly because "he is not committed to the recovery of Kashmir" and "he is not committed to the West Pakistan thesis of massive expenditure on the forces and continued hostility towards India."[62] American diplomats agreed, predicting that "if he achieves a position of power, Sheikh Mujib . . . would take all possible steps to restore full trade and commercial relations with India. He specifically mentioned the necessity of getting cheaper Indian coal for East Pakistan," as well as emphasizing the need for India's cooperation for flood control in East Pakistan.[63] Reporting on a meeting with Mujib after the elections, the U.S. consul in Dhaka wrote that "better relations with India will probably in fact be his most pressing concern since he sees at least partial solution to East Pak problems in expanded trade with neighboring India. Mujib, like many Bengalis, is not (except for record) particularly hard on Kashmir."[64]

Greater economic and disaster-management cooperation with India hardly spelled geopolitical collusion to destroy Pakistan, but that is how Mujib, the Awami League, and Bengali nationalists were perceived at large. Bhutto, the military, and the bureaucracy "feared that Mujib's constitutional scheme [Six Points] giving more political and economic freedom for the eastern region would allow East Pakistan to go close to India which would ultimately weaken Pakistan and kill the Kashmir issue for good."[65] As one journalist put it, Mujib's "theory of 'Bengali nation' was against the political conception of Pakistan. His advocacy for establishing trade and economic relations with India without the solution of the Kashmir dispute and the Farakka Barrage issue . . . was against the national interests of Pakistan."[66]

Behind this belief in collusion between Bengali nationalists and the Indian state was Pakistan's founding ideology, the "two-nation theory." This "theory" of religious nationalism claimed that the Muslims of South Asia formed a distinct community from its Hindus and thus needed a distinct political unit; in the words of Mohammad Ali Jinnah, Hindus and Muslims "belong to two different religious philosophies, social customs, literatures.

They neither intermarry not interdine together, and indeed, they belong to two different civilizations which are based mainly on conflicting ideas and conceptions. Their aspects on life and of life are different."[67] Partly as a result, and partly in spite,[68] of Jinnah's machinations based on this "two-nation" theory, Pakistan joined the comity of nations on August 14, 1947. As Devji writes of this development, "No other country has made of religion the sole basis of Muslim nationality."[69]

This foundational religious nationalism was, upon independence, the ideological glue for the new state. Scholars refer to concepts such as state-building nationalism, whereby the state promotes a common national identity to displace more parochial attachments.[70] This process is carried out by using public schools and the military, as well the creation and manipulation of symbols such as flags, anthems, and monuments,[71] to build a unified identity that coalesces around the state. For Pakistan, built on Muslim nationalism, it was but natural to adopt Islam as a unifying ideology in the face of religious and ethnic diversity.[72] While early rulers found these concerns pressing, it was Ayub Khan's regime (1958–69) that "began the process of official myth-creation in earnest," primarily through its control of textbooks, electronic media, and print media.[73]

The centrality of Islam to the identity of the state was contrasted with "Hindu" India, notwithstanding the latter's claims to being a secular state,[74] and cemented a stark division in Pakistan's conception of the nationalisms of itself and its neighbor, defined in civilizational, religious terms. Basic demographic facts, however, complicated this story: Bengali Hindus were a sizable minority in East Pakistan. As such, extensive "Hindu" or "Indian" influence in East Pakistan was a constant concern of paranoid West Pakistanis and manifested itself in their racist views of Bengalis well before 1971. For instance, during the 1960s, Bengal governor Monem Khan banned the songs of Nobel Laureate Rabindranath Tagore from being played on Radio Pakistan because he felt that Bangla was a "non-Muslim" language and was an agent of cultural domination of Indian Bengal.[75] One of Yahya's own ministers admitted that the regime thought of the so-called nonmartial Bengalis as "Muslims converted from lower caste Hindus."[76] According to Ayub Khan's autobiography, Bengalis, who "probably belong to the very original Indian races" had not known "real freedom or sovereignty" until the creation of Pakistan, before which "they have been in turn ruled either by the caste Hindus, Moghuls, Pathans or the British." Most important, "they have been and still are under considerable Hindu cultural and linguistic influence."[77] Even the December 1970 electoral success of the Awami League was thought to be a result of the large Hindu minority in East Pakistan,[78] even though it enjoyed strong support from Bengali Muslims too.

This conflation of "Hindu," "India," and "Bengali" translated into Pakistani perceptions that the Bengali nationalist movement enjoyed high levels of third-party support in 1971. In this simplistic view, "Hindu" stood for "India," and the "Hindu influence" on East Pakistan—symbolized by its substantial Hindu population, and cultural, geographic, political, and linguistic links to Northeast India—meant that the Bengalis were thought to owe their allegiance to the other "nation" that constituted the basis of the two-nation theory. The prism of religious bifurcation between "Muslim Pakistan" and "Hindu India" that the West Pakistani establishment saw events through, when combined with anti-Indian sentiment in the upper echelons of the same, meant that any Bengali uprising was perceived to be operating hand-in-glove with the Indian state. One Western historian, extremely sympathetic to the West Pakistani military and wider establishment in general, and Yahya Khan in particular, captured this sentiment when arguing that "East Pakistan, because of the predominance of the Bengali elements in its population, because of its very considerable Hindu minority of some 15 percent, and because of its physical separation from West Pakistan by hundreds of miles of Indian territory has for long afforded favorable conditions for the exercise of Indian influence."[79]

As a result of perceptions of full-blown Indian support for the Bengali nationalist movement, the Pakistani state responded with extreme brutality. The emotional implications of third-party support—pathological violence fueled by feelings of betrayal—revealed itself especially clearly in the collective repression carried out by security forces during the first stage of the war, from March to May. Commanding generals gave specific instructions to seek out Bengali Hindu villages to wipe out, and Pakistani soldiers—already indoctrinated with strong anti-Hindu and anti-Indian sentiment—efficiently followed orders.[80] During the early stages of the war, the U.S. consul general in Dhaka, Archer Blood, cabled Washington to report the "mass killing of unarmed civilians, the systematic elimination of the intelligentsia, and the annihilation of the Hindu population."[81] Indeed, U.S. officials in Dhaka were among the first to sound the alarm on the developing genocide, and the particular targeting of Hindus. "One of Blood's senior staffers privately noted 'evidence of selecting singling out of Hindu professors for elimination, burning of Hindu settlements including 24 square block areas on edges of Old Dacca and village built around temple.'"[82] Another was witness to the army lining up people outside their houses and shooting down in lines, "killing close to six hundred" in one go.[83] One diplomat in Dhaka plainly noted in April that "Hindus seem bear brunt of general regin [sic] of terror designed convince populace not cooperate with Awami League or anti-military forces in future."[84]

The Hamood-ur-Rahman Commission report, a judiciary-led inquiry into the war in its aftermath, reported that "there were verbal instructions to eliminate Hindus." Testimony such as that given by Lieutenant Colonel Aziz Ahmad Khan to the commission—"Gen. Niazi visited my unit at

Thakargaon and Bogra. He asked as to how many Hindus we had killed. In May, there was an order in writing to kill Hindus. This order was from Brigadier Abdullah Malik of 23 Brigade"—was commonplace.[85] Writing a series on the 1971 war for BBC Urdu, Colonel Nadir Ali recounted a conversation with his superior officer in the first month of the war. "The briefing officer said: 'Listen Nadir, we have got the root cause of this problem, and that is the Hindu. The decision was taken to kill Hindus. If Hindus are finished then this problem will be solved forever.'"[86] On the very first night of the conflict, the military made it a priority—alongside major military objectives, such as the disarming of East Pakistani Rifles and police and arresting Mujib—to target the Nawabpur area, where Hindu houses were alleged to have been converted into armories.[87] Even the decisions about which dormitories and halls at Dhaka University were to be targeted on March 25 were partly influenced by the "Hindu" factor, since Jagannath Hall, traditionally home to Hindu students, was one of the three main buildings attacked.[88]

The Pakistani military would attempt to ascertain whether locals were Hindu or Muslim before unleashing violence—as in Dhaka on April 16, where troops killed seven people after querying residents "are you Hindu or Muslim?" or as on a train from Mymensingh on May 18 where passengers were forced to recite the *kalma* to prove that they were Muslim.[89] The headmaster of a Catholic school in Nawabganj received a letter instructing him that "Hindus are trouble makers and you are not to give them any help."[90] There was a "common pattern" to the military's operations, "whereby troops move into a village, ask where Hindus live, and then kill male Hindus."[91] Even food relief for the largely peasant population stricken by civil war was denied to Hindus.[92]

Security forces on the ground in East Pakistan deployed paramilitary and irregular units in their aims, and the constitution of these irregular units offers a further clue to how the conflict was seen. Most conspicuous was the use of the Islami Jamiat-e-Taliba (IJT), the violent student wing of the Jamaat-e-Islami, a rightwing Islamist political party that gave its complete support to the army in its actions against "enemies of Islam."[93] The cooperation between the Jamaat and the army saw the formation of two paramilitary units drawn from the IJT called al-Badr and al-Shams—note the Arab/Islamic nomenclature—which aided and abetted the military's hunting of guerrillas and nationalists.[94] A Western observer noted during the crisis that West Pakistan's conflict with Bengalis "had overtones of a religious crusade or jihad . . . Western Muslims say the Hindus have corrupted Bengali Muslims" and that "one cannot be a Bengali and a Muslim" simultaneously.[95]

Contemporary diplomats' explanations for Pakistani aggression, especially against Hindus, corroborate the importance of perceptions of Indian support for Bengali nationalists. Speaking of the genocidal "naked, calculated and widespread selection of Hindus for special treatment," Blood wrote that "evidence suggests Pak military unable make distinctions between Indians and Pakistani Hindus, treating both as enemies. West Paks resident here in conversations with us often equate 'wicked Hindus' and 'wicked Indians,' using both terms interchangeably . . . it conceivable that soldiers from West Pakistan, where virtually no Hindus reside, inculcated with line that Hindus are responsible for secessionist currents in East Pakistan."[96] Similarly, summarizing their conversations with Pakistanis in Islamabad over the first two months of the conflict, the U.S. embassy cabled that "India is emotionally criticized as the principal culprit in the East Pakistan situation," which was deemed a conspiracy hatched by "only a 'small' hard-core of 'Bengali nationalists and Indian agents' . . . [who] should be dealt with summarily." Indeed, "the major criticism of the MLA [Martial Law Administration] is that Yahya showed too much patience and waited too long before striking down the Awami League."[97] A few months later, describing the "general mood in Karachi," American diplomats cabled that "to one and all, India is chief cause of trouble in East wing, major threat to peace in area, and warmonger determined to break up Pakistan. Intensity of anti-Indian feeling is hard to overestimate."[98] A U.S. cable relayed a conversation between a senior East Pakistan government official and two USAID officers, in which the official claimed that "the Hindu community in East Pakistan has always conspired against Pakistan and spoken and acted in such a way as to heighten distrust and hatred of West Pakistan by Bengalis."[99] Providing its explanation of the cleansing of Bengali Hindus one month into the war, the U.S. diplomatic mission in Islamabad noted that "there exists large body of West Pak opinion that Hindus leading element behind secessionist movement."[100] In mid-May, the same office wrote that "thinking of West Paks, especially Punjab is colored by an emotional anti-Hindu bias. This has been buttressed in recent weeks by thrust of GOP propaganda line about East Pak situation which has stressed alleged role of Hindus (and Indians) in creating crisis."[101] American consul Blood wrote at the same time that "we must allow for strength of army, and West Pakistan belief that Hindus in East Pakistan are subversive element, working with Indian movement and 'unpatriotic' Bengali Muslims to destroy integrity of Pakistan. Pak troops clearly look upon local Hindus as 'the enemy.'"[102]

These views were supported by contemporary American intelligence assessments. An intelligence memorandum written six months into the war explained that the Pakistani military's "wrath" turned toward Hindus was "apparently . . . because they were associated with India, which was thought to be responsible for the Bengali 'uprising,'" later noting that "Hindu residents were adjudged a permanent threat to security and apparently until that threat was reduced, i.e., until a sufficient number of Hindus had left the country, the government's repressive policy was to continue."[103]

Another memo suggested that "troops mostly from the West Pakistani Punjab (an area now almost 100 percent Muslim and strongly communal in outlook) appear have made Hindus, darkly suspected anyway of being Indian spies and secessionists, their special targets. In this virulent atmosphere, many Pakistani junior officers, enlisted men, and resident collaborators have become accustomed to mistreating the Hindu religious minority."[104] In May, the CIA reported that "Pakistani soldiers have almost certainly been encouraged in their extreme actions by the steady stream of anti-Indian, anti-Hindu propaganda put out by the Pakistani authorities, who claim that the trouble is India's fault and that they are only fighting foreign inspired subversive and secessionist plots."[105]

In an explosive article in the *Sunday Times* in June that detailed the extent of the army's atrocities in considerable depth, Anthony Mascarenhas spoke to soldiers and officers about the brutality. His article is worth quoting in some detail, for it captures soldiers' thinking at the time:

> "The Hindus had completely undermined the Muslim masses with their money," Col. Naim of 9th Division headquarters told me in the officers [*sic*] mess at Comilla. "They bled the province white. Money, food, and produce flowed across the borders to India. In some cases they made up more than half the teaching staff in the colleges and schools, and sent their own children to be educated in Calcutta. It had reached the point where Bengali culture was in fact Hindu culture, and East Pakistan was virtually under the control of the Marwari businessmen in Calcutta. We have to sort them out to restore the land to the people, and the people to their Faith."
>
> Or take Major Bashir. He came up from the ranks. He is SSO of the 9th Division at Comilla and he boasts of a personal bodycount of 28. He had his own reasons for what has happened. "This is a war between the pure and the impure," he informed me over a cup of green tea. "The people here may have Muslim names and call themselves Muslims. But they are Hindus at heart. You won't believe that the *maulvi* of the Cantonment mosque here issued a *fathwa* during Friday prayers that the people would attain *janat* if they killed West Pakistanis. We sorted the bastard out and we are now sorting out the others. Those who are left will be real Muslims. We will even teach them Urdu."[106]

As a serving officer in the 1971 war summarized, "Everyone thought that this secessionist activity was an Indian conspiracy."[107]

Accusations of Indian Support: Misperception or Propaganda? While it is quite clear that the soldiers and officers directly involved in the mass killings were convinced of the Indian-Hindu-Bengali triangle of subversion, the more difficult question is whether those in the higher leadership believed their own myth making.[108] Did the Pakistani leadership deploy propaganda—to the effect that the crisis was India's doing, acting primarily through the

Bengali Hindu community—that it entirely disbelieved? Was this a case of "genuine" misperception or deliberate dissembling? On the one hand, it is certainly true that leaders often use the "bogey man" of a foreign backer to distract the attention of their citizens and outside observers when clamping down on their own population; in a British telegram in early April, it was deemed "no surprise that the central government should use India as a scapegoat for any lack of progress in reimposing control in East Pakistan."[109] Perhaps the best evidence for this purely cynical view of the exaggeration of the "Indian threat" can be found in the tone and content of West Pakistani reports once censorship went into effect in late March, resulting in an almost comical level of concern with "infiltration" of "armed Indians" as well as movements of Indian troops and paramilitary forces on the border,[110] well before Indian forces were actually involved.

However, at the same time, it is likely that the military leadership believed at least some, and probably most, of what it was desperately trying to convince its population, and the rest of the world, of: that the Bengali movement was operating hand-in-glove with the Indian state. After all, they did not exist separately from the society in which such opinions were received wisdom. General K. M. Arif, a serving officer in the 1971 war, wrote about the ill-feelings Bengalis had toward West Pakistan by alleging that "initially, India played a subtle role in instigating such hatred. So did the Hindu minority in East Pakistan."[111] General A. A. K. Niazi, the commanding officer in the theater from April 1971, wrote that "India had been continuously assisting Mujib" and that "the vast majority of teachers in [East Pakistan] schools and colleges were Hindus."[112] "The teachers played an important role in moulding [sic] the ideas of the youth in their formative years. The West Pakistanis were painted as imperialists, exploiters, and tyrants. The seeds of discontent were sown."[113] He added that "thousands of Indians" entered East Pakistan during the unrest in early March, amidst the negotiations between Yahya, Mujib and Bhutto and that these thousands of Indians were actually military personnel who had crossed the border in civilian clothing to keep their identity secret.[114] While these recollections could be read as post-hoc justifications for their behavior during the war, such perceptions were confirmed by neutral observers. As U.S. ambassador Farland wrote in a secret telegram to Washington two weeks after Operation Searchlight kicked off, "Pak build-up of 'Indian threat' is probably a mixture of genuine concern and an effort to divert internal and external attention from Pak army actions in East Pakistan. I know the Paks [sic] are worried about India's intentions, and from info available through intelligence channels they have cause for worry."[115]

Pakistan's extreme brutality, especially in the first stage of the war, was typical of the emotional or pathological levels of violence that can result from perceptions of high levels of third-party support. Its "collective repression" strategy had its roots in how Bengali nationalists were seen: as acting on behalf, and with the full support, of the Indian state. Both the general slaughter, and the specific targeting of Hindus, can be attributed to the essentialism of leaders and soldiers. In turn, this racism was based on a civilizational conception of the difference between Hindu India and Muslim Pakistan, as captured by the two-nation theory. Niazi's description of the conduct of General Tikka Khan's forces the first two nights of Operation Searchlight is revealing in its choice of words: "Tikka let loose everything at his disposal as if *raiding an enemy*, not dealing with his own misguided and misled people."[116]

Indian Support for the Mukti Bahini and Pakistani Counterinsurgency. In addition to its emotional implications, the materialist effects of third-party support, which result in harsher state violence because it faces a tougher military fight, were also operative in 1971. Though Pakistan exaggerated, and believed some of its own exaggerations, concerning Indian involvement at the outset of the crisis, that does not take away from the fact that, within weeks of war breaking out, India verifiably began to provide support to the movement.

The Indian position in early April was, according to a British diplomat, "not to intervene militarily in either West or East Pakistan; to give assistance in the form of asylum and to allow supplies, short of war material, to the East Bengalis . . . the Indians are in no position to go further because they lack information of the development of the resistance movement in East Pakistan and of the progress made by the West Pakistan Army to secure control over the whole of East Pakistan."[117] Instead it would pay to wait, as another British cable in early April noted: "Time is needed for Bengali resistance to take organized form however and to work out strategy for longer term. Time is also needed to build up innatl support . . . nature of assistance India may provide when situation clarified will depend on circumstances."[118] Though there had been high-level political and military discussions of more direct intervention as early as March 26, initial support from the Indian side of the border in the early weeks was almost entirely unofficial or unconfirmed.[119]

However, India's involvement quickly stepped up.[120] In mid-April, American diplomats conveyed to their British colleagues that "the Indians are providing small arms and communications equipment to the East Bengalis" through the Border Security Force. Still, at that time "the Americans [did] not believe that the quantities are very large."[121] A week later, British diplomats reported that "reliable journalists" who had visited the border informed them that, in addition to supplying arms and communications equipment, the BSF "had crossed the border to blow up bridges when requested to do so by the resistance movement . . . [BSF] personnel spoke freely about their intention of setting up camps on Indian territory to give military training to East Bengalis. It was considered that the East Bengalis if properly trained could become effective guerrilla fighters."[122]

By the first week of May, British diplomats were reporting the "first reasonably authenticated case we have come across of supply of substantial quantity of arms from Indian side."[123] Indian arms factories were at this point manufacturing unmarked bullets for the Mukti Bahini.[124] A few days later, training camps were set up on the border by the recently "reorganized and expanded" BSF—previously under one inspector general, now under three IGs in each of West Bengal, Tripura, and Assam—leading diplomats to conclude that "present pattern of support seems to suggest direction by central government."[125] Indeed, the first evidence that training camps were being set up had arrived in late April.[126]

By the summer, the picture had changed appreciably from the beginning of the crisis, and Indian behavior had caught up to Pakistani perceptions and allegations.[127] By then, millions of Bengalis had poured into India, seeking refuge from the brutality of the Pakistani army. Among those crossing the border were thousands of defecting soldiers, police, and students, corralled into a guerrilla army, called the Mukti Bahini, by the Indian Border Security Force, which provided sanctuary, safe passage to its camps, food, money, small arms, ammunition, explosives, training, and intelligence to the insurgents.[128] The military commander of the Mukti Bahini was Colonel Osmani. Journalists who spent time with the Mukti Bahini were convinced "that most of their operations masterminded by the Indian intelligence and the Indian Army, who frequently gave fire cover to Mukti Bahini activities across the border."[129] Notably, men from the BSF or army themselves did not cross into Pakistan, notwithstanding official Pakistani accusations to that effect, though a State Department intelligence note did claim that it was "distinctly possible" that the Indian military had provided "advisors" on East Pakistani soil.[130]

India's direct support to the Mukti Bahini played an important role in the form and function of Pakistani counterinsurgency, especially in the post-monsoon phase of the conflict. First, India's strengthening of Mukti Bahini capabilities of insurgency and sabotage led to more guerrilla activity from the summer onward, resulting in vicious reprisal attacks from the army. Second, with its presence along, and shelling from, border positions, India ensured that Pakistan's army would necessarily be spread thinly, increasing its reliance on large-scale violence to control the population.

Indian support kicked in at a crucial time in the conflict: the West Pakistani military had largely asserted control of major towns, but had little presence in the countryside.[131] Additionally, while Bengali rebels did not lack resolve, they certainly lacked the material and technical capabilities to fight a guerrilla war. Finally, the monsoon was imminent.[132] These factors meant that Indian support ensured a significantly tougher fight for

Pakistani security forces than would otherwise have been the case; Mukti Bahini activity picked up considerably from the summer months.[133] Successful rebel attacks on security forces or infrastructure, such as bridges—possible partly because of India's "major role in training and supplying insurgents"—would invariably lead to vicious reprisals from the military, operating on the principle of collective punishment.[134] Commenting on how Indian support for the Mukti Bahini complicated their efforts in "counseling Paks against collective reprisals," the U.S. ambassador noted that "most of reprisals recently reported were in response to Mukti Bahini actions. Pak Army is caught up in vicious cycle of violence which cannot be halted solely by GOP restraint . . . this comment is not offered in any way as justification for harsh and stupid collective reprisals, however, and we shall continue to press for more rational army response."[135] When discussing the "primitive element in some of the army's actions," British officials gently impressed on Indian diplomats that "severe action was still likely in the border areas, particularly if there were any incursions or if the means of resistance were supplied from the Indian side."[136]

Moreover, the high levels of infiltration and coordination with forces from across the border necessitated the military guarding the long border with India, leaving it thin in the countryside towns and villages where the insurgency was centered.[137] Even before the summer, Pakistani leaders and military officials seemed concerned about Indian strategy and its encirclement in East Pakistan.[138] British diplomats reported a message from Yahya to the prime minister in which "the President had expressed apprehension about the Indian military forces in the states adjoining East Pakistan."[139] Similarly, Yahya complained to President Nixon in a letter on March 31 of "the deployment of nearly six divisions of the Indian Army not too far from the borders of East Pakistan" and expressed hope that Nixon would impress "upon Indian leaders the paramount need for refraining from any action that might aggravate the situation and lead to irretrievable consequences."[140] The Yahya regime constantly asked diplomatic representatives for information about Indian intentions vis-à-vis direct military intervention.[141] By the summer of 1971, Pakistan's worst fears began to be realized. As one American diplomat in Dacca summarized in July, "demands on Pak Army to defend border against India and protect its vital lines of communication may be out-running its capability. This gives insurgents who are willing to operate deep in East Pakistan territory opportunity that will be hard to pass up."[142] Blood summed up the trade-off facing the Pakistan military: "Concentration of searchs [sic] and purges in Dacca and contingency redeployment against Indian action would have effect of limiting army's freedom to control countryside, assuming it desired to achieve such control."[143] Shortly before India overtly intervened in the conflict, the "two-front" problem facing the Pakistan military became even more acute: Indian shelling and "probing" of the border "pins regular Pak army to the borders and gives them plenty to think about."[144]

Scholars expect militaries operating in counterinsurgency environments where their forces are stretched to adopt indiscriminate violence to spread fear, hoping they can sufficiently terrorize the local population in the hopes of subduing them.[145] As British diplomats noted in July, the problem the army faced was that "it must use its strength to compensate for its lack of numbers. It continues apparently to try to protect essential services against sabotage by instilling fear in the local populace that if the bridge or pylon near their village is damaged their village is going to suffer."[146] Reporting on a British journalist's visit to Tripura, a diplomat in Calcutta cabled that "his talks with refugees had convinced him of continued selective killing by Pakistan army of Bengalis and Hindus to terrorise population and also to establish wide deserted corridors along main communications routes and along Tripura frontier."[147]

Amidst the slaughter, India intervened overtly in the conflict, notwithstanding contemporary diplomats' concerns with such a step.[148] India's entry into the war can be laid almost entirely at the feet of West Pakistani decision makers, who believed so strongly in Bengali-Indian collusion that they helped bring it about, in a tragic self-fulfilling prophecy. The Indian state's casus belli to intervene was directly related to West Pakistani repression, especially at the beginning of the conflict. The heavy hand of security forces created a massive humanitarian and refugee crisis,[149] with millions of Bengalis fleeing across the border, mainly to the Indian states of West Bengal, Tripura, and Assam. The severe demographic and economic strain those states found themselves under, and the resulting domestic pressure imposed on Prime Minister Indira Gandhi to take action, led to India's overt entry into the war. It is an open question how much lower refugee flows would have been had the Pakistani military, correctly perceiving the "limited" third-party support Bengalis actually enjoyed, used a lighter hand at the outset of the crisis. It is beyond debate, however, that the extent of Pakistani repression eliminated both the prospect of any prominent Bengali politicians or leaders supporting the state, and induced India to directly intervene. Contrary to West Pakistani beliefs, India's actions were less a result of long-term planning and cooperation with Pakistani Bengalis and more an ad-hoc response to a growing crisis;[150] it saw an opportunity to weaken its primarily rival in the region and gleefully took it.[151] On December 16, 1971, lieutenant generals Niazi and Jagjit Singh Aurora signed the instrument of surrender of Pakistani forces, formally splitting the country into the independent states of Pakistan and Bangladesh.

An inescapable irony is that since its traumatic split in 1971, Pakistan has been more adept at defending itself. This increased territorial security is at least partly a product of military modernization, including the acquisition of nuclear weapons. However, Pakistan is also better able to defend itself because it is a more coherent state, at least territorially speaking, than it was before Bangladesh's secession. Indeed, one of the central predicaments facing Pakistani military decision makers between 1947 and 1971 was how to adequately guard both borders against India simultaneously; their solution to this problem—leaving the East almost entirely undefended, as in the 1965 war—was an important contributor to Bengali grievances.[152] In a sense, then, Pakistani leaders were, tragically and with great cost, wrong about the security effects of losing East Pakistan: secession decreased, rather than increased, the long-run chances of Indian invasion of Pakistan's territory. At the time they were making their decisions about whether and how much to repress Bengalis, however, Pakistani leaders could not have known, and did not believe, that losing East Pakistan would be beneficial for their security. They conceived of territorial loss in much more simplistic terms: losing land and people that were nominally tied to the Pakistani state was an unwelcome prospect to be resisted at all costs—and resist they did.

A few years later, the now diminished state of Pakistan would face another secessionist movement. This time, however, the military acted with more restraint, despite evincing a similar intransigence on territorial loss.

Defeating the Baloch Insurrection in the 1970s

Between 1973 and 1977, the Pakistan Army was ordered into Balochistan by Prime Minister Zulfiqar Ali Bhutto. Bhutto was unhappy with the fact that his party, the PPP, had little influence in the province, and he had uneasy relations with the parties in power in the provincial assemblies. He dismissed the assemblies, leading to Balochistan's secessionist moment, with the province rising in revolt, sparking an insurgency. The conflict continued for almost four years, and while there certainly was an element of repression carried out by the state, it was not at the level that it was during the 1971 civil war; in all, the four-year conflict between the state and the Baloch militias agitating for greater autonomy cost about nine thousand lives on both sides.[153]

The level of violence used at the time of the secessionist moment approximated "militarization." The reason for this response was that the dispute was seen primarily in domestic terms, and the movement was not considered a significant external threat. Third-party support for the Baloch rebels was "moderate": they enjoyed sanctuary and low levels of financial and military support from Afghanistan, a much weaker power than Pakistan, after Sardar Daoud Khan launched a coup, but little material support from major powers, including the Soviet Union. Other states, most notably Iran, backed Pakistan in the conflict. As such, the threat posed by the movement was deemed manageable without recourse to the levels of repression seen earlier in the decade.

EARLY TROUBLES

Balochistan's relationship with the center had always been rocky, and in fact could be traced to the British colonial era. British rule of the province was mostly indirect, exercised through the patronage of various tribal chiefs. Such policies empowered the tribes at the expense of local administration, and consequently Baloch tribal chiefs and leaders had a much stronger streak of independence than local actors elsewhere in British India.[154] The geography of the province has also facilitated the empowering of tribes: the large expanse—it is easily the largest by area in all of Pakistan—combined with the relatively low population, arid climate, and little fertile land resulted in a "nomadic pastoral" society. The long distances between settlements and desert environment made the execution of centralized authority difficult, thus fragmenting the society along tribal lines.[155]

Baloch tribal chiefs chafed under attempts to bring Balochistan into a wider body politic, whether under British or Pakistani administration. Ghaus Bakhsh Bizenjo, an important tribal elder of the Bizenjo tribe and the "principal spokesman for the independence forces," pointedly summarized Baloch nationalist sentiment in 1947 when he said that "we have a distinct culture like Afghanistan and Iran, and if the mere fact that we are Muslims requires us to amalgamate with Pakistan, then Afghanistan and Iran should also be amalgamated with Pakistan."[156] This streak of independent tribalism manifested itself in the Kalat State issue in 1947. Kalat was one of four princely states in Balochistan.[157] Upon the departure of the British, leaders of princely states were allowed a "third way"—an option other than acceding to either India or Pakistan, which is what the majority of states in British India faced. This third option was of independence, and unsurprisingly, many princely states opted for it, short-lived though it may have been.[158] The Khan of Kalat declared independence in 1947, with the support of the other princely states of Balochistan.[159] He was also supported by the Kalat State National Party, which was the majority party in the then Kalat House of Commons.[160]

Less than a year later, under considerable duress, Kalat acceded to the state of Pakistan. The accession was undertaken after the use of force by the Pakistan Army in putting down Baloch guerrilla forces. The coerced incorporation of Balochistan into Pakistan proper angered Baloch nationalists, resulting in rallies and protests in some parts of the province.[161] An alliance featuring various nationalist tribes and parties—including the Kalat State National Party, the Baloch League, and the Baloch National Worker Party—unsuccessfully attempted to lead a national liberation movement, and various "states" within Balochistan continued to assert their independence. It was not until 1954 that Balochistan was integrated both internally and externally as an official province of Pakistan.[162]

However, the troubled relationship between Balochistan and the center continued in the 1960s. Many of the underlying issues remained the same: Baloch leaders demanded autonomy or outright independence, owing to a sense of displacement due to the in-migration of Punjabis and Pashtuns in Balochistan, along with more longstanding grievances, such as underrepresentation of the Baloch in the military and bureaucracy and the exploitation by the center of Balochistan's plentiful natural resources.[163] The state, meanwhile, continued to bring Balochistan under even greater control. For instance, in 1955 the One Unit scheme was executed. One Unit realized the idea that the four provinces in West Pakistan—Balochistan, NWFP, Punjab, and Sindh—were a single administrative entity, while East Pakistan was distinct. It was aimed at neutering East Pakistan's numerical and demographic superiority, but for the purposes of Baloch nationalists, it was another instance of the center integrating Balochistan with the rest of the country despite their preferences to the contrary.

One Unit resulted in the second in a series of Baloch revolts. Guerrilla forces numbering about a thousand, primarily drawn from the Zehri tribe, first fought Pakistan military units in 1958 until the uprising was quelled.[164] But the cessation of hostilities proved sporadic. Skirmishes between the center and various tribes—including the Zarakzai, the Bugti, the Marri, the Mengal, and the Bizenjo tribes—continued intermittently throughout the 1960s, with major confrontations taking place in 1964 and 1965.[165] During this period, the Baloch movement was rocked by the Nauroz Khan incident, an episode which confirmed for future nationalists that the Pakistani state was untrustworthy and deceitful. In 1960, Nauroz Khan agreed to lay down his arms only on the condition that One Unit would be done away with, and that he and his men would be granted amnesty and safe passage. Having agreed to these terms, the military reneged on its promise, arrested Nauroz and his right-hand men, and hung five of his men for treason. Nauroz himself died in prison in 1964, and his imprisonment and death became an important symbol for the Baloch nationalist movement.[166]

THE SECESSIONIST MOMENT AND
PAKISTAN'S MILITARIZATION STRATEGY

For domestic political reasons, Bhutto had been unhappy with the provincial leadership of the main party in power in Balochistan, the National Awami Party (NAP). The NAP was a left-leaning nationalist party which also enjoyed power in NWFP.[167] The two provincial governments had troubled relations with the center throughout their tenure, with the NAP alleging that the federal government was intent on destabilizing the provinces in order to wrest control of them. The NAP leadership also raised concerns about the newly written constitution, which the PPP government had introduced with much fanfare.[168] In general, they "mistrusted Bhutto."[169] For its part, the PPP had little representation in NWFP and none in Balochistan; the main stakeholders in Baloch politics owed their allegiance to local tribal chiefs, such as the Bizenjos and Mengals, and not Bhutto's party.[170] Bhutto's leadership style was authoritarian, and he squabbled repeatedly with the NAP in his efforts to make them more subservient.

Even at the height of their "cooperation"—the spring of 1972—close observers predicted trouble between Bhutto and the NAP.[171] Sure enough, on February 12, 1973, he dismissed the provincial government, and that summer he would ban the NAP outright and arrest its leaders.[172] Bhutto fired the governor of the province, Mir Ghaus Bakhsh Bizenjo—"little purpose would be served" in explaining why, he wrote in his letter to Bizenjo—and replaced him with his confidante and ally Nawab Akbar Bugti, considered by many to be a traitor to the Baloch nationalist cause ever since.[173] He also dismissed Sardar Ataullah Mengal as chief minister, and in so doing ensured that two vital reservoirs of power in the province, the Mengals and the Bizenjos, strongly opposed his government.[174]

Bhutto used two episodes as justification for the move, and while conclusive proof is hard to come by, it is widely believed that his government was responsible for both. The first was trouble in Lasbela, which began in early 1973. According to the official PPP version, the localized violence was due to a dispute between the Marri and Mengal tribes, and it required central intervention in the form of army troops to restore order.[175] On the other hand, Baloch nationalists alleged that the government itself was "fomenting trouble" and "creating anarchical conditions in the provinces," and that "vested interests,"[176] such as federal home minister, Khan Abdul Qayyum Khan, "had a hand" in the "armed rebellion" in Lasbela, designed to "overthrow the elected and constitutional Government of Baluchistan."[177] As *Dawn*'s editorial on the Lasbela situation said, "It is almost impossible for any disinterested observer to form a coherent idea of the course of developments out of this welter of one-sided narratives and opinions."[178] Regardless, the center sent in its first batch of troops—their numbers to be increased manifold in the coming months—so that they could "restore law and order" in Lasbela.[179] Knowing Bhutto and his single-minded pursuit of power as the analyst armed with hindsight does, and knowing that the government had on its side the *jam* (tribal chief) of Lasbela, a staunch opponent of the NAP, it is more than reasonable to surmise that the incident was instigated by the central government itself. Certainly that is the view of those involved in the conflict, one supported by contemporary diplomatic correspondence.[180] A telegram from the British embassy in Islamabad, written during the Lasbela crisis, noted that "those people who theorised that

Mr. Bhutto had been encouraging Akbar Bugti and the other opponents of the Baluchistan Government to create trouble to provide an opportunity for the imposition of President's rule, may take this latest development as an indication that their theories are proving correct."[181]

The second and arguably more important justification for Bhutto's move was his revelation that Pakistan intelligence had recovered "a cache of 350 Soviet submachine guns and 100,000 rounds of ammunition in the house of the Iraqi political attaché in Islamabad."[182] Bhutto claimed that the arms were destined for Pakistani or Iranian Balochistan, but the Iraqi Embassy episode is, to this day, shrouded in mystery. After all, if the arms were destined for Southwest Pakistan or Southeast Iran, then using Islamabad, the capital city located in the northeast of the country, as a transit point made little sense, a point noted by the Bureau of Intelligence and Research (INR) in Washington and the U.S. embassy in Islamabad.[183] Interviews also pointed to the great likelihood that Bhutto's government was behind the whole episode.[184] All that can be said with assuredness is that the event was extremely convenient for Bhutto—an "uncanny coincidence" and "political windfall" according to the INR—which he used as a pretext to overturn the Balochistan and NWFP provincial governments.[185]

What was beyond contestation, however, was the fact that Bhutto's actions greatly angered Baloch nationalists, who rose in revolt, representing the movement's secessionist moment. Bhutto's actions were a catalyst—"he had created the Balochistan tragedy by his own overwhelming egomania"—but the underlying reasons for the revolt were more structural.[186] Balochistan remained a perilously underdeveloped region. Per capita income was easily the lowest of Pakistan's provinces, development projects instituted in the region often favored outsiders and settlers more than locals, royalties from valuable resources such as natural gas were extremely limited, literacy levels were the lowest in the country, and Baloch representation in the national and provincial governments was poor.[187]

An insurgency against the state got underway, featuring roughly between five and ten thousand armed insurgents.[188] It was by far the most serious challenge emanating from Balochistan in Pakistan's history. In response, Bhutto's government gave the Pakistan Army control over military operations; the military sent in eighty thousand troops to suppress the movement. The rebels were nominally united under the Balochistan People's Liberation Front and drew support from a number of tribes, but mainly the Marri tribe, in conjunction with the Mengal and Bizenjo tribes. They established bases of operation in Balochistan as well as in some parts of Afghanistan.[189] They were fighting what they deemed an army of occupation from Punjab and promised to keep fighting as long as their *sardars*, or leaders, remained imprisoned by Bhutto and as long as General Tikka Khan's troops remained in the province.[190] The Baloch tribesmen favored tactics such as cutting off the main transportation routes in the province, attacks on Western oil exploration teams, surprise attacks followed by quick retreats into the hills of Balochistan and even Afghanistan, and hitting military supply lines.[191] By July 1974, the rebels had succeeded in cutting off the majority of roads leading into the province and halting coal transportation from Balochistan to Punjab by repeatedly attacking the crucial Sibi-Harnai rail link. The guerrillas also attacked "colonial" oil exploration in the province, by targeting drilling and survey operations. More generally, as with most guerrilla groups, the Baloch nationalists focused on avoiding direct confrontation with the Pakistan Army, instead opting for ambush attacks.[192]

The Pakistan military, meanwhile, began its operations in the Marri and Mengal tribal areas.[193] It attempted to hold tribal leaders accountable for tribes' actions and imposed levies on tribes. It also used population transfers—an anti-insurgent technique imported from British tactics—in a bid to weaken the guerrillas from within. The most important element of the military's strategy, however, was air power. Air power was crucial in the largest and most important single battle of the conflict that took place in September 1974, when rebels fought a pitched battle against the army at Chamalang. The rebels set themselves up in a defensive formation to protect families and livestock. Benefitting from the maneuverability and firepower they provided, helicopter gunships, as well as F-86 and Mirage fighter jets, pummeled the rebel positions and, combined with ground forces, defeated the rebels soundly. Most of the guerrillas either escaped or were captured, and their livestock, including 50,000 sheep and 550 camels, crucial to their sustenance, were taken and sold to non-Baloch in Punjab. The Battle at Chamalang was a turning point in the conflict. After its conclusion, the war simmered at low levels since the tribesmen were unable to "regain the military initiative in the three ensuing years of . . . increasingly uncoordinated fighting."[194]

The conflict ended in 1977 when General Zia-ul-Haq withdrew forces after declaring victory. In total, the war cost about nine thousand lives on both sides.[195] The conflict was a small-scale war of attrition, fairly typical of civil conflicts in that the rebels were advantaged by the terrain, lack of communication links deep in the province, sound local knowledge, and a friendly population, while the state enjoyed greater military expertise, mobility, and firepower.[196] Though there were some echoes of General Yahya Khan's disastrous decision to use force in East Pakistan, the repression in Balochistan never approached the carnage on display in East Pakistan. Notwithstanding many Baloch partisans' attempts to draw the obvious analogy, the levels of force used in the two theaters simply were not comparable: one conflict resulted in hundreds of thousands dead (at least) in less than a year, the other, several thousand over four years. Bhutto sent eighty thousand troops into the province, but the violence was, by and large, contained to targeted action against militant camps and positions.[197]

"The major *sardars* [tribal chiefs] and other NAP leaders . . . were taken into custody by the government, charged with treason and subsequently brought to trial in Hyderabad"[198]—which may well represent repression but most assuredly a less extreme version than what Awami League leaders experienced, who were to be hunted down and killed on sight. Rather than the "collective repression" witnessed in the cities and countryside of East Pakistan, Balochistan witnessed Pakistani "militarization."

EXTERNAL SUPPORT FOR REBELS AND THE STATE

The most important consideration for the relatively low levels of violence and repression in Balochistan was that the movement did not represent a serious external threat. Baloch secessionists enjoyed only moderate support from Afghanistan, which was a weaker power than Pakistan. To the extent that that there was an external dimension to the conflict, it favored the state; the only major regional power to get involved was Iran, which, owing to its own "Balochistan problem," backed Pakistan against the nationalists. Given the source and type of external backing, the materialist effects of third-party support were not especially threatening, and the emotional implications were muted. As such, the Baloch movement was deemed manageable enough without recourse to such brutality as witnessed in East Pakistan. Doubtless, part of this tractability of the Baloch threat stemmed from basic material factors of the dispute, such as the low population base in the province. But insurgencies in even isolated, rural environs can attract vicious and disproportionate responses from state security forces, as occurred in Guatemala in the mid-1960s.[199] Moreover, rebellions in sparsely populated areas, such as Afghanistan, can pack quite a punch if they are wholeheartedly supported from abroad; at the extreme, such movements can defeat even the most powerful of states, as occurred in that country in the 1980s. That is, geographic and demographic factors, in and of themselves, do not determine the manageability of threat.

That the Baloch tribal insurrection was seen primarily as a domestic issue with no major external implications by the Pakistani state is an interpretation backed by various primary sources. First, contemporary media reports attest to Balochistan in the 1970s being a domestic dispute, waged by Zulfiqar Bhutto on the one side and recalcitrant NAP nationalists on the other, mainly over Bhutto's constitution and his authoritarianism. A few weeks prior to the deployment of troops, when the Federal Constitution was first presented to the National Assembly, Wali Khan, the leader of the NAP, demanded a debate on the question, with the main issue being how much power the prime minister enjoyed.[200] Bhutto, for his part, criticized the opposition for allegedly backing out of the constitutional accord the parties had reached the previous year, even though he had changed the terms of the agreement in favor of more power to the center.[201] The public wrangling over the constitution continued for weeks,[202] marked by talks at the end of January that ultimately failed to close the distance between the parties.[203]

Upon troops being deployed, the substance of the dispute did not change.[204] The day that headlines informed readers of troops being sent into Balochistan, Bhutto railed that Pakistan "must get a democratic constitution at any cost."[205] Bhutto's visit to the province in late February, and its aftermath, were dominated by concerns about the constitution.[206] Following the "discovery" of arms at the Iraqi embassy, Bhutto removed the NAP government in Balochistan and NWFP, only two days before parliament took up discussions on the constitutional bill.[207] By the summer of 1973, Bhutto was deliberating reaching a deal with the NAP—his constitution having passed, and Akbar Bugti being a less than useful puppet in the province—but he was unable to find one, instead arresting the NAP leaders (the charges, in the British ambassador's phrase, smelled "of the lamp"),[208] and it was at this point that the insurgency kicked off in earnest.

Second, contemporary diplomatic correspondence and intelligence reports point to the conflict's primarily domestic nature. As early as May 1972, foreign observers had noted the NAP's problems with the PPP's prospective constitution.[209] In August that year, American diplomats summarized that "the heart of the National Awami Party's dispute with the Bhutto regime involves (a) the degree of provincial autonomy to be provided by the new constitution, (b) the regime's alleged intention to set up an authoritarian one-party state, and (c) the regime's effort to undermine NAP's political position."[210] In March 1973, after Bhutto dismissed the provincial government, U.S. embassy cables from Islamabad reported that the "major domestic issue for Bhutto remains constitution"[211] and that "Bhutto meeting shortly with National Awami Party leaders from Baluchistan, which has become major obstacle to Bhutto both in securing all province consensus on constitution and in obtaining compatible provincial government."[212] In a handwritten edit to a confidential telegram in December 1972, the British ambassador noted that "the discussions now going on in Islamabad about the new draft constitution, in which the degree of authority to be enjoyed by provincial governments is a major item."[213] A research report prepared by the INR claimed that Bhutto's PPP "had only very limited strength in the Assemblies of NWFP and Baluchistan. Thus, much of the political conflict in Pakistan has revolved around President Bhutto's attempt to assert his control in these two provinces where he is politically weakest."[214] Similarly, a telegram from the U.S. embassy in Islamabad in April 1973 clearly located the cause of the dispute between Bhutto and NAP leaders as internal matters—the constitution and domestic reforms.[215]

Third, proceedings of the Hyderabad Tribunal from the middle of the decade—in which the entire leadership of the NAP, both Baloch and Pashtun nationalists, was on trial before the Supreme Court—speak to the conflict's domestic roots in Bhutto's bid for unbridled power and an unyielding NAP. While it is reasonable to question the reliability of testimony by major political players to the state's highest judicial body, the general tone and substance of the proceedings provide valuable clues as to how the conflict was seen at the time by its participants. On the one side, we get a clear picture of the government's—really, Bhutto's—version of events. The attorney general's background to the crisis is that "the new President [Bhutto] sought the help and co-operation of all political parties for the preparation of an Interim Constitution for the country with a view to restoring democracy and re-establishing democratic institutions." To secure this cooperation, Bhutto reached an accord with the NAP in 1972. "In spite of these agreements however, the Provincial Governments set up in these Provinces not only adopted an attitude of non-cooperation towards the Federal Government, but openly started violating their legal and constitutional obligations." Partly because the NAP did not subscribe to the ideology of Pakistan, and partly because it "resorted to methods designed to systematically destroy the infra-structure of the law enforcing agencies in the Province," Bhutto was impelled to send in the armed forces.

In response to these charges, the joint statement of NAP leaders claims that the government "falsely, frivolously and maliciously fabricated the allegations" against it in a bid to establish "naked one man's rule." Rather than the NAP being responsible for the "confrontation" between the provinces and the center, "it is, in fact, the Federal Government which had violated its constitutional obligations while Provincial Governments, on their part, had tried their utmost to cooperate with the Federal Government." Wali Khan's statement noted that Bhutto's conduct was "the design to achieve its political aim of setting up 'a one-man State.'" Marri made similar claims, arguing that Bhutto's government "started a campaign of vilification and vituperation against the N. A. P. so as to provide material for banning it, as it was the only effective political force in the country which could stand in the way of People's Party leadership and the latter considered it as its main political opponent and a serious hurdle in their way for establishing dictatorial one man's fascist rule in their 'New Pakistan.'"[216]

Fourth, interviews with those party to the conflict, either as insurgents or on behalf of the state, and other contemporary observers, painted a similar picture. Ahmed Rashid—then a member of the so-called London Group of leftists that fought in Balochistan—told me that the cause of the conflict was Bhutto trying to "demolish" the NAP's power.[217] Similarly, Rashed Rahman claimed the conflict got underway when Bhutto dismissed the provincial government in Balochistan, which he did because he was "an extreme centralist" who "wanted to reverse his concessions" on constitutional matters concerning provincial autonomy. Baloch nationalist Mohammad Ali Talpur agreed, saying that Bhutto resented the Baloch forming a government of their own, and that the main issue between Bhutto and the NAP was domestic power.[218] Shehryar Mazari, the son of prominent Baloch intellectual and political figure Sherbaz Mazari, said that Bhutto did not like the fact that his PPP was not in control in Balochistan, and that "he wanted to be in complete power, wanted to be Napoleon or Hitler."[219] Another member of the Mazari family stated simply: "Mr. Bhutto did not want to share power."[220]

Fifth, we can partly appreciate Bhutto's then-mindset by examining the memoirs of those PPP advisers closest to him, such as Kausar Niazi, Rao Rasheed, and Rafi Raza.[221] Our greatest clue about the relative manageability of the Balochistan dispute here is simply the absence of clues in the first place: they did not devote many pages to the conflict. For instance, Niazi's recollection of Bhutto's tenure mentions Balochistan only tangentially, with the dominant political issues being restricted to Punjab and Sindh, and Bhutto's hold on power more generally. When discussing the "four fronts" that Bhutto faced during Pakistan's quest for a nuclear weapon, a period coinciding with the Balochistan crisis, Niazi does not even mention Balochistan.[222] Rasheed gives more thought to Balochistan, but mostly in general terms, diagnosing the causes of discontent in the province, favorably comparing British administration of the province—who ostensibly tried to solve the issues of the people—to the Pakistani state's more negligent policies, and describing the tribal nature of Baloch society. Like Niazi, Rasheed does not mention Balochistan when discussing Bhutto's main challenges, instead focusing on his downfall at the hands of "industrialists, big landlords, traders, and religious people."[223]

Of the three party insiders, it is Rafi Raza that provides the most details about Bhutto and the Balochistan crisis, and his recollections only burnish the argument that the conflict was almost entirely domestically oriented. Raza discusses the background conditions for the crisis, noting that with the ascension of Ghaus Bakhsh Bizenjo and Ataullah Mengal to the positions of governor and chief minister, respectively, center-province relations were marked by confrontation, partly due to the Baloch tribal leaders' inexperience in formal government but mostly because of Bhutto's "failure to accept" the NAP-dominated government in Balochistan. Crucially, Raza describes how, during talks in the spring of 1973 between the dismissed NAP leaders and Bhutto, he (Raza) played intermediary and tried to impress on Bhutto the fact that his preferred client in Balochistan, the *jam* of Lasbela, did not have the political capital to maintain power and that continued military intervention in the province would be disastrous. Bhutto, however, remained apprehensive, and feared the consequences of retreat. In an attempt to placate him, Raza assured Bhutto that the constitution had sufficient safeguards in case the NAP-led government posed difficulties in the future.[224] That Raza felt the chief concern in Bhutto's mind vis-à-vis the NAP leaders was the constitution speaks volumes.

A related indicator of the conflict's domestic character is its failure to resonate strongly with the Pakistani establishment, manifested by a lack of literature and first-person accounts of the conflict, even by military personnel directly involved. Pervez Musharraf, who served as a major in the war, and is normally unafraid of media attention and speaking his mind, has exceedingly little to say about his experiences in Balochistan during the 1970s.[225] Bhutto, who wrote more than half a dozen books in his lifetime on politics, world affairs, his daughter Benazir, his jail sentence and anticipated judicial assassination, the 1971 war, and Islam, also has next to nothing to say about the Balochistan war. This is despite the fact that the war lasted longer than the East Pakistan conflict, and that Bhutto himself, more than any one individual, was responsible for the outbreak of war.

Viewed from the perspective of Bhutto's party confidantes, along with contemporary media, intelligence, and diplomatic reports, as well as court proceedings at the Hyderabad Tribunal and interviews with participants in the conflict, it is clear then that Balochistan in the 1970s was not a major crisis, threatening the existence of the state. Rather, it was a domestic political dispute over which parties enjoyed control of particular provinces, and how the NAP may or may not have threatened Bhutto's constitution and hold on complete power.

Baloch rebels were not deemed a challenge to Pakistan's external security not just because of the proximate causes of the dispute being entirely domestic in nature—the constitution and questions of autonomy—but also because of its geopolitical context. The most important regional or global power to get involved in the conflict, Iran, did so on the side of the state, not the secessionists. Owing to its own "Balochistan problem," the shah of Iran wholeheartedly supported Pakistan's attempts to defeat the movement,[226] calling for the movement in Balochistan to be "crushed." The shah's stance earned the ire of nationalists such as Mengal, Bizenjo,[227] and Wali Khan, who criticized him for interfering in Pakistan's internal affairs, pointedly noting that "the Shah had no right to decide which party should or should not rule in one or more provinces . . . if Iran can do this, why not China or the United States which have given more help to Pakistan than Iran?"[228] Indeed, the shah's concerns with events in Pakistani Balochistan may even predate Bhutto's—as early as the spring of 1972, when the NAP and PPP were still nominally allies, the British ambassador to Iran was delivered a message by the shah, who "was a bit concerned about the new 'federal' constitution in Pakistan. He hoped this would not eventually lead to what he had long feared, namely, encouragement of provincial dissidence and exploitation by the Russians of Pakhtunistan and Baluchistan separatist movements, working through Afghanistan in ways inimicable to Iran's interests."[229] The shah's concerns about Baluchistan were so extreme as to lead to Bhutto's privately expressed "mild irritation" on account of the shah's "hint of paternalism."[230]

With the benefit of hindsight, we can safely hypothesize that Balochistan generally and Bhutto's strategy for quelling trouble in the province specifically was a topic of discussion when the shah made his second visit to Pakistan in the middle of January—the first of several meetings with Bhutto in 1973—when the two leaders went on a duck hunt in interior Sindh.[231] The shah and Bhutto had met thrice the previous year, once in Pakistan and twice in Tehran.[232] A confidential British appraisal in late February claimed that the shah "offered military assistance in Baluchistan if requested to do so by Bhutto."[233] At the conclusion of the trip to the "brotherly country" of Pakistan, the shah captured the spirit of bonhomie between the two leaders in his farewell statement, in which he was "convinced that valuable discussions and the exchange of views we had together on matters of mutual interest will contribute to consolidate still further the close ties of amity and co-operation linking Iran and Pakistan."[234] The highly suspicious "capture" of arms at the Iraqi embassy in February 1973, which allowed Bhutto to scapegoat and paint as treacherous Baloch nationalists, took place less than a month after this "private" visit by the shah.[235] The timing of events lends credence to the belief that the two leaders were eager to strike at a common domestic foe.

Before Bhutto's return visit to Iran in the spring, the U.S. embassy in Tehran characterized the upcoming trip as "further indication of increasingly close relationship between Shah and Bhutto. In recent months and especially since Iraqi arms caper, security organizations of both countries have been working closely together with Iranians helping Pakistanis to penetrate and deal with what are perceived to be Iraqi/Indian/Soviet efforts at subversion in Baluchistan. Meeting will give Shah and Bhutto opportunity to compare notes on this problem which is high on Shah's agenda."[236] As predicted, the Iran trip was an outstanding one for Bhutto: he was given a warm welcome, and it yielded several diplomatic coups, such as Iran agreeing not to recognize the newly birthed state of Bangladesh until Pakistan did so,[237] "highly successful" summit-level talks that promised "tangible results,"[238] praise from the shah that bordered on fawning,[239] and most importantly for our purposes, strong promises of mutual defense and security cooperation, in which the two leaders "resolved that their countries would resolutely stand by each other in all matters bearing on their national independence and territorial integrity."[240] The shah also promised a return visit to Pakistan at a "convenient and early date,"[241] four months after his last trip. Commenting on Bhutto's Iran visit, the U.S. embassy in Tehran wrote that "we are struck with the unusually warm reception the Shah has given President Bhutto . . . in our opinion the Shah has made a very special effort to show in no uncertain terms that Pakistan's integrity and friendship constitute a principal facet in Iran's own security and well-being . . . visit has produced number rumors that Iran and Pakistan are developing closer military, even treaty, relationship."[242]

By August 1973, there were reports about Iranian military support to Pakistan.[243] Iran gave help mainly in the form of equipment. Specifically, Iranians supplied gunship helicopters and fighter aircraft to the Pakistan Army, which did not have such equipment at the time. By November 1973, the shah admitted to U.S. diplomats that he had in the previous month sent "two or three helicopters to add to the six or seven that were already there."[244] This help was crucial because it covered one of the most glaring weaknesses of the military: mobility. Just as the insurgency was getting underway, officials in the British embassy in Islamabad noted that "the Army also realizes it has insufficient tactical mobility to move its limited number of troops quickly between potential trouble areas."[245] Additionally, some Iranian pilots also flew helicopters used in Operation Chamalang in 1974, the most crucial of the entire campaign. Finally, Iran also supplied economic aid, specially directed to development in Balochistan.[246]

Interviews with military sources confirmed just how important this support was in the conflict. "Iran supported [Pakistan] openly," retired brigadier Asad Munir told me. "Chinook helicopter, troops carrier, logistics support, rations—all out support."[247] Another former security official told me that the shah's support was "very useful," especially because the helicopters allowed the state to more easily target Balochistan's large landmass, in which the little infrastructure that exists tends to be remote.[248] Hamid Hussain, a highly respected student of the Pakistan military, also spoke of the "significant effect" the shah's support had. Iran's state-of-the-art helicopter capabilities, he told me, allowed the army to negotiate Balochistan's harsh terrain. According to Hussain, while the state would have eventually fought the insurgents to a stalemate regardless of Iran's support, backing from its western neighbor helped Pakistan "speed up" the war; the Baloch would have inflicted more casualties and the conflict would have extended for a number of years without Iranian helicopters and pilots.[249] Absent Iranian air support, the Pakistan Army would have had to fight not just longer but differently too—more ground operations, with the attendant higher potential for ambush, a favorite insurgent tactic, and in turn a higher likelihood of vicious reprisals. The importance of Iran's support is underlined not just by military sources, but also by former insurgents; Ahmed Rashid, for instance, termed the shah's help as a "major boost for the army," stressing that the Pakistani military did not enjoy mobile artillery until the Iranians gave it to them.

While the state enjoyed considerable external backing, the rebels did not enjoy any significant diplomatic or military support.[250] India could not support the Baloch due to simple geography. As one former Indian intelligence official wrote, Balochistan "did not have a contiguous border with India. Any Indian support could have been only by sea. This was not feasible."[251] The potentially most viable and consequential patron was the Soviet Union, the superpower from whom the Baloch groups never got the support they were looking for.[252] This was not from a lack of effort: Baloch groups made several overtures for the support of the Soviets but were rebuffed.[253] Though the Soviet Union was keen to support separatist movements with leftward tendencies, which the Baloch movement undoubtedly was, its material and functional support was simply not forthcoming. The Soviets maintained a greater interest in goings-on in Afghanistan at the time, "a much bigger piece of the chessboard" for the communist superpower.[254] The Soviets simply "weren't interested in the Balochistan issue," according to Baloch nationalists, because it was too peripheral a conflict to occupy their strategic vision. As one former security official who served in Balochistan in the 1970s summed up, there is "no evidence that [the] Russians supported these people."[255] Contemporary American intelligence reports confirm the lack of Soviet involvement, noting that "although both Tehran and Islamabad have alleged that Moscow is supporting separatist movements in Iran and Pakistan, there is no evidence to support these charges; on the contrary, the Soviet Union has on occasion attempted to restrain Iraq's activities against Iran."[256]

While material support was not forthcoming from the Asiatic superpower, its client state in the region, Afghanistan, did provide sanctuaries and some aid for Baloch rebels.[257] Camps in and around Kabul and Kandahar allowed rebels to regroup "after bouts of fighting. As well as allowing the camps to exist, the Afghans provided the rebels with modest amounts of financial support.[258] Supplementing this sanctuary and financial support, Daoud Khan, who had recently come to power in a coup, "supported the Baloch tribal leaders with propaganda and small arms."[259] This level of "moderate" support made the Baloch movement stronger than it would have been otherwise but was not cause for significant alarm. As a member of the Mazari family told me, "If anyone would be supporting the Baloch, it would be the Afghans, a tiny government."[260] Afghanistan's weakness relative to the two main states involved in the fighting in Balochistan—Pakistan and Iran—was a theme emphasized also by military sources.[261] Asad Munir noted that "Afghanistan was not in a position to help them, they didn't have [a] strong army, they could not support, the only country that could have supported them, Iran, was on our side."[262] Other sources have emphasized that Afghanistan's own relative poverty, and closer identity relations to Pakistan's Pashtun community, meant whatever material support it extended to Baloch rebels was limited. As Mohammad Taqi told me, "The fact is, Afghanistan never did arm or train rebels to the extent that India did with Mukti Bahini . . . if Afghanistan would arm anyone, it would be the Pashtun nationalists," rather than the Baloch. In Balochistan, by contrast, Kabul's backing was mostly restricted to "moral and political support."[263]

This lack of external support played a crucial role in keeping the threat from the Baloch nationalists limited and translating into a fairly manageable job for the state. As a Mazari family member told me, "A tribe can't take on the Pakistan army."[264] Multiple interviews emphasized the lack of training and modern equipment the Baloch rebels enjoyed, weaknesses that external states would and could have covered up had their sponsorship been more forthcoming. While the majority of Baloch tribesmen were armed in their villages, their weaponry was not sophisticated enough—for instance, they did not have automatic weapons.[265] Crucially, there was never a threat of invasion from abroad in the Balochistan case,[266] a stark departure from what the military had experienced in East Pakistan, which meant that military did not have to spread itself thinly. The confluence of significant support for the state, and the near-complete lack thereof for the rebels, meant that its counterinsurgency efforts did not need to be extended particularly far.[267]

Despite rhetoric that cast the Baloch separatists as aided by external enemies, Bhutto and the leadership in Pakistan knew that this particular insurrection was mostly domestically based, especially at its inception. That is, the state's allegations of foreign support, made well before Daoud even came to power, were not perception but propaganda. These allegations began apace in early 1973, led primarily by Akbar Bugti, to the considerable consternation of Baloch nationalists. However, as the British high commissioner in Islamabad delicately noted,

> It is difficult to know how much to believe of his stories of foreign arms: anything that Bugti says at the moment must be highly coloured by his desire to topple Bizenjo and the NAP Government and take their place himself . . . . We have no reliable information to indicate that they [the reports] are true . . . . There are those who believe Bugti and Bhutto are working hand in hand on this . . . to stir things up, and for the Central Government to intervene later as a Deus ex Machina.[268]

American diplomats described unsophisticated propaganda tying the NAP to Soviet-backed Iraqi groups, in the form of pamphlets and maps of "Greater Balochistan" that were several years old, as "merely another information minicstry [sic] attempt to keep up propaganda pressure on NAP," while at other times noted "clumsy" and "apparently contrived" attempts to tie domestic opposition to foreign conspiracies with "concrete evidence" of foreign complicity "notably absent."[269] United States embassy cables from March 1973 also give strong indication that the allegations of external support were tendentious, designed as political theater, and that the bone of contention remained the constitution.[270] Bhutto was doubtless concerned about the Baloch conflict *becoming* an international war and attracting the support of Baghdad, Kabul, Delhi, or Moscow, but did not believe that it actually was one at the time. In June 1973, Bhutto sent a letter to his governor in the province, Akbar Bugti, and wrote that "perhaps Khair Bakhsh Marri is trying to play a miniature Bangladesh. Perhaps he wants to get some Marris across the border . . . to internationalise the problem. We must therefore bottle up the migration even if it is a handful of Marris."[271] What this statement clearly shows is that at the time, Bhutto did not consider the Baloch insurrection an "internationalized" dispute in the first place. Unlike the East Pakistan case, public allegations of third-party support for rebels in Balochistan were almost entirely political theater, rather than reflective of genuine belief.

Certainly, the relatively low military threat from the Baloch was also a function of pure demographics: estimates suggest their organized fighting forces numbered between five and ten thousand, due in part to the revolt being mainly carried out by the Marri and Mengal tribes rather than a cross-section of society in Balochistan.[272] Moreover, the insurgency's geographic spread was restricted to eastern Balochistan, in the mineral-rich districts of Kohlu, Khuzdar, and Dera Bugti; by contrast, the Pashtun-speaking towns of the province, such as Sibi, Zhob, Loralai, and Pishin districts, did not participate in the rebellion.[273] There is little doubt these factors helped mitigate the threat the state faced from Baloch nationalists.

On the other hand, geographically restricted insurgencies in rural areas with low levels of popular support are not always treated kindly by states. Consider Guatemala. Two decades before its gruesome civil war claimed a hundred thousand lives, the country witnessed a smaller-scale insurgency, extinguished with "shockingly brutal"[274] methods. The number of active guerrilla fighters in the mid-1960s did not exceed five hundred—a tenth of the fighting force in Balochistan—and yet the Guatemalan government employed a "massive counterinsurgency program" in Zacapa and Izabal, which included modernized weaponry, a vast intelligence network, mobile military police, and "sophisticated" torture techniques.[275] Most notably, the government used right-wing death squads, the most active of which was the Mano Blanco, which tortured and murdered large numbers of peasants and possible sympathizers.[276] This "pacification program" led to the deaths of around ten thousand peasants in a short period (1965–67): "Entire villages were razed to the ground. Mutilated bodies were left in public places as a warning to others."[277]

Of course, the context and conditions of insurgency in Guatemala were different than those in Balochistan, but the case bears noting if only to demonstrate that revolts in rural, sparsely populated regions do not necessarily see relatively sedate responses from states. Moreover, a rebel force of between five and ten thousand fighters is hardly an insignificant figure when compared to other insurgencies worldwide; the Bengali insurgency took until May or June of 1971 to have that many men under arms. As the secretary of finance in Balochistan told one British official, the security situation in the province "was really potentially very serious. He could not say what sort of casualties the army was taking, but a friend of his had seen the bodies of 20 soldiers in the Hospital only last week and numbers of this sort were by no means unusual. He did not think that the Baluch, who were experts in guerrilla tactics, were taking anything like these casualties."[278]

Indeed, it is unlikely that a fighting force of between five and ten thousand rebels with experience fighting the Pakistan Army and with strong external state backing would have presented such a manageable challenge for the Pakistan military. A thought experiment can help build the case: assume that, instead of being concerned about a Greater Balochistan, Iran was wholeheartedly behind its development. Under such circumstances, it is easy to imagine a significantly tougher rebel movement in Balochistan, and an attendant increase in the Pakistani state's brutality.[279] When I put this hypothetical to a former security official, he claimed that the threat posed by the rebels would have been significantly stronger with such support.[280] For obvious reasons, few interviewees would explicitly concede that the state would have employed more indiscriminate violence as a consequence. But as one student of the Pakistan military noted, "If the insurgency is stronger, then [the] state's response would be more serious."[281] Commenting on the manageability of the Baloch threat in the 1970s, a retired three-star general noted that, "unlike today," the relationship between India, Afghanistan, and Balochistan then did not involve "weapons, training, systems, money."[282]

The extent to which the Baloch movement enjoyed outside support, then, was intimately tied to how grave a threat it posed to the state, which in turn guided how repressive the state was in its dealing with the movement. Prima facie, a movement resting on a longtime historical dissatisfaction with the state, featuring between five and ten thousand rebels in rugged terrain, would pose a significant issue for any state. However, because the roots of the conflict were entirely domestic in nature, and because the movement enjoyed only moderate support from a weaker power—in stark contrast to the state, which enjoyed the fruits of its partnership with its powerful western neighbor, Iran—the degree to which the movement was deemed a threat was reduced considerably. As such, the conflict never represented an existential danger to the central Pakistani state and consequently required less violence to quell it than the Bengali insurgency of 1971.

Alternative Explanations

No single study that I am aware of has tackled the Bengali and Baloch secessionist conflicts side by side, but we can adduce a number of general and context-specific arguments for why Pakistan might have responded to this pair of movements differently, insofar as levels of violence and repression are concerned. How well do these arguments explain the observed variation?

It is unclear how much the reputation argument from the literature on secessionist conflicts can account for Pakistan's strategies in East Pakistan and Balochistan, simply because its different strands point to different predictions. On the one hand, this argument expects states to be more violent against movements appearing earlier, because the state has more of a reputation to create then. This, indeed, is what took place in Pakistan, with the Bengalis in 1971 subject to genocide, while Balochistan in the middle of the decade saw less harsh measures. On the other hand, scholars making this argument also point to changes in leadership as crucial: reputation concerns aggregate at the level of individuals in power.[283] If this is the case, then, the military in 1971 and Bhutto in 1973 would have faced similar incentives to establish "tough" reputations, and thus we would expect similar levels of violence. Even if one is generous to this argument, and discounts the mixed predictions it generates, the causal story it proffers was simply not relevant to these conflicts: there was little indication that the leadership in *either* conflict was concerned with sending messages to other domestic ethnic groups. This is precisely why process tracing is valuable—it allows for researchers to check for spurious correlations, unlike in large-n work.[284]

Insofar as the argument for domestic veto players is concerned, the institutional setup of the Pakistani state did not experience the kind of metamorphosis between 1971 and 1973 that would have changed the responses to nationalist movements so drastically.[285] While it is true that Pakistan experienced a nominal transition from military to democratic rule, it is important not to overstate the effects, or even substance, of this transition. A more accurate reading would be that Pakistan went from military to civilian authoritarianism; the number of impediments to centralized decision-making did not change between 1971 and 1973. Furthermore, the veto-player argument is valid only in those situations when decision makers wish to make concessions but cannot do so for institutional reasons, but in these conflicts, the state was not much interested in concessions in the first place.

Moving away from general explanations for secessionist violence, there are a number of context-specific arguments that could possibly account for the observed variation. The most obvious of these would be that Balochistan was simply an easier fight than East Pakistan: the population to be subdued was smaller and the terrain and weather more forgiving. There is assuredly something to this argument, especially in accounting for the military's violence in Bengal after the summer monsoon of 1971, when it tried and failed to pacify the Bengali countryside. Militarily, however, the Baloch were arguably a stronger force than the Bengalis at the outset of the respective crises, which was when the decision to use force was made, and indeed, one of the reasons for the military's overwhelming force in East Pakistan was its persistent belief in Bengali pusillanimity and decided lack of martial strength. The Baloch had about ten thousand men under arms when their province was occupied by the Pakistan military. In addition, Baloch tribes had experience of fighting pitched battles against the Pakistan Army in the 1950s and 1960s. By contrast, the Bengalis were in disarray in March and April of 1971; their strength in numbers was similar to the Baloch insurgents, drawn from the deweaponized East Pakistan Rifles, the East Bengal Regiment, and policemen, but they faced important handicaps to the extent that they lacked firepower, adequate transportation and communication, and commanding officers to lead the insurgency,[286] and had to wait until well into the civil war before training, arms, and logistical support from the Indian state bestowed them with the capabilities to be a viable military force.

Another alternative argument is that the Pakistani military acted with overwhelming force in East Pakistan out of a pathological hatred for Hindus and non-Muslims. There is no doubt that emotion was an important factor in the response in East Pakistan. When commanding officers refer to the actions of their men as going "berserk,"[287] we can reasonably deduce that strategic concerns were not responsible for all that happened in 1971. Nevertheless, we must ask why racism and emotion mattered so much more in Bengal than Balochistan. After all, the Pakistani military has historically been dominated by the "martial races" of Pashtuns and Punjabis, and both Bengalis and Baloch were deemed unworthy of fighting by both the colonial British as well as the postcolonial Pakistani state.[288] Why was the Pakistani state more racist against Bengalis than the Baloch? The distinction in the two cases lies in that the "other" race in East Pakistan was perceived to be close to India, Pakistan's biggest and most significant rival—culturally, linguistically, and geopolitically. The Baloch were not conceived of in these terms.[289] That is, even if pathological racism was at work in East Pakistan, that racism was operating through the lens of geopolitics. A simple thought experiment will bear this point out. Consider a situation where Balochistan borders India and its population shares strong political, ethnic and linguistic ties to citizens across the border. Conversely, imagine "East" Pakistan bordering Afghanistan and Iran, two states that either do not have the ability or willingness to threaten Pakistan's security from without, and that have never fought a war against Pakistan. Is it reasonable to surmise that Pakistani racism and hatred would be directed against Balochistan more strongly than in "East" Pakistan in this hypothetical?

A third context-specific argument would be that the West Pakistani leadership was chastened as a result of civil war and the dismemberment of the country in 1971, causing it to tread more carefully in Balochistan later that decade. Such an inference would be incorrect. First, Baloch insurrections—even those before the 1971 civil war, such as those in the 1950s and 1960s—had *always* been treated with more direct and focused military action, rather than the widespread and indiscriminate repression on hand in East Pakistan. Second and more important, there is sparse evidence that the memories of 1971 played any significant role in Bhutto's or the military's decision-making.[290] Individual officers who had fought in East Pakistan were either eased off into retirement or were prisoners of war when the fighting broke out in Balochistan. Meanwhile, at the institutional level, there was no strategic review or internal analysis of the military's mistakes following the loss of East Pakistan.[291] The one verifiable area in which the memory of 1971 did reverberate was in Bhutto's decision to have ethnically mixed regiments in Balochistan, as opposed to the purely Bengali regiments found in the former East Pakistan,[292] but the effect of this was minimal on the actual decision-making pertaining to the conflict itself. The basic elements of the logic behind the decision to use force to put down a rebellion rather than grant concessions were the same—the only difference was in the intensity of the response. If the leadership was truly chastened, it would have been reluctant to use force in the first place, not calibrate it to a lower level.

Finally, a materialist explanation would expect Pakistan to fight harder in more resource-rich regions, but this explanation predicts the opposite of what actually occurred. Balochistan was and remains the most resource-rich province of Pakistan and is an important source of natural gas, minerals, copper, uranium, gold, coal, silver, platinum, and potential oil reserves for the Pakistan state;[293] by contrast, East Pakistan did not hold much potential for material wealth.

This chapter has asked the question of why the Pakistani state was so much more indiscriminate and extreme in its use of violence against Bengali secessionists in 1971 than Baloch secessionists three years later. It showed that the primary reason for the variation in state strategy was the perceived differential in third-party support: the Bengali movement was deemed to be operating hand-in-glove with the Indian state, receiving full-blown political and military support, while by contrast, the Baloch only received sanctuary from Afghanistan. This distinction between moderate and high levels of third-party support meant that the Bengali movement was deemed a much more significant threat to Pakistan's external security than the Baloch movement was. Consequently, decision makers and soldiers on the ground were more aggressive and violent in East Pakistan than they were in Balochistan.

CHAPTER 3

India's Strategies against Separatism in Assam, Punjab, and Kashmir, 1984–1994

India is hardly a stranger to separatist conflict—no state has experienced as many secessionist movements.[1] I explore three movements that took place within half a decade of each other—Assam (1985–92), Punjab (1984–93), and Jammu and Kashmir (henceforth Kashmir, 1989–94). These movements represent the three "hotbed" regions of ethno-national separatism in India. Muslim and Sikh nationalism in Kashmir and Punjab dominated regional, national, and even international headlines for years. The Northeast, meanwhile, has proved problematic for India to placate for decades, featuring both ideological (primarily leftist or Marxist) and ethnic-based conflicts, and Assam is the central state in the region. I focus on these cases because of the two basic clusters of secessionist movements in India—immediately after independence, and in the late 1970s through the 1980s—we have better data and simply know more about the latter period. Moreover, by maintaining consistency from the previous chapter in both the region and period covered, South Asia in the 1970s and 1980s, I can control for larger, structural changes in international politics, such as regional dynamics or the Cold War. Finally, because the cases display variation on both the independent and dependent variables, and in Punjab's case, variation over time, there is a theoretical, as well as empirical payoff to juxtaposing these conflicts.

Separatist conflict in India, broadly speaking, is a function of the country's extreme size and ethnic diversity, on the one hand, and the state's long-running stand that it would not acquiesce to the loss of territory based on ethno-national claims on the other (see map in chapter 2). This strict insistence against secessionism is often thought of as the product of the precedent-setting logic, whereby India fights separatists because it fears that concessions would only encourage other groups to stake similar claims. The thinking goes that, in a state as heterogeneous as India, such a policy would lead to a domino-effect, and the internal destruction of the state. There is certainly something to this idea, and Indian leaders often invoke the danger to the state's secular constitution that territorial concessions to ethnic or religious groups would entail. However, the emphasis on the precedent-setting effect of fighting separatists has probably been overstated. India has other reasons to foreclose the possibility of secession when faced with such movements. Its urgency to keep territory within the Indian Union is also a function of external factors: the interplay of its rough neighborhood, its ambitious regional and global agenda, and its collective view of the causes of its colonial subjugation.

India perceives itself as a major global power, competing for hegemony in the region with China. The major narrative sustaining Indian foreign and security policy in the latter half of the twentieth century, according to Garver, was that "India is a great nation whose radiant influence molded a wide swath of the world beyond its boundaries," and that it deserves a "place of eminence in the world."[2] Jawaharlal Nehru's deep belief in India's destiny to be a major player in world politics shaped his rhetoric and actions as India's long-running first prime minister and foreign minister.[3] Even before independence, Nehru argued for a Security Council seat for India on the basis that "it is absurd for India to be treated like any small power in this connection . . . India is the center of security in Asia."[4] Notwithstanding its lack of a formal strategic doctrine and its claims that it is not hegemonic, scholars argue that India's behavior is in keeping with its own version of the United States' famous Monroe doctrine, whereby it seeks to bar foreign powers from exercising influence and sees itself as the guarantor of stability in the region.[5]

The Indian state has been sensitive to the issue of territory since birth, when it consolidated itself by bringing under its ambit, in a matter of weeks, more than five hundred "princely states" crisscrossing it, bequeathed by a clumsy British retreat from the subcontinent.[6] Nehru and the Indian leadership were more than aware that India was only a potential major power, not an actual one, and that the realization of its promise depended on its size, both geographically and demographically.[7] In 1949, Nehru told the Constituent Assembly that there was an "inevitability of India playing an important part by virtue of her tremendous potential, by virtue of the fact that she is the biggest political unit in terms of population today and is likely to be in terms of resources also. She is going to play that part." Nehru believed that alongside the Soviet Union, the United States, and China, "the obvious fourth country in the world is India." This belief that its size and population are central to its claims and potential for great power status are generally widespread among Indian leaders.[8]

The main threat to these ambitions to become a major power and exercise influence in the region and beyond were internal and external subversion from its neighbors.[9] India's grand view of its place in the world is complicated by its strategic environment, where it is the third node in the Sino-Indo-Pak triangle.[10] It has had numerous confrontations and wars with both China and Pakistan, including a devastating defeat in a border war in 1962 against China that shook not just the security and foreign policy establishments, but the entire body politic.[11] China and Pakistan enjoy deep strategic ties, and each actor in the Sino-Indo-Pak triangle has been a nuclear power since at least the 1980s.[12] Historically, China and Pakistan have forced Indian planners to confront the possibility of a two-front war,[13] though the introduction of substantial nuclear arsenals in the region complicates such plans. Pakistan has launched conflict over Kashmir several times, and continues its revisionism over the territory today.

That internal and external security are an "overriding consideration" for India's political elites stems from the widely shared view of its colonial history, where its two-hundred-year servitude to the British crown was attributed to its longstanding lack of internal cohesion.[14] For Nehru and the newly independent Indian state, therefore, the greatest threats to its security came from within, not without.[15] This view has survived decades. Analysts argue that strategic thought in India sees a "close relationship between internal security and outside aggression," most obviously encapsulated in the issue of Kashmir and Punjab,[16] as I discuss below, but also historically in places such as Nagaland and Mizoram. India conflates internal and external security with good reason: its internal vulnerabilities mark an opportunity to upturn the balance of power against it, one that each of its main rivals has taken repeatedly in its Northeast and Northwest over decades. India's neighbors would gain considerably by cartographically cutting it down to size, forcing the loss of territory and population, and its geopolitical ambitions demand that it must be consistently on guard against such behavior. For India, secessionism is therefore as much an external threat as internal, and it consequently denies the possibility of its various ethnic or nationalist groups becoming independent. As Indira Gandhi pointedly noted, "If there is friendship, well, all the borders can be soft, not just Kashmir!"[17] The absence of "friendship" with both China and Pakistan has meant that India cannot afford compromise against separatists and must ensure their defeat, lest its security and ambitions be threatened.

While a combination of concerns about the balance of power and precedent setting may explain why India refuses to acquiesce to secessionism in general, we are still left with the puzzle of why the extent of coercion India used against separatists in the 1980s varied widely. In Assam, the Indian government practiced a mix of policing and militarization: it delegated strategy to the state government led by the Asom Gana Parishad (AGP), itself a product of a concessionary accord with the center, for dealing with United Liberation Front of Assam (ULFA), an avowedly secessionist organization. Its delay, short duration, and limited intensity of military operations against ULFA were backed up by repeated offers of talks with "moderates." In Punjab, the government's initial strategy was policing, encapsulated by an accord with "moderate" Sikhs in the Akali Dal (L) Party in 1985, before it

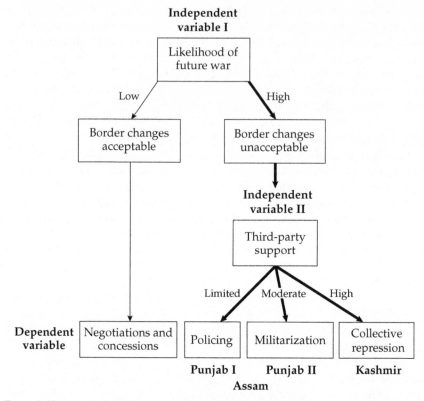

Figure 3. Variation in India's responses to secessionism in the 1980s

escalated to militarization in 1987, when the Punjab police assumed center stage in the conflict. In Kashmir, in contrast to both cases, the state used collective repression at the outset of the crisis, in the winter of 1989–90.

This variation can be explained by these movements representing external threats to varying degrees, since there were dissimilar levels of third-party support. Kashmir was the main prize in a territorial dispute between India and Pakistan—two wars had been fought over it previously—and religious, political, and military ties between the Pakistani state and the Kashmiri secessionists meant that perceived third-party support was "high." Conversely, Indian strategy in Assam was less repressive because the movement, owing to third-party support that was "limited" from a significantly weaker power, Myanmar, did not represent a significant external threat, freeing various central governments to alternatively ignore the problem, or treat it with low levels of coercion. Indian strategy in Punjab, meanwhile, followed shifts in Pakistani support. In 1985, when there was "limited" support for Sikh nationalists, and the government saw the problem through a domestic prism, it adopted policing, a mixture of low-level coercion and concessions to moderates. However, the passage of time saw Pakistani involvement in support of Punjabi secessionists rise to "moderate" levels, and in 1987, India responded with militarization. Figure 3 graphically represents the argument proffered in this chapter.

The main alternative theories outlined earlier in this book cannot explain the variation in India's strategies against separatists in the 1980s. Internal deterrence arguments that privilege the reputation-building effects of using violence would predict that the earlier movements—those in Assam and Punjab—would see more repression than Kashmir. Arguments for political institutions, meanwhile, cannot explain the observed variation simply because India's status as a constitutional democracy and the number of "veto factions" within the polity did not change in the period examined, but state policy assuredly did. Additionally, arguments specific to the Indian context, such as those based on natural resources or the extremism of the movement's demands, also offer unsatisfactory answers. A focus on external security allows us significantly greater analytical traction on secessionist conflicts in India than we had previously.

Assam, 1985–92

We first turn our attention to the Northeast of India, encompassing the states of Assam, Nagaland, Manipur, Tripura, Meghalaya, Mizoram, Arunachal Pradesh, and Sikkim, home to decades of insurgency and instability. In total, there are about one hundred rebel groups active in the region. Much of the violence in the Northeast is autonomist or secessionist in nature, but there is also violence among the states themselves, among different tribes within states, between tribal and nontribal groups, and between native sons of the soil and "outsiders."[18] Indeed, the conflict-ridden nature of politics in the region is reflected in the title of a book on it: *Durable Disorder*.[19]

Given the wide-ranging panoply of groups and ethnicities in the region,[20] I focus my attention on Assam, one of the states in question. Why Assam? For one, it is the most populous state in the region.[21] For another, the fact that it borders every other Northeast sate renders it, at least geographically, the region's core.[22] Finally, of the seven major urban centers of the region, Assam is home to four—Guwahati, Jorhat, Dibrugarh, and Silchar.[23] It is thus fair to characterize Assam as the "heart of this region"[24] and consider it an apposite window to understand secessionist conflict in the restive Northeast.

The Indian state was fairly restrained in its use of force in Assam relative to ethno-national movements in other parts of the country. In the period under study, the center faced two different types of actors: a student-led sons-of-soil agitation in the mid-1980s and a full-blown separatist insurgency at the turn of the decade. Neither saw sustained aggressive Indian military action. Instead, the former was treated with a negotiations and concessions strategy by the Rajiv Gandhi government, which signed an accord with the All Assam Students Union (AASU) in 1985. However, because AASU fell well short of a true autonomist or secessionist organization, the center's conduct toward it is not a true test of my argument. On the other hand, ULFA was a more typical secessionist organization, and while it was assuredly the target of military campaigns unlike AASU, coercion in Assam, compared to Kashmir or Punjab, was delayed in implementation, restrained in intensity, short in duration, and targeted in scope. For years, the center delegated its dealing with ULFA to the AGP-led state government that enjoyed close ties with the organization. When force finally came in the early 1990s, talks with moderate elements of the movement were continually emphasized, and in one case, elected state governments were in charge when the campaign was ordered, in contrast to Punjab and Kashmir. As such, I consider Indian behavior in Assam between 1987 and 1992 as falling between policing and militarization.

This "soft" coercion had its roots in the fact that unlike in Punjab and Kashmir, ethno-national movements in Assam did not pose a significant external threat to the Indian state. Third-party support for both the students of AASU as well as the separatists of ULFA was negligible from the usual suspects, Pakistan and China. Bangladesh provided sanctuary and support to ULFA, but this support began in the 1990s, after, not before, the Indian military campaigns to flush militants out of Upper Assam that I focus on. ULFA's third-party support in the time period in question was restricted to a handful of bases in Myanmar, a significantly weaker power than India, and as such can be categorized as "limited." The lack of support from threats to Indian security meant that, first, the center's attention was distracted from the ULFA problem to more urgent matters elsewhere in the country, where external involvement was higher. Second, when the center did decide on coercion, such as in operations Bajrang and Rhino in 1990–92, it calibrated it to the relatively low levels needed to neutralize an organization lacking significant third-party backing.

RELATIVE DEPRIVATION AND DISAFFECTION AGAINST OUTSIDERS AND MIGRANTS

The major structural cause of Assamese dissatisfaction with the Indian state revolved around socioeconomic concerns.[25] Literacy and per capita income were lower in Assam than national averages, and roads, communications, access to piped water, and industrial development lagged well behind the rest of the country.[26] From the perspective of native Assamese, what was especially galling about the state's relative poverty was that the state possessed plentiful natural resources, without substantially benefitting the local population. Instead, royalties from oil, plywood, and tea were siphoned off to the center.[27] Exacerbating this sense of exploitation was that central and state administrations were dominated by outsiders—those that were not "sons of the soil."

More immediately, what led to Assamese agitation in the late 1970s and 1980s was the pace and extent of migration into the state by nonlocals, upturning the demographic balance and allegedly "turning the indigenous people of Assam into a minority."[28] The roots of migration into Assam go back 150 years. The British colonial administration encouraged migration from places such as Sylhet and Mymensingh in present-day Bangladesh, as well as Bihar, Orissa (present-day Odisha), the Central Provinces (present-day Madhya Pradesh), the United Provinces (present-day Uttar Pradesh), and Tamil Nadu because it needed a cheap and effective labor force for its interests in tea, oil, communications, and economic modernization. In turn, these demographic changes led to a desire for more direct administration in Assam, leading to greater demand for educated labor to occupy clerical and administrative positions in government. The English-speaking population of Bengal fit the bill, resulting in even greater immigration of non-Assamese to the state.[29] Around this time, formal opposition to immigration began to develop, such as with the formation of the Assam Protection Association in 1926.[30] Partition brought another mass influx of nonlocals, to the chagrin of Congress's chief minister in Assam, Gopinath Bordoloi, whose opposition to the settlement of Bengalis in the state relented only when Prime Minister Nehru threatened withholding federal development funds.[31] A similar story played out when a civil war in Pakistan between its east and west wings spilled over into India, leading to significant migration from Bengal to Assam and the rest of Northeast India (chapter 2). This episode of migration into Assam set the stage for the crisis of the late 1970s.

Reliable figures on the exact rate of migration into Assam are difficult to find precisely because immigration was such a politicized issue, and illegal immigrants are hardly likely to leave a paper trail on official forms and the census. However, some broad inferences have been made, given that population growth in Assam consistently outpaced growth in India overall. Between 1971 and 1981, Assam's population grew by 36 percent while India's grew by 25 percent. In the previous decade, the respective figures were 35 percent and 25 percent. Between 1951 and 1961, Assam experienced population growth of 35 percent and India of 22 percent. In the decade before that, it was 20 percent and 13 percent respectively. One estimate notes that had Assam's population grown at the same rate as India's throughout the twentieth century, Assam's population in 1971 would have been half of its 15 million.[32] While hardly conclusive, this disparity suggests that Assam attracted migrants at a much higher rate than the rest of India. Organizations directly involved in the anti-immigrant movement claimed that there were between 4.5 and 5 million illegal aliens in Assam, about a third of the total population, in the 1970s. This was probably an exaggeration. A lower-end estimate put the number of illegal foreign nationals in Assam at about 1.6 million, or 11 percent of the state's population.[33] Regardless of its precise extent, native Assamese found immigration troubling for both cultural and socioeconomic reasons: Bengali Hindus and even Muslims tended to dominate the public sector as well as professional jobs, and there was a fear amongst Assamese property owners that the generally impoverished peasants could radicalize their native counterparts.[34] Most important was the electoral impact of migration, which disproportionately benefitted the Congress Party and its "vote bank" among Bengalis.

THE AASU AGITATION AND RAJIV GANDHI'S ACCORD

In April 1979 Hiralal Patowari, a parliamentarian from the Mangaldai constituency, one with a significant Bengali Muslim population, died.[35] The voter rolls for the resulting by-election included large numbers of foreigners; a court found forty-five thousand voters to be illegal aliens, or about one-sixth of the overall list.[36] The Mangaldai election put into sharp relief an issue that had been simmering for years and had even gained national prominence, and led to organized opposition to illegal aliens led by the All Assam Students Union (AASU), which kicked off a statewide strike to protest the infiltration issue in June 1979.[37] Two months later, it joined the All Assam Gana Sangram Parishad (AAGSP), an umbrella organization counting in its midst several regional parties and organizations. Their leaders had one specific demand: use the 1951 National Register of Citizens as the baseline to ascertain which Assam residents were legally living there and which were not, and deport all identified noncitizens.[38]

The center and student leaders held a series of negotiations in the early 1980s on this question of detection, disenfranchisement, and deportation of foreigners, but the devil was in the details: who, exactly, was to be considered a foreigner? In discussions with the prime minister and the Home Ministry, the AASU-AAGSP pressed that all immigrants who entered the country after 1961 be classified as illegal. The center countered with 1971 as the cutoff date, mainly because of a cooperative agreement signed between Indira Gandhi and Mujib-ur-Rahman which impelled India to settle all refugees who entered the country before 1971.[39] From the center's point of view, readily giving in to the nationalists would exact a significant political cost: it would imperil its Bengali immigrant vote bank,[40] and treating Hindu immigrants from what had been East Pakistan as illegal aliens would have courted disaster in mainstream Hindu circles in the rest of the country. The "obvious" solution to this problem—of making an exemption for Bengali Hindus while declaring Bengali Muslim immigrants illegal—would open a unique can of worms, drawing into question the secular nature of the Indian republic as well as alienating Muslims at large, an important constituency for Congress. Finally, expelling Bengali immigrants would spell trouble for India's relations with Bangladesh.[41]

Consequently, neither side conceded much for years, as Assam became home to strikes, disturbances, and instability. State governments, devoid of legitimacy due to election boycotts and contested electoral rolls, repeatedly collapsed after a few months in charge.[42] Even Chief Minister Hiteshwar Saikia, an ethnic Assamese and a "most dynamic and astute" politician who knew local Assamese politics well, could not stem the agitation after coming to power in the 1983 State Assembly elections. The polls were marred by an AASU boycott—adhered to in Assamese areas and ignored in Bengali constituencies—and significant communal violence, especially in Nellie, where some fourteen hundred Bengali men, women, and children were killed by a mob of about twelve thousand people.[43] A year after the Nellie massacre, a young tribesman told the *New York Times* that "our people are itching for another confrontation. They tell us that peaceful methods haven't worked for these four years."[44]

This juncture fell short of a true secessionist moment, given AASU's demands did not involve greater autonomy or statehood, but the escalatory rhetoric and disturbances forced the center to confront this ethnic movement. The strategy of Rajiv Gandhi's government was negotiations and concessions, promising a "new initiative" and talks with agitation leaders in January 1985 that began the next month.[45] By June, the two sides had agreed on all but one issue.[46] By August, optimism was pervasive and Rajiv appeared jubilant.[47] Despite a last-minute hitch, an accord was signed, and its fortuitous timing allowed the prime minister to announce it in his Independence Day speech at the Red Fort in Delhi on August 15, 1985.[48]

On the big question of voter rolls, the center conceded and decreed that January 1, 1966, would serve as the base year for ascertaining residents' citizenship status. Anyone who entered the state after January 1, 1966, but before March 25, 1971, would be removed from electoral rolls for a period of ten years. Anyone who entered Assam after March 25, 1971, would be deported. The government also pledged to ramp up border security. Acknowledging the long-running sociocultural undercurrents in the Assamese movement, the government promised that "constitutional, legislative and administrative safeguards, as may be appropriate, shall be provided to protect, preserve and promote the cultural, social, linguistic identity and heritage of the Assamese people." Finally, the government agreed to "review with sympathy and withdraw cases of disciplinary action" against those who had transgressed in the agitation and to pay compensation money to survivors of those who had been killed. In return, the AASU and the AAGSP agreed to halt its agitation.[49] The accord was signed by R. D. Pradhan, the home secretary, and AASU president Prafulla Mahanta and general secretary Bhrigu K. Phukan.

As was the case in Punjab (see below), Rajiv Gandhi's "decisiveness" garnered a great deal of credit. Unlike his mother, who "disliked making decisions," Rajiv "hears his people and decides quickly—often immediately in the cabinet meeting."[50] The "fundamental difference" between the two was that while Indira was more interested in protecting Congress' majority, Rajiv cared less about the party's interests and wanted to be seen as a problem-solver.[51] Western headlines and editorials cooed in admiration for Rajiv's "willingness to rethink seemingly intractable problems, open dialogue, and after hard bargaining, reach agreements that give promise of providing solutions," which was a "fresh approach that leaders in other troubled areas of the world would do well to emulate."[52] Rajiv himself struck a triumphant tone: "Ten months ago, the world was watching whether India would disintegrate into pieces. Today, that question does not arise."[53] Notwithstanding opposition from Assamese Muslims who felt "betrayed," and politicians in West Bengal, who played up the fear of a mass migration of Bengali Hindus into their province, overall sentiment toward the accord and Rajiv was almost entirely positive, with some going as far as calling it "a magna carta for peace."[54] For their part, the leaders of the agitation were also recognized, marking their return from New Delhi at a euphoric rally at Judge's Field.[55] They formed a new party, the Asom Gana Parishad (AGP), bringing into their fold two regional parties, the Assam Jatiata Badi Dal and Purbanchalia Loka Parishad, and delivered a dominant performance in the elections of December 1985, winning 64 out of 126 seats.[56] Mahanta became the youngest chief minister in Indian history and promised that illegal immigrants would be "deported immediately after their detection."[57] "The accord will definitely be implemented," he warned Bengali immigrants. "If that antagonizes them, we cannot help it. There will definitely be no compromise on that aspect."[58]

From the center's point of view, the accord defanged the student agitation, bringing it into mainstream politics. However, the center's accommodationist stance, and the resulting tenure of the AGP government, created the space for the development of a significantly stiffer test for the Indian state in Assam. Interestingly for our purposes, even the United Liberation Front of Assam (ULFA), an avowedly secessionist organization, was treated with relative restraint.

THE RISE OF ULFA

The AGP record in power was, to put it mildly, disappointing.[59] Less than two years into the AGP's tenure, the *Times of India* commented that "the ruling Asom Gana Parishad (AGP) seems to have lost much of its initial enthusiasm for change . . . the AGP is slipping into the familiar role of a traditional political party in power which is affected by internal rivalry and faced by disillusionment among its earlier support base."[60] The AGP failed for many reasons. First, their leaders were inexperienced, unprepared, internally divided, and corrupt.[61] Second, despite claiming that they would "reach out to other Indian citizens who have doubts about our intentions" their strict insistence on antiforeigner drives and assertion of Assamese identity created the conditions for rebellions by tribals, such as the Bodos, led primarily by the All Bodo Students Union (ABSU).[62] Third, the task of detecting and deporting illegal immigrants proved challenging, both due to the difficulty of separating illegal immigrants from their ethnic brethren who were present legally, and because the Congress government in the center could not be accused of expending all its energies in aiding the AGP in fulfilling the conditions of the accord, leading to considerable rancor from Mahanta.[63]

The upshot of these developments was that by 1988, observers were referring to the accord as a "crumbling document," propelling support toward ULFA.[64] ULFA was a secessionist organization that fought on behalf of "the people of Assam," unlike AASU, which fought on behalf of the "Assamese people."[65] This distinction was born of an idea to expand ULFA's potential support base and to include not just those drawn from the Ahom ethnic stock, but all ethnicities and religions contained on Assam's land; "they realized you can't take on the Indian state without 30–35% of the population."[66] In the words of an organizational spokesperson, "The ULFA is not a chauvinist organization and [we] treat all sections of people staying in Assam as equal."[67] ULFA drew cadres and support both from nationalist groups such as the AASU and AAGSP as well as leftist groups such as the Assam Jatiyotabadi Yuba Chatro Parishad (AJYCP). Largely dormant during the agitation from 1979 to 1985, its activities restricted to bank robberies and isolated assassination attempts, ULFA stepped up its violence in response to the failures of the AGP government. Though it is difficult to pinpoint one secessionist "moment" for this movement, contemporary reports record it having a significant presence in Upper Assam, where it originated, and throughout the Brahmaputra Valley by 1987.[68]

In the five years of AGP rule, ULFA killed about a hundred high-value targets, such as Assamese businessman Surrendra Paul, politicians belonging to Congress or UMF such as UMF leader Kalipada Sen, and police officials such as Dibrugarh superintendent Daulat Sing Negi.[69] Its activities, including violence, extortion—especially of tea producers, who closed factories and tea gardens and evacuated scores of executives—and bank robberies were considered serious enough to postpone general elections in the state in November 1989.[70] By December 1989, it was said to "run a flourishing parallel government in many rural areas of Assam," focused especially on the districts of Nalbari, Barpeta, Lakshmipur, and Dhemaji.[71] In November 1990, the *Times of India* argued that "the depredations of this secessionist and terrorist outfit have reached such a stage that the ruling Asom Gana Parishad has ceased to govern in all but name."[72]

THE CENTER'S STRATEGY AGAINST ULFA

For years, in part compelled by greater external threats elsewhere covered later in this chapter, the center adopted a hands-off policy and outsourced the task of dealing with ULFA to the AGP state government. When it did escalate to militarization, it chose a relatively mild form. Crucially for our purposes, the Indian state made splitting the separatists into moderate and extremist camps a central part of its strategy, a hallmark of policing. As such, it would be fair to characterize India's strategy against ULFA from 1987 to 1992 as a mixed one, between the poles of policing and militarization, but tending to the former.

Despite demands from toughness from the Hindu right, the center explicitly left matters up to the AGP state government on dealing with ULFA between 1987 and 1990.[73] This was a curious strategy given that the close relations between the AGP and ULFA were widely acknowledged.[74] At the same time as Prime Minister V. P. Singh was unleashing Governor Jagmohan and Indian security forces in Kashmir, he adopted conciliatory rhetoric and offered the carrot of oil refineries and financial munificence to placate Assamese dissatisfaction—and was applauded by observers both in Delhi and in Assam for doing so.[75] Meanwhile, the AGP "strategy" to deal with the situation was comically undercooked: police were "asked to take prompt and effective steps" to improve law and order, alongside a "publicity blitz" to counter ULFA propaganda.[76]

It was a change of government, to Prime Minister Chandra Shekhar, combined with the threat to international tea producers and sellers, that brought about closer center attention to ULFA and Assam, starting around August 1990.[77] Another possible factor, unconfirmed, was an alleged video shown to the prime minister in which a senior AGP minister was caught having discussions with an ULFA leader, the last straw for the government.[78] Increased central attention to the problem resulted in two military operations in close succession: Bajrang in late 1990, and Rhino in late 1991, which killed or captured a great proportion of ULFA's senior leadership.[79] Bajrang began in November 1990, when Shekhar instituted president's rule and outlawed ULFA.[80] He said that "any country cannot afford that secessionist elements go on scot free."[81] A senior government official was blunter, warning that "these fellows are really going to get it in the neck. They've been getting away all these months with murder, extortion, and worse."[82]

Though there was some alarmist rhetoric upon the announcement, fear and uncertainty amongst the general public, and reports of human rights abuses,[83] the Indian security footprint in Assam was relatively light, especially when contrasted to events in Punjab and Kashmir. Security forces mostly focused on capturing ULFA cadres alive and dismantling camps.[84] One indicator of the moderate nature of Indian coercion in Assam was the short duration of military operations. Bajrang was phased out after less than three months, mainly because of ULFA's ceasefire declaration.[85] Foreign tea companies such as Unilever, often a litmus test of stability and order in the state, had returned even earlier, by February.[86] Bajrang brought substantial numbers of ULFA cadres to the negotiating table after the organization had previously claimed it would not settle for anything less than full independence.[87] Five months after Bajrang had begun, the center considered Assam's situation "normal" enough to announce that it would hold general elections in the state.[88] By April, the army had completely suspended Bajrang; by June, elections had been held, with Congress and its chief minister designate, Saikia, emerging as the big winners.[89]

The Indian state was compelled to act once again when, a few months later, ULFA kidnapped several important personalities, including state government employees and a Soviet mining expert.[90] Eventually it decided on more military action in the form of Operation Rhino in September 1991, again focusing on Upper Assam.[91] One important distinction from Bajrang, as well as many other Indian military operations including those in Kashmir and Punjab, was that Rhino was conducted with an elected state government in power, symbolizing delegation from the center. Indeed, Chief Minister Saikia was an important player, mediating between various levels of government and the secessionists throughout the crisis.[92] As with Bajrang, it did not take long for ULFA to cry uncle. By December 1991, its "backbone was broken," a "virtually decimated" organization.[93] It announced a unilateral and indefinite ceasefire in anticipation of talks with the Narasimha Rao government in Delhi, and released six major hostages in its custody.[94] In turn, this quick retreat by ULFA allowed the center to halt military operations in January 1992 and pursue a soft strategy of talking, which began in February.

A crucial part of the government's strategy was to induce fissures in ULFA, and it took less than two weeks of Rhino for these splits to occur.[95] In fact, there were so many reports of factionalization within the organization that its leaders felt compelled to clarify that no such thing was happening.[96] By March 1992, a formal split was all but complete, with one side favoring talks and the other fighting.[97] The breakaway moderate faction, called S-ULFA (S for surrendered), began negotiations while the more extremist camp, led by Arabinda Rajkhowa and Paresh Barua, continuing to face military action.[98] This factor, of both national and state leaders continually emphasizing that talks with extremist organizations were acceptable, is another that distinguishes the center's strategy from other parts of the country, such as Kashmir in the early 1990s or Punjab in the late 1980s and early 1990s.[99] Meanwhile, India's softer side was shown in the center's promises for establishing an Indian Institute of Technology in North

Guwahati, infrastructural development, support for a fourth oil refinery at Numaligarh, and Finance Minister Manmohan Singh's assurances that "that the center would do everything possible to put the state's economy on a sound footing."[100]

A policing strategy entails selective coercion against hard-line elements alongside tactical concessions to moderates, while a militarization strategy includes targeted counterinsurgent operations. India's strategy against ULFA from 1987 to 1992 included elements from both. Its delegation to the AGP government between 1987 and 1990, its delay of military operations, and its consistent emphasis on talks with moderates all fell under a policing strategy.[101] Meanwhile, the very fact that it had to launch counterinsurgent campaigns, albeit limited in scope, duration, and intensity, means that it escalated to militarization, at least temporarily.

THE LIMITED ROLE OF EXTERNAL SECURITY IN ASSAM

The Indian state faced two types of nationalist movements in Assam, and neither saw significantly harsh repression. The state's response to the first movement, against the student agitators, was a negotiations and concessions strategy involving an accord between Rajiv Gandhi and AASU in 1985. There were few external implications attached to the student movement; the Indian state's concerns in the run-up to the Assam accord were almost entirely domestic in nature. Congress leadership in the mid-1980s believed that "a negotiated peace in Assam was important for gaining better political control over the Northeastern cluster of states as a whole." The "national leadership was confident that the post-accord election would strengthen Congress rule in Assam. Even if Congress were to lose the election, its replacement could be expected to lend support to the national system."[102] Indeed, this is precisely what occurred. The Assam crisis was also an opportunity for Rajiv Gandhi to reaffirm his "problem-solving" reputation, which at least temporarily was a boon to Congress.[103]

However, the state's response to the AASU movement is not a true test of my theory, given that, while based on a conceptualization of ethnic difference, it was not aimed at a separate homeland, or anything close. AASU's demands are consistently described as existing within the confines of the Indian constitution.[104] As one analyst put it, "The student leaders of the Assamese movement were fighting not so much to assert their separate identity as to return to the bosom of Mother India."[105] Indeed, AASU explicitly needed the Indian state to accept its point of view on Bangladeshi migrants for it to succeed in its political goals.[106] As such, it is not surprising that the Indian state did not use even low-level force against the movement.

More relevant for my argument is the state's treatment of ULFA. India faced a far tougher challenge against this avowedly secessionist organization, but partly because of a lack of external support, even this was treated with relatively soft hands. Contemporary reports declared that, "unlike in Punjab and some other states, there is, according to military and civilian intelligence sources, no evidence of state-level foreign involvement in Assam."[107] Local journalists confirmed in interviews that ULFA did not get direct support from outside India.[108] Instead, ULFA received training from other insurgent groups in the Northeast, mainly the Nationalist Socialist Council of Nagaland (NSCN), and relied on illicit private Chinese networks to procure arms.[109] While China had earlier supported assorted rebel groups in the Northeast, especially in Nagaland, it had ceased to do so by the early 1980s. Indeed, "repeated efforts by the ULFA and the NSCN in the late 1980s to secure Chinese help did not lead to any direct assistant from Beijing," mainly because by then China, under Deng Xiaoping's leadership, was seeking to mend relations with India, and saw the "export of revolution" as undesired "baggage of a Maoist past." Pakistan too had supported groups such as the Naga National Council and the Mizo National Front in the 1960s but overtly leftist groups were not generally supported by the Pakistani state.[110] Most important, Pakistan's ability to offer support to secessionists in India's Northeast was severely hampered when it lost East Pakistan in 1971, denying it a border connection to the region.[111] Simple geographic proximity meant that Pakistan could support movements in Kashmir and Punjab much more robustly than those in the Northeast; the distance made it challenging for insurgents to go to Pakistan.[112]

While ULFA would go on to receive significant external support, it would be after operations Bajrang and Rhino, not before. Those cadres who did not see fit to surrender escaped to Myanmar, Bangladesh, and Bhutan, where they enjoyed sanctuary and eventually financial and military aid.[113] The connections with Bangladesh were especially important after the formation of the Khaleda Zia government, one more friendly to Pakistan and the ISI than Awami League regimes led by Sheikh Hasina, which were closer to India.[114] Indeed, Khaleda Zia's tenure saw a two-pronged effort, both by Bangladesh's DGFI as well as Pakistan's ISI, to support ULFA.[115] But until the early 1990s, the period covered in this chapter, the external implications of nationalist movements in Assam were muted, with the only possible concern rumors of ULFA's sanctuaries in Myanmar, a much weaker power than India. Even the extent of these bases is disputed, and interviewees noted that ULFA's sanctuary presence in Myanmar was minimal relative to what it achieved in Bangladesh after the early Rhino. As such, I code third-party support for the movement in Assam as "limited."

A lack of significant external support had several implications for softening India's strategy against ULFA. First, it ensured that Indian action in Assam was delayed, because of more pressing external concerns elsewhere in the country.[116] In the words of a national editorial, "the total collapse of law and order in Kashmir and the continuing violence in Punjab" meant that the "grave situation in Assam is largely going unnoticed."[117] According to a local journalist, "national symbolism" and the "Pakistan obsession" had a great deal to do with India's lack of attention to the Northeast: "Kashmir is a high issue, while Northeast India is a low issue." Because there are important electoral constituencies in the Hindi belt, including Bihar and Uttar Pradesh, there is an element of playing to the galleries insofar as insurgencies on the western border were concerned. As he told me, "These [Kashmir and Punjab] were the important insurgencies, but Northeast is a fringe insurgency."[118]

Second, the lack of external support for ULFA meant that when military action did come, it was relatively brief. ULFA's material base suffered from a lack of foreign sponsorship, dampening the level of force required to defeat it.[119] It was "not very advanced" when it came to military capabilities, and "no match" for the Indian army.[120] And unlike Kashmir or Punjab, Assam is surrounded by other Indian states, providing a buffer from China, thus making it easier to deal with.[121]

Third, the lack of "emotional" connections to India's main security rivals mitigated the possibility of pathological violence by security forces. As one journalist remarked, "In Kashmir, it's perceived as a war against Pakistan. In Punjab also, it was supported from across the border. If ULFA was let's say a Muslim group, my impression is it [Indian use of force] would have got more amplification."[122] While the Kashmiri Muslim is looked at as a "closet Pakistani," Assam's heavily Hindu population makes it less likely that security forces would see locals as being in bed with an enemy state.

In Assam, then, India faced movements which enjoyed no support from major threats such as China and Pakistan, and even minor powers, such as Myanmar, only provided sanctuary. As such, the threat the movements posed was relatively muted, which meant that the Indian state adopted relatively soft methods to deal with them. It adopted negotiations and concessions against AASU, encapsulated by an accord in 1985. Against ULFA, the center adopted a mix of policing and militarization, as seen in its delegation of strategy to the ULFA-friendly AGP state government; its delay of military operations because of distraction with other more pressing threats; the short duration and limited intensity of its military operations when they finally did kick off; and its emphasis on talks with moderate elements of the movement.

Punjab, 1984–93

The interaction between the Indian state and Sikh nationalists in the 1980s is perhaps the most complex of the cases in this chapter, simply because it saw the largest degree of internal variation in strategy. While Assam saw a mostly hands-off center and only sporadic military action, and Kashmir witnessed consistent brutality, Punjab was the target of different policies by the Indian state. When opposition to the state among Sikhs became wide-spread after the attack on the Golden Temple in June 1984, marking the secessionist moment, Rajiv Gandhi treated the problem with a policing strategy, stressing the difference between "moderates" and "extremists." This strategy resulted in a generous, negotiated accord with the Akali Dal (L) in the summer of 1985. However, violence continued to fester in the state, and in the spring of 1987, India escalated to militarization, when it imposed president's rule and loosened the leash to the Punjab police led by K. P. S. Gill.

Overall, this case, more than others, highlights the limits of monocausal explanations and the need for analytical humility. My theory can shed light on important aspects of the variation in state strategy in Punjab. Rajiv's concessions to Sikh nationalists in 1985 were based largely on a domestic political logic, staged within a context in which Pakistani support for the movement was muted ("limited"). By 1987, when Pakistani support was more robust ("moderate"), the Indian state instituted a harsher strategy. While at least some of this covariation is causal, in that Pakistani support made for a tougher militant movement and consequently a more coercive policy, external security considerations were only part of the story. There were at least two equally important contributors to the tough fight the Indian state faced: the long-term institutionalization of British and Indian essentialist beliefs in Punjabi Sikhs' martial capabilities, which imbued them with the very same, and the splintering and factionalization of the militant movement in the late 1980s. These factors, along with Pakistani arming, training, and sanctuary of Sikh militants in the late 1980s, com-bined to produce an insurgency whose lethality required significant coer-cion in response.

THE ORIGINS OF SIKH NATIONALISM

A number of factors, structural and more immediate, were responsible for the outbreak of Sikh mobilization in the 1980s. First, Punjab had a rela-tively even demographic split between its Sikh and Hindu populations,[123] concentrated in the countryside and cities respectively. The rural Sikh com-munity was itself divided between more prosperous, landowning Jats on the one hand, and the traders, former refugees from Pakistan, scheduled castes, and landless laborers on the other. The Akali Dal Party, an ethno-religious party purporting to represent Sikh interests, generally attracted the vote of the landowning Jat Sikhs, while Congress's main supporters were Hindus and poorer, urban Sikhs. Congress, as a result, had a larger vote-bank than the Akalis; the latter would benefit if it were able to unite the Sikh population, both rural and urban, poor and rich, to form one voting bloc.[124]

Then there was the matter of provincial boundaries. Since independence, Akali leaders had demanded a Punjabi province. But because India's governing ideology was marked by a Nehruvian distaste for "communalism" or any hint of religious demands, Congress at both the national and state level succeeded in delegitimizing Akali demands by casting them as based on a Sikh, rather than Punjabi, identity. In their dismissal of Punjabi-centric demands as a Sikh Trojan horse, the center was calculatedly aided by Punjabi Hindus, who in the 1951 and 1961 censuses, declared their personal language to be Hindi, rather than Punjabi. However, with the deaths of Nehru and his successor Lal Bahadar Shastri, along with Sikh sacrifices in India's wars against Pakistan and China in the 1960s, the mood within Congress—led by Indira Gandhi—shifted. On November 1, 1966, the province was carved out, featuring 41 percent of the land and 55 percent of the population of the old one, but the absence of many Punjabi-speaking areas, such as Abohar-Fazilka, and the fact that Chandigarh, the state capital, was administratively a Union territory, to be shared with Haryana, rankled.[125]

Agriculture was a third structural factor. The Green Revolution disproportionately benefited richer Jat farmers at the expense of lower castes and landless laborers, polarizing society on socioeconomic lines.[126] More narrowly, the center allocated 75 percent of Punjab's water for nonriparian states despite Punjab providing, in 1980, 73 percent of the central government's food grain reserves and contributing handsomely to the country's rice, cotton, and sugarcane production. Canal irrigation did little to soften the blow,[127] and as a consequence, Sikhs demanded greater allocation of water from the Ravi-Beas, at the expense of states like Haryana and Rajasthan.[128]

Finally, as Delhi became the scene of "fawners and flatterers," Prime Minister Indira Gandhi centralized power to ward off threats from within and outside her party and declared Emergency, suspending constitutional provisions and rights. As a result of these actions by Indira, the Akalis, as one of the only groups to directly take on her authoritarianism, saw their leaders imprisoned.[129] These factors contributed to large-scale mobilization in the state, but it took some myopic and foolish decisions from Congress leaders for Punjab to reach its secessionist moment.

OPERATION BLUESTAR AND THE SIKH SECESSIONIST MOMENT

Upon winning control of the central government in 1980, Indira Gandhi dismissed a number of state governments controlled by the opposition, including Punjab, and sought fresh elections in each of them.[130] The Akalis, turned out of government, won a paltry 27 percent of the vote, which in turn allowed Indira to paint them as unpopular. Armed with the Anandpur Sahib resolution, which explicitly laid out their grievances on water,

Chandigarh, and territory, the Akalis turned to more agitational politics. They were, in essence, forced to do so. On the one side, they had to make their presence and demands felt to the center. On the other, they were being squeezed by Jarnail Singh Bhindranwale.

Bhindranwale was a relatively unknown figure until the late 1970s; his main claim to fame came from being elected the head of the Damdami Taksal, a religious educational institution, in 1977. His role was essentially that of a traveling evangelist, encouraging a more ascetic tradition among Sikh youth, proscribing clipping beards, smoking, alcohol, or drugs, and baptizing hundreds of men and women.[131] His rise to prominence—"from a village preacher to national figure"—was a result of violence between orthodox Sikhs and a breakaway sect known as Nirankaris in the late 1970s.[132] Bhindranwale recruited gangsters, criminals, and unemployed young men execute hits on regular Nirankaris at first, and then expanded their target list to include Nirankari sympathizers, dissident Akalis, Congress members, police officers, and Hindu journalists.[133]

Bhindranwale created an extreme flank of Sikh agitational politics, even if he did not enjoy widespread popularity or legitimacy.[134] Bhindranwale's behavior generated "a game of one-upmanship," compelling moderates to adopt extremist rhetoric, if not methods.[135] Interestingly, Bhindranwale's role as an extremist that would pressure the Akali Dal was envisioned and cynically deployed by Congress itself, mainly for electoral reasons. To attract Jat Sikh peasant voters and discredit the Akali Dal Party, Congress leaders—including those at the very top, such as Giani Zail Singh and Sanjay Gandhi—encouraged Bhindranwale's violence.[136] Such behavior is typical of mainstream Indian political parties, which often seek the "production" of communal violence in advance of elections, usually in the form of riots, so that voters may be polarized into secure voting blocs on religious lines.[137]

In the midst of Hindu-Sikh communal violence pushed by the likes of Bhindranwale, there was a series of negotiations between Indira and Akali leaders such as Sant Harchand Singh Longowal over the status of Chandigarh, water rights, territory, and a recognition of Sikh grievances more generally.[138] At times, a deal appeared imminent, but Indira would back off, generally acting on the political advice of her close confidantes who wanted her to appear tough minded. Meanwhile, communal and terrorist violence increased at a slow rate. Between 1981 and 1983, 101 civilians were killed, with 75 of those deaths occurring in 1983.[139] Particularly concerning was that Bhindranwale and his men started smuggling arms and hiding out in the Golden Temple, one of Sikhism's holiest sites. From there, they acted with de facto impunity.[140] Bhindranwale, in characteristic bluster, warned that "if the authorities enter this temple, we will teach them such a lesson that the throne of Indira will crumble. We will slice them into small pieces . . . *lohe ke chane chabayenge* (they'll be forced to chew iron lentils, i.e. bullets)."[141] Indira and Congress faced pressure to do something about the worsening law-and-order.

The result was Operation Bluestar. On June 2, 1984, the Indian government officially ordered the army to "check and control extremists and communal violence in the state of Punjab and the Union Territory of Chandigarh, provide security to the people and restore normalcy."[142] Punjab was sealed off from the rest of the country, and troops using tanks and heavy artillery surrounded the Golden Temple complex.[143] It took about four days for the entire area to be neutralized. At least hundreds of people, including Bhindranwale, died. The operation was deemed a bad idea across the political spectrum, with the typical comment referring to it as a "major mistake."[144] K. P. S. Gill, the man given credit for eventually eradicating violence in the state as director general of police in Punjab, and who generally espouses a fairly no-compromise attitude with regard to terrorists in his writings on the conflict, termed the operation "ill-planned, hasty, and knee-jerk . . . the damage Bluestar did was incalculable."[145] Lieutenant General J. S. Aurora, a decorated veteran of the military, said in an interview that "the government showed no sense, no sensibility in handling the crisis."[146]

Bluestar was the point at which Sikh dissatisfaction with the center became congealed, becoming widespread from a relatively tiny group of militants and extremists to a more general feeling in Sikh society.[147] That is, Bluestar's aftermath represented Sikh nationalism's secessionist moment. For Julio Ribeiro, a former senior police official, Bluestar was "the trigger for the Khalistan movement, it affected all ordinary Sikhs."[148] According to a journalist, "Bluestar was a watershed in the history of Sikhs, Punjab, and possibly India" because of the role it played in uniting Sikhs who were otherwise more divided into pro-Congress, pro-Akali, and pro-militant camps; "almost every Sikh felt alienated and hurt."[149] Khushwant Singh pointedly noted that "only a miniscule proportion of Sikhs subscribed to Khalistan before the temple was stormed." The *New York Times* reported that "before the raid on the Golden Temple, neither the Government nor anyone else appeared to put much credence in the Khalistan movement."[150] A measure of Sikh dissatisfaction was the desertion of four thousand soldiers in the aftermath of the twin operations.[151] Sharper still was the assassination of Prime Minister Indira Gandhi in October 1984 by two of her Sikh bodyguards. Anti-Sikh riots kicked off in all areas of the country but were especially acute in Delhi, where the Sikh community became the target of mob violence. In an echo of its pre-Bluestar activities, Congress officials connived with local authorities to fuel the riots.[152] More than two thousand Sikhs were killed and ten thousand left homeless in Delhi alone.[153]

Facing Punjab's secessionist moment was Rajiv Gandhi, who took over the prime minister's office the day his mother was assassinated before riding the backlash and ethnic mobilization conjured up by that event to win a sweeping election victory in the winter of 1984–85. His initial strategy of policing failed to quell the violence, partly due to Pakistan's increased meddling, which caused the Indian state to escalate to militarization in 1987.

POLICING IN PUNJAB: ACCORD WITH THE AKALI DAL (L)

Punjab was atop incoming Prime Minister Rajiv Gandhi's to-do list. Though he veered into a hawkish stance early in his tenure, saying in December that the Anandpur Sahib resolution was unacceptable and that separatists would be "crushed," Rajiv essentially adopted a conciliatory stance.[154] "My government will give top priority to the problem of Punjab," he said. "The Sikhs are as much a part of India as any other community."[155] He stressed that "we must go beyond the prevention and suppression of violence. We must cure the minds where hatred and prejudice arise."[156]

Rajiv adopted what Wallace calls "a process of political accommodation" by opening dialogue with Akali representatives and making "significant concessions in all major areas of concern."[157] In fact, Rajiv not only conceded essentially everything his mother had rejected between 1982 and 1984, but went further still.[158] The central government agreed to turn the city of Chandigarh over to Punjab. It appointed a commission to determine which Hindi-speaking areas would be transferred to Haryana, further cementing the status of Punjab as a Punjabi province. The dispute over the river waters was referred to a judicial tribunal. The Anandpur Sahib resolution, for so long the bane of the center, was referred to the Sarkaria Commission on Center-State Relations.[159] That was not all. Earlier in 1985, starting around March, the Rajiv government released senior Akali leaders from prison. An inquiry into the killings of Sikhs in Delhi was ordered and a ban on the AISSF was lifted. Economic assistance to the state was also promised.[160] Finally, the Rajiv government also planned to hold state elections in Punjab which, presumably, the Akalis would win, and thus would constitute a transfer of power.[161]

The accord was signed with hopeful language, with the signatories—Rajiv Gandhi and Longowal—declaring that "this settlement brings to an end a period of confrontation and ushers in an era of amity, goodwill and co-operation, which will promote and strengthen the unity of India."[162] Both Rajiv and Longowal earned considerable goodwill within and outside Punjab, and optimism was pervasive. The *Times of India*'s report on the accord began, "The Punjab problem has been solved."[163] The *Chandigarh Tribune* glowingly commented that "statesmanship, courage, a judicious blend of diplomatic finesse and administrative firmness and purposeful mediation" all contributed to Rajiv's agreement with Longowal, one that "represents the collective triumph of sanity and good sense over sectarian sentiments and mutual hatred."[164] A week after the accord the governor, Arjun Singh, claimed that "normalcy was returning to Punjab at a fast pace."[165]

With respect to my argument, India adopted a policing strategy, where state violence is restrained, and instead tactical concessions—especially to those nationalists deemed "moderate"—are employed to deal with the movement. Indeed, the distinction between the "moderate" Akali Dal (L) faction and those actors deemed more extreme, both in the AD (L) and broader Sikh movement more generally (e.g. AD [United], AISSF), was one Rajiv consistently played up. In public appearances, he credited Longowal for isolating terrorists, expressed gratitude for his reciprocation of his good faith, and emphasized that "the other group was the extremists and we will deal with them as such."[166]

As my theory would predict, these concessions could be made only within a context of depressed external vulnerability. Most explanations for Rajiv's accommodationist stance explicitly credit a domestic-political logic. For example, scholars such as Kohli and Brass cite the heavy electoral victory Rajiv and Congress won in 1984–85 as the primary cause of the concessions to the Akalis, since Rajiv could concede from a position of strength and be unconcerned with a backlash in the Hindi belt, having swept into power on the back of a massive and convincing electoral victory.[167] A biography of Rajiv Gandhi's also notes that the accord brought the prime minister a "great deal of kudos and the respect of friend and foe alike," reaffirming his early reputation as a problem-solver.[168]

It is true that allegations of Pakistani support to Sikh militants were common in 1984–85, but contemporary media reports suggest that rather than reflecting "true" perception, such accusations were propagandistic, deployed for political gain and discrediting adversaries. Indira Gandhi's warnings about "foreign forces" at work in Punjab after Bluestar were politely dismissed as carrying "the odour of election propaganda in them."[169] Similarly, a *New York Times* report soon after Bluestar summed up the prevailing wisdom on the authenticity of accusations of external involvement, which pointed to not just Pakistan but also the CIA. It wrote that "the Government has yet to provide proof of foreign complicity to overcome doubters among Indians and Western diplomats," noted that "in the past, attacks on Pakistan have been politically popular among the Hindi-speaking tier of northern India, which has become a crucial arena for elections expected to be called around December," and quoted both opposition politicians, such as the BJP's Atal Bihari Vajpayee, and anonymous diplomats, as dismissing the Pakistani connection.[170] The *Washington Post* reported that "the only indirect evidence of a Pakistani link that has surfaced so far has been the confiscation of weapons smuggled across the border into Amritsar with markings indicating they came from the arms pipeline that normally services Afghan guerillas operating on Pakistan's western border,"[171] while another Western paper informed its readers that "specialists say there is little evidence thus far that Pakistan is supplying armaments to extremist Sikhs in the Punjab."[172] Indian security officials claimed to the media, based on the testimony of one arrested truck driver, that Pakistan was training "15,000 Sikh youths" in "subversive activities,"[173] an outlandish figure. One item of proof ostensibly demonstrating Pakistani complicity was the discovery of two circumcised men at the Golden Temple.[174] A media report quoted an army officer admiring the cleverness of Pakistani support to Sikh militants, noting that they "have covered their tracks so well that it is difficult to pinpoint them,"[175] eliding the possibility that their tracks were nonexistent because they had not yet walked the soil. Indeed, the weapons that were coming from across the border into Punjab around the time of Bluestar were the product of smuggling networks rather than full-throated official support.[176] Given that the Pakistani angle appears to have been publicized more as a product of cynical electoral and political objectives rather than apparent wholehearted belief, it seems reasonable to code Indian perceptions of Pakistani support in 1985 as "limited."

For the Indian government, then, the combination of Rajiv's domestic incentives and muted external support allowed for a relatively restrained policy, where the center made significant concessions to "moderate" elements of the nationalist movement. Elections held soon after the accord featured a high turnout and were dominated by the Longowal wing of the Akalis, suggesting that mainstream Sikhs were satisfied with the accord.[177]

Unfortunately, the extremist fringe of the Sikh movement did not accept the deal. An ominous sign was a police subinspector's killing in Amritsar the day after the accord.[178] The "United" Akali Dal assailed the pact as a "sellout" and claimed that the leaders of the Akali Dal (Longowal) did not represent Sikhs.[179] Less than a week after the accord, there were gunfights between Akali Dal factions at the Golden Temple, where AISSF cadres were distributing pamphlets describing Longowal and other Akali Dal (L) leaders as traitors to the Panth.[180] AISSF cadres disrupted Akali Dal meetings with anti-Longowal and anti-accord slogans.[181] Meanwhile, Longowal pleaded with less moderate party allies to not air their differences with him and the accord in public.[182] Eventually, those party allies would come around, but tragically only on the day Longowal was shot dead.[183] Longowal's assassination took place less than a month after the accord; it was "hard to imagine a more lethal blow to the cause of peace and harmony in Punjab."[184] A drumbeat of murder and violence ensued. The accord became controversial, with Hindu hard-liners, such as the BJP's L. K. Advani, criticizing it for hurting the interests of Haryana and Rajasthan, and its implementation, or lack thereof, becoming a cause of recrimination between the state government and the center.[185]

Following its election victory in September, the AD (L)-led state government proved unable or unwilling to arrest the violence.[186] The Akali Dal's administrative control of the state was always tenuous, caught as they were between religious militants accusing them of being stooges and a center impatient with their inefficacy in quelling violence.[187] There were several illustrations of this predicament, one not dissimilar from what the AGP faced in Assam. In February 1986 for instance, Chief Minister S. S. Barnala claimed that it was up to the executive committees of the Akali Dal and the SGPC (a religious institution) to decide on how best to clear the Golden Temple of militants, rather than the elected state government which he headed.[188] Twice in the next year, Barnala was hauled up by the Akal Takht (Sikh religious authority) on account of his religious misconduct,[189] blurring the lines of authority in the state. Militants were widely perceived to have considerable sympathy and outright support of many within the police and the Akali Dal (L) Party itself, compromising Barnala's ability to mobilize political support to take Sikh terrorism head on.[190] As such, the center's next major step was to institute president's rule in May 1987.

ESCALATION TO MILITARIZATION

President's rule had been on the cards months earlier. In December 1986, the *Times of India* editorialized that, given the law and order situation, "the case for President's rule in Punjab has become pretty strong."[191] The Hindu right was regular in its demands that it be imposed, warning of "unprecedented bloodshed" absent "drastic steps."[192] By May, disappointed in the state government's efforts in bringing order, the center was ready to pull the trigger. It dismissed Barnala and the Akali government, marking the coda to the Punjab accord's political arrangement.[193] Alongside president's rule, the center instituted the draconian Terrorist and Disruptive Activities (Prevention) Act.[194] Rajiv promised that under the new regime there would be "no compromise with terrorism" and "no leniency" would be shown until "this terrorism ends and this issue is solved."[195] His firmness was supported by brokers in Delhi.[196] Almost immediately after the imposition of president's rule, security forces launched a major offensive against militant hideouts in Tarn Taran.[197] In response, the militants too stepped up their attacks, marked by an especially horrific attack on dozens of Hindu commuters riding a bus in July.[198]

These measures represented an escalation from policing to militarization, the Indian state's admission that it was fighting a war. As Julio Ribeiro said at the time, "We are in the thick of a battle."[199] For him, the Indian state had to react to the militants' increasing violence.[200] Similarly, K. P. S. Gill wrote that by 1987, "the conflict had certainly escalated to the level of warfare."[201] Under his much-discussed leadership, the Punjab police instituted a harsher, tougher strategy, a "ruthless but effective police campaign," marked by operations such as Black Thunder in May 1988 (aimed at clearing the Golden Temple), massive search and cordon operations, and Operation Rakshak in November 1991, which called for a "catch and kill" policy for alleged militants.[202] The so-called Gill doctrine, "grounded in hard-headed

Clausewitzian principles," emphasized "kinetic counter-terrorist measures," or in plain English, aggressive force.[203] As one analysis states, Gill "did not waste time trying to engage them in theological debates. Instead he appealed directly to their natural instinct for survival. Gill offered the terrorists a stark choice: they could either die for their idea of God, or live for themselves. There was no third option."[204] The early 1990s, especially, saw Gill and the Punjab police given *"carte blanche* power to confront militancy without interference from legislators or state administration" following the election of Prime Minister Rao.[205] Predictably, human rights violations piled up: Indian security forces, "and the Punjab police in particular, summarily executed civilians and suspected militants in custody, engaged in widespread disappearances and brutally tortured detainees" during the conflict's worst years. Gill dismissed concerns about such methods, noting that "if an officer has done something wrong, it is between him and his maker."[206]

There were two main trends that were responsible for rising militancy in the state, and in turn Indian escalation to militarization: increasing Pakistani support, and the Sikh insurgents' lack of unity. When Sikh militants first crossed into Pakistan after Blue Star, they were disappointed at their cool reception: "The Pakistani state initially denied them military aid and imprisoned them so as to control their movements better. It was not until the Sikh insurgency truly began to organize in 1986 that the Pakistani secret services considered supporting the insurrection in earnest."[207] Pakistan's initial hesitation sprung from the militants' lack of discipline and the fact that Punjab "was not Kashmir" and simply not as important. As such, hundreds of Sikh militants were held in a Faisalabad jail, while some potential leaders were given villas in Lahore. Indeed, not only did Pakistan not support these militants initially, but it did not even allow them to go back to India, leading to a failed prison-escape in Faisalabad. "It was not until the first Sikh political-military structures were formed in 1986 that ISI really began to back these insurgents' war effort," achieving real momentum only after 1988.[208]

Similarly, a journalist with close ties to the Indian security establishment argues that Pakistani "support seems to have been generally low-grade prior to 1984," and it took until the early 1990s for Pakistan to "become a significant player."[209] Elsewhere he notes that while "we do not know precisely when and how Pakistan arrived at the decision to back terrorists" in Punjab, it is only in 1987 when the Kalashnikov rifle and "hundreds of terrorists" crossed the Indo-Pak border.[210] One former security official corroborated that Pakistan's supply of the dreaded Kalashnikov rifle did not reach appreciable levels until 1988.[211] It was in response to the 1989 Brassstacks crisis that Pakistan further opened the "terror tap" when "small arms flows, in particular, increased dramatically."[212] This support included the supply of assault rifles, including the AK-47 and AK-56, RPG-7 rockets,

Chinese-origin machine guns, night vision equipment, communications equipment, training, and leadership of Khalistani groups by Pakistani intelligence personnel, thus qualifying Pakistani support in 1987 as "moderate" by my framework.[213]

The importance of Pakistani support in the late 1980s for Indian counterinsurgency can be gleaned from a variety of sources. K. P. S. Gill told me that "the impact of [Pakistan-supplied] AK-47s was very grave," that absent Pakistani backing, the insurgency would have ended "much earlier" and been "treated on par with aggravated dacoities, on par with criminal issues" rather than the war that it was fought as.[214] As he wrote, the militants' collective ability to kill was "directly connected with the gun-power available" to them through Pakistan.[215] Another former security official told me that Pakistani support, including "finances, weapons, training, explosives" gave the Sikh militant movement greater "lethality and punch," and was like "oxygen" for the Sikh militants. "We tried to choke that supply of oxygen."[216] Specifically, he discussed a two-pronged strategy, whereby K. P. S. Gill went "hammer and tong" in the heartland, while on the border the erection of a fence beginning in 1988 drastically cut "hardcore terrorist numbers." Pakistani external support meant that even relatively low numbers of militants—Julio Ribeiro claimed there were between three hundred and five hundred terrorists operating in 1986—could paralyze India's most prosperous state because the large number of arms and ammunition that flooded Punjab were far superior to what the Indian police then possessed.[217]

Alongside this increasing Pakistani support, the splintering of the Sikh movement—"there was no common leadership, no common manifesto"— meant that there were innumerable militant groups, whose violence took on as much a criminal as ideological color.[218] Each area would see a different, local organization come up, with no central command coordinating between the many leaders and groups.[219] One estimate was that there were 162 militant groups active at some point during the insurgency.[220] Recent scholarship on civil conflict has emphasized how fractionalization of national movements generates higher levels of violence; fragmentation results in actors using violence to outflank rivals within the movement, and it precludes attempts by movement leaders to end hostilities when peace agreements are signed.[221] Both processes, outbidding as well as spoiling, were in evidence in Punjab after the accord.

These two trends—splits from within, and support from without—took on greater potency in the wider context of Sikh martial capabilities. Both the colonial British state, as well as the Indian Republic (less explicitly), subscribed to a belief in a theory of "martial races," whereby some ethnicities are considered better fighters than others. Punjabis—and especially Punjabi Sikhs—have long been overrepresented in the Indian armed forces (at partition, Punjabis were 6.5 percent of the population and 54 percent of the army).[222] This belief has become a self-fulfilling prophecy because it helped endow Sikhs with greater-than-average levels of military training and combat experience. These longstanding policies caught up to, and deeply compromised, the Indian state in the 1980s, since it afforded militant organizations a steady stream of possible recruits who could provide organizational, tactical, and weapons skills. Indeed, the heaviest violence in Punjab took place in precisely those districts where the army is most heavily recruited (Amritsar, Gurdaspur, and Tarn Taran).[223] As one journalist told me, militants in Punjab were "very tough" and "would not bend in interrogation," and that gun battles were "very long" between security forces and militants.[224] The fighting in Punjab often took place "between Jat Sikh and Jat Sikh" often drawn from the same village, one fighting for the police and one for the militants.[225]

India's escalation from policing in 1985 to militarization in 1987 can be clearly seen in the annual death tolls from the conflict. In the years preceding the accord, "terrorist" fatalities were relatively low: 14 in 1981, followed by 7, 13, 77 (a gross underestimate), and 2 in 1985. These low numbers were consistent with a strategy of policing. In 1986, there was a rise to 78, before a massive increase to 328 in 1987, then 373, 703, 1,320, 2,177, 2,113, and 798 in 1993.[226] Put differently, when Pakistani support for the militants was essentially nonexistent, between 1981 and 1985, the average number of annual deaths (including civilians, militants, and law enforcement) in the conflict was 138. The corresponding figure for the period between 1986 and 1992, when Pakistan support was more robust, was 2,841.[227] Though correlation does not imply causation, the difference in casualty rates in the two eras is massive, and testimony from analysts, journalists, and former security officials all point to the centrality of Pakistani support in generating a stiff insurgency.

Generally, the Punjab case observes the theoretical predictions of this book. When the Punjabi movement was viewed through a domestic lens—that is, when external support for the separatists was relatively low—the state's response was policing. Despite the best intentions of the Rajiv-Longowal accord, the extensive raw material for, and splits within, Sikh militancy, alongside Pakistan's increasingly active role in the late 1980s in Punjab, led Indian strategy to become more heavy handed over time.

Kashmir, 1989–94

The third crisis under study in this chapter is the one that took place in Kashmir, beginning in the winter of 1989–90. This crisis was set off by a fraudulent election in 1987, which pushed Kashmiri nationalists to launch a secessionist struggle. Unlike the Assam and Punjab cases, however, the center employed collective repression at the outset of the crisis. The principal driver of the overwhelmingly violent response by the state was that Kashmir was center stage for the Indo-Pak rivalry. In particular, Pakistan had twice before tried to take over Kashmir in the decades prior to the secessionist struggle and was widely perceived to be behind the rebellion in the early 1990s, especially by Indian security forces on the ground. For the Indian state, Kashmir's separatist movement posed a greater external threat, and as a consequence, it acted as the theory proffered in this book would predict—with heavy-handed repression, with both emotional and materialist effects of "high" third-party support operative.

A BUFFER STATE SINCE BIRTH

Contestation over Kashmir and its future began during the drive for, and in the immediate aftermath of, independence from the British. Under the terms of the British withdrawal, Muslim-majority provinces such as those in Northwest India and the northeastern province of Bengal were to become part of Pakistan; the rest would become the independent nation state of India. The grey area in between was occupied by the so-called princely states, which were governed by monarchs nominally independent of the British crown but who still paid allegiance to it. The leaders of these princely states were given three choices: join India, join Pakistan, or become independent.

The unique factor about Kashmir was that it was a Muslim-majority province with a Hindu leader, Maharaja Hari Singh. From a strictly demographic perspective, it probably should have acceded to Pakistan, but Hari Singh opted for independence, not wishing to subject himself to larger powers. As a result, a tribal rebellion broke out in Kashmir in July 1947. Sensing an opportunity, Pakistan sent bands of its own forces to support the rebellion later that year,[228] leading to Hari Singh asking for Indian help to quell the disturbances. India promised aid only on the condition that he formally accede, a condition he agreed to. India's forces faced off against Pakistan's, in what became the first war over Kashmir. The war ended in an essential stalemate, and the ceasefire line drawn by international mediators in the fall of 1948 left Pakistan with about one-third of Kashmir and India the rest.[229]

Over the next few decades, the Indian center's interventionist practices caused Kashmiri disaffection.[230] For instance, state elections in the rest of India began in 1952, but Kashmir had to wait until 1962 for legislative assembly elections and 1967 for national assembly elections to be held. Moreover, the elections that were held were typified by irregularities, rigging, and fraud, aimed at ensuring that the center's chosen affiliates maintained power.[231] It took until 1963 for the formal offices of the governor and the chief minister to be introduced, and for the Indian Election Commission and Supreme Court to exercise jurisdiction in Kashmir.[232] Additionally, India failed to hold a plebiscite Prime Minister Nehru had promised

Kashmir in November, 1947.[233] By the mid-1970s, Shaikh Abdullah, the most popular leader in the province, had ceased his demand for a plebiscite, having been in jail for close to two decades, and signed an accord with Indira Gandhi.[234] Ominously, these developments were not taken in stride by Kashmiris, who began to question whether personalities such as Shaikh Abdullah truly spoke for them. Shaikh Abdullah's administration was highly corrupt and authoritarian, all the while doing little for the socioeconomic development of the state, which was marked by increasing unemployment among educated youth.[235]

The 1983 elections represented a crucial turning point. Shaikh Abdullah had passed away, replaced as party head by his son, Farooq Abdullah, who was not blessed with his father's charisma and political acumen.[236] Though there were some irregularities and violence during the election, most broadly accepted the National Conference's comfortable victory—resting mainly on Muslim support in the valley—with one important exception: Indira Gandhi.[237] When in May 1983, Farooq Abdullah joined a national alliance of anti-Congress parties, the die was cast. Up to this point, Kashmiri politicians, even relatively nationalist ones, concerned themselves mainly with developments within the state. The approach onto the national stage was uncharted territory, and it was one that was not appreciated by the prime minister.[238] She dismissed the Abdullah government, with incoming governor Jagmohan informing Abdullah that he had "lost confidence" of the state assembly. In his place, Congress installed a puppet regime led by Abdullah's personal rival, and brother-in-law, G. M. Shah.[239] However, G. M. Shah himself soon outgrew his usefulness and was dismissed. Farooq Abdullah, desperate to return to power, reached an agreement with the center to contest the forthcoming elections in an alliance with Congress.[240]

Predictably, Kashmiris did not react amiably to this alliance, which they perceived as a sellout to the center, similar to Farooq's father's act in the mid-1970s. A conglomerate of parties under the banner of the Muslim United Front (MUF), led by the Jamaat-e-Islami, called a strike after the alliance was announced, and on March 23, 1987, hundreds of activists were arrested.[241] The MUF would be the primary opposition party contesting the now-infamous 1987 elections, widely deemed to be rigged and fraudulent.[242] More generally, Kashmiris began to shed their previously docile acquiescence to the maneuvering by the center and the National Conference Party, their mobilization driven by a more literate citizenry and greater access to media. Kashmiris could no longer be bought off with the ease with which they once were.[243]

1987 ELECTIONS

The Congress–National Conference alliance swept to an overwhelming victory in 1987, in an election widely acknowledged to be rigged. An anonymous source in the Indian Intelligence Bureau told one scholar that thirteen seats were stolen. Two weeks before the election, six hundred opposition party workers were arrested in stronghold areas. Despite the pervasive allegations of fraud, watchdog institutions such as the Election Commission and the High Court of Jammu and Kashmir were silent.[244] The importance of the 1987 election rigging can be inferred from the fact that the leaders of the Kashmir insurgency, when it finally came in early 1990, were all polling agents for the MUF in the 1987 elections. These included Shabir Shah, Yasin Malik, and Javed Mir.[245] Abdul Ghani Lone summed the 1987 rigging this way: "It was this that motivated the young generation to say 'to hell with the democratic process and all that this is about' and they said 'let's go for the armed struggle.' It was the flash point."[246]

Under pressure from the opposition and with increasing agitation in the state by 1989, Farooq Abdullah began to lose control. The unrest was fueled by global developments, such as those in Eastern Europe, where the Soviet empire was collapsing and giving rise to free and independent states.[247] Becoming increasingly assertive, the main insurgent organization in the state—the Jammu and Kashmir Liberation Front (JKLF)—kidnapped the daughter of the Indian home minister in December 1989 and successfully used her as a bargaining chip for the release of five members of their group.[248] The following month, Farooq Abdullah's government was dismissed and Kashmir was brought under direct rule by New Delhi.

This was Kashmir's secessionist moment. Kashmiris were expectant of a new era; "they thought it was the beginning of what they've been asking for."[249] The Indian state would follow with a highly repressive response, beginning with the installation of the hard-line Jagmohan as governor and the banning of foreign journalists from the valley.[250]

COLLECTIVE REPRESSION IN KASHMIR

The extent of the repressive response to separatism in Kashmir can, at a first glance, be discerned from the language deployed to describe Indian behavior from 1990 to 1994. Scholars and journalists have variously described Indian actions as "stringent repressive measures," "undirected repression," "nonsurgical," "unleash[ing] its iron fist," "ferocious," "tenacious," "often unruly," and "bare-knuckled."[251] State officials directly involved in the violence have also guardedly betrayed the high levels of state violence in the early 1990s: secessionists "required a credible display of the might of the State to put things in proper perspective," and it was crucial to "give sharp teeth to the machinery against terrorists."[252]

What, precisely, are these descriptions of? First, there was a high level of military and paramilitary participation in the state. By January 1990, just as the Kashmir issue was becoming a national concern, there were already over 80,000 troops in the state, and the Kashmir "valley had been virtually handed over to paramilitary forces."[253] By the middle of 1993, these figures had increased to an estimated 175,000 soldiers and 30,000 paramilitary personnel in the province.[254] By the mid-1990s, the number had increased further still, to 400,000, a number which represents more troops than all but sixteen countries' entire active-duty personnel in 1995.[255] These forces were overwhelmingly non-Kashmiri and non-Muslim,[256] meaning that not only did the Indian government blanket the state with security forces from an early juncture, but also that these soldiers were generally deemed to be outsiders.

Second, Indian forces were afforded a great deal of latitude, and absolved of any accountability, when it came to the security operations.[257] "The Armed Forces (Jammu and Kashmir) Special Ordinance, introduced in July 1990, provided the security forces with extraordinary powers to shoot and kill, and search and arrest without a warrant, all under immunity from prosecution 'in respect of anything done or purported to be done in exercise of power conferred by this Act.'"[258] It also introduced the Disturbed Areas Act to supplement existing emergency laws in the state, as well as the Terrorism and Disruptive Activities (Prevention) Act. However, as Bose notes, "most Indian counterinsurgency operations in the Valley made no reference to *any* framework of law."[259]

Alongside the liberal use of curfews, often accompanied by shoot-on-sight orders, crackdowns were the main ingredient in the stew of Indian counterinsurgency.[260] Crackdowns involved large groups of heavily armed security forces arriving in jeeps and trucks and cordoning off a village or neighborhood. All men would then be asked to step outside their homes and congregate in an open space, where local informers—often tortured into flipping to the government's side—would identify militants and those who helped and harbored them. Meanwhile, soldiers would carry out house-to-house searches for weapons and explosives; allegations of theft, vandalism, and sexual assault of women and girls were commonplace during these searches. These crackdowns "would last a whole day or longer, even in harsh winter conditions."[261] Those that were identified as militants or supporters of militants would be driven to "interrogation centers" which grew rapidly in Srinagar and the Valley in general. "Torture, often in gruesome forms, became routine and widespread . . . numerous people returned from interrogation either physically crippled or mentally disturbed, or both; others never returned at all." Journalists and rights organizations estimate that a few thousand persons disappeared after being taken into custody throughout the duration of the conflict.[262]

More serious was the series of massacres of unarmed civilians in Kashmir, especially during the early months of the crisis. In January 1990, a large group of unarmed civilians gathered at Gawakdal Bridge to protest searches conducted at Chota Bazar and Guru Bazar that morning. The protestors were shot at with live ammunition from either side of the bridge, and more than a hundred died in what is considered one of the worst massacres in

Kashmiri history.[263] In fact, in just three days in late January, Indian security forces killed more than three hundred unarmed protestors.[264] In March 1990, similar demonstrations were shot at by police forces, and more than forty people died.[265] When Maulvi Mirwaiz Farooq, chief preacher at Jama Masjid in Srinagar, was assassinated in May 1990, his funeral procession passed through Islamia College, where the Sixty-Ninth Battalion of the CPRF was stationed. The security forces fired at the crowd and killed between sixty and one hundred people. Mirwaiz's coffin was also struck with bullets. As a close aide of Governor Jagmohan said, "They just went berserk and emptied all the bullets they had."[266]

Neutral observers assiduously recorded Indian repression, including summary executions, reprisal killings, torture, rape, the destruction and looting of civilian property, arson of residential neighborhoods, and lethal force against protestors.[267] They described Indian behavior in places such as Handwara, where the BSF burned down three dozen houses and two hundred shops and fired into a crowded market in October 1990; or in Phazipora in August 1990, when Indian army soldiers killed twenty-five civilians in a village in retaliation for a militant attack two kilometers away; or in Pattan, also in August, where soldiers fired from their convoy into a crowded market, despite no provocation.[268] International media also high-lighted the importance of collective punishment for Indian counterinsur-gency, noting its reliance after July 1990 on arson—witnesses described seeing "men in khaki sprinkle gunpowder, light it, then keep firefighters away at gunpoint"—and gang rape as a response to militant attacks.[269]

It is important to reiterate that these policies were carried out at the beginning of the crisis, representing the state's primary response to Kash-miri nationalists. Furthermore, notwithstanding Governor Jagmohan's hard-line reputation, this response was "supported by virtually the entire spectrum of Indian political opinion."[270] According to a news report, "'Action first, political initiative later.' This is the line of thinking that is emerging among various political groups in the State," while another relayed Rajya Sabha parliamentarians' demands for a "ruthless crackdown on the militants."[271] Even when Jagmohan resigned in the spring of 1990, there was no letup, with Saxena, his replacement, clarifying that "there is no change of policy" and that he would be "very firm" in Kashmir.[272] The Indian response of collective repression, which targeted both insurgent groups as well as civilians, took a heavy toll, with estimates of tens of thou-sands dead in the first few years of the conflict.

INDIAN STRATEGY IN KASHMIR: THE PAKISTAN CONNECTION

As soon as the crisis hit the Valley, the Indian state blamed Pakistan for its "direct incitement to subversion, violence and terrorism" in Kashmir.[273]

Indeed, it would be difficult to make sense of the Indian response in Kashmir without accounting for how the region figured into the interstate tension between India and Pakistan.

Kashmir was valued highly by both India and Pakistan at independence, with neither state prepared to relinquish its claim.[274] For India, the state mattered a great deal for its self-perception as a secular republic, as opposed to its bitter rival, Pakistan, which is often thought of as the product of communal and religious agitation. As the only Muslim-majority state in India, Kashmir is often regarded as the emblem of India's secularism. In a 1951 address, Nehru summed up this feeling when he said that "Kashmir has become the living symbol of that non-communal and secular state which will have no truck with the two-nation theory on which Pakistan has based itself." On another occasion, he commented that "Kashmir is symbolic as it illustrates that we are a secular state; Kashmir with a . . . large majority of Muslims nevertheless of its own free will wished to be associated with India." Pakistan too felt the acquisition and control of Kashmir was a sine qua non of its existence as a state because the idea of Pakistan as a home for South Asian Muslims simply did not make sense without holding all Muslim-majority states in the Indian subcontinent. As M. A. Gurmani, Pakistani minister for Kashmir affairs noted in 1951, "We are fighting for Kashmir on the same principle as that on which we fought for Pakistan."[275]

Pakistan's first salvo for Kashmir took place in the winter of 1947–48, when it supported a tribal rebellion in an effort to win control of the state. Less than two decades later, it tried, and failed, again, launching Operation Gibraltar, which called for Pakistani troops bearing the sharp teeth of a domestic uprising and seizing the entirety of Kashmir.[276] These wars rendered Jammu and Kashmir the most sensitive border state in India and made Congress and other mainstream parties in India regard any opposition emanating from Kashmir as inherently suspicious.[277] This suspicion was exacerbated by citizens of Indian Kashmir playing up Pakistan relations; for instance, it was common to see the Pakistan flag hoisted on 14 August (Pakistan Independence Day) and a black flag on 15 August (Indian Independence Day), and locals tended to back Pakistan in hockey or cricket matches against India.[278]

Pakistan did not cause Kashmir's secessionist moment, but certainly took advantage of it, as it became "deeply involved in the uprising and provided training, arms, and sanctuary," along with fighters themselves. As one analyst put it, the "situation in Srinagar appeared like a dream come true" for India's neighbor.[279] Initially surprised by the scale of Kashmiri unrest and dissatisfaction, Pakistan moved quickly. What was different about its intervention in 1990 from what came earlier was that this time, Pakistan waited for Kashmiris to act first. As one local journalist put it, "the insurgency in Kashmir was imported, not exported."[280] What aided Pakistan was a decade of practice in the anti-Soviet conflict in Afghanistan—the so-called

Afghan model—which entailed training, arming, and funneling money to antistate guerrillas from across the border. The Pakistan Army and its Inter-Services Intelligence (ISI) set up training camps and used much of the same personnel it had used in Afghanistan, who, conveniently, were available for action given the Soviet withdrawal from Afghanistan in the late 1980s.[281] Joshi provides details on Pakistani training:

> When insurgency began, training tended to be elementary, spanning just about a week to ten days and involved learning the use of AK-47 rifles, pistols, throwing grenades and laying explosives. Trainees were shown how to take apart a rifle or a pistol, clean it and put it together again. Later, the course was increased to two and a half weeks and the syllabus was upgraded to include the use of RPG-7, light machine-guns as well as techniques of concealment, camouflage, reconnaissance and intelligence gathering.[282]

Pakistan did not uniformly back every insurgent group operating in Kashmir. While at the outset, Pakistan supported groups demanding independence, such as JKLF, as well as those demanding accession to Pakistan, such as Hizb-ul-Mujahideen (HM), it quickly grew to favor the latter. Eventually, by cutting off financial and logistical support for JKLF and overwhelmingly siding with its insurgent rivals, Pakistan ironically aided India in decimating the most viable organization for winning independence.[283] This unevenness in support emanated from the ISI and Pakistan military's natural partiality to those groups that shared their goals—unity with Pakistan, rather than independence, which would conceivably cut into Pakistani-controlled Gilgit-Baltistan. Moreover, the JKLF was more of a secular, nationalist organization, while HM and its allies were more Islamist in nature, fitting better with the ISI worldview and ideology.[284]

Relative to Punjab and other secessionist "hot-spots," the Kashmiri nationalist movement saw more Pakistani support. One Kashmiri journalist told me that "Kashmir is an altogether different ballgame," compared to other separatist conflict in India, and another stated simply: "No country backed Punjab like Pakistan backed Kashmir."[285] One defense analyst informed me that there was a "huge difference" in scale between the Khalistan and Kashmiri insurgencies, marked especially by the large numbers of young men going across the Line of Control in January 1990 and the equally large number of weapons coming back. Additionally, the Kashmiri insurgency was almost entirely funded by the ISI while the Punjab insurgency was largely financed autochthonously.[286] A newspaper analysis in May 1990 commented that the Kashmir insurgency was "totally different" from others India had faced because there had never before "been such a massive involvement of a neighboring country."[287]

All this is to say that Pakistan exercised a great deal of control over the direction and strength of the insurgency in Kashmir. However, even before reliable intelligence had been collected, Indian officials were convinced that Pakistan was behind the insurgency. The first indication that India interpreted Kashmir as an external conflict was that it moved thousands of troops from its border with China to Kashmir and the Pakistani border.[288] Less than two months after Rubaya Sayeed's kidnapping, intelligence sources claimed that there were five hundred Pakistan-trained militants in the valley, supplied with "sophisticated arms and explosives."[289] Jagmohan repeatedly mentions the importance of Pakistan in his memoirs. He writes that when he assumed his role, he faced "an intensified onslaught of the terrorist campaign which Pakistan intended to fan vigorously," that "powerful forces, both internal and external, were operating, at various levels, to frustrate whatever I was doing, or intended to do," and that of the forty-four distinct militant organizations operating in Kashmir, "almost all" of them came from across the Line of Control; "it came to be known that there were at least 39 training centers in Pakistan-occupied Kashmir and Pakistan."[290] According to him, "Pakistan provided not only moral, political and propaganda support to the subversionists in the Valley, as it itself admitted, but also actively helped them in training in guerilla warfare and techniques of contemporary terrorism . . . sophisticated weapons and finances were made available."[291]

Other state officials were on a similar page. Sudhir Bloeria, who served in various roles in the Kashmir bureaucracy, wrote that when he arrived in the area in April 1990, he had to "launch an immediate and vigorous exercise to . . . assess the impact of the sustained and strenuous efforts of the Pakistani ISI and its cohorts."[292] He discovered that "an unspecified number of sympathizers and motivators had been activated by the ISI operators along the border and in the interiors."[293] The "fire and smoke" in Kashmir, he claimed, was caused by the "machinations of Pakistan and its notorious ISI," and there "were unmistakable signs as well as confirmed intelligence reports that ISI was making strenuous efforts to foment trouble" in Kashmir.[294]

In October 1990, Governor Girish Chandra Saxena summarized the status quo by noting that "the number of militants is very large. Weapons available to them are also sizable. And the situation on the ground is not frozen. Pakistan is trying to push more and more people."[295] A similar snapshot of the Indian security establishment's bleak view during the first months of the insurgency is captured by A. S. Dulat, a former senior intelligence official, in his recent memoirs:

Things were going badly in the Valley: Kashmiris began to sniff azaadi, for they were taken in by the ISI's bluff that if they started something big enough, the Pakistan army would come and liberate them from India, much in the way India had helped Bangladesh's liberation from Pakistan. Insurgency in Kashmir was masterminded by Gen. Zia-ul-Haq and his henchmen

as revenge for Bangladesh. Kashmiris were crossing the border in droves . . .
we were in a mess. The Pakistanis were enjoying watching Kashmir burn.[296]

The Indian state, then, believed Pakistan was behind developments in
Kashmir;[297] third-party support was perceived as "high." As my theory
would predict, there were two aspects of this support that led to a more
vicious Indian reaction. First, violence from security forces on the ground
was more indiscriminate because of their seeing the entire local population
as disloyal and traitorous, in bed with an enemy state. Second, Pakistani
support led to a more challenging fight, since it meant a stronger Kashmiri
nationalist movement alongside the potential for a Pakistani invasion. This
tougher fight generated a more vicious counterinsurgency.

According to Bose, "In the eyes of the several hundred thousand soldiers and paramilitary troops flooding the Valley, the whole population
was suspect—not just disloyal to India, but, much worse, in league with
the enemy state across the LOC [Line of Control] . . . for the average Indian
soldier fighting insurrection in the Valley, 'the face of the Kashmiri has dissolved into a blurred, featureless mask. He has become a secessionist-
terrorist-fundamentalist traitor.'"[298] Representatives of the Indian state
themselves make the case for violence being intensified due to suspicions
of divided loyalties amongst the local population. As Bloeria wrote,
"Those who had been swayed by the propaganda and sustained efforts of
the ISI and had embarked on the path of militancy, anti-national activities
and challenging the integrity of the country, required a credible display of
the might of the State to put things in proper perspective . . . the aim was
to send a clear message to the militants and their supporters that they
would not be in a position to carry out their nefarious activities unchal-
lenged and the retribution would be swift and severe."[299] Saxena, who
succeeded Governor Jagmohan as the lead administrator in Kashmir,
noted that "because of a proxy war being conducted from across the
border and sponsoring of terrorist violence on a large scale, it was at times
difficult to ensure targeted responses by the security forces. There were
occasions when there was overreaction or even wrongdoing."[300] The distinction between ordinary Kashmiris and Pakistanis had all but vanished
for those in charge.[301] BSF personnel argued that, given the presence of
Pakistani agents in Kashmir, "judicious suspicion" was an "essential" part
of their duty.[302]

Yasin Malik, one of the top commanders of JKLF, alleged that when held
in captivity, "They called me a Pakistani bastard. I told them I want my
rights, even my vote was stolen."[303] This treatment was not restricted
merely to those who took up arms. A moderate Kashmiri politician said
that "we are branded Pakistanis. We have always been objects of suspicion.
Even if we pick up the Indian flag, and start shouting *Jai Bharat ma*, the suspicion will remain. They do not trust us. Our elders fought against the

Pakistanis in 1947, we fought against them in 1965 and 1971, but I do not know why we are still not trusted."[304] When a labor leader was tortured and attempted to tell soldiers about his Indian friends, they replied that "Humme sab kuch pata hai. Tum sab Pakistani ho" (We know everything. You are all Pakistanis).[305] A four-member fact-finding team visited the state in March 1990 and concluded that security officials "suffer from the paranoiac feeling that the entire population of the valley are pro-Pakistani 'terrorists.' Dictated by such suspicions, operations to maintain law and order have invariably led" to Indian counterinsurgency "wreaking vengeance on the innocent masses of the valley."[306]

Veteran Kashmiri journalists pointed out how due to their perceived pro-Pakistani leanings, Kashmiris were seen as an "enemy" by security forces; "for India, every Kashmiri is a Pakistani agent, or at least anti-India. Their loyalty is in doubt."[307] Younger Kashmiri journalists, explaining the intensity of Indian counterinsurgency in Kashmir, agreed that it was an emotional reaction, rooted in "the baggage of partition" and the fact that Kashmir is an overwhelmingly Muslim state.[308] Journalists and analysts based in Delhi backed these assessments, arguing that there was "no question" that Pakistani support led to a tougher, more emotional, and more vicious Indian response, as it hardened Indian resolve.[309] Another suggested that the Indian state had a "panicked" reaction to the insurgency because Kashmir was an issue "attached to Pakistan," with its Muslim-majority population.[310]

One aspect of the Kashmiri-Pakistani threat conflation that bears mentioning, commented on by several interviewees, was the rise of right-wing Hindu nationalism in India during this period. One former security official who served in Kashmir emphasized this angle at length. According to him, what explained the Indian reaction in Kashmir was the national context within which it took place, including the rise of Hindu fundamentalism and religious polarization in mainstream politics, with the rise of the BJP, the Ayodha mosque incident, and communal riots in Bombay.[311] As a result, violence in Kashmir from both insurgents and the state became colored with a religious tinge, especially since a substantial proportion of Kashmiris were demanding or fighting for accession to Muslim Pakistan. Notably, during the midst of the crisis, the Hindu right, led by the BJP, insisted on tough measures against the Kashmiri movement—in part as a signal to Pakistan. The BJP claimed that only the "strongest possible measures" including a "bullet for bullet approach" could salvage India's unity and integrity, arguing against any "political moves" given that the "the first priority should be to check and curb Pakistan's interference in the affairs of Jammu and Kashmir."[312]

Other sources shed light on the second important implication of Pakistani support: that it resulted in a more challenging fight for the Indian state. Similar to Indian support for Bengali separatists, Pakistani support for the Kashmiri national movement set up a two-front problem for the Indian state, whereby it had to practice counterinsurgency internally while guarding an international (de facto) border from which it regularly received fire.[313] This meant that the security forces were as concerned with infiltration of insurgents into Kashmir as it was with their activities once crossed.[314]

At the outset of the crisis, it was deemed that the Indian state's solidarity was under threat from a "Pakistan-backed insurgency [that] has assumed alarming proportions."[315] As far as Indian decision makers and soldiers were concerned, they needed to fight very hard to keep Kashmir within the union. A former Congress Party official told me that the period between 1989 and 1992 saw "extreme brutality" because Kashmir was "a bone of contention between India and Pakistan, India will defend it no matter the cost. Suspicion of Pakistan support from the beginning gave legitimization for extreme violence."[316] Another former official said that the Indian state's response to the Kashmir rebellion "was that a portion of Indian territory is under attack and needs to be defended."[317] A Kashmiri Pandit who fled the valley claimed that matters escalated faster in Kashmir than in Punjab or Assam because unlike those territories, in Kashmir the combination of a history of border war with Pakistan, and the fact that it was "a Muslim country providing [help to] Muslim citizens" of India, meant that the state was on high alert.[318] As one contemporary analysis argued, "most Indians, for security reasons, would tolerate a level of repression in Kashmir that they would protest if it occurred elsewhere in the country."[319]

The seriousness of the external threat in Kashmir necessitated strong resolve. Referring to Pakistan, Prime Minister V. P. Singh noted in April 1990 that "they want to achieve their territorial goals without paying the price of war. You can't get away with that. You will have to pay a heavy cost. We have the capability to inflict that cost."[320] He made clear that there would be no compromise with "anti-national elements" who were "getting assistance from external forces," and that "no force, either external or internal, will ever be permitted to alter" Kashmir's status in the Indian union.[321] Dispelling the impression that security forces' actions in Kashmir were excessive, the prime minister pled for a proper understanding of the threat that necessitated such a response: "Let us not underestimate the very deep conspiracy across the border."[322] Similarly, his successor, Chandra Shekhar, argued for "strong measures" in Punjab and Kashmir to ensure that the militants not receive Pakistani help.[323] A diplomat summarized the Indian position succinctly: "We have pulled no punches in our messages to the Pakistani leadership . . . we have told them clearly to stop interfering in Kashmir and that we will not allow the secession of any part of India."[324]

Jagmohan himself justified his repression as a response to the territorial threat India faced, noting that "now I am saving the union. How many people did Abraham Lincoln kill? If I have to use force, there's a moral legitimacy to it."[325] Home Minister Mutfi Mohammad Sayeed, one of the principal architects of India's Kashmir policy, similarly argued that "no slackness" would be shown to the "terrorists" of Kashmir.[326] He warned Pakistan that "any attempt to destabilize the nation will be fought back with full determination and fortitude," that "we have the capacity and determination to fight out this undeclared war," so that it may "defend every inch of Kashmir."[327] Even ousted chief minister Farooq Abdullah claimed that an "iron hand" was needed in Kashmir to adequately deal with the "evil designs of our neighbor."[328]

Former security officials also focused on the material implications of Pakistani support. Some emphasized that insurgent organizations need military leadership for purposes of planning and analysis of military operations, and pointed to the importance of training across the LOC in the early years of the insurgency, which gave insurgents the ability to take on, and in certain cases, be militarily superior to, state security forces. Put together, the cocktail of training, command and control support, and sanctuary meant that security forces' "hands were full."[329] Others argued that a movement as large-scale as the Kashmiri insurgency could not be sustained without the level of support the Pakistani state proffered.[330] The sophistication of the arms Pakistan was supplying, for instance, necessitated an upgrade in Indian security forces equipment in both Kashmir and Punjab.[331]

This position was shared by the press. An editorial in a national newspaper urged the Indian nation "to gear itself for the very long haul in Kashmir" given that Pakistan was now imparting "control and direction of the movement in the Valley."[332] It cheered "the tough line being taken by the home ministry against militants and secessionists," which dealt significant blows to "the ideologues of the Pakistan-sponsored movement."[333] Pro-union Kashmiri newspapers urged their readers to consider this "a time when every patriotic Indian should have supported the efforts of Governor Jagmohan in dealing with the terrorist menace [and] restoring peace and tranquility in the valley."[334] Security forces' "excesses" may be troubling, "but in a kind of situation that we face in the valley today and in view of the increase in the militants' attacks on the security forces, it will be difficult to altogether avoid" them; the deaths of innocents' was "inevitable" when security forces came under attack from "groups of militants numbering 50 to 100."[335] The *Kashmir Times* argued several times that Pakistani support for the insurgency necessitated toughness from the Indian state, and latitude for Jagmohan's repression. In February 1990, it solemnly noted that "in view of [the] serious threat of militants in the valley and threatening posture of Pakistan the country is facing a serious situation in the border state . . . any letup in the efforts being made to combat terrorism and face the challenge to the country's integrity is unthinkable."[336] Similarly, in March, it argued that "what we face today is a war-like situation with the neighboring country planning infiltrations, arming the militants and providing them every kind of assistance including finances and sophisticated arms in addition to crude propaganda to boost the morale of the subversives . . . in such a situation the security forces in the State cannot take things lying down . . . what is important at this juncture is a clear-cut Kashmir policy by New Delhi and free hand to the Governor to fight the terrorist menace in Kashmir."[337] President's rule in the summer of 1990 was "inevitable because of the continued attempts by Pakistan to push more and more militants and arms into the valley."[338]

High levels of perceived support from Pakistan to the Kashmiri nationalist movement, then, helped generate collective repression by the Indian state in response. Pakistani aid to, and affinity with, the local population meant that they were seen as a disloyal fifth column, leading to more indiscriminate violence on the ground. Pakistani support also meant that Indian security forces faced a tougher fight than they would have otherwise, both within the valley and across the LOC, which resulted in more violence.

Alternative Explanations

The two main theoretical alternatives to the view given in this chapter do not fare well in the Indian case. The argument for institutional veto points fails to explain the observed variation because India's governing structure did not change in the period in question while its strategy assuredly did. To the extent that political arrangements with varying degrees of centralization were imposed, such as president's rule, these were consequences, not causes, of India's decision-making. The precedent-setting argument, meanwhile, has been often employed by Indian leaders when justifying their stance against secessionism. Typically, leaders will refer to the noncommunal and secular nature of the Indian state when denying the possibility of independence to ethnic or religious groups, arguing essentially that if the Muslims go, what will stop the Christians or Sikhs? An argument for cascading secessionism being the state's overriding concern would expect the most violence and repression in the crisis which chronologically appeared before the others. However, the Indian state employed concessions and policing to deal with the first two crises in Assam and Punjab, which took place in the early and mid-1980s, and employed the more brutal response in the conflict that arose last.

More context-specific arguments also offer unsatisfactory answers. For instance, one could argue for a natural resource–based explanation, where a state fights harder for richer lands, but this would also fail to explain the variation examined here, since it was Assam that was the most resource-rich province of the three, not Kashmir. Assam contains large oil reserves and is also a massive producer of tea. One could make the case that even Punjab is more resource-rich than Kashmir, given the reliance of the Indian state on Punjab for agricultural production.

It could also be reasoned that the movement in Kashmir had the most extreme goals (full independence, rather than autonomy) and thus saw more violence. This view ignores that the ULFA, treated with relative restraint, was an explicitly secessionist organization. More generally, this argument ignores "strategic bluffing" by separatist movements, an exceedingly common tactic:[339] movements demanding independence sometimes do so only to set a high initial price, while movements demanding autonomy could do so as the first of a series of "salami slice" claims. Prima facie, it is difficult for states to distinguish between the two types. Past a certain baseline of organizational and political strength, which all three movements displayed in spades, the state must treat the movement's demands with seriousness. In turn, the seriousness with which the state takes each individual movement is dependent on how much it can threaten the state, which rests on how much third-party support it enjoys.

One could also point to varied levels of democratic political institutions in each of the states examined here, with Kashmir featuring a much higher degree of centralization of power, as a more powerful explanation for variation in violence. There is no doubt that a decaying institutional framework gave fuel to dissatisfaction on the ground to rebels and their supporters, especially in Kashmir. However, from the perspective of the state's decision-making—the object of inquiry here—differences in institutionalization was as much a consequence as a cause of its calculus. It was precisely *because* Kashmir was viewed through an external lens that the center could ill afford to take chances with allowing greater democratic representation to its citizens. In Assam, by contrast, rebel parties such as the AGP could be brought into the political fold because of the lower level of threat the movement posed, and state governments in both Assam (1987–90) and Punjab (1985–87) could be trusted to tackle militancy when the external threat was relatively low.

A final counterargument to mine could reason that I overstate the variation in Indian strategy across space and time. One specific version of this claim would point to Operation Bluestar, and question why the death of hundreds at the hands of state security forces would not be considered harsh coercion. I consider Bluestar the very event that led to the Sikh secessionist moment, and as such, do not include it as part of the Indian state's strategy against separatists. To the contrary, until 1985, Sikh agitation was restricted mainly to Bhindranwale and a relatively tiny group of militants, in part encouraged by the Congress government itself. As such, the Indian government's actions at the Golden Temple in 1984 should be seen as an overcompensatory corrective to its cynical deployment of religious criminals for electoral gain, rather than as part of a strategy against a full-blown separatist movement. A more general version of this counterargument, meanwhile, would make the claim that "India has always been very brutal" in its counterinsurgency, pointing to, for instance, Indian strategy in the

Northeast in the 1960s, and dispute whether there is a significant difference between its conduct in places such as Assam and Kashmir and Punjab.[340] A more general assessment of Indian counterinsurgency lies outside the scope of this book. However, it bears noting that during the much-discussed period of Indian brutality in the Northeast, the 1960s, insurgents enjoyed significantly more Pakistani and Chinese support than in the period examined here. For example, groups in Nagaland began receiving weapons and training from East Pakistan in 1958.[341] This support was intensified after China's victory against India in the 1962 war, after which it began its wholehearted support of Naga insurgents, making Indian counterinsurgency considerably more challenging from the mid-1960s onward.[342] It was Pakistan's loss of its eastern wing in 1971 that severely compromised its ability, and China's, to support groups in the Northeast,[343] explaining why, during the 1980s, the scale and intensity of Indian counterinsurgency in the Northeast did not approach its behavior on the western border.

The comparison of Kashmir with Punjab and Assam is instructive. In Assam, the Indian government was willing to escalate to only mild coercion, while signing accords with both political and militant representatives of the ethnic group. In Punjab, similar to Assam, the government was willing to be accommodationist when it viewed the conflict through primarily a domestic lens; it was only when Pakistani support for the Sikh separatists increased that the Indian state went to a more aggressive strategy. In the Kashmir case, however, at the first signs of trouble, the center imposed president's rule, sent in the hard-line Jagmohan, and when he proved to be a disastrous choice, replaced him with the equally hard-line Saxena. High levels of violence were evident from the very beginning of the crisis. The Indian state simply could not afford to do anything other than smash the insurgency, given that it believed Pakistan was behind it, and that a serious and significant threat to the territorial status quo between the two states had developed.[344]

   As my theory would expect, the movement that represented the greatest external security threat, Kashmir, received the most repressive strategy—collective repression. Conversely Punjab was a more mixed case: a strategy centering on policing at the initial secessionist moment, and then an escalation to militarization when Pakistani support increased to moderate levels. The movement deemed the least threatening externally due to limited levels of third-party support, Assam, was dealt with the softest hands, with a mixture of policing and militarization.

The Ottoman Empire's Escalation from Reforms to the Armenian Genocide, 1908–1915

In the first decade and a half of the twentieth century, Ottoman treatment of its Armenian community changed in step with changing threats to the polity. The Armenian nation had no pivotal secessionist "moments" as such during this period. Rather, the state of Armenian demands and nationalism was a near constant phenomenon: significantly greater autonomy, up to and including statehood. As we shall see, the Ottoman response to these Armenian demands ebbed and flowed. Upon deposing the sultan and assuming power in 1908, the Young Turk movement dealt with the Armenians peacefully, with the promise of administrative reforms. However, once World War I broke out, and Turkey joined the Central Powers, the Armenians faced genocide. Seven years apart, the same regime, facing the same ethnic group, used strategies as vastly different as "negotiations and concessions" and "collective repression." Why?

The increased external vulnerability brought about by Turkey's involvement in the war was crucial in the escalation the Armenians faced, particularly given relations between Russia, the Ottoman state, and the Armenian community. When the Young Turks first rose to power, they had a relatively optimistic outlook on the state's future in Europe. More important, they conceived of Ottoman identity as including the presence and participation of Armenians. These beliefs supplied the confidence necessary for a strategy of negotiations and concessions. However, by 1914–15, their treatment of Armenians changed dramatically, with two factors relating to external security especially relevant. First, the changing shape and form of the Ottoman Empire between 1908 and 1914—it lost essentially all of its European territory—meant that the state's identity became based more on a narrow Turkism than an accommodating Otto-manism. Shifts in Ottoman identity ensured that Armenian nationalism was no longer considered indifferent to the national core but actively opposed to it and caused the regime to view Armenian demands in a more

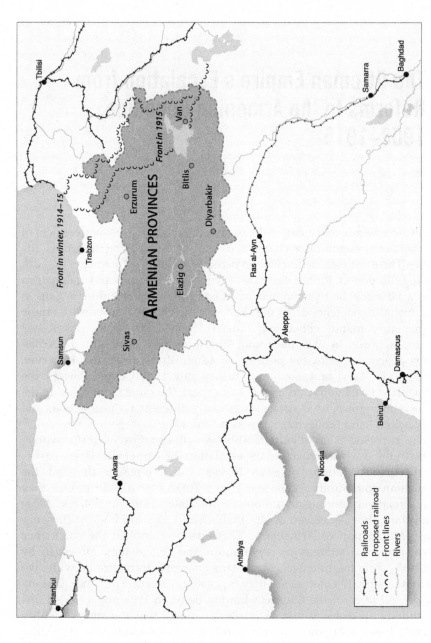

Map 2. The Armenian provinces

existentially threatening light. Second, the fact that the Ottomans and Russians were on opposite sides in the war meant that when the latter's support for Armenians shot up, it did so at a time when the very survival of the Ottoman Empire was in peril. Strong support by Russia for the Armenians had both material and emotional consequences, whereby the Ottoman Empire faced a significantly tougher fight in World War I thanks to Armenian collaboration and acted angrily in the face of perceived betrayal. In conjunction, these factors—the adoption of a more exclusivist and paranoid nationalism by the Young Turk regime, which shifted the identity distance between the two groups from "indifferent" to "opposed," and "high" Russian support for the Armenians during the Great War—translated into genocide.

I believe this case is worthy of investigation for a number of reasons. First, "extreme" cases, or those where either or both of the independent and dependent variable lie far from the median, can prove instructive.[1] The Ottoman-Armenian case certainly fits this description, with state strategy spanning from "negotiations and concessions," wide-ranging and substantive reforms to the Armenians, to "collective repression." Insofar as the independent variable is concerned, it is difficult to imagine a more externally threatening environment than the one the Ottoman Empire faced during World War I.

Second, because the Ottoman case was not one of a modern nation-state, but an empire in the midst of dissolution, its inclusion increases the breadth of the sample tested thus far. Unlike most other European empires—the British, French, Dutch, Portuguese, and Spanish—the Ottoman Empire was geographically contiguous, with no body of water between the metropole and the periphery. This meant that it "looked" like a state more so than the Western European empires (see chapter 1).

Third, scholars suggest dividing a single case into two subcases, a technique known as "before-after research design," in order to gauge the effects of changes in one significant variable.[2] Leveraging the variation in Young Turk strategy with respect to the Armenians in 1908 and 1915, when little about the case changed other than the appreciably different external environment the state faced, allows for a fruitful examination of the effect of external security conditions on state strategy with respect to separatist minorities.

Before proceeding, it is important to note that the historical origins of the Armenian genocide are strongly contested. As the title of one book suggests, the Armenian genocide is a "disputed genocide."[3] There are essentially two interpretations on what transpired between the Ottoman state and its Armenian nation. First, there is the belief that, absent World War I, the Armenian genocide could not and would not have happened. This view is generally forwarded by Western historians, who argue that the Ottoman position and performance in the war was intimately tied to its decision to organize the deportations of hundreds of thousands of people in bad weather and through rough terrain, without protection against marauders or disease, resulting in the murder of a million Armenians. The oppositional view, generally forwarded by Armenian historians, is that the genocide was a premeditated act, planned well before World War I.[4] There is a third view, proffered primarily by "official" Turkish historians,[5] who argue that there was no deliberate mass-targeting of the Armenian community in the first place,[6] and to the extent that there was violence committed against Armenians, it was part and parcel of the fog of war. Such "scholars" understate levels of violence against the Armenians;[7] overstate Armenian responsibility for the violence; claim that rather than ordering massacres, the Young Turk regime wanted to provide both food and security to the deportees;[8] argue that the Armenians suffered no more or less than other communities in the state during the Great War; and practice frankly bizarre forms of false equivalence, where small-scale incidents such as murders and seizures of banks occupy the same moral space as the deaths of hundreds of thousands of people.[9] This third view has been thoroughly discredited, and as such, I will not engage with it at length here, except to merely note its existence.

I side primarily with the first camp. Although the leadership in the Ottoman state may well have harbored considerable ill-will toward their Armenian citizens before the war and was uneager to ensure their safety once deported, it was only the security exigencies of the Great War that caused the genocide. In particular, the real and perceived partnership between Russia and the restive Armenian population made the senior Ottoman leadership believe that their prospects of survival in the war were nonexistent if they did not first tackle the Armenian "problem."

The main factors to consider in favor of this argument are: the perilous situation the Ottomans found themselves in the spring of 1915; the location of major Armenian population centers, occupying important territory along Ottoman lines of communication and supply as well as possible lines of Russian invasion; and the timing and escalation of the major deportation orders by Talaat and Enver Pasha. As we shall see, Armenian population centers were concentrated in the Ottoman rear, especially with respect to two of their three major fronts in World War I—the Caucasus campaign against Russia and the Palestine and Mesopotamian campaigns against Britain. During the spring and summer of 1915, when the Ottoman Empire was considered to be on its last legs, and faced Allied and Russian incursions in three theaters as well as internal insurrections, its leaders ordered deportations both *when* and *where* it faced the greatest security threat. In conjunction with corroborating public and private testimony from the main Ottoman decision makers, the implication is that the Ottoman state was concerned with the prospect of the Armenian fifth column attacking its vulnerable supply and communication lines, or alternatively, joining advancing Russian or Western forces, both fears that were realized in a number of cases. On a wider temporal scale, the onset of the war, and considerable territorial losses in the years running up to it, at once solidified the existence of threats emanating from abroad, and hardened Ottoman resolve to deal with them.

For the purposes of the general argument forwarded in this book, then, external security considerations for the Ottoman state were the crucial driving variable for the escalation from its accommodationist policy to widespread slaughter. In 1908, the revolutionary Young Turk government attempted "negotiations and concessions" to solve the Armenian issue because they had an optimistic view of the state, both internally and externally. By the time the war began, however, and the external threat that the Ottoman state faced ramped up due to changes in national identity and the wider geopolitical context, its policy of "collective repression" was put in place. Figure 4 summarizes the argument I forward in this chapter.

The main theoretical alternatives to mine outlined in the introduction cannot explain the observed variation in this case. The reputation argument

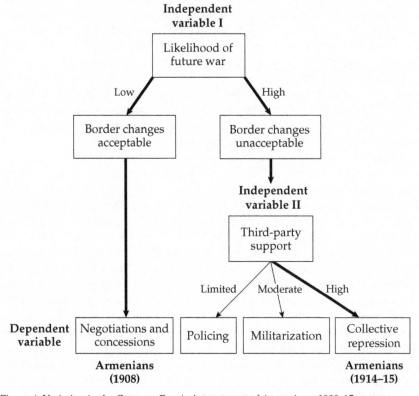

Figure 4. Variation in the Ottoman Empire's treatment of Armenians, 1908–15

would predict that the earlier movement would face greater violence, but the opposite took place. Meanwhile, Young Turk leaders' concentration of power between 1908 and 1915 would have been relevant for the veto points argument—as long as they preferred a policy of concessions, only to be stymied by a lack of credibility with the minority. However, in the spring of 1915, the Young Turk leaders were flatly uninterested in concessions to the Armenians, rendering theories centering on domestic institutions less than useful in explaining the Ottoman escalation to genocide. The main alternative, context-specific argument would be that external security considerations were merely correlated, rather than causally related, with Ottoman decision-making, and that the leadership had decided on genocide well before the Great War. Such a view does not withstand empirical scrutiny, as we shall see.

Antecedent Conditions of a Tripartite Rivalry

In the early 1800s, historic Armenia was scythed up between the Russian and Ottoman empires, and the Russians supplemented those gains in the coming years by snapping up territory through wars, conquests, and treaties.[10] By the middle of the century, the Ottoman state was left with just over 2 million Armenians under its control, more than half of which lived in six *vilayets*, or provinces: Van, Bitlis, Erzurum, Diyarbakir, Kharput, and Sivas, where they outnumbered both ethnic Turks and Kurds. Armenians were also concentrated on the Mediterranean coast at Cilicia.[11] The geographic distribution of Armenians mattered greatly because the Ottoman authorities, in trying to dampen calls for reform, would attempt to minimize the number of Armenians in particular areas.[12]

Armenian demands in the latter half of the nineteenth century had not yet escalated to full independence. Rather, they sought guarantees of life and property. Armenians often fell victim to marauding Kurds, who would attack entire villages and extort local merchants. This practice forced a system of double taxation on Armenian communities, who paid high taxes to the state on account of being non-Muslim, even before they were subjected to violence and intimidation from Kurds. Moreover, the laws and regulations of the Ottoman system imposed additional hardships on the Armenian community: Christians were not equal before the law and judicial system, and they were barred from serving in the higher levels of the government and military. Worse still was that the perpetrators of attacks against them were never punished, which in turn encouraged yet more attacks. In fact, the Turkish-Armenian conflict actually began as a Kurd-Armenian conflict; the latter were generally defenseless against Kurdish violence and extortion, and it was the refusal of Ottoman authorities to do anything about it that greatly angered the Armenians.[13]

The Armenian community was generally more economically advanced than most ethnic blocs under the Ottomans. In this, they were aided by the fact that Muslims in the state were discouraged from merchant or trade-reliant careers. Moreover, the Armenians' geographic clustering and religious identity led to a stronger sense of nationhood and common identity than among most other groups. As a consequence, it was easier for them to forward demands as a unified community in the face of discrimination. Reform on security, administrative matters, taxes, and property were the central Armenian demands in the latter half of the nineteenth century, with independence or autonomy not a major concern as yet.[14] From the state's point of view, the Armenians were not considered the most pressing internal problem either, to the point that they were famously considered the "most loyal community" among Ottoman Christian citizens in the nineteenth century.[15]

In 1877, war broke out between Russia and the Ottoman Empire. The Ottomans allied with Britain, which itself was wary about Russian ambitions in and around Asia Minor, Persia, and India. However, Britain's support did not extend to lending a military hand to the sultan, and Russia won the war relatively easily. In fact, they entered Constantinople and were six miles from the Porte before French and British forces compelled the Russians to stop their advance. The war resulted in Russia annexing the border regions in the Caucasus. The 1878 Treaty of Berlin marked the end of the war, and with it ensured independence for Serbia, Montenegro, and Romania—that is, the Ottomans lost most of their Christian citizens. In addition, Bulgaria won greater autonomy and reforms were promised to Macedonia, eastern Roumelia, Salonika, and Kosovo.[16]

These developments reaffirmed Ottoman perceptions of Russia seeking to weaken it from within by supporting the independence efforts of ethnic groups in their midst, particularly if they were Christian.[17] More generally, they fueled resentment at Western intervention in the state's domestic affairs.[18] Russia's actions did not allay these concerns. It put its cards on the table when it pledged to withdraw from annexed Ottoman territory only when reforms targeting Armenian grievances were put in place.[19] Perversely but unsurprisingly, international intervention in Armenian efforts toward reform provided mixed results at best—while the recognition of their strife led to a greater sense of national consciousness among the Armenians, European interference tended to give the Ottoman leadership more reason to clamp down on them.[20]

Russia's ambitions for Ottoman Armenians were not very grand or wide ranging. Contrary to Ottoman perceptions, Russia did not prefer Turkey's empire to dissolve or be partitioned out of existence; rather, Russia preferred a weak but still viable Ottoman state. With regard to Armenian aspirations, Russia wished for the sultan to enact relatively moderate reforms—concessions too weighty would be problematic for the Russians too, since they had their own politically active Armenian minority.[21] Although Russia's geostrategic focus turned partly from the Balkans and Near East to Persia and the Far East, it still considered its "historic" tasks in the Near East important. These objectives were that no third state should control the Straits, which were key for Russian commerce, and a natural launching point for control of the Balkans and the Black Sea; statehood for Balkan Christian peoples; and a general, non-negotiable sphere of influence in the Near East.[22]

Regardless of Russian interference and provocation, when the Young Turks rose to power, their first interactions with Armenians were hardly marked by antipathy, or anything close to it. To the contrary, their relationship was, at least at the outset, marked by cooperation and mutual optimism.

Young Turks Ascension to Power and Accommodation of Armenians

The Young Turks assumed control of the state in a revolution in 1908 that featured "astonishingly little bloodshed."[23] The revolutionaries were an eclectic group: modern thinkers, intelligentsia, liberals, and naval and military officers, organized under various political groups, most prominent of which was the Committee of Union and Progress (CUP). The CUP was inspired by the French Revolution and Japan's Meiji Restoration, which imparted to the Young Turks the lesson that constitutionalism was the key to state strength. In this simplistic view, constitutionalism was considered a panacea, "a recipe for alleviating ethnic strife, ending nationalist separatist movements, propelling economic growth, and instituting legal rationality in the military and the civil administration."[24] The organizational antecedent for the Young Turks was the Ottoman Union, a secret group formed in 1889 by medical students in Istanbul, which operated underground and worked to establish contacts with liberal-minded members of the sultan's regime as well as oppositional figures abroad, particularly in Western Europe. Ahmed Riza was the main leader in charge of the organization that was to develop into the CUP.[25] Riza was based in Paris—many of the Young Turk movement's leaders resided abroad—and led calls for constitutionalist government. He also decried foreign interference in Turkey's internal affairs.[26] Additionally, dissatisfied military officers were an important component of the Young Turks and the CUP. One scholar has characterized the entire transition to constitutionalism as "overwhelmingly military in character" and the revolution as "the corroboration of the ideas and activities of a handful of idealists who leaned upon the military for its prompt and smooth execution."[27]

The Young Turk movement had been the subject of persecution from the sultan's regime throughout the 1870s and 1880s but its organizational strength and activism grew in the 1890s to the point where it was a latent revolutionary threat to the regime.[28] The elements behind the Young Turks even attempted a coup in August 1896 but were thwarted at the last moment, throwing their entire secret organizational structure into chaos and forcing a temporary retreat.[29] The Young Turks finally staged their revolution in 1908, with July 24 signifying the end of autocratic rule and the beginning of the era of the Second Constitution.[30] Ideologically, what united the movement was their common goal of a comprehensive modernization program and a fervent belief in Ottoman nationalism and identity, building on ideas first carried forward by the Young Ottomans.[31] Their principal aim was to restore the constitution and depose the sultan's government, which was too theocratic and regressive for their modernist world view.[32]

Even before their revolution, the Young Turks had foreshadowed a spirit of cooperation that was to mark their relationship with Armenian nationalists in 1908. Despite differences of opinion, representatives from nationalist parties such as the Hanchaks, including Stepan Sapah-Gulian, M. Boyadjian, and Arpiar Arpiarian, met with Young Turk leaders Nazim and Behaeddin Shakir. As Kirakossian writes, the two sides found a mutually beneficial framework: the Young Turks "agreed with the idea of establishing autonomous Armenia: she was not to be separated from Turkey but could have a European governor. . . . Ahmed Riza and others expressed readiness to meet Armenian requirements on the condition that Huntchaks assist in resolving general state problems."[33] Consistent with these expectations, when they finally rose to power, the Young Turks dealt with the Armenian community peacefully. Their strategy was rooted in both a reasonably secure regional environment and, more importantly, a belief that Armenians were an important component of Ottoman national identity.

The Young Turks assumed power with the wholehearted support of the two main Armenian revolutionary parties, the Hanchaks and the Dashnaks.[34] In terms of their goals, the Hanchak Party was more radical than the Dashnaks, who unlike the former group, did not advocate for full-blown independence, but rather reform within the empire.[35] Though there was much to unite the elements that made up the nascent state, there was one important division, which was to matter a great deal a few years down the road. Specifically, how would the state be organized administratively? Ahmed Riza called for greater centralization, while the decentralist group, which was led by Prince Sabahaddin, the sultan's nephew, called for political and economic liberalization along the Anglo-Saxon model.[36] The Armenian community, naturally, supported the Sabahaddin camp.[37]

At the time, however, Armenian nationalists and the Young Turks put their differences aside. It was not just a common foe that united them— though it remains trivially true that neither had any love lost for the sultan. Rather, the promise of a constitution and a more modern Ottoman Empire held appeal for each set of ideologues, the Armenian nationalists as well as the Ottoman state builders. This was why "Armenians took great satisfaction in the victory of the army and its CUP commanders. . . . The downfall of the sultan and the restoration of the constitution of 1876 was everything and more that they and their parties such as the Dashnaks had hoped for."[38]

In the aftermath of the July Revolution, the CUP reached out to all non-Turkish communities, including the Armenians, Greeks, and Macedonians, to institutionalize cooperation on the question of candidates for the upcoming elections, bringing them into the CUP fold.[39] From the perspective of the CUP, it was imperative, right from the beginning, to portray a friendly and tolerant image toward the Christian communities within the empire and to do away with internal divisions. Their message was clear: the aim was a constitutional regime, and all communities organized against the sultan's regime were not just welcome but necessary.[40] To that end, the Young Turk regime's initial months were marked by greater liberalization in the entire state, including lifting censorship of the press, disbanding the sultan's internal intelligence network, amnesty for political prisoners, and the dismissal of corrupt government and palace officials.[41] Citizens of "all denominations marched in the streets under banners bearing the slogan 'Liberté, Egalité, Fraternité' in various languages, and welcomed the age of freedom and democracy."[42]

Aside from this general trend of liberalization, the Young Turks made several substantial concessions to the Armenian community. Armenians contested seats in parliament, as full Ottoman citizens of the state, rather than as part of a separate *millet*, or nation. The Armenian national assembly was convened after being banned under the sultan. Schools and libraries were opened, and newspapers were allowed to circulate. Kurdish raids and violence were scaled down. Exiled notables, such as the deposed patriarch of Constantinople, Madteos III Izmiriliyan and the writer Grigor Zohrap, were welcomed back home. Enver Pasha, Talaat, and other Young Turk leaders went to Armenian churches, schools, and graveyards, where they paid respects to fallen Armenians who had died in the antisultan struggle, and made powerful speeches pointing to cooperation between Turks and Armenians. Enver told "children that the old days of Moslem-Christian strife had passed forever and that the two peoples were now to live together as brothers and sisters." The changes that took place were slow moving, but they were substantive, and recognized as such—even by revolutionary Armenian parties.[43] The Hanchaks went so far as to claim that the Ottoman parliament was a "genuine spokesman of the yearnings and will of the subjugated element, staunch supporters of its human rights and the champion of the fatherland's freedom."[44] Sapah-Gulian, one of their leaders, wrote that "when the constitution was proclaimed, the majority of Armenians and myself among them, became Ittihadists. Our common belief was that the party that proclaims the constitution is heart and soul for the progress and development of the entire country and all her people."[45] Parties such as the Dashnaks would participate fully in Ottoman politics, cooperating with the CUP, playing an active role in the first parliamentary elections, and mobilizing Armenian support in favor of the constitution.[46] As Suny summarizes, "The 1908 revolution proclaimed a new era for the empire, a progressive step into a European-style modernity based on constitutionalism, equality, fraternity, and personal freedom," and therefore "Ottoman Armenians and other minorities joyfully greeted the restoration of the liberal Constitution, hopeful that the new government would provide a political mechanism for peaceful development within the framework of a representative parliamentary system."[47]

CUP's rhetoric and actions spoke to the accommodationist stance they held toward the Armenian community in the early days of their regime. To use my theoretical framework, the state used "negotiations and concessions" when dealing with Armenian demands for autonomy. This strategy was undergirded by confidence in their future security; Young Turk leaders were not preoccupied with foreign relations but sharply focused on internal reform. They could maintain such a focus first because they had a base optimism about the future of the Ottoman Empire. Specifically, in 1908 "the Young Turks believed in the possibility of their empire's becoming a full member of European international society, convinced that it could represent the harmony of Eastern and Western civilization," and went about cultivating diplomatic contacts in various European capitals, seeking to cement friendships with major powers such as Britain, France, and Germany.[48]

More important than this optimism about their regional environment, the Young Turks' conceptualization of Ottoman identity was consistent with, and welcoming of, the presence of Armenians, and called for their greater political participation. The Armenian and central leaderships shared ideological goals, and Armenian demands for autonomy were not seen as unreasonable or problematic. The basic belief upholding their reforms was that if the Ottoman Empire could unite its various nationalities from within, its relations with Europe and the world would, in essence, take care of itself. For the Young Turks, unlike previous Ottoman regimes, Armenian identity was not "opposed" to that of the central state, but "indifferent."

Ottoman nationalism, particularly in the early period of the Young Turk regime, implied the privileging of Ottoman identity over and above communities' parochial identities. As Kayali notes, "In the euphoria of July 1908 the Unionists believed that the non-Muslims would be won over to the CUP's Ottomanist platform in the new parliamentary regime. They hoped that religious and ethnic differences would be superseded by a broader Ottoman identity."[49] In other words, Ottoman concessions to Christian communities generally and the Armenians specifically grew out of a belief that all Ottoman citizens owed their allegiance to the state, and as such, their primary identity should be tied to it. The antecedent arrangement of separate millets, or nations, starkly recognized, and contributed to, the ethnic differences between different groups of Ottoman subjects,[50] distinctions which the Young Turks aimed to extinguish. This shift in worldview mirrors the so-called soup versus salad debate on immigration in contemporary politics, where some advocates argue that all communities must subjugate themselves to a larger identity, as ingredients mix in a melting pot of soup, while others argue for the maintenance of (respectful) boundaries between different ethnic or religious groups, akin to vegetables in a salad bowl, such that each maintains their unique character in a larger ensemble.[51]

The Young Turks initially opted for a soup model. As Enver Pasha memorably claimed, "We are all Ottomans." The general philosophy they espoused was one of unity "without distinctions of race" and the "peace and safety of the common homeland" alongside the abandonment of "particular purposes." The state would be organized along the "secular and universalist principle of the equality of all subjects, who all owed equal loyalty to the empire."[52] As the CUP wrote to one Bulgarian politician, "This country belongs neither to the Turk, nor to the Bulgarian or Arab. It is the asset and domain of every individual carrying the name Ottoman. . . . Those who think the opposite of this, namely those who try to sever the country into parts and nations, even if they are Turks, are our adversaries, our enemies."[53]

This fervent belief in Ottomanism is referred to by detractors of the regime as "fascist," but in reality, the Young Turks were simply behaving as other European powers, where the creation, imposition, and sustenance of national and uniform identities became state projects.[54] Nationalism, as it existed in contemporary Europe, swept into the Ottoman state around the middle of the nineteenth century, and came hand in hand with a more general belief in transporting the dominant ideas about politics at the time, from reforms aimed at strengthening the bureaucratic nature of the state, to the liberalism of Montesquieu, Rousseau, and Smith.[55] It was the very lateness of this arrival of nationalism that forced on the Young Turks such decisions about the "official" state identity.[56]

Terms such as *centralism* and *decentralization*, therefore, should be treated with caution, as they are often taken to mean things that they do not. For instance, it would be easy to fall into the analytical trap of conflating "decentralization" with positive reforms toward the Armenian community. In fact, *centralist* ideas lay behind the concessions: the notion that all citizens were Ottomans first and foremost meant that the CUP was eager to ensure equality in treatment. For the Young Turks, Armenian nationalism was not opposed to Ottoman identity, it was to be seamlessly subsumed under it.

The Young Turks' view of their national identity, which had a welcome place for the Ottoman Armenian community, when combined with the relatively relaxed external environment the state faced in 1908, opened the possibility of significant concessions. Soon, however, both the Ottoman Empire's regional security, as well as its conception of Armenian nationalism, would undergo drastic changes—with severely deleterious consequences for Armenians.

Radicalized Identity, Deteriorating Neighborhood

The spirit of bonhomie and mutual cooperation between the Young Turks and the Armenian community lasted less than a year. The 1909 Adana massacre, where roughly twenty thousand to thirty thousand Armenians died following a temporary countercoup by the sultan, and the general slow pace of reform notwithstanding promises to the contrary, put paid to Armenian hopes. For their part, the Young Turks' view of the Armenian community would also change drastically over the next half-decade, with two episodes particularly responsible.

First, the Ottomans' defeats in the Balkan wars of 1912 would irrevocably change both the physical and ideological nature of the state. Losing its European and Christian territories meant that the Ottoman Empire pursued an increasingly Turkified nationalism, as a result of which Armenian identity assumed a much more sinister and threatening shape. These developments caused the shift in Ottoman perceptions of Armenian identity from "indifferent" to "opposed." Second, the 1914 Mandelstam Plan, named after a Russian diplomatic official, which called for Armenians' autonomy being guaranteed by foreign powers, mainly Russia, cemented in the leadership's collective mind that Armenian nationalists were a fifth column not to be trusted. Together, these developments ensured that the Ottoman leadership began to see Armenian nationalism as a significant security threat, one whose dangers escalated drastically once World War I broke out and Russian support for Armenians rose to "high" levels.

THE BALKAN WARS' TERRITORIAL AND IDEOLOGICAL CONSEQUENCES

The first major episode that shifted Young Turk perceptions of Ottoman Armenians was the Balkan wars. In October 1912, Serbia, Montenegro, Greece, and Bulgaria declared war on the Ottoman state. "Out-powered, demoralized, unprepared, and poorly equipped, the Ottoman army fought fourteen battles and lost all but one of them."[57] Within a few years, due to war losses and successful separatist movements, the Ottomans lost about 40 percent of its landmass and about 25 percent of its population. The first domino to fall was Bulgaria, which declared its independence, followed by Austria-Hungary's annexation of Bosnia and Herzegovina. Having fought a war against Italy in 1911, due to which the Ottomans lost Libya, the Balkan wars in 1912 ensured that Turkey was essentially no longer in Europe.[58]

What proved pivotal was not just the extent of territorial loss, but also its nature. Having lost almost all its European and Christian territories, the multinational and multiethnic character of the state lay in tatters, moving the center of gravity of the Ottoman Empire east, toward Anatolia. The Balkan provinces had been the "heart of the Empire, its provinces being by far the most advanced and the most productive. They had always provided much of the Empire's wealth and had long been the recruiting ground for the army and the bureaucracy."[59] This was no longer the case. The loss of European territories precipitated a crisis for the Ottoman state; one scholar claims that "it is no exaggeration to state that the effect of the Balkan wars on Ottoman society was nothing short of apocalyptic."[60] There were a number of reasons for this.

First, and most important, the territorial losses and European opportunism narrowed the Young Turks relatively pluralistic Ottomanist ideology to one espousing Turkish identity and nationalism.[61] After all, simple demographics meant that with the exit of the Albanians, Greeks, and Slavs, the Turks were numerically dominant in a way that they were not before 1908. Moreover, the very fact of territorial losses "strengthened the hands of centralizers and of Turkish nationalists/Islamicists against liberals and Christians—a stronger, more loyal state was needed."[62] As a consequence, the state saw a transition, from the "seemingly liberal, egalitarian Young Turks into extreme chauvinists, bent on creating a new order."[63] One exemplar of this trend was Ziya Gökalp, one of the key intellectual and ideological figures behind the new Young Turk movement, who believed that state strength comes from homogeneity. A nation, he wrote, "must be a society consisting of people who speak the same language, have had the same education and are united in their religious and aesthetic ideals—in short those who have a common culture and religion."[64]

This paradigmatic shift in the regime's conception of the state's identity would have significantly adverse consequence for the Armenian community down the road. Armenians were now perceived as directly opposed to the Ottoman national core, after previously being seen as unthreatening to, and being subsumed under, it. As Bloxham notes, what eventually drove the Armenian genocide was the "the impulse 'to streamline, make homogenous, organize people to be uniform in some sense. . . . CUP nationalism was . . . shaped by, and in reaction to, the ethno-nationalist movements in the Balkans."[65] Melson concurs, noting that "by 1912, certainly by 1915, the Young Turks were not particularly benign or dedicated to pluralism. They had become xenophobic integral nationalists for whom the identity and situation of the Armenians were sufficient proof of their treachery and potential threat to the continuity of the empire."[66] War losses generated a significant shift in the Young Turks' outlook on questions of identity.

Second, the Balkan losses increased the salience of any seditious activity in Anatolia, which now constituted the Turkish heartland.[67] As Abdullah Jevdet, a CUP leader, said: "Anatolia is the well spring of every fiber of our life. It is our heart, head, and the air we breathe."[68] The Young Turks considered disloyalty from its secessionist citizens as the primary cause of military defeat. The positive reforms they had instituted had, in a sense, sown the seeds of the state being scythed up.

> More than the failure of the Ottoman army to mobilize and defend the empire, many observers saw treason at the heart of this tragic defeat. Local Christian civilians and armed bands in Macedonia had aided the onslaught of the Balkan States. The eviction of hundreds of thousands of Ottoman Muslims from Macedonia and Kosova entailed the forfeiture of countless homes and hectares of land to the Christian victors. Ottoman Christian subjects still under Istanbul's rule were not immune to blame . . . the complicity of both Christian and Muslim Albanians in establishing an independent Albanian state in November 1912 confirmed to many in the government the duplicity and seditiousness of their former countrymen.[69]

Finally, the losses in the Balkan wars led to the predominance of external security concerns for the CUP, which "weighed heavily on the minds of the Young Turks immediately after the fighting ended."[70] No longer was the neighborhood deemed safe enough to risk policies that could result in border changes. The losses in the Balkan wars created a "new sense of crisis" for the state and its Committee of Union and Progress leadership.[71] As Üngör argues, the issues of external security, a more fervent Turkish nationalism, and ethnic separatist mobilization were inextricably bound up with one another:

> Most of all, the Young Turks' perception that the catastrophe of the Balkans should never be allowed to happen to the remaining territories of the Ottoman Empire, especially the eastern provinces, would give birth to unprecedented forms of population politics and social engineering. One major outcome of these processes was a deep fear, or perhaps a complex, of loss. The fear of losing territory was a persistent phobia of both late Ottoman and Turkish political culture.[72]

Crucially, this increase in levels of fear the regime faced was directly due to the behavior of outside powers. As the U.S. ambassador during the war noted in his memoirs, "Of all the new kingdoms which had been carved out of the sultan's dominions, Serbia . . . is the only one that has won her own independence. Russia, France, and Great Britain have set free all" the other

Christian peoples in the Ottoman Empire.[73] The realization of external vulnerability led the triumvirate of Enver, Talaat, and Jamal to make military restoration a serious priority on reasserting strong control of the Ottoman state in 1913. They wished to modernize the military corps, increase their spending on defense, acquire better equipment, and build modern naval ships. They also recruited German officers, thought to be the best officer corps in Europe, for army training purposes, as well as the British and French for the navy and reorganizing the gendarmerie respectively. The Russians, owing to the transparency of their designs on Ottoman territory, were not considered.[74]

Turkey's territorial losses in the Balkan wars were significant from the point of view of the Armenian nationalists too, serving as valuable learning experiences. They thought great powers might help resolve their national question just as had been the case with other Christian peoples under the Ottomans.[75] An article in a Russian newspaper argued that "all the Turkish Armenians regardless of their membership of a party . . . see Russia as their sole defender and savior and are envious of the peaceful life of the Russian Armenians."[76]

In sum, the losses in the Balkan wars made the Young Turks more wary of external security concerns, more suspicious of any secessionist activity in its homeland, and more narrowly nationalistic in its outlook. Territorial losses changed how the ruling regime saw the state as well as how it saw the Armenian community: identity relations shifted from "indifferent" to "opposed." Moreover, all these changes took place in an environment of internal upheaval for the CUP.[77] Within this context of geopolitical weakness—a shrinking state facing ethno-nationalism from within and, from without, rapacious European powers with whom it suffered an imbalance of economic and military power—the Armenians and Russians pushed for a reform plan.[78] The Mandelstam Plan hammered the nail in the coffin of Ottoman-Armenian relations.

THE MANDELSTAM PLAN

By the time the Balkan wars were over, the Armenians had essentially given up on eliciting concessions from the Turks without external intervention, their hopes from the 1908 revolution dashed.[79] The obvious patron was Russia, whose reasons for supporting Armenian reforms were strategic. Unlike the 1890s, when they expressed greater trepidation at the prospect of Armenian independence or autonomy owing to a fear of nationalistic conflagration, Russia was more firmly behind this round.[80] Previously, Russia was fearful that Armenian uprisings in the Ottoman Empire would spread to Armenian territories in Russia, a problem that it could do without. By the early 1910s, however, Russia's strategic calculus had reversed. With Western powers, including Germany and Britain, taking an increasing interest in the region's division of spoils, Russia became more assertive in its traditional preference for the strategic benefits of the territories in question. This was especially because Russia's main rival in Europe, Germany, was deepening its footprint in the region, with schemes for railways in Persia and greater military cooperation with the Ottomans.[81] Russia also had domestic political reasons to push for reform. Russia still faced its own restive Armenian community despite some minor efforts in placating it. Russia feared that Ottoman Armenians would use the example of other beleaguered nationalities under the rule of the Ottomans, rise to independence, and attempt to include Russian Armenians in an independent state.[82] To dampen their rebellious spirit, Russia wished to advance the cause of their Armenian "brothers" across the border, so as to show that they had the community's best interests at heart.

Russia therefore took the lead in designing and proposing a plan, which originated in the Armenian National Assembly, for reform aimed at Ottoman Armenians. The reform plan, named the Mandelstam Plan after the chief dragoman of the Russian embassy, was seen as a way to extend Russian influence in the region. In a secret notice sent by the Russian vice consul at Van to Russian ambassador Giers, in Constantinople, the need to take the initiative was made clear: "We must not allow Britain to oversee the realization of reforms in Kurdistan and Turkish Armenia which lie in the sphere of our political influence. A Russian protectorate for Turkish Armenians is a must; this gives the possibility for the Russian government to have a permanent influence in Turkey. This is one way to penetrate by peaceful means."[83]

The Mandelstam Plan was signed between Russia and the Ottoman Empire in February 1914 after almost a year of deliberations between the two principals as well as Britain, Germany, and France. The negotiations were testy because of the stakes involved, with each power keenly aware of its interests in the region. Russia wanted to expand its influence and placate its Armenian minority; Turkey wanted to minimize foreign involvement on its territory above all else; Germany sought to gain a foothold in the region; and Britain wanted to ensure that neither Russia nor Germany gained too much.[84] The plan that was finally agreed on entailed the creation of two Armenian "zones"—one in the six eastern Armenian *vilayets* and one consisting of Trebizond on the Black Sea—to be administered by two neutral European inspectors at the Porte. The foreign inspectors, nominated by European powers in conjunction with the Ottoman state for a term of five years, were to ensure the execution of liberalization reforms toward the Ottoman Armenian community.[85] The administrators would have the right "to appoint and dismiss all officials and provisional judges" as well as "the command of the gendarmerie and the disposal of the military forces for the maintenance of order." They would govern in consort with a "consultative council," which would include European advisers.

Armed elements of the state such as the police and gendarmerie were to be drawn from the local population, half of which were mandated to be Christians. Official Kurdish militias were to be disbanded. Both Christian and Muslim communities were granted elected assemblies for which they could nominate representatives.[86]

Germany, Britain, and France looked on this plan with considerable trepidation, viewing it as the first step toward the dismemberment of the Ottoman state and a violation of its sovereignty.[87] During the negotiations, German ambassador Wangenheim reported in a cable that "Russia desires an autonomous Armenia . . . [but] autonomy is to be thought of as one step on the path that ultimately leads to Istanbul."[88] Wangenheim claimed elsewhere that "the Armenian question is the key that will open the Straits for Russia," giving a clear indication of the prevailing wisdom in Germany on affairs in Turkey.[89] The plan had also called for a "regional military service" that would ensure order and stability in those regions most susceptible to uprisings, but this element was shot down by the other European powers, who saw it as a step too far.[90] The accord was signed by Turkish and Russian representatives in February 1914.[91]

The Ottoman leadership bristled under the external involvement in their internal affairs. In their collective mind, the Armenians were to blame for internationalizing a domestic issue, and thus causing embarrassment to the state.[92] In addition, it greatly angered them that the reform question was brought up by the Armenians at a time of great national loss for the Ottomans, who had lost considerable swathes of territory in the Balkan wars of 1912. As one minister said, the defeats in the Balkan wars had "turned the heads of Armenian politicians," who saw the confirmation of Turkey's external weakness as an opportunity to press for the redress of grievances at home.[93] Moreover, the constant interference from abroad was difficult to accept for a regime that so prized its national, independent, and modern identity.

That it was the Turks' historical and traditional enemy, Russia, which was behind the chipping away of Ottoman territory and prestige only exacerbated matters.[94] Indeed, the CUP government saw the Mandelstam measures as Russian preparation for annexation of the six Armenian provinces and increased control of the areas bordering Persia. As an editorial in the regime-affiliated newspaper *Tanin* put it, "Europe's intervention and Europe's desire to control our internal affairs is a warning to us to ponder the fate not only of Rumelia [Balkans], but also eastern Turkey, for it will be impossible to spare eastern Turkey the fate awaiting Rumelia."[95] Simple geography played a key role; "the fact that the Christian communities who revolted lived in the border regions of the Empire and that Empire progressively lost territories from the border regions were primary factors determining the policies" of the regime.[96] Armenian allegiance with Turkey's "national enemy" in humiliating the Ottomans ensured that the cognitive conflation between its external enemy and restive minority was all but complete.[97] This conflation would have devastating consequences once the war began, and Russian support for Armenians shot up to "high" levels. Recent research in political science backs this assessment: rather than a long-standing ideological conviction on the part of Ottoman leaders, it was "Russian, and later French, military and diplomatic support of the Armenians—rather than merely the cultural or religious difference between Armenians and Turks per se—that transformed the perception of this group in the eyes Ottoman ruling elites and set the stage" for the genocide.[98]

Overall, then, the "initial rapprochement between the CUP and Armenian nationalists during the Revolution of 1908 in the name of 'Brotherhood and Unity'" gave way to widespread suspicions that the Armenians were poised for a mass uprising, buoyed by the Ottomans' losses of its European provinces as well as increased contact between Russian forces and Armenian dissidents.[99] This fear, often exaggerated but still deeply held, led to drastic and genocidal measures when the level of external threat ramped up with the Ottoman entry, and disastrous losses, in World War I.

The Escalation to Genocide

By the end of 1914, the territorial and ideological changes in the Ottoman state, alongside the scarcely concealed alliance between Armenian nationalists and Russia, increased the baseline level of threat the center perceived from the Armenians. Peaceful reforms were now anathema, the prospect of an Armenian state or anything approximating it deemed impermissible.[100] Gone were the days when the Young Turks considered Armenians a valuable and integral part of the tapestry of the revolutionary state. Now, Armenian identity was deemed directly opposed to the Ottomans' concept of nationhood. Furthermore, the Young Turks' optimism about their external environment had given way to the cold realization of their empire's vulnerability.

With the outbreak of the Great War, which heightened considerably the baseline threat the Armenians posed to the Ottoman Empire, the idea of making concessions that could lead to an Armenian state was out of the question. The security consequences of such an eventuality were simply too grim, as Enver Pasha noted:

In my opinion this is a very big mistake. *If today in the Caucasus a small Armenia possessing a population of five to six hundred thousand and sufficient territory is formed, in the future this government, together with the Armenians that will come mainly from America and from elsewhere, will have a population of millions.* And in the east we will have another Bulgaria and it will be a worse enemy than Russia because all the Armenians' interests and ambitions are in our country. Consequently, in order to remove this danger, the formation of even the smallest Armenian government must be prevented.[101]

The Turks were wary of the prospect of an Armenian state not just because Armenians themselves could cause them great harm in the future, but also because they could partner with others to the same end. For instance, there were concerns expressed that the British and others would use Caucasian Armenia as a base from which to drive out the Turks from eastern Anatolia.[102] Even their decision-making at the end of the war betrayed Ottoman leaders' central preoccupation with the security implications of an Armenian state, when in a bizarre diplomatic volte-face, they *supported* its creation, on one condition: that ethnic Georgians and Azeris join them. This was because at that point, it was clear an Armenian state would come into existence; the only question was its composition. Behind the Ottomans' seemingly curious policy was a transparent aim, to weaken the Russian state from within. More to the point, where the Armenian state was essentially a fait accompli, the Ottoman diplomatic corps attempted to limit the size of the Armenian army, a signal that it was concerned with the security ramifications of Armenian independence.[103]

Before an Armenian state became a cartographic fact, however, the Ottoman Empire used a strategy of "collective repression" in 1914–15 to forestall its creation. This was because Armenian nationalists were supported at "high" levels by Russia during World War I. In other words, Ottoman leaders perceived that cooperation between Russia and the Armenians extended to them fighting side by side. Armenians' collusion with Russia meant that when the war began, they were targeted for extermination and deportation by the Ottoman authorities. During the spring and summer of 1915, both materialist and emotional implications of "high" third-party support were operative. The threat of Armenian collaboration and rebellion, especially given the community's location, ensured a tougher fight for the Ottomans against the Russians. Additionally, "the collective stereotypes of Armenians as grasping and mercenary, subversive and disloyal, turned them into an alien and unsympathetic category that then had to be eliminated."[104] Armenians had been the subject of massacres and violence before, most notably under the regime of the sultan,[105] but the level, intensity, and length of time that they were made victims of genocidal policy was something unprecedented. At the center of it all was the Armenian-Russian partnership, and what it meant for Ottoman security. Below, I develop this argument in four steps.

First, the circumstances under which the genocide unfolded, particularly relating to Russian-Armenian collaboration, need to be closely examined. Second, a look at Ottoman leaders' statements and quotes captures their decision-making processes at the time. Third, the timing of deportations is indicative of the importance of the external peril facing the Empire. Fourth, the location of the major Armenian population centers, on the path of oncoming Russian or British thrusts, alarmed the Ottomans because it exposed their vulnerable supply lines and threatened collaborationist attacks. Taken together, these items constitute strong evidence for the argument that the Armenian genocide was directly related to the Ottomans' external security concerns.

Before we proceed, it is important to note two points. First, the question of whether the Armenian genocide was "preplanned" is contested in the historical literature. There are essentially two views. One claims that the genocide was planned and prepared for before the war broke out, and that the Ottoman authorities waited until the war only to use it as an excuse to carry out a long-held preference for the extermination of the Armenian nation, perhaps to create "space" for a Pan-Turkic empire. This is a view most often, but not exclusively,[106] expressed by scholars sympathetic to Armenia.[107] The other side argues that though the Armenians were subject to much violence and coercion before World War I, the policy of *genocide* and *deportation* arose only as direct responses to conditions of international war. I side with the latter group, and in the following pages show that this side has greater claims to historical accuracy.

The second note to make is to reiterate that an explanation for genocide is in no way commensurate with its justification. My purpose in this chapter is to understand the factors that led to the Ottoman genocide of Armenians, but it is certainly not to suggest that such strategic decisions are moral or excusable under any circumstances. There simply can be no justification for the slaughter of a million noncombatants. Even if one grants the Ottoman state the concession that there existed security exigencies concerning the Russian-Armenian alliance, the reaction to those exigencies was wildly disproportionate. As one historian notes, the allegations of disloyalty and treason aimed at the Ottoman Armenian community were "wholly true in as far as Armenian sentiment went, only partly true in terms of overt acts, and totally insufficient as a justification for what was done."[108] Perhaps more important, the Ottomans' perilous security position in 1914–15, both externally and internally, was in large part its own doing: it joined the war of its own volition to fulfill revisionist aims despite its military and economic weakness relative to European powers, and through decades of vehemently resisting reforms that would improve the lot of its Armenian community, drove it into the arms of its longtime enemy, Russia. Cruelly, the most vulnerable actor in the Russia-Ottoman-Armenia triad was the one that bore the brunt of great power machinations.

WAR, COLLABORATION, AND GENOCIDE

Initially, the Ottoman Empire was neutral in the war, but the desire to oppose Russia was too great, given past hostilities. On October 20, 1914,

Enver Pasha, as the minister of the navy, convinced Jamal Pasha to bombard Russian ports and ships with German ships. As a consequence, Russia declared war on the Ottoman Empire on November 2, 1914. The British and French followed suit on November 5.[109] It would be the tenth time that the Ottomans and Russia were at war in two centuries, but this time, the former's traditional allies, Britain and France, were on the other side. Czar Nicholas II conveyed Russian war aims to the French ambassador: to expel the Turks from Europe, to bring Constantinople under a neutral administration, and to annex Armenia.[110]

Meanwhile, the Ottoman's central concern in the war was to reclaim lost territories and, more broadly, to reclaim its status as a great power—to fight off British and French control of its fiscal policy and European violation of its sovereignty. The Armenian reform agreement signed just the previous year was particular cause for angst, and overturning it, or ignoring it altogether, was one of the driving decisions to enter the war.[111] Barely a month after the Ottomans' entry into the war, the two European inspectors required by the Mandelstam Plan, L. C. Westenenk from the Netherlands and Nicolai Hoff from Norway, were sent home, and the plan as a whole was torn up, by way of an imperial rescript.[112]

Once the war began, the Armenian community was dealt with on the basis of security: would it help provide it, or prove to hinder it? Armenian representatives from all the *vilayets*, but particularly in the Caucasus, rejected the Young Turks' suggestions on cooperating during the war.[113] Their refusal cemented the belief that Armenian nationalism was a proxy of European great powers and morphed into a stereotype of Armenians as collaborators. Upon the war's commencement, Ottoman leaders received reports from the provinces about Armenian collaboration with advancing Russian forces. One telegram from the Interior Ministry to the eastern provinces in August 1914 referenced "completely reliable reports to the effect that the Russians have, through the assistance of the Armenians in the Caucasus, incited the Armenians among us . . . additionally, they have brought weapons and munitions with the intent of depositing them at certain places along the border." Another cable to the eastern provinces evinced considerable concern with Armenian-Russian cooperation, requesting officials "investigate and report back soon . . . on how many Armenian families have as of now left for the Caucasus and whether or not there is such a revolutionary movement or sensibility as this is present among the Armenians living there or if it is limited."[114] In November 1914, the government "was already requesting lists of those of its subjects who had voluntarily gone to Russia, as well as members of their families."[115]

The feelings of suspicion and the belief that the Armenians were fifth columnists were widely held. One cartoon that appeared in a satirical Turkish paper during the war summed up the dominant view in this regard, showing one Turk questioning another about where he gets his news. "I do not need war news," the second Turk replied. "I can follow the course of the war by the expression on the faces of the Armenians I meet. When they are happy I know that the Allies are winning, when depressed I know the Germans had a victory."[116] Certainly the Ottoman authorities had reason to believe that they would face a two-pronged attack, from both within and without.[117] Though Armenians had valiantly fought for the empire in its various wars in the past, the level of Armenian desertions to, and collaboration with, invading Russian forces was rising. Particularly in eastern Anatolia, the Ottomans had justifiable fears of an Armenian revolt being tied to external threats. Up to thirty thousand Armenians formed bands, and were armed and trained across the border in Russia, before returning when the war began.[118] To cite an example of the eagerness with which the Russians and Armenians embraced each other, the czar traveled to the Caucasus to make plans for Russian-Armenian cooperation in preparation for the winter conflict between Russian and Turkish forces in the region. The president of the Armenian National Bureau in Tiflis said in response:

> From all countries Armenians are hurrying to enter the ranks of the glorious Russian Army, with their blood to serve the victory of Russian arms. . . . Let the Russian flag wave freely over the Dardanelles and Bosporus. Let, with Your will, great Majesty, the peoples remaining under the Turkish yoke receive freedom. Let the Armenian people of Turkey who have suffered for the faith of Christ receive resurrection for a new free life under the protection of Russia.[119]

At the onset of the war, the czar also notably promised the Armenian catholicos Kevork V that "a most brilliant future awaits the Armenians" if they allied with the Russians against the Turks.[120] In September, the czar told Armenians that "the eve of liberation from Turkey was nigh," and Russian military plans included the formation of "armed Armenian bands under military command in the Caucasus at Olty, Sarikamish, Kagysman, and Igdyr, and, in Persia, bands at Choi and Dilman under the authority of the Russian military and the Choi consulate."[121] Within the specter of war, however, these promises of support from the Russian side and desertions from the Armenian side spelled disaster for the Armenians, since it completed the cognitive tying together of their cause with the Russians: perceptions of third-party support were locked at "high" levels.

It is important to note that Turkish accusations of desertions and Armenian soldiers passing over to Russian territory are corroborated by American, German, and Austrian sources, as well as prominent Armenian nationalists themselves, like Nubar. The historical record shows, among other instances, that the well-known Armenian partisan Andranik helped the Russian forces invading Saray, east of Van province, from Persian Choi, and that another group of Armenian volunteers joined the Russian forces in occupying Bayazid, in the north.[122] In a cable from early February 1915, Ambassador Wangenheim conveyed to officials in Germany that "I constantly come up against an opinion among the Turks, which until now has not been refuted by the behavior of the Armenians, that if Turkey is defeated, the Armenian population would definitely join the winner's side."[123]

Young Turk leaders, then, "were convinced that all Armenians were potentially disloyal and likely to be pro-Russian."[124] Such Armenian-Russian collaboration was deeply concerning to Ottoman leaders—enough for Talaat, at the beginning of the war, to demand that Germany offer Russia parts of occupied Poland if it would translate into Russia's withdrawal from any part of the Ottoman Armenian *vilayets*. He also asked that the Germans evacuate parts of Flanders as a quid pro quo for the British to leave Iraq.[125] At the same time, the Ministry of War created the Secret Organization for the purpose of dealing with security threats throughout the empire. One of the first tasks that the Secret Organization concerned itself with—in addition to the Greek community in western Anatolia—was how to disentangle the Armenian community in eastern Anatolia from the territory in question, owing to its proximity to Russia.[126] Prominent members of the Armenian political community and intellectuals were to be closely monitored.[127] In addition, the Ministry of War, under Enver's direction, also created a series of paramilitary youth groups, supplying them with arms and ammunition for the "defense of the fatherland." Enver also ensured that the CUP maintained greater control of the military than previously by culling the old regime of officers—he fired eleven hundred in January 1914 alone—and promoting hundreds of loyalists to high-ranking positions.[128]

The killings of Armenians started in the late summer of 1914. In the border regions of the Caucasus and Persia, Armenian property was looted and plundered, and Armenian men were rounded up and killed, by militias and small bands of forces. At that point, the killings had not yet attained the massive scale they would later. Rather, the genocide proper began in the spring of 1915 as a series of massacres in sensitive border regions most vulnerable to external intervention.[129] The killings then spread south and west from eastern Anatolia, where the largest share of the Armenian population lived. In all, more than 1 million Armenians died in the genocide, more than two-thirds of whom met their fate as a direct result of being deported.[130] Most of the violence was carried out by paramilitary organizations and through secret orders.[131]

Balakian summarizes how the genocide unfolded:

> Armenians were rounded up, arrested, and either shot outright or put on deportation marches. Most often the able-bodied men were arrested in

groups and taken out of the town or city and shot en masse. The women, children, infirm, and elderly were given short notice that they could gather some possessions and would be deported with the other Armenians of their city or town to what they were told was the "interior." Often they were told that they would be able to return when the war was over. . . .

A map of the Armenian genocide shows that deportations and massacre spanned the length and width of Turkey. In the west the major cities included Constantinople, Smyrna, Ankara, and Konia. Moving eastward, Yozgat, Kayseri, Sivas, Tokat, and Amasia were among the large cities of massacre and deportation. Along the Black Sea, Samsun, Ordu, Trbizond, and Rize were killing stations where Armenians were often taken out in boats and drowned. In the south, in historic Cilician Armenia, Adana, Hadjin, Zeitun, Marash, and Aintab were part of the massacre network. The traditional Armenian *vilayets* in the east—Sivas, Harput, Diyarbekir, Bitlis, Erzurum, Van—with hundreds of villages and dozens of cities, where the majority of the Armenian population of the empire lived on their historic land, were almost entirely depleted of their Armenian populations.[132]

The forced marches exacted such a high toll because they were through rough terrain in difficult weather, with no medical support or protection against marauders.[133] First person testimony is sparse for obvious reasons, but some survivor's tales have made it through the test of time. One memoir, for instance, describes a typical scene following a deportation order:

> As I now recall that day, there is a trembling in my body. The human mind is unable to bear such heaviness. My pen cannot describe the horrors. Confusion! Chaos! Woe! Wailing! Weeping! The father kisses his wife and children and departed, sobbing, encrazed. The son kissed his mother, his old father, his small sisters and brothers, and departed. Those who went and those who remained sobbed. Many left with no preparation, with only the clothes on their backs, the shoes on their feet, lacking money, lacking food, some without even seeing their loved ones. Already thousands of men had gathered in the appointed place, and like madmen, others were joining them.[134]

THE MINDSET OF OTTOMAN LEADERS IN 1914–15

Why did the Ottoman Empire commit genocide against its Armenians? Ottoman leaders were obsessed with the prospect of territorial loss, and the potential of Armenians to aid in their state's dismemberment by collaborating with Russia. The specific personalities behind the policies that led to genocide offer a clue as to its origins: by most accounts, Enver Pasha, the minister of war, and Talaat Pasha, the minister of interior, were behind the mass deportations, lending credence to the belief that the deportations were a security issue, rather than an ideological one.[135] Unfortunately, it is difficult to ascertain the exact processes by which the triumvirate of Enver, Talaat, and Jamal made decisions because archival records within the Ottoman state were either lost or destroyed in a period of chaos.[136] However, that these leaders consistently maintained both publicly and privately that their drastic measures against the Armenian population were primarily due to the wartime situation and the existential threat the state faced given Armenian-Russian collusion is instructive. Their particular emphasis on the threat posed by Armenians in their rear, as they faced the Russians in the Caucasus and the British in Palestine, suggests that the material effects of "high" third-party support were especially important. Alongside this material effect of Russian backing, Talaat's and Enver's statements also stress the emotional consequences of collusion that Armenians experienced: an angry and betrayed state.

Take, for instance, Talaat's warning to an Armenian representative in a moment of candor: "We will do whatever Turkey's interests demand, it is a matter of one's fatherland. There is no place for personal attachments. Do not forget how you jumped at our throats and stirred up the problem of Armenian reforms in the days of our weakness."[137] Elsewhere Talaat stated that "it was deemed necessary, in order to avoid the possibility of our army being caught between two fires, to remove the Armenians from all scenes of the war and the neighborhood of the railways."[138] After the Armenian uprising at Van, timed to coincide with the Russian invasion, Enver revealingly told Ambassador Morgenthau in a private meeting that

> the Armenians had a fair warning of what would happen to them in case they joined our enemies. Three months ago I sent for the Armenian Patriarch and I told him that if the Armenians attempted to start a revolution or to assist the Russians, I would be unable to prevent mischief from happening to them. My warning produced no effect and the Armenians started a revolution and helped the Russians. You know what happened at Van. They obtained control of the city, used bombs against government buildings, and killed a large number of Moslems. We knew that they were planning uprisings in other places. You must understand that we are fighting for our lives . . . and that we are sacrificing thousands of men. While we are engaged in a struggle such as this, we cannot permit people in our own country to attack us in the back. We have got to prevent this no matter what means we have to resort to. It is absolutely true that I am not opposed to the Armenians as a people. I have the greatest admiration for their intelligence and industry, and I should like nothing better than to see them become a real part of our nation. But if they ally themselves with our enemies, as they did in the Van district, they will have to be destroyed.[139]

As Enver said, treatment of secessionist minorities in war time obeyed different logics than during peace, when the external threat was not as significant: "During peace times we can use Platonic means to quiet Armenians and Greeks, but in time of war we cannot investigate and negotiate. We must act promptly and with determination." On another occasion, he reiterated the importance of war and external security on their decision-making process: "Our situation is desperate, I admit it, and we are fighting as desperate men fight. We are not going to let the Armenians attack us in the rear."[140] In a cable to most of the Ottoman provinces, Talaat echoed this logic, writing that "the objective that the government expects to achieve by the expelling of the Armenians from the areas in which they live and their transportation to other appointed areas is to ensure that this community will no longer be able to undertake initiatives and actions against the government, and that they will be brought to a state in which they will be unable to pursue their national aspirations related to the advocating for a[n independent] government of Armenia."[141]

Talaat stuck to similar themes in conversations with Morgenthau: "These people refused to disarm when we told them to. They opposed us at Van and at Zeitoun, and they helped the Russians. There is only one way in which we can defend ourselves against them in the future, and that is just to deport them."[142] He later drew a direct connection between the Armenian relationship with the Russians on the one hand, and the Turkish performance in the war: "They have openly encouraged our enemies. They have assisted the Russians in the Caucasus and our failure there is largely explained by their actions. We have therefore come to the irrevocable decision that we shall make them powerless before this war is ended."[143] After a private meeting with Talaat during the war, U.S. ambassador Morgenthau reported that "he [Talaat] explained his [Armenian] policy on the ground that the Armenians were in constant correspondence with the Russians."[144] Enver was similarly forthcoming with Morgenthau: "If the Armenians made any attack on the Turks or rendered any assistance to the Russians while the war was pending, [I] will be compelled to use extreme measures against them."[145] Those words proved to be prophetic.[146]

TIMING OF GENOCIDE: MOMENT OF NATIONAL PERIL

One could reasonably object to the above with the proposition that Enver and Talaat were employing justificatory rhetoric for decisions that had little to do with security. If their statements were mere window dressing, however, then how is one to explain that the timing of the genocide coincided with a security emergency for the Ottomans?

Indeed, it was only by the summer of 1915 that a clear and coherent policy of empirewide killings and massacres even developed. The deportations, the single leading cause of death of Armenians in World War I, began a full seven months after Turkey's entry into the war.[147] Generally speaking, the policy of genocide was instituted only in a period of national peril, between April and June 1915, when the Ottomans were on the back foot in the war. As one international relations scholar notes, "The radicalization [of Ottoman policy] seems to have occurred in large part in response to the Turks' rapidly deteriorating military situation."[148] Part of the Turks' worsening security was down to their own strategic myopia—Enver Pasha, for instance, chose the wintertime in 1914–15 to launch an attack on Russia's Caucasus region. Despite some initial success, he lost more than seventy-five thousand out of ninety thousand men, mainly due to the weather. Moreover, the Russian general Yudenich foresaw Enver's encirclement strategy, was prepared adequately, and dealt a crushing blow to Enver's forces.[149] It must be noted, however, that the Russians were aided in considerable part by six Armenian volunteer units, of eight to ten thousand men each, who were familiar with the terrain, and were useful as scouts, guides, and advance guards. After the Battle of Sarikamish, which effectively ended the Turkish fight in the Caucasus, the Armenian units received high praise from Russian military commanders and even the czar. The loss at Sarikamish, and the wider loss in the Caucasus generally, was pinned on Armenians by Enver—even if his own decision-making was largely to blame.[150] Regardless of culpability for the loss, the bottom line was that "the disaster at Sarikamish left just some fifty-two thousand Ottoman soldiers spread over a six-hundred-kilometer front facing the much better equipped Russia's Caucasus Army with roughly seventy-eight thousand effective combatants."[151] In addition, immediately after Enver's failure in the Caucasus, the Ottoman army's campaign in Persia failed. Enver's brother in law, Jevdet Bey, was compelled to withdraw and retreat from Tabriz.[152] The devastating battlefield losses in January 1915 planted the first seeds of what was to come.[153] As a result of the defeat, and in conjunction with earlier desertions, Armenian soldiers were disarmed and Armenian villages were massacred by retreating Turk forces,[154] the first set of large-scale massacres against Armenians during the war.

More generally, the spring of 1915 was a time of considerable danger for the Ottoman state, since it faced invasion on three fronts: the British and French in the West, at the Dardanelles; the British in the South, in Iraq; and the Russians in the east.[155] In February the Royal Navy launched the first attack on the Dardanelles. Britain and France had planned an amphibious assault, aimed at taking the Dardanelles on the way to Istanbul, establishing a "critical supply route to Russia."[156] Concomitantly, the allies were bombarding, and later landing, on the beaches north of Çanakkale. These allied movements "led the Unionists to believe that the end of the empire was certainly at hand."[157] Ottoman forces were also compelled to retreat from the Suez Canal in early February, while the British Indian Army attacked the Ottomans through central Iraq, occupying Basra in November. All the while, the weakness and lack of development insofar as the Ottoman economy and infrastructure was concerned only exacerbated the status quo, since it meant that provisions from the capital to the periphery declined both in quality and quantity.[158]

March 1915 was a turning point, with the Dardanelles attack in the foreground along with a Russian move toward Van. Concurrent with "the British coming up from the south, and the British and French landing at Gallipoli in April," the government prepared to move the capital from Istanbul to the east and make a "last stand" in the Anatolian interior.[159] As one scholar puts it, "The Ottoman Empire was being pinched in three directions at once. The Fourth Army in Syria and the Sixth in Mesopotamia were both in danger of being cut off owing to partisan attacks . . . in the worst position of all, however, was the Third Army facing the Russians, who were advancing against a beaten and battered enemy on both the northern (Erzurum) and southern front (Dilman-Van)."[160] These developments "cast panic into the hearts and minds of the CUP leaders" because they reaffirmed their fears of a "nightmare scenario in which potential Armenian disloyalty would pave the way for an Allied incursion into Anatolia." Consequently, the Special Organization—in charge of irregular paramilitary units—was reorganized and expanded to deal with the increasing threat.[161] As Suny argues, Ottoman leaders were both fearful and angry: afraid of the future of their state and angry "at the perceived betrayal metamorphosed into hatred of those who by their nature were devious and treacherous."[162]

Deportations were a result of this toxic mix of fear and anger. On April 8, there were "targeted" deportations from Zeytun and Maras, both sites of Armenian uprisings. On April 24–25, the night of the Allied landings at Gallipoli, Armenians in Constantinople were arrested and, more important, Talaat and Enver issued decrees ordering the reduction of Armenians to less than 10 percent of the population in frontier districts and frontline areas. On May 2, after the rebellion at Van, the entire Armenian population of Van was removed. Later, these relatively ad-hoc measures, gave way to "more systematic overtones."[163] First, the deportees from Zeytun, Maras, and Van were rerouted from the original destinations to Urfa and Aleppo, before it was decided to send them even further south, to the Syrian desert. Then, Talaat issued his famous decree of May 31, which called for the deportation of Armenians in the six eastern provinces away from frontline areas, to areas at least twenty-five kilometers away from rail lines. In June and July, Armenian uprisings behind Ottoman lines led to the deportation net being thrown wider still: it now included Samsun, Sivas, Trabzon, and the port cities on the Mediterranean, Mersin and Adana.[164]

The timing of the first deportation orders, and their ensuing escalation, lends strong support to the argument that external security considerations were a key driving force for the genocide. It was only when the Ottoman Empire was on the back foot in the war—after disastrous losses in the winter of 1914–15 and the prospect of being pinned between three fronts in

CHAPTER 4

March–April 1915—that Ottoman leaders began their policy of "collective repression" against their Armenian community. That the timing of this escalation so closely coincided with wartime fears of the end of the Ottoman Empire draws into sharp question the view that the Armenian genocide was unrelated to security concerns.

LOCATION OF DEPORTATIONS: SUPPLY LINES AND ALLIED INCURSIONS

Talaat stated that "if war is declared, Armenian soldiers will take shelter on the enemy side with their arms. If the Ottoman army advances, [they will] remain inactive, if the Ottoman army retreats, [they will] form armed bands and hinder transport and communication" (quoted in Bloxham 2003, 163). There is considerable evidence that the Armenians provided exactly such support, impeding the Ottoman war effort. The threat of Armenian collaboration was especially problematic because they were concentrated in locations that alternately posed a threat to Ottoman supply lines, or could serve as springboards for landings and incursions by the Russians, British, and/or French. As such, even the slightest suspicion of collusion was enough to radicalize Ottoman leaders during wartime—the stakes were simply too high, and the costs of being insufficiently concerned too weighty, to contemplate half measures.

The geographic logistics of the Ottoman war effort are crucial when understanding the roots of the genocide. Erickson sums up the Ottoman predicament:

> The Ottomans were fighting the Russians on the Caucasian frontier, and the British in Mesopotamia and Palestine. The lines of communication supporting those Ottoman fronts ran directly through the rear areas of the Ottoman armies in eastern Anatolia that were heavily populated by Armenian communities and, by extension, by the heavily armed Armenian revolutionary committees. Importantly, none of the Ottoman armies on the fronts in Caucasia, Mesopotamia, or Palestine were self-sufficient in food, fodder, ammunition, or medical supplies and all were depending on the roads and railroads leading west to Constantinople and Thrace for those supplies. Moreover, none of these forces had much in the way of prepositioned supplies available and all required the continuous flow of war material. The Armenian revolutionary committees began to attack and cut these lines of communication in the spring of 1915.[165]

Rebellious Armenians threatened Ottoman prospects in war because of where the war was being fought and where the Armenians were concentrated: at the rear of the major fronts the Ottomans were fighting on. As Suny notes, "The Caucasian front was the longest front for the Ottomans and the most difficult to defend and supply. The Ottoman-Russian border stretched 280 miles, but the zone of fighting extended twice that distance, deep into Ottoman territory and Persia," a "frontier region with porous borders."[166]

Armenian regions posed special dangers to the empire's rail system, the Ottomans' "'Achilles Heel' because it served almost the entire logistics needs of the three Ottoman field armies in the Caucasian, Mesopotamian, and Palestinian theaters of operations (the Third, Sixth, and Fourth armies respectively)."[167] The fact that Talaat's deportation orders emphasized Armenians be resettled "at least twenty-five kilometers away from the Baghdad railway lines running to the frontier as well as away from other railway lines" is instructive: such a distance would be near impossible to traverse safely in one night's darkness, suggesting that security was a key imperative for Talaat's orders.[168] The region of Dortyol, for instance, was a pressing concern both because it was located on the Mediterranean, and thus inviting to Allied incursions, and also because it was where the so-called "Berlin-Baghdad" railway split. Troubles in Dortyol occupied the attention of security bulletins and cables from Enver and Talaat in March and April in 1915, resulting in the deportation of Armenian communities from Dortyol and the nearby Alexandretta, Adana, and Bilan districts. In addition to the rail network, sizable Armenian populations were located on or close to the main road links from Sivas to Erzurum, which supplied the Ottoman Third Army in the Caucasus.[169] The relative importance of these supply lines increased in the aftermath of Enver's loss at Sarikamish, which moved the front to the lowland Urmia region. Urmia lay at the intersection of the Ottoman, Russian, and Persian empires, "ground zero in the Russo-Turkish espionage and propaganda wars over the loyalties" of Kurds, Armenians, and Assyrians.[170] As such, Ottoman leaders' deportation orders in the spring of 1915 could legitimately be seen as securing the "tactical rear of the Third and Fourth Armies" in the Caucasus and Mesopotamia/Palestine (see map 2).[171]

Aside from these general concerns about supply lines and railroads, Armenian uprisings in several prominent locations catalyzed Ottoman paranoia and fear, as the massacres in Van illustrate. Van was a crucial strategic location, important for its connection to Russian military plans, as well as its ability to rise up militarily based on it being armed and trained. It could be used by Russian forces launching into Mesopotamia and interior eastern Anatolia from Persia, or by the Turkish forces in the opposite direction.[172] It was a significant military pivot, and its importance grew only after the defeat at Sarikamish. Specifically, as the center of gravity of the Ottoman-Russian war shifted south from the winter to the spring, the Ottoman defeat at Dilman in late April increased the significance of Van, which was now "directly in the path opened up by the Russian victory at Dilman."[173] Van had a dense Armenian population, and a significant Armenian Revolutionary Federation presence, one that had established prewar connections to the Russian consulate. Demographically, the Armenian population was greater than the Turkish and Kurdish population combined, further increasing its importance.[174]

In the spring of 1915, the CUP correctly anticipated a massive Allied offensive: while Russia was preparing to launch aggressively in the Caucasus, the British and French were expected to stage landings at Gallipoli on April 25. Turkish commanders had often spoken about the threat of insurrection in Van, and when news spread of Armenian collaboration with Russian forces, Ottoman forces turned their attention to the region. As preemptive measures, the authorities carried out mass arrests in the Armenian parts of Van on April 24, similar to the mass arrests carried out in Trebizond on April 19, which immediately preceded the Russian attack on the port of Kerasond/Giresun on April 20.[175] These arrests represented the first step in the escalation in Van. Along with the arrests, the government demanded that the city hand over four thousand Armenian men for the army's labor battalions. Van's leaders surmised that those men would ultimately be killed, since that was the usual fate of Armenians in labor battalions all over the empire, and asked that the men instead be used for combat duty, but their request was refused. The Armenians then counteroffered with a proposal of handing over four hundred men, with the justification that the rest were exempt due to payment of a tax, but Jevdet Bey, now the governor of Van province, refused to budge.[176] Concomitant with the mass arrests, the Armenian community in Van staged an uprising. On April 20, 1915, four thousand Armenian fighters fired at police stations, set alight Muslim houses, and set up a barricade behind which they stayed on the defensive. An additional fifteen thousand Armenian refugees soon joined the rebellion. Turkish forces suffered huge losses in trying to stamp out the rebellion and inflicted mass casualties of their own. The fighting went on for a month.[177]

With their ammunition running low, the Armenians were saved by the advancing Russian army, which forced the retreat of the Turkish units. The Russians' advance itself was aided in considerable part by both Russian and Ottoman Armenians. Armenian units were especially useful as bands of shock troops, as well as guides to the area, and were crucial to the Russian advance. The entire episode—from the initial insurrection to the joint invasion of Van—was believed to be a coordinated rather than a random coincidence, even by foreign diplomats on the scene sympathetic to the Armenians. This, then, crystallized for the Turkish state the belief that the Armenians were traitors against whom strong action would be justified.[178]

During the conclusive days of the fighting in Van, the Ottomans brutally followed the Russian line of attack with massacres and deportations. As U.S. ambassador Morgenthau cabled in June 1915, "Because Armenian volunteers, many of them Russian subjects, have joined Russian Army in Caucasus and because some have been implicated in armed revolutionary movements and others have been helpful to Russians in their invasion of

Van district, terrible vengeance is being taken."[179] German diplomats also backed this interpretation. On May 8, Ambassador Wangenheim cabled that "despite efforts by Armenian circles to diminish the significance of the riots which have broken out over the past few weeks in various places or to put the blame on the measures taken by Turkish authorities, there are increasingly more signs that this movement is more widespread than presumed up to now and that it is being encouraged from abroad with the help of Armenian revolutionary committees . . . it cannot be denied that the Armenian movement has taken on a worrying character over the past few weeks, which has given the government cause to introduce severe repressive measures."[180] As Reynolds notes, "At the same time as the Van rebellion was unfolding, the Russians were entering from the east, the British pushing on Baghdad from the south, and most ominously, the British and French were storming ashore at Gallipoli. The simultaneous attacks stretched the wobbling Ottoman army to breaking point."[181] Van was a crucial step in the escalation to genocide mainly because it confirmed the worst suspicions of the Ottomans, and that too at a strategically vulnerable time in the war.[182] One historian of the genocide calls the Van insurrection the "turning point" as far as the deportations and massacres were concerned.[183]

Van was not the only geographic area where massacres and deportations followed the external security threat. One can also consider Cilicia. At the end of March 1915, the Ottomans feared that the Russians would make incisions through eastern Anatolia in a bid to capture the port city of Alexandretta/Iskenderun, because it represented the shortest route to bisect the empire and acquire a Mediterranean port. Indeed, the Russians themselves had advertised this strategy before the war. The Armenian population in Cilicia had a complicated history with respect to inviting outsider intervention to help their cause, and Ottoman authorities claimed that an uprising was to be timed to coincide with the Russian invasion. Some historians have dismissed those claims as pure propaganda, but Nubar was in contact with the British military in Egypt and floated the idea of the Armenian community in Cilicia being a bridgehead for invading Entente forces. The British had asked the Armenians to "revolt to make things more difficult for the government, and support the British by hindering [the government's] efforts to mobilize."[184] Cilicia was consequently targeted with massacres and deportations.[185]

There was a similar story in Zeytun, where the fear of desertions and collaborations fed into the stereotype of Armenians as the "enemy within."[186] Before the war even began, there were signs of organized revolt; Armenians in Zeytun refused to be conscripted in the Ottoman Army and organized a corps of volunteers in order to disrupt Ottoman lines of communication. During the war, in May 1915, there was a second uprising in Zeytun, an episode which led to the formal introduction of deportation laws on

May 27, with the purpose of drawing Armenian populations away from strategically important areas.[187] As Enver told Ambassador Morgenthau, "We shall not permit them to cluster in places where they can plot mischief and help our enemies. So we are going to give them new quarters."[188] This was essentially the final nail in the Armenians' collective coffin, since the general deportation orders spelled doom for the community. By June, the deportations were in full swing across the empire; only 20 percent of the deportees would even reach their desert destinations.[189]

The case of Adapazari, in northwest Anatolia, where the deportations began in July 1915, also followed this trend. Enver and Talaat believed that an Armenian rebellion was being planned in conjunction with an expected Russian landing on the Black Sea. "Talaat's memoirs, as well as other wartime publications, offered evidence of escalating guerilla activity on the provincial border between Bursa and Izmit, as well as the discovery of hidden weapons caches throughout the region. Indeed, several secret telegrams confirm cases of Armenian bandit activity in Bursa and Izmit in 1915 and 1916," though it should be noted that these reports were filed after the deportations had already begun.[190]

That the massacres and violence were proceeding in step with the external threat is shown not just by where the violence occurred but where it failed to occur.[191] For example, between March 5 and March 17 in 1915, there was to be a joint British and French attack on the Dardanelles, to relieve pressure on Russia's forces in the Caucasus. As a preemptive measure, authorities were given orders to carry out deportations—which, we must remember, almost always meant death for the deportees[192]—in the region between Constantinople and the new provisional government base in Eskishehir. The point was to ensure that the Armenians did not join invading forces and conduct reprisal operations against the population transfer of citizens, as the Ottomans wished to move their capital from Constantinople given the expected Anglo-French attack. But when the anticipated breakthrough did not occur, the population transfer, and attendant massacres, also failed to materialize, suggesting that "Armenian policy was still contingent on the course of the War, and was not fully proactive or general across the empire."[193]

Certainly once the genocide achieved its own momentum, it bore less of a relationship to an external threat, especially after June 1915. It is also true that the cleansing of Armenians served the purpose of creating a more ethnically homogenous territory on which to base the modern Turkish state.[194] Finally, there is little doubt that the Ottoman leadership could have arranged for deportations that did not necessarily result in mass death, but chose not to, almost assuredly due to a vicious antipathy against Armenians.[195] But these qualifications aside, the spread of violence in 1915 shows that the escalation to deportations and massacres occurred as preemptive measures against a foreign military threat. "High" levels of Russian support for Armenian nationalists resulted in a tougher fight for the Ottoman Empire, owing primarily to Armenians' location and potential for insurrection, as well as angry and emotional leaders bent on vengeance. As German ambassador Wolff-Metternich reported after a conversation with Talaat in late 1915, "In the districts on the Russian border and near Aleppo, mass displacements had been necessary on the grounds of military security. A Russian-engineered large-scale conspiracy among the Gregorian Armenians in the border areas and near Aleppo had been discovered. Attacks on bridges and railways had been planned. It had been impossible to single out any individual culprit from the masses of these people. Only the deportation of the whole could ensure security."[196]

Moreover, in addition to the direct effects of collaboration, the indirect effects were important for external security too. The very existence of Armenian revolts in the empire meant that Turkish forces were often withdrawn from the front to deal with the uprisings, thus rendering them even more vulnerable to the external threat.[197] For example, the rebellion in Van forced the Turks to reposition forces from strategically vulnerable campaigns in the Caucasus region and Persia to suppress the insurrection, fueling the belief that the Armenians were causing them considerable losses in the war.[198]

When the violence took place, where it took place, and where it did not take place—each of these factors supports Enver and Talaat's claims that the Armenian genocide was a product of external security considerations. The Ottoman Empire escalated to deportations only at the height of its external vulnerability, after battles at Sarikamish and the Dardanelles. Its policies were first enacted in those areas most vulnerable to Armenian sabotage and collaboration with oncoming Russian forces and were not executed where the external threat was deemed less important. The Ottoman Empire used a policy of collective repression against its Armenian community because of "high" levels of support from Russia, whose men often fought alongside or in sequence with Armenian bands, in a war that threatened the very existence of the state. Because this war and the Russian-Armenian alliance closely succeeded the Balkan wars and the Russian-dictated Mandelstam Plan, which cemented CUP beliefs that the Armenians were both a short-term and long-term threat to Ottoman security, the Armenians were targeted with genocide.

Scholarly consensus supports these views. According to Holquist, when it came to the slaughter of the Armenian population, "Russia's role—both in terms of intended and unintended consequences—was greater than that of any other party, aside from the CUP itself."[199] As Bloxham notes, "The stereotype of Armenians as proxies of the Great powers in peacetime was extended into a stereotype of military collaboration during warfare: the 'inner enemy' and the 'outer enemy' were now fully merged in the Ottoman mind."[200] Even those scholars that believe the genocide was "premeditated" concede the importance of the external security angle, as Kirakossian does when he writes that the Young Turks "were positive that in the forthcoming war the Armenians would become a threatening force in the enemy camp and considered it urgent to prevent them from taking unified action."[201]

Generally, Western scholars maintain that the deportations and massacres were not an a priori plan of action, but rather a result of a series of more limited measures that culminated in genocide.[202] They were instituted because of the "mortal danger from without" that the Ottomans faced, in combination with Armenian collaboration.[203] Gwynne Dyer, one of the foremost historians on the genocide, puts it thusly:

> there was a genuine, though mistaken, belief among the Ottoman leaders in Istanbul that there was a deliberate and coordinated Armenian uprising in the East, with Empire-wide ramifications. . . .
>
> When more work is completed on the period, I believe historians will come to see Talaat, Enver, and their associates not so much as evil men but as desperate, frightened, unsophisticated men struggling to keep their nation afloat in a crisis far graver than they had anticipated when they first entered the war (the Armenian decisions were taken at the height of the Dardanelles), reacting to events rather than creating them, and not fully realizing the extent of the horrors they had set in motion in 'Turkish Armenia' until they were too deeply committed to withdraw.[204]

Armenian historians often claim that the deportations were a result simply of anti-Christian nationalism, but they are unable to explain why the Young Turks "cast both Muslims (Turkish-speaking or otherwise) and Christians in the same sinister light."[205] There simply does not exist strong historical evidence to suggest that before the war broke out, the Ottoman state planned for or wished to carry out genocide. In northwestern Anatolia, for instance, "CUP policies towards Armenians were intertwined with aims that were more operational in nature than ideological. The logic encased within state directives from this period emphasizes, above all things, the need for security within this critical region."[206] As Mann sums up, initially the policy of forcible deportations "was designed to move potentially disloyal Armenians away from the theater of war so that they could not interfere with it."[207]

Alternative Explanations

The main theoretical alternatives to mine cannot explain why the Ottoman Empire went from a policy of peaceful concessions to genocide. The reputation argument would predict more violence earlier in the Young Turks' tenure to establish a deterrent; in this case, the opposite took place. The argument for veto points, meanwhile, cannot explain the observed variation because the Young Turks' increasing centralization of power meant that there were fewer veto points to stop their offering concessions— had they wished for such a course. Under conditions of a low number of veto players, the domestic-institutions argument would expect the possibility of concessions to be negated by their incredibility to the secessionists due to the absence of veto points. However in this case, the leadership did not even consider such a concessionary policy, let alone desire it.

The principal competing context-specific explanation—that the Armenian genocide was "preplanned" sometime between 1910 and 1912—does not stand up to historical scrutiny. Scholars who wish to make this case rely on "secret" schemes and speeches given at the CUP congresses in 1910 and 1911, records for which do not exist. Notwithstanding the CUP's less pluralist nature over time—there was increasing talk of "Turkifying Armenians"—this view does not imply an intent to murder an entire community.[208] As Bloxham states, "Despite the great deterioration of CUP-Armenian relations, there is little evidence that a policy physically to destroy the community was forged prior to the First World War."[209] Scholars from the "preplanned" camp overstate the consistency of Young Turk policy between 1908 and 1915; their repeated efforts to find the proverbial smoking-gun evidence of orders for extermination of a people does not convince.[210] Moreover, the very notion of a single turning point in the fate of the Armenians is problematic from a historiographical perspective, since rather than resulting from one decision on a given date, the genocide unfolded cumulatively as a process, or "cascading sequence of events."[211] "Pre-planned" scholars' approach tends to be teleological" as Mann notes. "Early events, early decisions are too often read back from the ghastly known end result."[212] These analysts employ as a starting point the final destruction of the Ottoman Armenian community and works backward to locate "violent expressions in the perpetrators' early speeches and writings, treating them as a 'serious declaration of intent.'"[213] It is difficult to accept for some that such a far-reaching set of decisions could be made on a relatively contingent basis, without any grand purposes of social engineering behind it and affected primarily by the ebbs and flows of war, but the historical record suggests that is exactly what happened.

The theoretical framework employed in this book goes a long way in explaining variation in the Young Turks' strategy to deal with the so-called Armenian question. When they first ascended to power, the Young Turks forwarded a more universalist, Ottoman identity for all subjects of the empire and dealt with Armenian demands peacefully. The indifferent identity division, combined with a general optimism about the future of the modernizing Ottoman state, allowed for a policy of negotiations and concessions, reflected in the support they got from Armenian revolutionary parties.

However, between then and 1915, two major changes occurred from the regime's perspective. First, Armenian demands were now cast in a more threatening light—since they were the only main Christian community left in the empire, their demands now threatened the ideational basis of the new, more narrowly defined Turkish nationalism of the empire. That is, the identity division between Ottomans and Armenians became "opposed." Additionally, a series of territorial losses changed the erstwhile optimistic outlook of the Ottoman leadership to a more insecure one. This meant that the prospect of a future Armenian state suddenly assumed graver security implications. Second, World War I, and in particular, its alliance patterns, which saw Russia against the Ottoman Empire, threatened the very existence of the Ottoman state. This external threat was given a considerable boost, both in reality and in perception, by Armenian nationalists, who fought alongside Russian forces. Because the level of third-party support they enjoyed was "high," there were to be no distinctions drawn between the Armenian "citizens" and the foreign enemy of Russia. As far as the regime was concerned, Armenians and Russians were one and the same. As such, when the state's security was at its bleakest, in the spring of 1915, the vicious policy of deportations was instituted across areas of the empire deemed most vulnerable to external intervention.

Peaceful and Violent Separatism in North America, Europe, and the Middle East, 1861–1993

Can my theory explain secessionist violence, or the complete lack thereof, in vastly different regions and eras? To that end, I proceed in three sections.

In the first, I turn my attention to the Israeli-Palestinian conflict since the 1980s. This conflict allows a direct comparison of my theory with its primary competitor, the reputation argument. As a binational state, one that is a "liberal" democracy no less, Israel would be expected to treat an independence movement with little recourse to violence. Given there is no possible ethnic group other than the Palestinians that would demand statehood on land controlled by Israel, it need not be concerned with establishing a tough reputation against independence movements. My argument would predict the opposite, given Israel's security concerns with the prospect of an independent Palestine. Second, despite being one of the most important geopolitical disputes today, easily fulfilling the "intrinsic importance" criterion whose use methodologists encourage,[1] students of secessionist violence have strangely ignored it. This may be because the Israeli-Palestinian dispute may not strike some as obviously "secessionist"—notwithstanding datasets on secessionism including both the first and second intifadas.[2] Such a view would be wrongheaded, however: the fight between Israel and Palestinians is over whether the latter can establish a state on territory controlled by the former, the very definition of a secessionist conflict. As I discuss below, Israel's coercive response to Palestinians' secessionist moment, the first intifada, is consistent with my theory's expectations, when it chose such a strategy because of security fears. These fears sprung from its rough neighborhood, featuring a history of warfare with its neighbors, and its essentializing of Palestinian nationalism, subsuming it under an "Arab" identity. In keeping with its "policing" strategy, coercion was relatively low, and Israel additionally offered tactical concessions to moderate Palestinian nationalists, at Oslo, that fell well short of statehood. That said, it is important to acknowledge that factors that lie outside the explanatory range of my theory, such as the rise of the religious-nationalist settler lobby in Israel, and the Palestinians' ability to manufacture violence despite little third-party support, are also important to the development of the conflict, especially in the last two decades. Nevertheless, the issue of security generally looms large when one considers Israeli intransigence in the face of Palestinian demands for a state, both in the twentieth and twenty-first centuries.

I then examine two of the handful of completely peaceful major secessions to occur in the twentieth century, one in 1993 that dissolved Czechoslovakia into its constituent units, and the other in 1905 that separated Norway and Sweden. It is important, after all, that a theory purporting to explain the variation in state response to secessionism is able to offer insight on the cases in which the state did not seriously consider violence, let alone use it. Methodologists have noted that social science should be "concerned not only with cases where something 'happened,' but also with cases where something did not."[3] A number of previous chapters showed how my argument can deal with genocidal violence, as well as less intense forms of coercion, but what about instances in which separatism generated only peaceful negotiations and concessions? As I show below, the muted external security implications of Norwegian and Slovak separatism facilitated their respective host states peacefully negotiating their exit from the polity. The "Velvet Divorce" that split the Czech and Slovak republics in 1993 was made possible by the collapse of the Soviet Union, the end of the Cold War, and the unification of Germany, all of which signaled the changing geopolitics of Central Europe. Combined with the relatively muted history of conflict between Czechs and Slovaks, ensuring that there were no deep identity divisions between the two, this benign regional environment allowed Czech leaders to peacefully acquiesce to Slovak nationalism. Similarly, almost a century earlier, the insulation of Scandinavia from traditional European power politics, and Norway's pledge to destroy border forts as a condition of its independence, mitigated any threat Sweden might have faced from the establishment of a fully sovereign Norway. As a consequence, Sweden and Norway peacefully went their separate ways.

Finally, I investigate the U.S. Civil War, even though it neither took place in the twentieth century, nor was it, strictly speaking, ethnic in nature. Nevertheless, the very fact that it does not fit the profile of the type of secessionist struggle I discuss in this book makes it a useful litmus test—if my argument can account for elements of a dispute that lies outside its original scope conditions, we can gain even greater confidence in its explanatory power. As I show below, Union leaders denied Southern independence in part based on concerns about the prospect of a geopolitically divided North America were the Confederacy to secede. They were further rankled by British and French interference in the crisis, which compelled Lincoln to escalate to a "militarization" strategy at Bull Run, setting the stage for a

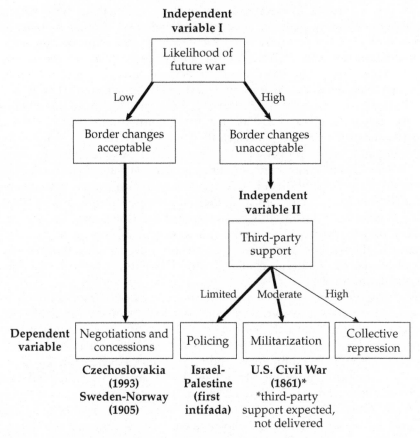

Figure 5. Variation in state response to secessionism in the Middle East, Europe, and North America, 1861–1993

larger conflagration. However, the case does not fit my theory in one important sense. Usually, the intensity of coercion is determined by how much third-party support is delivered, but in this case, such support had not actually materialized. Rather, Union leaders chose to escalate to *preempt* third-party support, undergirded by a belief that a more forthright response would signal to, especially, Britain that it should not interfere. Figure 5 summarizes the argument I develop in this chapter.

Israel-Palestine: A Unique Separatist Conflict

The Israeli-Palestinian conflict is by any measure one of the most important in international politics today. It is also one of the most controversial: it touches on themes as visceral as nationalism, colonialism, territoriality, historical memory, religion, identity, and inequity. Though scholars of secessionism have generally shied away from studying this dispute, such inattention is mistaken. At bottom, I submit, the conflict is separatist: a nationalist group (the Palestinians) under the control of a state (Israel) wishes to establish a state of its own on the territory which it inhabits, and the state in question has used a variety of methods to ensure this eventuality does not come to pass.[4] This picture is slightly complicated by the fact that some of the territory on which the Palestinians live is not fully incorporated into Israel "proper," but for our purposes, this technicality is just that. Israel controls and exercises authority over the Palestinian territories, and has incorporated them into its administrative web after its victory in the six-day war of 1967.[5] In turn, the indigenous Palestinian population has carried out a liberation struggle against the Israel, aimed at the creation of a new state.[6] This makes it a separatist movement in the strict sense of the term. As such, theories of secessionist conflict should have a great deal to say about this conflict, if little about how to solve it, an admittedly daunting task.

As it stands, however, the main alternative theory to mine is unable to provide significant analytical traction on this dispute. Arguments that revolve around internal deterrence and demography would predict peaceful concessions from Israel, up to and including a Palestinian state possessing military, paramilitary, and police forces. Given it is a binational state, comprised almost entirely of Jews and Arabs, Israel should have no precedents to fear were it to grant autonomy or independence to the Palestinians. Which ethnic group in Israel, after the Palestinians, will rise up and demand a state of their own? Unfortunately for these theories, this state of affairs has not materialized. To the contrary, Israel has used varying levels of repression to deal with the Palestinian movement and has been unprepared to acquiesce to an independent, Weberian state. Meanwhile, the institutions argument does explain important elements of this case, providing a framework to understand the influence of Israel's religious-nationalist settlers and their political supporters. However, the importance of the far right has markedly increased in the twenty-first century. In the immediate aftermath of the first Palestinian intifada, the main object of study here, Israeli religious nationalists exercised less influence over events, with Israeli policy in the hands of centrists: a unity government, followed by a center-left government led by Yitzhak Rabin. Even these "moderate" elements, however, dismissed the possibility of a fully-sovereign Palestinian state. The question then becomes: why did this "liberal" democracy, with no other ethnicities in its midst that would conceivably rise and demand statehood, not allow for the creation of an independent Palestine?

Consistent with my theory, Israel's coercive strategy of "policing" in response to the first intifada was conditioned by its lack of trust that its external security would not be violated by the creation of a Palestinian state, were it to come to fruition. This lack of trust related to its rough neighborhood, one of the most militarized in the world,[7] in which it has been the victim of Arab state aggression, especially early in its life as an independent state. In combination with this collective memory of conflict with Arab neighbors, an essentializing logic that subsumed Palestinian nationalism under the rubric of general Arab hostility to the state ensured that Palestinian identity is necessarily seen as "opposed" to Israel's founding Jewish nationalism. Together, Israel's conflict-prone environment and calcified view of Palestinian/Arab identity rendered it incapable of acquiescing to an independent Palestine. Simply put, Israel feared that granting a Palestinian state would result in further security problems for it. Given this logic, it was advisable to repress Palestinians in the present, pay the limited but rising reputational costs associated with such policy, and live to fight another day.

That said, we should be careful to ascribe Israeli behavior only to external security concerns, especially in the last two decades, a period in which my argument has more limited explanatory power. The rightward turn in domestic politics in Israel since the 1970s, and its acceleration since the mid-1990s, is organized around the related desire for colonizing land in "Judea and Samaria," or the West Bank, which also helps explain its strident reaction to Palestinian nationalism. This increased prominence of the Israeli far right has added an ideological and religious dimension to a territorial conflict, and made Israeli leaders from both the right and left loathe to yield even slightly in negotiations with Palestinians. Such domestic developments lie outside the bounds of my theory. My theory also struggles to explain Israel's "militarization" strategy in the second intifada. I would expect such a strategy only under conditions of at least "moderate" third-party support, but Palestinian groups had little material backing from external powers in the early 2000s. Nevertheless, I maintain that even in the twenty-first century, concerns about security are one of the prime drivers of Israeli intransigence on the question of a Palestinian state.

There are two questions organizing this case. First, how do we classify the Israeli response to the Palestinian quest for statehood, especially in the immediate aftermath of the first intifada? Second, to what extent was this response determined by external security considerations? Before we get to these questions, however, we must go slightly further back in time.

TERRITORY, NATION, AND STATE IN ISRAEL-PALESTINE IN THE TWENTIETH CENTURY

It was at the end of World War I that European countries sliced Arab lands, previously under the control of the defeated Ottoman Empire, into colonial trusteeships called "mandates." Each of these mandates, including Palestine, witnessed a general national awakening.[8] Unlike the others, however, the Palestinian national movement had to contend with competing claims to the same land. The movement for Jewish nationalism, known as Zionism, considered the ancient Kingdom of Israel the most apposite location for a modern Jewish state and inspired waves of migration, leading to an increase in the Jewish population, from 24,000 in 1882, or 5 percent of the population of Palestine, to 85,000 by 1914.[9] Palestinian concerns escalated in 1917, when the Balfour Declaration—bearing the name of Foreign Secretary Balfour, who had written in a confidential memo in 1919 that "Zionism, be it right or wrong, good or bad, is rooted in age-long traditions, in present needs, in future hopes, of greater import than the desires and prejudices of the 700,000 Arabs who now inhabit that ancient land"—privileged Jewish over Arab nationalism. As a consequence, Palestinians would turn their attention to convincing the colonial power to abandon the commitment to a Jewish national home.[10]

Between 1921 and 1929, Jewish land possessions, settlements, and businesses multiplied in Palestine. The Jewish community, known as the Yishuv, increasingly appeared as a protostate: it had an elected national assembly, an armed defense force, an institutional architecture related to agricultural collectives, waves of new immigrants, and banking. The community's highly skilled human capital, urban nature, ideological homogeneity, and financial and political support from abroad additionally stood it in good stead. By contrast, Arabs in Palestine had no such support, nor had they built internal institutions to the same extent. Moreover, the leaders of the Palestinian national movements were drawn from only a narrow sliver of the elite and were internally divided. Palestinians simply fell short of achieving the level of cohesion and political advancement of the Jewish community, with even the revolt of 1936–39 marked by fragmentation.[11]

The 1930s saw substantial immigration into Mandatory Palestine by European Jews escaping Nazi persecution, while Hitler's genocide during World War II deepened and broadened support for Zionism among both Jews and non-Jews.[12] Meanwhile, Jewish militant groups successfully attacked British targets in Palestine, forcing Britain to transfer its mandate to the UN in 1947. In November of that year, the UN General Assembly passed resolution 181 dividing Palestine into two states, one Arab and one Jewish. The Yishuv accepted the plan, but the Arabs' representatives, along with Arab states, rejected it. The basis of this rejection was that Jews were a third of the population and owned less than 10 percent of the land, and yet were awarded 56 percent of Palestine, including territory which was 45 percent Arab.[13]

This state of affairs led to two separate but related conflicts: one between the Jews and Arabs of Palestine, and the other between the nascent state of Israel and independent Arab states. The former began almost immediately after the passage of Resolution 181, with Arab offensives repelled by the superior Jewish forces. By March 1948, about 75,000, mostly urban middle-class Palestinians fled the violence and chaos. More would follow with a Jewish offensive in the spring, with entire towns and villages being impelled to escape by episodes such as the Deir Yasin massacre. In all, between 250,000 and 350,000 Palestinians were expelled or fled in this first phase of the war. On May 14, the state of Israel was established, which led to five Arab states waging war on the Jewish state. Israel decisively won the war the next year, by which time the total number of Palestinians that had become refugees reached about 700,000—representing about 60 percent of the Palestinian population. Israel meanwhile controlled 78 percent of Mandate Palestine, about half more than it was allotted by Resolution 181. Egypt won the Gaza Strip on the southern Mediterranean coast, while Transjordan, which would become the Hashemite Kingdom of Jordan later that year, took over the West Bank.[14]

The year 1948 represents a watershed moment in Palestinian history; the massive refugee outflow as a result of war is known as *naqba*—catastrophe. Before the war, Arabs had constituted a majority in the area between the Jordan River and the Mediterranean, making up approximately 1.4 million out of 2 million people, and were a majority in fifteen of the sixteen subdistricts of Mandatory Palestine. By the end of the war, half had fled or been expelled, and about 150,000 Palestinians remained in Israel. As Israel's "new historians" working with archival evidence opened in the 1980s showed, "most Palestinians left because they were forced to do so either by direct Israeli attacks on their cities and villages or due to conditions of extreme insecurity." Indeed, it was known to Zionist leaders even in the 1920s and 1930s that the creation of a Jewish state within Mandatory Palestine, required the wholesale "transfer," or expulsion, of Arabs.[15]

Palestinians had become a Diaspora nation overnight: 10 percent were in the East Bank, 39 percent in the West Bank, 26 percent in Gaza, 14 percent in Lebanon, 10 percent in Syria, and 1 percent in Egypt. From the Israeli perspective, too, 1948 was a key moment, cementing the importance of external security in national narratives. After all, what could be more traumatic for a state's collective memory than a multipronged assault immediately on gaining a state, one created less than three years after Nazi death camps at Auschwitz, Majdanek, and Jasenova were closed? The conflicts affirmed for Israel the "myth in which the Jews are in existential danger of annihilation and must be ready to fight in the wars that are imposed on them against their will."[16]

The 1960s and 1970s saw an increasing indigenization of the Palestinian cause, with the birth of the Palestinian Liberation Organization (PLO) especially symbolizing control of the movement being wrested from Arab states by Palestinians.[17] Israel's borders and regional environment, meanwhile, continued to be marked by danger. As a result of the Six-Day War of 1967, when Israel routed the armies of Egypt, Syria, and Jordan and seized control of the West Bank from Jordan, the Gaza Strip and the Sinai Peninsula from Egypt, and the Golan Heights from Syria, a further 250,000–300,000 Palestinians became refugees.[18] The 1967 war represents a critical juncture in the Israeli state's approach to land. It marked the point at which "revisionist Zionism," or the political movement aimed at incorporating the entire ancient Land of Israel, gained greater legitimacy domestically, and "set the stage for a war of position over the shape of the state."[19] Indeed, in many ways, Israel's victory in 1967 was a poisoned chalice, summed up in a memorable exchange. After the victory, Prime Minister Eshkol held up a "V"-sign, only to be chastised by his wife: "Have you gone mad?" He replied: "No, this is not a V sign in English. It is a V sign in Yiddish! *Vi Krishen aroys*?" The phrase translates to "How do we get out of this?"[20]

For their part, groups such as the PLO used terrorism and "fedayeen" raids from bases in Jordan—until September 15, 1970, when Jordan's army began a move to crush them, expelling the PLO entirely by the next year— as well as Lebanon, whose southeast was so completely in the PLO's hands that it was referred to as "Fatahland" in Israel.[21] Israel's sensitivity to these cross-border attacks was evinced in its full-scale invasions of Lebanon in 1978 and 1982,[22] from which the Israeli military did not disengage until two decades later. In addition, Egypt and Syria, eager to reclaim lost territories in the Sinai and Golan Heights respectively, attacked it in 1973, catching Israel unaware and leading to the Yom Kippur War.[23] These border troubles helped cement the notion of vulnerability within sections of the Israeli body politic, which would have severe consequences for Palestinian nationalists two decades later, when their hopes for a sovereign state were denied.

THE FIRST INTIFADA AND ISRAEL'S POLICING STRATEGY

When the first mass uprising in Occupied Palestine took place in the late 1980s, the PLO's leadership in Tunisia, along with Israel, was caught by surprise, and indeed threatened by the prospective development of an alternative, local, and younger leadership of the national movement.[24] The Palestinian intifada began early in December 1987, when an IDF vehicle crashed into a van transporting Palestinian workers back to Gaza, killing four and injuring seven. Rumors spread to the effect that the collision was deliberate. Matters were compounded when Israeli forces opened fire on demonstrations after the funerals the next day. In response, the Palestinians staged a national uprising, the intifada, one that constituted their secessionist moment. It was an almost entirely homegrown movement that began as a series of protests and demonstrations against "unbearable" economic conditions. Conversely, the Palestinian territories saw considerable sociopolitical development, including a burgeoning of civic institutions that formed the institutional backbone of the intifada, such as trade unions, professional associations, students' committees, charities, newspapers, research institutes, and women's groups.[25]

Several reasons explained the timing of the uprising.[26] First, both the Gaza Strip and the West Bank suffered major economic slumps in the 1980s. Between 1981 and 1985, per capita GNP fell almost 2 percent annually in Gaza and 0.7 percent annually in the West Bank. Second, Israel's control and occupation of the territories became more enveloping. For example, twenty-five hundred settlers in Gaza, constituting 0.4 percent of the population, controlled 28 percent of state land, and on average, West Bank settlers used twelve times as much water as Palestinians did. Third, Israeli policies predictably placed Palestinian development subordinate to Israel's economic needs, with the territories operating effectively as a "slave market" for the Israeli economy. Fourth, settlements expanded at pace, with the Jewish population in the West Bank almost doubling between 1984 and 1988, from thirty-five thousand to sixty-four thousand. More generally, there existed an "all-pervading element of humiliation" resulting from "the protracted state of political subjugation and economic dependence, and the day-to-day realities of military occupation [which] meant a continuous trampling of the basic rights and dignity of the inhabitants."[27] As Israeli historian Benny Morris sums up: "The rioters of December 1987 and the years that followed wanted to get rid of the Israeli occupation and to better their economic conditions. Most Palestinians certainly regarded independence and the establishment of their own state as a further, major objective."[28]

Palestinians threw stones at soldiers and tanks and boycotted jobs in Israel; shopkeepers stopped accepting Israeli goods and paying taxes and were eventually even joined by Palestinians in Israel.[29] Rioting first began in Gaza's refugee camps and spread to camps in West Bank, before it extended into towns in both Gaza and the West Bank.[30] Though emanating from the ground up, this movement soon coalesced around an umbrella organization named United National Leadership of the Uprising (UNLU) that coordinated Palestinian political activities in the territories, before giving way to PLO leadership by the summer of 1988.[31] The main decision maker—the "single most important national symbol and arbiter of Palestinian politics"—leading the movement at this point was Yasser Arafat.[32] Importantly, Palestinians mostly refrained from violent methods in the intifada, both because doing so would play into Israeli hands but also to retain global sympathy as the oppressed party.[33]

The intifada represented Palestinians' secessionist moment. The state's response was a policing strategy. It used relatively soft coercion while also making tactical concessions, all the while ruling out complete statehood, or anything approximating it, for the Palestinians. This strategy was undergirded by Israel's lack of faith in its future security should a militarized Palestine come into fruition, colored by its history of warfare with its Arab neighbors and its essentializing of Palestinian identity, reducing it to "Arab."

Israel's calibration of coercion was typical of policing: it used mass imprisonment, torture, and other coercive methods of interrogation, but did not escalate repression to a point where substantial casualties resulted.[34] It "gradually introduced police-style riot-control techniques and equipment, deployed nonmilitary measures such as cutting of the telephone lines and economic restrictions, and created special undercover units to hunt down the uprising's most extremist factions."[35] Though there was a mass influx of troops in the territories, and shoot-on-sight orders during some curfews, Defense Minister Yitzhak Rabin instituted his "beatings policy," which called for the intensive use of clubs and sticks to break up riots. The idea behind this strategy was that broken bones were better than dead bodies and funerals, which provided further opportunities to riot and meant bad publicity abroad. However, while the policy did achieve its goal in keeping the number of dead relatively low—roughly a thousand in five years—many thousands of Palestinians were seriously injured, and many became handicapped. Israel's most favored coercive measure was arrest and detention, imprisoning 1,000 people for every 100,000 Palestinians in the West Bank and Gaza. As a comparison, the figure for the United States, widely considered to have an unusually high incarceration rate, is 426. For Northern Ireland it was 120, for South Africa 240, and for the Soviet Union, at the apogee of the gulag era, 1,423.[36]

Alongside the use of coercion, the intifada forced Israel to hold talks with Palestinian negotiators, which were held both in public in Madrid and in secret in the Norwegian capital of Oslo, culminating in two accords, signed in 1993 and 1995. Israeli concessions in these agreements were limited to recognizing the PLO as the legitimate representative of the Palestinian people. In addition, the accords created some institutions of self-government, in the form of the Palestinian Authority, in 60 percent of Gaza and 17 percent of the West Bank.[37] Such granting of limited autonomy can be seen as tactical concessions to "moderates" embedded within a larger policy of denying the Palestinians a future state, a balance typical of policing strategies. Indeed, it would be a serious mistake to conceptualize Israeli concessions at Oslo as a deal or process that was to pave the way to a Palestinian state, despite hopeful rhetoric at the time. According to a Palestinian academic, Oslo was a "very brutal political compromise" and there "wasn't any indication formally or informally that the accord was leading to a two-state solution."[38] As one diplomat told me, "we were naïve" at Oslo.[39]

That Oslo was not seen as laying a path to a Palestinian state is attested by the fact that in its aftermath, Israel built settlements and roads that divided Palestinian land; tightened restrictions of travel between the West Bank, Gaza, and East Jerusalem; and disallowed a "safe passage" between these territories,[40] rendering the possibility of a Palestinian state more unlikely. In interviews, Israeli researchers, journalists, and activists consistently maintained that the question of a Palestinian state at Oslo was a bridge too far and had never been seriously contemplated or envisioned by the Rabin government. Rather, in this perspective, the aim of the accords was considerably less ambitious: the creation of a framework within which trust could be built between the parties, culminating in Palestinian self-determination by the end of the decade, and preparing the Israeli public for the endgame with gradual steps.[41] As several interviewees reminded me, it had been illegal for Israeli citizens to even talk to a PLO member until Oslo; the idea of a Palestinian state was simply unthinkable for the Israeli leadership. Notably, major concerns such as borders, the "right of return" of Palestinian refugees, the division of Jerusalem, and Israeli settlements were not negotiated in the accords. Instead, these so called final status issues—"landmines waiting to be blown up" in one evocative phrase[42]—were left for a time when greater confidence and trust existed between the Israeli state and its Palestinian interlocutors. As one study puts it, Oslo "frontloaded benefits for Israel and backloaded them for Palestinians" and "did not provide much sense of urgency to Israelis to take the steps necessary for Palestinians to achieve those backloaded benefits, or even reassure Palestinians that they would actually materialize."[43] As such, it is difficult to make the claim that Israeli concessions at Oslo signaled the creation of a state.

The bottom line is that in response to the Palestinian secessionist moment, Israel responded with a policing strategy, using a mix of soft coercion, centering on beatings and imprisonment rather than killings or massacres, as well as tactical concessions that fell considerably short of statehood. This Israeli strategy of policing represents a puzzle for existing accounts of separatist violence. Reputation-based arguments would predict that a state such as Israel, with no other national group in its midst that could conceivably demand independence after the Palestinians, would be happy to make substantial concessions, including independence. Arguments centering on veto points also fail to explain Israeli strategy, since at the time Rabin led a center-left government that had the support of left-wing and Arab parties in the Knesset. That such a coalition was unable to even contemplate significant autonomy or statehood speaks to a wider unease with the concept in the Israeli body politic.

PALESTINIAN NATIONALISM AND ISRAELI EXTERNAL SECURITY

I argue that a major factor that stood behind Israeli reluctance to grant a state, or anything close to one, in the aftermath of the first Palestinian intifada were concerns about external security. Consistent with my theory, Israel could not trust that a sovereign Palestine would not create problems for its security in the future, given first its militarized history with neighbors and, second, deep identity divisions between Palestinian Arabs and Israeli Jews.

Security-based fears of a Palestinian state have generally been important for the center right (Likud) and center left (Labor) mainstream parties and leaders in Israel. As Rabin said in a major speech to the Knesset in 1992, "When it comes to Israel's security, we will not concede a thing. From our standpoint, security takes precedence over peace."[44] Both traditional parties in Israel have been "deeply opposed to Palestinian nationalism and denied that the Palestinians had a right to national self-determination" and "unconditionally opposed to the establishment of an independent Palestinian state."[45] Israel's insistence that Palestinians not win their own state, according to scholars, is rooted in "enormous anxiety," guarding against "further misfortune,"[46] conditioned as it was by Arab states' aggressions against it early in its life, as well as centuries of persecution of European Jews. For the larger Israeli security establishment, its surrounding Arab population have "represented first and foremost a military threat."[47] As insiders put it, "Israel's national security policy has been predicated on the assumption that the nation faces a realistic threat of both politicide (destruction of a state) and even genocide. Six wars, numerous major confrontations, and ongoing violence, from low-level terrorism to massive rocket attacks, have been basic features of Israel's external environment. A sense of nearly unremitting Arab enmity prevails, of a conflict of unlimited hostility and objectives. . . . National security issues in Israel are commonly addressed in existential terms."[48]

In the Israel-Palestine case, both "trip wires" to state coercion are set off: not only does Israel live in a dangerous neighborhood, by one metric the second-most militarized region during the twentieth century,[49] but it also has deep identity divisions with the Palestinians, based on a history of conflict and a collective essentialization that subsumes Palestinian identity under a general Arab one. As my theory would expect under such circumstances, the state cannot countenance independence for separatists, lest the new state threaten its security in the future, either directly or in consort with other regional states. Israel's behavior against the Palestinians is consistent with this expectation. The mainstream of the Israeli body politic views the creation of a Palestinian state as an apocalyptic threat, despite the massive gulf in capabilities dividing the two entities. According to one veteran Israeli journalist, security is the main issue when it comes to Israeli stubbornness against the Palestinians—despite no Arab army having confronted Israel for years, the sense of fear from Arab hostility is "very high." For the Israeli right wing and even center, the prospect of a Palestinian state "is a direct threat on Israel," since organizations such as Hamas are thought to be primed to take over the West Bank and launch missiles at Tel Aviv and Ben Gurion Airport on their ascent to power.[50] Other journalists agreed with this sentiment, noting that "most of the public feels concessions will end in specific disasters for Israeli lives and families."[51]

This fear of a Palestinian state results partly from Israel's primordialist, essentialist understanding of Arab identity, through which both peaceful and violent Palestinian mobilization is subsumed under a larger feeling of victimization by its neighboring Arab states. As current Israeli prime minister and longtime opponent of Palestinian statehood Benjamin Netanyahu wrote, to make sense of the national movement, "it is necessary to go beyond the pretense that 1967 and the 'occupation of the West Bank' are the starting point of 'resistance' against the Jews. The Arab war against the Jews is in fact as old as this century."[52] Similarly, former Israeli prime minister Golda Meir famously remarked that "it was not as though there was a Palestinian People in Palestine considering itself as a Palestinian People and we came and threw them out and took their country away from them. They did not exist."[53] Moshe Feiglin, a Likud politician, incredulously reacted to the very notion of a Palestinian. "'Palestinians'? Do you know about a nation without a history? How can a nation exist without history? They are Arabs. They identify with a big Arab nation, and there are many Arab tribes."[54] As a result of Palestinian identity being folded under a wider Arab rubric in this way, Israel's assessment of the risks of a future Palestinian state rest on the security threats it has faced from Arab states in the past.

Evidence for the claim that security was the main driver of Israel's refusal to concede a state can be found at the Madrid talks that preceded the Oslo negotiations, where Israeli hawks pressured Prime Minister Yitzhak Shamir, insisting "that the West Bank was an important buffer between itself and Jordan, and a Palestinian entity, let alone a Palestinian state, would represent a military threat to Israel's existence."[55] Though Shamir and Likud were was soundly defeated by Rabin's Labor and other left-leaning parties in 1992, the two "differed more in style than substance"[56] when it came to negotiating. Rabin's strategy at Oslo was to go only so far as to grant administrative control to those territories unimportant to Israel's security, as well as "retain final military control throughout the *whole* of the occupied territories."[57] Indeed, security issues were the "hardest nuts to crack" in the Oslo negotiations according to contemporary reports, with one Labor Knesset member warning that "the negotiation is not just a perpetual festival of Israeli gestures. It's based on give and take, and in this case, give and take means they accept our terms as far as security arrangements are concerned."[58] That security was the overarching Israeli concern during Oslo is also revealed by the fact that, against tradition, Rabin assigned major negotiating responsibilities to serving generals in the IDF; this reliance on serving officers was a "natural" outcome when, as one retired officer put it, "problems of security are so predominant in any of the negotiations." Besides, for the broader Israeli public at the time, "the sight of

IDF officers rather than politicians shaping the peace accord is reassuring. The average Israeli will judge peace with the Palestinians by one criteria—personal security—and 'the public feels better if security arrangements are negotiated by generals rather than by [Deputy Foreign Minister] Yossi Beilin.'"[59]

In consonance with this theme, Benjamin Netanyahu, then leader of the Likud Party in opposition, claimed that "Palestinian autonomy, although not a Palestinian state, was something that he could accept and even support on the condition that it provided for exclusive Israeli responsibility for security, external borders and foreign relations," which was not the case with the agreements then.[60] When Netanyahu gained power in 1996 after severely criticizing Oslo and promising to undo the accords, one anonymous government official was blunt about the changes in the offing: "The whole world can jump up and down, but there is no way to achieve a Palestinian state under Likud. This is the red line."[61] As the *Financial Times* noted in 1996 after Netanyahu and Arafat visited the White House, "The underlying problem is that the Israeli prime minister does not accept the principles behind Oslo. . . . He believes security requires a buffer of occupied land insulating the Jewish state from its Arab neighbors." As a consequence, "he has told his supporters at home he will go no further along the route charted by the Rabin and Peres governments which was leading to a Palestinian state."[62] Sure enough, with Netanyahu's election "the Oslo process effectively came to an end."[63]

Indeed, more than most, Netanyahu—the dominant figure in Israeli politics over the last two decades—personifies the views connecting a history of conflict with Arab neighbors to predictions of security problems an independent Palestinian state will pose. The same year he was elected leader of Likud, Netanyahu published a book in which he "viewed Israel's relations with the Arab world as one of permanent conflict, as a never-ending struggle between the forces of light and the forces of darkness." Compromise with the PLO "was completely out of the question because its goal was the destruction of the State of Israel. . . . The PLO was 'constitutionally tied to the idea of Israel's liquidation.'" The very title of the chapter on the PLO in Netanyahu's book *A Place among Nations* speaks volumes: "The Trojan Horse." He wrote that it was "all too easy for anyone familiar with Israel's terrain to imagine, precisely as Arafat promises, that a PLO state implanted ten miles from the beaches of Tel Aviv would be a mortal danger to the Jewish state." For Israel to secure its cities, it must militarily control essentially all the territory west of the Jordan River. "To subdivide this land into two unstable, insecure nations, to try to defend what is indefensible, is to invite disaster. Carving Judea and Samaria out of Israel means carving up Israel."[64]

We can find evidence of the centrality of Israel's dangerous neighborhood and history of conflict not just in its refusal to grant a state, but also in its specific demands during negotiations with the Palestinians. For instance, while Oslo divided Palestinian sovereignty into several sectoral and geographic zones, Israel controlled security not just for Israeli areas, but also for the "mixed" zones—the so-called Area B—while Palestinians were given control of security in Area A only, about 3 percent of the landmass of the occupied territories.[65] More tellingly, throughout the Oslo process, Israel's view of a future Palestinian state entailed an Israeli military presence in the Jordan valley as well as a Palestinian state that would be demilitarized.[66] In my interviews, Israeli journalists and former negotiators emphasized that a demilitarized Palestinian state was a sine qua non for the Israeli body politic to even consider territorial concessions. These interviewees were often puzzled when I even brought up the question of demilitarization, given how "obvious" Israeli demands were on this issue relative to thornier issues, such as Jerusalem, refugees, and settlements.[67] In this view, the presence of another Arab army in the West Bank is a red line for Israel's security, given the Jordan Valley's importance to Israel historically. Importantly, this insistence that Palestine be demilitarized is not just deeply but also widely felt, with both left and right subscribing wholeheartedly to it. For instance, at the infamous failed accord of Camp David under the supervision of Bill Clinton, Ehud Barak of the Labor Party ostensibly made "the most far-reaching Israeli concessions ever made"—but still insisted that an independent Palestinian state be demilitarized and that Israel control a "thin strip" of the Jordan valley for security purposes.[68]

For their part, Palestinian interviewees, including journalists covering the Oslo talks as well as negotiators and scholars, made clear to me that their side was well aware of Israeli resolve on this question. In their telling, the Palestinians felt compelled to agree to nonmilitarization as a signal of assurance to the Israelis that they were interested only in gaining a state and not using it to fight wars, happy to delegate their future border security to international actors.[69] In this telling, a Palestinian army would be of little use in a conflict against the militarily superior Israelis or any of the major Arab states.[70] As such, it was smart strategy to put their future security in the hands of outside actors—"bear-hug the international community to provide security" in one Palestinian analyst's words—and reassure Israel of its peaceful intentions in the future to the extent possible.[71]

Doubtless, the idea that the Palestinians must assure Israel of its security in order to win a state justifiably appears "twisted logic" to some.[72] Is it not the case that the Palestinians are a stateless minority oppressed by a powerful state enjoying a regional nuclear monopoly as well as the unflinching backing of world's only superpower? How can an actor so weak assure a state so strong? Such a viewpoint, reasonable as it is on the surface, ignores the difference between absolute and relative power. As a regional hegemon, Israel is assuredly more powerful than, and continues to assert dominance over, the Palestinian nation. However, as IR scholars point out, states care deeply about not just absolute power but also relative power. Were the Palestinians to win a state, Israel's security environment would become more challenging, at least marginally. An independent Palestine would still be vastly weaker than Israel, but because of the military, economic, demographic, and institutional benefits of statehood (chapter 1), it would have caught up relatively. More importantly, even if the leaders of an independent Palestine were solely interested in peaceful relations with Israel, the thorny question of nonstate actors and militant groups, using such a state as a base for attacks, would be left unanswered. As such, Palestinian statehood represents an adverse shift in the balance that would be unpalatable for a state like Israel, which having fought numerous interstate wars and nonstate actors, is consistently obsessed with maintaining its security.

Indeed, the tragedy from the point of view of common Palestinians is that there is only so much they, and their leaders, can do to placate Israel. Israel's history of conflict with Arab states in its early years of statehood, which Palestinians bear little responsibility for, has had significant path-dependent effects, leaving Israel suspicious of any changes in the regional balance of power.[73] Such rapid changes in the balance of power, as I argue in this book, inhere in any separatist demand. Palestinian negotiators seem to be aware of this dynamic; their relative comfort giving up claims to an army in negotiations—as opposed to their strident stance on issues such as Jerusalem, refugees, and settlements—are explicitly aimed at providing assurance to Israel. Nonetheless, there are elements of independence that the Palestinians simply cannot negotiate away, such as internal sovereignty and the existence of "hard" international borders, which necessarily reduce Israeli security. As one Israeli peace activist told me, even if the threat of Arab armies from Iraq, Jordan, or Syria crossing the Jordan River through the West Bank is largely "fantastical" today thanks to a peace agreement with Jordan and the geopolitical weakening of Iraq and Syria, the threat of "military terrorism," that of militant groups inside an independent Palestine, such as Hezbollah, showering Israel with rockets and mortar fire remains. This leads to the belief that holding on to the West Bank as a security buffer is "worth it," given the alternatives.[74] Even the prospect of international forces, including troops from the United States, being stationed on the border as a "trip wire" would not satisfy this insecurity, since Israel prefers operational flexibility to handle its own security, which international border forces would limit, and sound public and technical relations with the United States, which might be threatened by the presence of American forces on their border.[75]

For mainstream Israeli leaders, then, concerns about external security led to a refusal to grant the Palestinian national movement a state in the 1990s. Conditioned by wars both at its birth and early in its life as a state, Israel saw its surrounding Arab populations as implacably hostile to it. Given it saw Palestinians as Arabs first and foremost, it should not surprise us that Israel feared the security consequences of a new "Arab" state on its border. As such, Israel sought to ensure the lack of meaningful territorial concessions to the Palestinians under its control. It further stipulated that to the extent that Palestinians enjoyed any autonomy, they would not exercise sovereign control of their borders, nor would they be allowed an army, meaning that even if a Palestinian "state" were to somehow come to fruition, it would still lack some of the core elements of widely accepted definitions of the modern, Weberian state. These demands reveal a great deal about dominant Israeli concerns with the prospect of a Palestinian state: its future external security.

SINCE THE FIRST INTIFADA AND OSLO

Since the failed Oslo process in the 1990s, Israel has become even more wary about the security consequences of territorial loss. In interviews, Israeli journalists, academics, and activists, even those from the left, have emphasized the unhappy experiences after concessions elsewhere, including the Sinai, Lebanon, and Gaza. From this perspective, the state has already experienced a proverbial trial run of an independent Palestine, after the withdrawal from Gaza in 2005, the results of which were not encouraging: an increase in rocket attacks from the territory. As Benny Morris noted, "Israel's leaders quite naturally feared that a similar unilateral pullout from the West Bank would be followed by a far more dangerous rocketing of the state's main population centers, Jerusalem and the greater Tel Aviv area. It is today clear that no Israeli leader will initiate a pullout from the West Bank—unilaterally or in agreement with the Palestinians—before the IDF acquires the technological capability to protect its population centers from short-range missile attacks."[76] My interviews revealed just how widely pervasive the view that transferring control of territory only invites more aggression is in Israel today, rendering the traditional "land for peace" equation dicey from the Israeli perspective—how can they be sure, given their history, that conceding land will actually lead to peace?[77] Overall, the right wing's views that "they want to destroy us, they want to finish us" are very popular today.[78] Indeed, on the eve of the 2015 elections, two-thirds of Israelis strongly or moderately agreed with the claim that "no matter which party forms the next government, the peace process with the Palestinians will not advance because there is no solution to the disagreements between the sides."[79] In 2010, 80 percent of Israeli Jews believed that "the Palestinians have not come to terms with Israel's existence and would destroy Israel if they could" and 74 percent agreed that "there will be no change in this position even if a peace agreement is signed."[80]

Alongside Israeli fears, Palestinian frustration has also increased manifold since Oslo. This is because the empowering of the religious-nationalist settler lobby within Israel in the last two decades has added an ideological dimension to an already complicated territorial conflict, pushing the country toward "fanaticism and radicalism"[81] and making concessions even less likely. Right-wing religious nationalism has risen in Israel since the 1967 war and even more so since the 1977 elections—partly a consequence of a more politically active community of lower-class Sephardic Jews. Included in this group are mainstream rightwing parties such as Likud and the National Religious Party, as well as radical nationalist parties such as Tehiya, Kach, Moledet, and the National Union Party in the 2000s.[82] In recent times, this religious-nationalist camp has "through different political parties, far exceeded its proportionality" in the Israeli Knesset.[83] They view the Jews as the chosen people, the rightful owner of the land between the Jordan River and the Mediterranean. That is, they are advocates of so-called Greater Israel, precluding territorial concessions to the Palestinians, who are considered aliens in this land, untrustworthy, and the sworn enemy of Israel and the Jewish people. This "subculture," equal parts religious nationalism and racist fanaticism, was born out of Israel's successes in the 1967 war, which included the conquest of the West Bank— known as Judea and Samaria to the adherents of this subculture—which convinced "many Orthodox rabbis and teachers that they were living in a messianic era and that salvation was at hand."[84]

This rightward turn has been responsible for one of the primary impediments toward a solution of the Palestinian-Israeli conflict: the issue of settlements. The Israeli policy of establishing Jewish settlements in occupied territories began in earnest by the Labor government after the 1967 war, was accelerated considerably since 1977, when Likud came to power,[85] and has shown precious little signs of abating, up to the present day. As such, Israeli leaders' decisions on how to deal with Palestinians are not just conditioned by Israel's checkered relationship with its Arab state neighbors, as my theory would predict, but also by a fear of crossing an increasingly vocal and racist coalition in domestic politics.[86] Naftali Bennett, a rising star within the far right movement and one with serious chances to become prime minister soon, put it simply in 2012: "There are certain things that most of us understand will never happen: 'The Sopranos' are not coming back for another season, and there will never be a peace plan with the Palestinians. . . . I will do everything in my power to make sure they never get a state."[87]

The right-wing and settler lobby made a show of strength after Oslo, when it did "everything within their power to obstruct the spirit and letters of" the accords.[88] According to interviews with both Israeli and Palestinian journalists and researchers, the open-ended nature of the agreement, with final-status issues kicked down the road, left considerable time and space for spoilers from both sides to dent and possibly extinguish the potential of a Palestinian state.[89] Israeli settlers considerably quickened their takeover of Palestinian land as a preemptive measure, their population doubling in the territories during the 1990s.[90] From eighty thousand before Oslo, the number of settlers in the West Bank and Gaza today is half a million. Jewish settlements in the aftermath of Oslo created "facts on the ground," meaning that while the final status of a Palestinian state was suspended midair, so to speak, the territory on which such a state would be organized was taken over. These settlers were given political backing by right-wing Israelis, including those from secular parties such as Likud's Ariel Sharon, both in and out of government. Most damagingly, an Israeli settler named Yigal Amir assassinated Rabin in late 1995—a "knockout blow" to the peace process.[91] Amir's murderous act ended the life of the one Israeli leader from the center left with the gravitas and standing to stand up to the settler lobby—Rabin had served in Israel's war of independence and led it to dramatic victories in the 1967 war—and thus ended any possibility of meaningful Israeli concessions toward a Palestinian state, even a demilitarized Bantustan version of it. Between the security-motivated views objecting to Palestinian independence, personified by Netanyahu, and the religious-nationalist angle, personified by Bennett, arguably more important than security concerns since the turn of the century, the prospects for Palestinian statehood seem very grim indeed. Even more unfortunately, the unique nature of the conflict means that the option usually considered by restive minorities second-best to independence—assimilation in the host state, or in this case, a "one-state solution" where Palestinians enjoy rights as full citizens of a binational state—is also not on the cards.

THE SECOND INTIFADA AND ISRAEL'S MILITARIZATION STRATEGY

Within this general context of Israeli fears and Palestinian frustration, another uprising erupted in the early 2000s. The collapse of the Oslo process led to an impasse that forced Bill Clinton to convene a summit with Israeli Prime Minister Ehud Barak and Palestinian leader Yasser Arafat at Camp David in 2000. The summit was a failure. Later that year, Ariel Sharon, the Likud leader of the opposition, visited the Temple Mount, which provoked demonstrations that day and the next. These demonstrations marked the beginning of the second intifada: once more, the Palestinians rose to "shake off" the Israeli occupation. Israel's response to the second intifada, a "militarization" strategy, is a failed prediction of my theory, which would only expect such an escalation in the presence of "moderate" third-party support, which the Palestinians lacked in this instance.

The second intifada saw more violence than the first, with the IDF adopting a "more hard-line approach," closer to a militarization strategy than policing.[92] The casualty rate of the second intifada was double that of the first.[93] In the earlier episode, the IDF's central message was that "there is no military solution to the intifada, only a political solution," while in the second, it preferred "exacting a price." Security forces killed more than a hundred Palestinians in the first month alone, the large majority being unarmed civilians.[94] "By the second week it had opened fire with all the weapons in its arsenal: in addition to using snipers, it shot missiles from Apache helicopters on demonstrators and their buildings, and it fired from tanks on Beit Jallah and Ramallah in response to small-arms fire on Giloh and Psagot." Such force "would have been more appropriate in a war against a standing army but was totally out of place against stone-throwing civilians."[95] Indeed, Israel viewed the second intifada much more as a war than the first. It used air power to a considerable extent, and then launched a number of "invasions" of West Bank towns, resulting in significant numbers of civilian casualties.[96] This calibration of violence had support from Israeli society, which in fact demanded even more forceful action.[97] From the Israeli perspective, "this was war, not a case of a nation seeking to overthrow its oppressors, end its occupation, or struggle for liberation."[98] As a result, casualties soared: "The first 18 months of the second intifada, ending February 2002, witnessed nearly as many deaths (1,136) as the 69 months of the first intifada (1,265)."[99]

My theory would expect that the increasing intensity of the Israeli response between the first and second intifadas, from policing to militarization, would be due to differences in third-party support for the Palestinians. While we have sound reasons to believe that certain elements of the Palestinian movement, especially Hamas and Hezbollah, enjoyed financial and military aid from hostile regional powers, such as Iran or Syria,[100] my interviewees stressed the nonimportance of third-party support in explaining Israeli behavior in the second intifada. Respondents emphasized that to the extent that the involvement of third-parties was invoked by the Israeli leadership, it was a public relations tactic more than a whole-hearted belief in the perils of regional involvement.[101] Instead, there were three main considerations when explaining the harsher Israeli response in the second intifada. First, the movement it was responding to was itself deadlier: while Palestinians staged a peaceful movement in the late 1980s, mostly throwing stones and Molotov cocktails, the second intifada was considerably more violent, led by Hamas and featuring suicide bombers within Israel "proper."[102] Second, there were differences in domestic politics.[103] The reaction to the first intifada was in the hands of a unity government and a center-left government, while in the second intifada, it was the right-wing Likud Party led by the hawkish Ariel Sharon that was mostly in charge.[104] Third, there was already an Israeli security presence in the territories in the first intifada, while the second was more akin to an "invasion," with Israeli tanks and troops moving in to Palestinian cities and towns.[105] As such, the form and function of Israeli policy in the second intifada was significantly different from what occurred a decade prior.

While my theory can explain Israel's choice of coercion over concessions in the second intifada, it fails when explaining the intensity of coercion. Specifically, the conspicuous absence of "moderate" third-party support in explaining Israeli escalation from policing to militarization is a drawback for my argument and serves as a reminder of the necessarily imperfect fit of general models to specific empirical contexts in social science. That said, even unmet expectations can sometimes prove constructive for scholars, if theoretically useful answers can be found for the argument's failed prediction. In this case, one clear lesson is that the intensified lethality of rebel violence resulting from higher levels of third-party support, pushing governments to escalate from "policing" to "militarization," can be just as easily produced from other sources. For instance, the Palestinian Authority "accumulated tens of thousands of guns during the 1990s," which were used in the second intifada,[106] signifying that vast increases in material capabilities can be generated from within under some circumstances. Second, the failed prediction shines a light on the importance of the splintering of the Palestinian movement, similar to the role factionalization played in Indian Punjab in the late 1980s (chapter 3). The factionalization of the Palestinian movement generated incentives for various organizations to increase violence, unlike when the movement was relatively unified in the first intifada.[107] Finally, Palestinian militants also adjusted tactics, employing suicide bombing more regularly than ever before. During the 1990s, there was an average of three suicide attacks per year, which increased to over twenty a year during the second intifada.[108] These developments in conjunction meant that the Palestinian movement had a level of lethality that a movement in other circumstances may have required "moderate" third-party support to reach.

Overall, my theory has a great deal to say about the Israeli-Palestinian dispute. Confronted by the first intifada, the Israeli state responded by refusing to countenance an independent, Weberian state on the Palestinian territories, adopting relatively light coercion to keep in check a movement enjoying "limited" third-party support, and making tactical concessions to "moderates" that fell well short of statehood. Consistent with my argument, this "policing" strategy had its roots in Israel's militarized history with its neighbors and its deep identity divisions with Palestinians, who it considers no different to the "Arabs" that it fought over decades, leaving it fearful of the security consequences of a new state on its borders. These security fears, exacerbated by Palestinian militant violence aimed at independence, continue to dominate to the present day and render the prospect of a Palestinian state, in control of its borders and security, an exceedingly unlikely prospect. However, developments that lie outside the explanatory range of my theory—such as the rise of the religious nationalist settler lobby in Israel, and the ability of Palestinian movement to generate significant violence in spite of no significant third-party support—have also played an important role in the continuation of violence, especially in the aftermath of Oslo. Most important, my theory cannot explain why the second-best option usually available to ethnic groups denied independence, that of assimilation in the host state, is denied to the Palestinians. This implausibility of a one-state solution, alongside Israel's rejection of "two states for two peoples" partly due to security fears, has created the perfect storm of pessimism and despair that so pervasively mark the Israeli-Palestinian relationship.

Peaceful Secessions in Northern and Central Europe

Completely conciliatory responses by states to separatist movements, where the center is prepared to relinquish territory during peaceful negotiations, are quite rare in international politics. When they do occur, such "negotiations and concessions" strategies often result in the ethnic group expressing satisfaction with the state's concessions, as in contemporary Quebec or Scotland. In exceptional circumstances, however, the ethnic group will continue pressing demands for an independent state in the face of concessions, in which case a peaceful split should occur.

I expect these peaceful splits, and peaceful responses to secessionism by states more generally, under a relatively narrow set of conditions: only when governments do not foresee security troubles, from either regional rivals or the newly created state, in the future. Such a positive prognosis of the state's external security would require residence in a relatively pleasant neighborhood as well as a lack of deep identity divisions between the two actors. Historically, these conditions are most likely to obtain in the comfortable, optimistic, post-security regions of North America and Western Europe in the twenty-first century, which is why we see, for instance, Britain not consider violence against Scottish secessionism nor Canada against the Quebecois. The question posed in this section is: to what extent did these conditions match those in Czechoslovakia at the end of the twentieth century and Scandinavia at the beginning of it? The relative paucity of the nonviolent strategies in the empirical record increases their importance when evaluating any theory of separatist conflict; if my argument has trouble accounting for these cases, we should have serious doubts about its plausibility.

In Czechoslovakia's Velvet Divorce, external security considerations were taken off the table, creating the conditions under which Czech leaders could concede territory unworryingly. For one thing, the regional security environment underwent dramatic changes in the lead-up to the secession, with the end of the Cold War, the collapse of the Soviet Union, and the unification of Germany. For another, the Czechs had little to fear from an independent Slovak state, given the relatively warm historical relations between the two groups; identity relations were at worst "indifferent." Additionally, the Czechs handsomely won the separation agreement, which granted them a massive preponderance of military power. Given their economy was much weaker than the Czechs', the Slovaks could not have plausibly closed that gap. With military and security considerations side-lined, the focus turned to economic and diplomatic issues. On these measures, the Czechs were only too happy to let the Slovaks secede, since they believed, correctly, that the Slovaks would dilute their reform agenda and shift their desired focus away from Western Europe and Western institutions more generally. Thus the Czechs acquiesced to Slovak demands for separation eagerly and peacefully.

Similarly, my theoretical argument sheds lights on two main aspects of the Scandinavian case. First, the region enjoyed an extremely and atypically benign security environment, which rendered future security threats less important, thus opening up space for a potential peaceful response. Second, the Swedes only took coercion against Norway off the table in 1905 once they were assured of a demilitarized zone along the new international border and the destruction of the latter's forts, speaking to their concerns about a future dyadic threat.

THE VELVET DIVORCE: CZECHOSLOVAKIA SPLITS IN 1993

The Velvet Divorce in the former Czechoslovakia, which birthed the Czech and Slovak republics, was by no means inevitable, given that the ethnic divisions in the state were not as pronounced as others in the region.[109] But the Slovaks, or at least their political representatives, argued for and demanded greater freedom and autonomy once communism collapsed in the late 1980s. The Czechs did not get in their way. When the breakup did occur, officially on midnight of January 1, 1993, it was a completely peaceful outcome; "virtually painless" and without "a nose being bloodied."[110]

This peaceful split could have occurred only in an environment of minimal external threats, where border changes were almost meaningless for security. Indeed, that is precisely where the Czechs found themselves in the early 1990s. The dissolution of the Soviet Union, the unification of Germany, and the end of the Cold War rendered the region's environment wholly benign. Additionally, the Czechs had little reason to fear an independent Slovak state. The relatively warm relations between the two ethnic groups over the previous century resulted in muted identity divisions, especially compared to other ethnic dyads in the region. As such, when the Slovak leader Vladimír Mečiar used his electoral victory in 1992 to press for (at least) a confederal state, Václav Klaus and the Czechs were only too happy to acquiesce to a split.

The Czechs and Slovaks shared a common history to the extent that both republics were part of the Habsburg Empire that collapsed at the end of World War I. There were, however, significant differences in the ways they had been controlled: the Czech lands were more loosely governed from Vienna, while the Slovaks were strictly ruled by the Hungarians. There were significant differences in the social and economic makeup of the regions too. The Czech region was a thriving, industrial region which contributed nearly 70 percent of the Habsburg Empire's industrial output, while the Slovak region was generally organized along more feudalistic lines, where a rural economy dominated. Largely as a consequence of these historical differences, the Czechs were known for their "urbane and secular culture," whereas Slovaks practiced a "deeply religious (mainly Catholic) brand of nationalism."[111] The Czechs developed a society with full literacy by the nineteenth century that contained an industrial working class and a bourgeoisie that evinced cultural, social, and intellectual capital. The Slovaks, on the other hand, were more impoverished and agrarian, and often pejoratively described as "economically and politically primitive."[112]

When the Habsburg Empire collapsed in 1919, the independent state of Czechoslovakia was born. Almost immediately, there was cause for consternation for the Slovaks. The first would-be president of Czechoslovakia, Thomas Garrigue Masaryk, signed an agreement in Pittsburgh in 1918 that promised a considerable degree of autonomy to the Slovaks, including the provision of their own Diet, administration, and the use of Slovak as a language of instruction in schools as well as officialdom. Unfortunately, the Pittsburgh Agreement, as it came to be known, was never implemented.[113]

Twenty years later, the republic's life came to an abrupt end, when Nazi Germany occupied the Czech lands. The Slovaks enjoyed a brief period as a nominally independent state under the stewardship of a fascist priest named Jozef Tiso. The taste of independence was never forgotten in Slovakia, providing the impetus for a drive to greater autonomy and freedom in later decades.[114] It is noteworthy for our purposes, however, that the Czechs and Slovaks never fought one another during the war, though they were technically on different sides from 1939, when Nazi Germany occupied Bohemia and Moravia, until 1944, the year of the Slovak uprising. This lack of violent conflict paved the way for muted identity divisions down the road.

After the war, the state was reunited as Czechoslovakia and brought under the ambit of the Soviet Union. Under communism, the Slovak lands especially saw Soviet-style industrialization, with the introduction of heavy steel and armaments factories. Politically, the state lay securely within the sphere of influence of the Soviets, who crushed various uprisings and revolutions, most brutally in 1968. The so-called Prague Spring of 1968 was important also because of its impact on intra-Czechoslovak institutions and relations. In the lead-up to 1968, the Czechs and Slovaks were working on plans to make the state a federation, with one central government and two republican governments, one for each ethnic group. Up to that point, the Slovaks had a state government but the Czechs did not, lending credence to the Slovak belief that the central government was, in fact, a Czech enterprise. A similar structure was prevalent with respect to the Communist Party: there was a Slovak wing and a central wing, but no specific Czech wing. The reforms being discussed at the time would have created a Czech state government as well as a Czech wing of the Communist Party. The Soviet invasion changed those plans, at least in part: the plans for revamping the state went through, but party reforms were squashed. Following the late 1960s, Czechoslovakia formally became a federal state.[115]

The communist era was notable for cementing the status of the Czech region as more preeminent than Slovak lands. "During 42 years of communist rule, everything went through Prague," leading to a Slovak sense "of being at the end of the line, not at the front of the line."[116] By the late 1980s, Eastern Europe was thrown into turmoil by the domino-like revolutions that evicted the Soviet presence in the region. The Czechoslovakian manifestation was the Velvet Revolution of 1989, led by playwright turned dissident, Václav Havel, which released the Soviet shackles from Czechoslovakia. It is to that period we now turn.

FROM VELVET REVOLUTION TO VELVET DIVORCE

After the fall of communism in Eastern Europe, the newly free Czechoslovak state went about instituting a series of economic reforms, making the country more promarket and capitalist. These reforms affected Czech and Slovak societies unequally. The more educated and economically advanced Czechs benefited greatly from the market-oriented direction of the new state, while the Slovaks disproportionately suffered. By the early 1990s, the unemployment rate in the Czech lands was amongst the lowest in Europe—only 3 percent—while in Slovakia it was about four times higher. Growth rates in the Czech regions were higher than those in Slovakia too. The uneven nature of the impact of economic reforms was the primary stumbling block in Czech-Slovak relations and eventually caused the dissolution of the state.[117]

Such an outcome was not foreordained, however. There was an air of optimism after the first elections in postcommunist Czechoslovakia in 1990. The recently imprisoned dissident Václav Havel led a new federal government. The main winner in the Czech lands was the Civic Forum, and its sister organization, Public against Violence, dominated the vote in Slovakia. The state governments in the Czech lands and Slovakia were led by Petr Pithart and Vladimír Mečiar, a former communist.[118] After the 1990 elections, the state promised to address many of the main Slovak complaints as they pertained to the institutional makeup of the state. Havel, who held considerable sympathy for many Slovak grievances, held negotiations with Slovaks on the formation of new federal and republic constitutions. But his promises would not go far enough for Slovaks, who felt that Prague was not sufficiently helpful in dealing with its economic crisis.[119] Polls showed that the feeling was mutual for the Czechs, and both ethnic groups thought that the state behaved more favorably toward the other ethnic group. In January 1992, for instance, 52 percent of Slovaks believed that the federal government benefited the Czech nation while 41 percent of Czechs believed the same about the Slovaks.[120]

Levels of general dissatisfaction with the political and economic status quo began to grow more acute by 1992. By May, three-quarters of the Czech population and 86 percent of Slovaks were unhappy with the overall political situation. This created space for populists to conflate ethnic with economic concerns, particularly in Slovakia.[121] Mečiar, especially, held the Czechs responsible for the lack of development and growth in Slovakia, and favored a more personalist, statist form of government and economic expansion, perhaps predictably, given his communist background. These competing visions to choose from—a promarket, pluralist policy favored by the Czechs and a more nationalistic and ethnically defined state favored by the Slovaks—set the stage for the 1992 election. Mečiar sought to exploit nationalistic sentiment in Slovakia with an economic populist message,[122] though he was careful not to campaign on a platform of independence, keeping his goals ambiguous.[123]

The elections proved to be Slovaks' secessionist moment and paved the way for the separation of the state.[124] In Slovakia, Mečiar's party, now named Movement for a Democratic Slovakia, after Public against Violence had been disbanded, won 37 percent of the vote for the Slovak parliament and 33.5 percent of the vote in the federal parliament. In total, Mečiar's party won 74 out of 150 seats in the Slovak parliament. "We need a politician like this right now," said one voter in Bratislava. "Meciar is a tough guy. He can defend us. Things must be put in order vis-à-vis the Czechs. They must stop getting a better deal."[125] Notably, no parties that were allied with major Czech parties won more than a negligible percentage of the vote. In the Czech lands, meanwhile, the Civic Democratic Party, led by the promarket reformer Václav Klaus, won similar totals, with 30 percent of the vote for the Czech legislature and 34 percent for the federal parliament.

After winning in their respective regions, Klaus and Mečiar began negotiations. Mečiar pushed for a separate constitution for the republics, which would take precedence over the federal constitution. Indeed, Mečiar had demanded a separate constitution for the Slovaks as far back as September 1991.[126] Moreover, the very fact that Klaus was the leader of the Czechs made Mečiar even more intransigent, since a large proportion of Slovaks held Klaus personally responsible for the economic reforms that had damaged their region. Klaus, however, refused Mečiar's solution, arguing that such a step would invalidate the unity of the country.

The pair exercised considerable influence on events after the election, without input from wider institutions such as parties or interest groups.[127] This lack of popular participation was significant because by most accounts, support for a complete split, if gauged in a referendum, would have been around 30 percent at the most, and probably closer to 20 percent.[128] As one voter said, "I voted for Mečiar. Lots of people voted for Mečiar. But they definitely did not vote for a split."[129] Indeed, polls showed that small majorities in both regions favored a solution other than secession, though a majority of Slovaks did desire greater distance from the Czechs, possibly in a confederal state.[130] However, this opposition to the split was mostly silent, with civil society not deeply established and formal mechanisms for dissent not in place. As such, common people against the split resigned themselves to their lack of influence and delegated all decision-making to Klaus and Mečiar.[131] Both Klaus and Mečiar had personal agendas too, eager to exercise power and be "masters of their own domain."[132]

Though the negotiation took place between "two tough-minded guys," it was carried out in a "calm, civic way."[133] At bottom, the issue was that each side's most preferred option for the future direction of the state—the Czechs preferred a strongly centralized unitary state, the Slovaks a loose confederation—were directly opposed. However, each side's second-most preferred option was the same: the dissolution of the state.[134] A strategy of "negotiations and concessions" saw the two leaders reconcile themselves to a split, pledging to ensure its peacefulness. The timetable for dissolution was laid out in advance, with three agreements signed on July 23, August 26, and October 6, each of which dealt with the particulars of the divorce.[135] Finally, the Czechs and Slovaks peacefully separated at midnight on December 31, 1992. Hilde's succinct summation of the divorce is well-put: "The problem of finding a new model for the common Czech and Slovak state, while at the same time reforming not only the economy but the whole of society away from the socialist model, proved to be too heavy a burden."[136]

EXTERNAL INSECURITY: CONSPICUOUS BY ITS ABSENCE

There were a number of reasons the split between the Czech and Slovak ethnic groups was as peaceful as it turned out. One central factor was the benign regional environment that the state found itself in.[137] In the lead-up to the Velvet Divorce, external security considerations were simply not a significant part of the calculus of the main players, especially on the Czech side.[138] As Kraus notes, "The sense of euphoria surrounding the altogether unexpected collapse of communism and the end of the Cold War temporarily eliminated any sense of external threats to Czechoslovakia."[139] Interviews of former diplomats; political officials; Czech, Slovak, and Western academics; and other observers of the region unanimously confirm that security issues were neither discussed by the principals nor a major concern during the negotiations to split the country.[140]

There were two elements that encapsulated the shifting geopolitics of the region. First, the end of the Cold War and the collapse of the Soviet Union, the entry of a unified Germany into NATO, and the signing of the Maastricht Treaty brought about a pervasive optimism in the region, and especially in central Europe. For this region, the dominant notion that suffused this period of European integration was that outside threats were diminishing and that there was little reason to worry about borders.[141] In Czechoslovakia, Soviet troops as part of the Warsaw Pact were removed in a matter of months—unlike in places such as Poland, where the process took years—supplementing the feeling of the "return to Europe" that was the main driver of Czech behavior. With the Czechs' erstwhile major threat, the Soviet Union, no longer on the map, alongside the unification of Germany, the Czechs' security environment represented a sea change.[142] Three-fifths of their borders were suddenly with German-speaking Europe, with which the Czechs felt a closer cultural affinity, as well as buffers in the form of Slovakia and Ukraine between it and the still-transitioning Russia. In fact, the environment had changed to such an extent that the major threat the Czechs faced from the east involved further unrest in, and disintegration of, the Russian state, following the putsch attempt against Yeltsin, rather than a military assault from it.[143] Unlike in 1919, when the Czechs actually believed they were too small to survive in Europe on their own, there were no such concerns in the 1990s.[144]

To the extent that any party was even slightly concerned about the external implications of separation, it was the Slovaks, not the Czechs. The active and anxious 600,000-large Hungarian minority in the Slovak lands, combined with the revanchist rhetoric of Hungary, whose leader loudly proclaimed that he was the prime minister of 15 million Hungarians—that is, Hungarians in both Hungary and Slovakia—and a dispute over a dam on the Danube, all constituted cause for concern, but certainly not to the Czechs.[145] To the contrary, Havel and Jiří Dienstbier, the Czech foreign minister, believed so strongly in their external safety that they momentarily believed NATO would follow the Warsaw Pact into oblivion: the continent was safe, aside from the threat of instability from breakup of Soviet states.[146] Perhaps the most revealing measure of how sanguine the Czechs were about the security environment were the drastic cuts in its armed forces: before the divorce, the united state had a military of 200,000, while the independent Czech Republic's army was a tenth of that size.[147]

Second, and relatedly, the Czechs were eager to turn to the west politically, economically, and socially. A senior Foreign Ministry official put it simply as the divorce was being finalized: "Eventual membership in the European Community is the No. 1 foreign policy objective of the Czech

Republic."[148] Czechs saw themselves as integrated members of Western European culture—as one American diplomatic official reminded me, Prague is further west than Vienna—and saw Slovaks as closer to Russia.[149] A split would leave most of the Czech Republic bordering German-speaking Europe, while Slovakia would continue to share 90 percent of its borders with other Visegrad group states (Czech Republic, Poland, and Hungary).[150] More important than social-cultural divisions, the Czech leadership, especially the so-called Chicago school economist Klaus and his promarket allies, saw their future in the EU and in Western institutions and markets more generally.[151] Slovaks, at least those such as Mečiar, saw them themselves tied to Russia, not least because of significant gas and oil imports from there,[152] and were more skeptical of Klaus's "shock-treatment" market reforms.

This goal of "Returning to Europe," was, according to Czech scholars, not conducive to an escalation of political violence.[153] For their part, Western institutions such as NATO organized training programs for military, civilians, and parliamentarians, and extended aid.[154] As part of these efforts, NATO extended assurances to the new states about their future security, especially regarding territorial defense.[155] Former NATO officials with extensive experience in Eastern Europe told me that the peaceful dissolution of Czechoslovakia "would have been a different story had both institutions [NATO and EU] maintained closed doors. . . . If we didn't have those institutions, I don't think it would have ended up like it did, they were necessary but not sufficient conditions for such a [peaceful] transition."[156] While one should not overstate the role of NATO—a former U.S. ambassador to Slovakia with extensive experience in Czechoslovakia before the split told me that "we weren't pushing them to join NATO" due to concerns about the reaction in Russia,[157] and some Czech leaders, as mentioned, thought NATO was on the way to being obsolete—it is fair to say the pull of the European Community, and European institutions more generally, rather than NATO specifically, exercised a significant influence on the Czech leadership.

While the general regional security environment was unthreatening, what made the Velvet Divorce truly possible was the complete lack of dyadic threat a future Slovak state would pose to a future Czech one. For one thing, Slovakia would lack the capabilities to mount a serious threat to the Czechs, given the particulars of the separation agreement. Specifically, discussions in the lead-up to the divorce suggested that federal assets would be distributed territorially—in this case, possession was 100 percent of the law—while all other assets would be divided in a 2:1 ratio favoring the Czechs, in proportion to their population advantage. From a military point of view, this would be wholly beneficial to the Czechs, since 80 percent of military assets were located on their territory.[158] Additionally, it was not just quantity but quality of hardware that was crucial. At the time of the separation, "roughly 95 percent of all Czechoslovak combat aircraft were still deployed in Czech lands, and the only planes based in Slovakia were some obsolete MiG-21s. All the federal army's antitank helicopters were deployed in Bohemia, as were 70 percent of its main battle tanks and armored combat vehicles, including all modern ones. Moreover the Czech Republic was well protected by a mix of short-, medium-, and long-range air defense missiles, whereas Slovakia was only partly covered."[159] The reason for this lopsided nature of military installments was that the Czechs were closer to the East-West dividing line in the Cold War, and as such, the best and most modern forces, equipment, and bases were stationed there. Slovakia would also have to start from scratch with respect to creating a defense ministry and a military command and organization.[160] These terms were not especially appealing to the Slovaks, but they could object little under the circumstances.[161] Nor could they easily make up the difference in capabilities, given that their economic strength was well behind that of the Czechs, and the gap between them was only expected to grow after independence.[162] The only military advantage the Slovaks had over the Czechs was a more-than-proportionate share of the officer corps of the army,[163] but even here, the Slovak advantage was mitigated. During the split, many Slovak officers elected to stay in the Czech Republic, typified by one Slovak officer explaining that, "I am neither a good Slovak nor a bad Slovak. I'm an army officer. My wife and children are Czech. It makes no sense for me to return to Slovakia."[164] This position, shared by many of his colleagues, left the Slovak army, according to a former NATO official, with "the B-team in terms of officer corps."[165]

More important than the imbalanced terms of divorce was the muted identity division between the Czechs and Slovaks. There was no history of violent conflict between the two ethnic groups, no bloodthirsty calls for revenge for crimes past.[166] A *Washington Post* editorial captured this notion when it noted that "having had a very different history, Czechs and Slovaks will proceed differently from the way Serbs and Croats did. Yugoslav-style mayhem is not the danger in Czechoslovakia."[167] Almost all my interviewees cited a lack of historical enmity and violence between the Czechs and Slovaks, especially relative to other ethnic dyads in the region, as the primary cause of the peacefulness of the split.[168] In fact, by the standards of Eastern Europe, the two ethnic groups had fairly cordial relations. They were briefly on opposite sides during World War II, when the Czech lands were occupied by Nazi Germany, while Slovakia was an independent state for the duration of the war under fascist Jozef Tiso, who hoped to win territory in the eventuality of a Nazi victory, but Slovaks' uprising in 1944, which cost sixty thousand lives, "cleansed their soul."[169] More important for our purposes, there were no mass atrocities akin to the Yugoslavian Croat-Serb dyad during or after the war. That type of intense, inter-ethnic hatred simply did not exist in the Czech-Slovak case.[170] As one Slovak nationalist said in the run-up to the 1992 elections, "Our sovereignty movement is like a grown-up son moving out and looking for his own apartment. It doesn't mean he is angry with his parents. But he just wants to speak in his own name, have his own identity."[171] Journalists reported that the general mood characterizing the 1992 election was "of passive anger rather than hysteria."[172] This relatively muted history of conflict translated into identity relations that were at worst "indifferent," resulting in a sanguine outlook on the future by Czech leaders. The warm relations between the two independent republics since, stretching to over two decades, confirms the Czech prognosis.[173]

Thus, when it came to both military capabilities and intentions, the Czechs had little reason to believe the Slovaks would prove a security problem in the future. Combined with the benign regional environment, this meant that security considerations were relegated to a tertiary—if that—concern for the Czechs, and economic and cultural considerations came to be dominant.[174] My interviewees were unanimous that economic considerations are what drove the split for both sides: Klaus and the Czechs wanted "shock treatment" economic reforms, while Mečiar wanted a more gradual shift from a command economy. The Czechs felt that Mečiar and the Slovaks would slow the pace of reform. With that in mind, Czech leaders such as Klaus were not just tolerant of Slovak secession, but positively eager. They believed that economically speaking, they would be better off without the Slovaks than with them. They would no longer have to subsidize Slovakia's weaker economy to the tune of $1 billion annually, about 7 percent of the national budget.[175] As Kramer notes, "Klaus's determination to consummate the split as rapidly as possible in 1992 was based in part on his judgment that attempts to retain a unified state would merely cripple his economic program and make Slovakia even more of an economic burden."[176] The institutional makeup of the state, with ample veto points in the legislative process, shared equally between Czechs and Slovaks, juxtaposed with the election results that gave right-of-center reformers power in one region but a former communist in another, meant that "almost no form of cohabitation [was] feasible."[177] Moreover, the Czechs felt, correctly as it turned out,[178] that Mečiar's authoritarianism would be problematic for admission to European institutions, and that this goal could be achieved more rapidly going alone. As a *Financial Times* report summarized, "The likelihood is that the western Czech lands of Bohemia and Moravia, freed of the need to subsidize the economically weaker Slovakia, will now move faster on economic and other reforms. Such policies should allow them to fulfil the preconditions for membership of the E[uropean] C[omission] while Slovakia, with its inefficient heavy industries, risks sliding backwards economically."[179] An influential Prague weekly, *Respekt*, printed a headline that captured the prevailing attitude: "Alone to Europe or together to the Balkans."[180]

For the Czechs, then, Slovak demands for separation, far from representing a threat, were an opportunity to pursue political and economic goals that might not have been possible otherwise. To describe their response as sanguine would be understating it; they positively welcomed the chance to separate, once the Slovaks had set the process in motion. But this outcome was possible only because security concerns were taken off the table, in turn due to assessments of Slovak capabilities and intentions in the future. The existence of a benign security environment and the muted identity divisions between the two ethnic groups meant that the state could peacefully negotiate secession.

In addition to muted external security considerations, however, there were other factors at play that allowed for a peaceful split. Some interviews emphasized the importance of the Czech leadership and its enlightened character, especially when it came to Havel—"if he was [Slobodan] Milosevic, you would've had conflict"—and how drastically it differed from contemporary Eastern European politics.[181] These interviewees emphasized that, unlike in other parts of Eastern Europe, such as Poland, the revolution in Czechoslovakia was led by intellectuals based in Prague coffeehouses. These enlightened leaders yearned for democracy, "the institutionalization of freedom" in their words, and sought to build "a democracy without adjectives."[182] It is important, however, not to overstate the case for enlightened leadership playing a decisive role in the peacefulness of the split. Havel served more as a "guiding light" or a moral force and had "almost no influence" on actual events in 1992.[183] He did not get along with Klaus, who ensured that Havel was shunted from the negotiations. Additionally, he was considerably more popular in the Czech lands (and the rest of the world) than he was in Slovakia, whose heavy armaments industry suffered considerably from his dictum that the state, after the collapse of communism, would no longer be an exporter of arms.[184] Unlike Havel, the two personalities directly involved, Mečiar and Klaus, were not especially enlightened. Mečiar, while not a full-blown fascist, had rightist, "proto-authoritarian" leanings; according to Western diplomatic officials, he was "a nasty piece of work" with a background in intelligence services. Meanwhile, Klaus, who in retrospect was just as authoritarian and nationalist as Mečiar, was an "egomaniac" similar to Donald Trump, according to a Western diplomatic official.[185] The main difference between the two was that the people behind Klaus were not as uniformly authoritarian as those behind Mečiar.[186] Regardless, the decision makers involved in the split had more nationalistic, authoritarian tendencies than the coffeehouse intellectuals that led the Velvet Revolution.

A factor probably more important than the leadership involved was the neat dividing line between the two groups, their "clear, undisputed frontiers" in Martin Bútora's words.[187] Several interviewees commented that there were "historical" borders between the Czech and Slovak lands; there was no "fight for the furniture."[188] Additionally, there were few ethnic enclaves left over, with Czechs being 1 percent of the population in the Slovak lands and Slovaks making up 4 percent of the population in the Czech lands. As such, there was no fear about the fate of conationals left behind an enemy state's borders,[189] a fear much more strongly prevalent in the former Yugoslavia. The absence of these fears, and security fears more generally, allowed Czech leaders to accept territorial loss with little trepidation, signing off on the country's Velvet Divorce less than half a decade after its Velvet Revolution.

SEPARATION IN SCANDINAVIA: NORWAY-SWEDEN IN 1905

After spending nearly a century together, Norway and Sweden separated into independent nation-states in 1905. Norway had been loosening the knot that bound the two for decades, and the early twentieth century saw it untied. Notably, it was a completely peaceful event. Though there was, temporarily, a threat of military action by the Swedes, King Oscar and his government decided against the use of force, and Norway gained its statehood in a negotiated settlement. The separation is generally considered to be one of the very few cases of peaceful secession in the twentieth century.[190]

While several idiosyncratic factors facilitated the peaceful dissolution of the Norway-Sweden union, limiting the number of generalized lessons we can draw from it, the case forms important material to test my argument because we have so few cases of a state employing a "negotiations and concessions" strategy against secessionism. Can my theoretical claim, that states will adopt peaceful methods against separatists only when they are unconcerned about future war, be sustained given the evidence from events in Scandinavia in 1905? For instance, we would have cause for concern if Sweden's peaceful response to Norway's demands for independence took place amidst intense interstate rivalry or a militarized history between the two peoples. To the contrary, as I detail below, the muted nature of geopolitical competition in the region, along with Norway's pledge to demilitarize its border and raze its forts, helped create the structural conditions—a sanguine sense of external threat—under which Sweden felt assured acquiescing to territorial loss.

The story of the Norway-Sweden union began in 1814, after the Napoleonic wars. For more than four centuries, Norway had been part of Denmark, but that arrangement came to an end when Denmark foolishly dragged the union into the Napoleonic wars and declared war against Sweden. Norway consequently had to face an onslaught from a much stronger Sweden, which it did a fair job of repelling, despite worse military equipment and training. At the same time, Sweden lost a third of its territory to Russia in 1809, including Finland, setting off panic in Sweden about its vulnerability. The Swedes deposed their king and joined the alliance led by Britain and Russia, which defeated France in 1812. In return for its help in victory, Sweden's two great power allies agreed that Sweden should get compensation for its loss of Finland. Relatedly, Sweden's military threatened Denmark and requested that Norway be handed over to it. Owing to its weakness, Denmark agreed and gave Norway to Sweden by the Treaty of Kiel on January 14, 1814.[191]

As was standard practice in the high politics of warfare and territorial exchanges in contemporary Europe, nobody had bothered to ask Norway whether it wished to be part of this union. This was especially important because the timing of the transfer took place just as nationalism was beginning to take root and spread on the European continent.[192] Norway would have much rather been independent, or at the very least enjoyed more autonomy than it did under Denmark. Negotiations to that end led to a standoff, which in turn resulted in a short, sharp military battle, in which Sweden asserted its superiority. Along with military dominance, Sweden also enjoyed the support of Russia and Britain. Mindful, however, of maintaining goodwill with the people it aimed to assert sovereignty over, Sweden pressed for a negotiated settlement early in the conflict, and Norway finally relented. On August 30, 1814, the union between Sweden and Norway was established by the Treaty of Moss, with its designated head of state the king of Sweden.[193]

Union wasn't easy. It took until 1875 for the two political units to share a common currency and coinage. Their bodies of law were distinct, despite sharing ancient foundations. Their economies were so similar that their primary trade partners were other states in Europe, not each other. The two units had a common foreign policy, it is true, as well as cooperation in areas such as railroads, communication, and shipping, but most other instruments and levers of power were located at the state level, including legal supremacy, budgetary decisions, trade policy, citizenship, civil service, ministries, and the courts.[194] That said, autonomy had limits, given that "the acts of the Norwegian parliament would require approval of the Swedish King-in-Council."[195] Overall, Norway resisted attempts aimed at greater political integration, such as plans for a confederal legislature in the 1850s or closer cooperation in 1871.[196] Most important, the two units retained independent militaries.[197] This would have important consequences when push came to shove at the beginning of the twentieth century, as we shall soon see.

THE PRELUDE TO DISSOLUTION

The main issue dividing Norway and Sweden was the former's lack of separate consular services, and more generally, where constitutional and legal control of diplomatic and consular officials within the union would lie. Norwegians believed that their shipping and trade interests were misrepresented by Swedish consuls, who were biased in favor of Sweden,[198] an important concern given Norway's "growing merchant marine, which by the late nineteenth century was far larger than Sweden's and heavily engaged in the carrying trade between foreign ports. There were differences as well between Norwegian and Swedish trade policies, especially when Sweden in 1888 established protective tariffs while Norway continued to favor free trade."[199] The issue was not just economic but also symbolic, given foreign affairs was the area in which Sweden exercised power over Norway most clearly.[200]

Matters escalated in 1892. The Norwegian minority government, led by the Conservative Party and Emil Stang, reached an agreement with the Swedes on the larger question of representation in foreign policy. The deal would leave the nationality of the foreign minister undefined—but assumed to be Swedish—and would make him responsible to a union council featuring three Norwegians and three Swedes. The compromise, however, was not satisfactory to the so-called pure wing of Venstre Party, the most radical party in Norway at the time. Venstre leaders such as Wollert Konow and Carl Berner unequivocally rejected the agreement. The Storting, Norway's legislature, passed a resolution that proclaimed "Norway's right to safeguard its foreign affairs in a constitutionally adequate manner." Stang interpreted the resolution as a vote of no confidence and resigned, and in his place the Swedish King invited the radical Venstre to form the new government led by Johannes Steen. Upon assumption of power, Steen and the radicals, supported by the moderates and the conservatives, passed a resolution in the Storting that asserted its right to legislate on a Norwegian consular system, voted in a law for separate consuls, and appropriated budgetary funds for their functioning. Such a unilateral move was anathema to King Oscar, who was aware that the Swedish cabinet would resign if he countenanced the developments taking place in Norway. The king predictably vetoed the resolution, which in turn led to resignations from Steen and his fellow ministers, kicking off a three-year political crisis that lasted until June 1895.[201]

What helped end the crisis was the threat of military action by Sweden. In February 1895, the Riksdag, Sweden's legislature, almost unanimously rejected Norway's consular service demands. More ominously, the king called a meeting of the Secret Committee, which had last been brought together during the Crimean war. Military supplies for unspecified purposes were voted for, and we know now that the Swedish General Staff had detailed plans prepared for moves against Norway. It was evident that Sweden was sending a message, and by June 1895, Norway received it. The Storting, in a lopsided 90–24 vote, called for a reopening of negotiations on the matter.[202]

There is little doubt that Norway's relative military backwardness was the main cause of its retreat.[203] With the memory of its acquiescence to perceived Swedish bullying in sharp relief, Norway went about modernizing and improving its military capabilities. More attention, and money, was budgeted for the army. The navy was updated, including the purchase of warships. Norway also built fortresses along its southeastern border with Sweden and stockpiled munitions.[204]

NORWAY AND SWEDEN GO THEIR SEPARATE WAYS

A crisis remarkably similar to the one from 1892 to 1895 took place in 1905, but with a dramatically different result: Norway's independence.

Just as in the 1890s, the main issue was whether Norway would enjoy separate consular representation. There was initial promise in working out a compromise between the two hardened positions, as Sigurd Ibsen, son of the well-known playwright, put together a plan for separate consular establishments under one single diplomatic staff for two kingdoms. A joint commission was put into place—itself an advancement after Norway's insistence in the mid-1890s that there was nothing to negotiate—and there was genuine promise in the commission's deliberations. It all came crashing down, however, when Swedish premier E. G. Boström played spoiler by inserting six clauses in a prospective agreement that would have confirmed Norway's dependent position in the union in 1904.[205]

On February 7, 1905, the Joint Cabinet recognized the failure of the negotiations, and the Norwegian coalition government, which had been elected on a platform to negotiate, was disbanded. According to one contemporary observer, Norwegian anger was widely palpable, and citizens were "united with a determination to repudiate every Swedish encroachment."[206] In mid-March, a new coalition government led by Christian Michelsen took charge and displayed its resolve immediately. The Storting once again passed a resolution calling for the establishment of a separate consular service, knowing full well that the king, as in 1892, would veto it. Sure enough, he did, and in a prearranged move, the entire Norwegian cabinet resigned en masse. The king refused to accept the mass resignations, since a replacement government could not be formed.[207] The Norwegians went ahead with their final step, which included the Storting unanimously resolving to dissolve the union, owing to "the king's ceasing to function as king of Norway."[208] It was a bold and provocative step, Norway's secessionist moment.

At this juncture, Sweden faced a choice: to use coercion or not. Norway had, after all, just unilaterally declared itself free of the Swedish king's sovereignty. Sweden did temporarily consider military action to keep the union alive, but thought better of it. Crown Prince Gustav summed up the prevailing attitude in Sweden, arguing that "Sweden should herself propose a divorce rather than to be, so to speak, kicked out of the union."[209] The Rikstag followed suit and accepted the dissolution of the union, so long as Norway met four conditions.[210]

Two of these conditions had more to do with Sweden's pride than anything else: it demanded that Norway hold a plebiscite on the question of independence—to ascertain that it was truly what the people wanted, and not merely a product of the machinations of politicians—and that Norway submit itself to bilateral negotiations without any reference to the unilateral actions taken earlier. The third related to organizing a conference that dealt with the logistics of the separation, including access to transfrontier watercourses and guarantees for the unimpeded migration of the nomadic Lapps. The fourth was the most important, and most interesting for our purposes. It called for the demilitarization of the border zone up to ten kilometers, as well as the destruction of all the Norwegian forts on the border.[211] Ultimately, Norway came to accept each of these demands, and though hard feelings lingered on both sides, there was also a great deal of relief. By the fall of 1905, the disunion was final, and Norway was an independent state, all down to Sweden adopting "negotiations and concessions" as a strategy at Norway's secessionist moment.

SWEDEN'S SANGUINE SUMMATION OF ITS SECURITY

This case highlights and illustrates certain important aspects of the theory I proffer in this book. First and most important, a completely peaceful secession such as the Norway-Sweden dissolution could take place only in a very benign security environment. The region was not a battleground for power politics; as Parent puts it, "Sweden and Norway generally stayed out of world politics, and world politics generally returned the favor."[212] Throughout the nineteenth century, Scandinavia was involved in "very little international conflict . . . from 1864 to 1914, Sweden and Norway were not involved in any notable international incident; the union hardly had a foreign policy."[213] For the most part, Sweden assumed a position of neutrality in intra-European affairs.[214] As such, it is reasonable to assert that Sweden had little to fear from rapacious European powers when it came to the security consequences of losing substantial territory. Moreover, in the same year as the disunion, the great powers' focus was on other matters, most notably the fallout from the Russo-Japanese war as well as burgeoning colonial rivalries in Morocco.[215] The overall external environment, from Sweden's perspective, was benign, thus affording it greater latitude in its dealings with Norwegian nationalism.

Second, it is instructive that Sweden did not reconcile itself to a peaceful split until after it attained guarantees regarding the status of the forts Norway had constructed on the border. Lindgren describes the forts' importance, noting that "their thin line of guns and masonry walls pointed directly into Sweden from the sea on the south to almost the sixty-first parallel north of Hamar. They barred Swedish armies from a direct attack on Oslo and could be breached only by fierce fighting and heavy losses of men."[216] Indeed, one contemporary media report conveyed that the destruction of Norway's forts was the central Swedish concern during negotiations.[217] The Swedish demand to raze the forts directly stems from the commitment problem that makes granting statehood such a thorny proposition: a host state needs to be confident that the separatists will not turn its new guns on it for it to consider concessions that could ultimately lead to letting go of its territory.

On the other hand, while confidence that its future security would not be violated set the stage for Sweden's response, there were additional causes for the peacefulness of the split. One factor unique to the Scandinavian case was the relatively weak political and administrative ties between the two units, which made the split more acceptable than it otherwise would have been. More important, the fact that each side had its own military was crucial in Sweden acquiescing to territorial loss. The was because as scholars almost unanimously point out, Sweden did briefly consider military action to keep the union alive, but backed off, in part owing to little chance for long-term military and political success.[218] It is important to underscore why exactly Sweden's prospects for military success were not assured. As mentioned above, Norway spent the decade before the 1905 crisis revamping and modernizing its military capabilities. It raised loans to build its two first ironclad warships and constructed additional forts on its coasts. It also budgeted more money for annual military purchases and stockpiled munitions. By strengthening its defenses before moving for disunion, Norway ensured that an invasion by Sweden would not result in an easy Swedish victory. While helpful to its cause in the immediate term, this military strength would have posed a problem for Norway's demands for independence had it not been accompanied by credible assurances that Sweden would not fall victim to it in the future. Norway had to thus reassure Sweden, explaining its decision to destroy its forts along the border.

The American Civil War

Perhaps no secessionist war has been studied as much as the U.S. Civil War. It is the only conflict in this book that has entire academic journals dedicated to its study.[219] Interestingly, despite this attention, and notwithstanding some notable exceptions, little research has focused explicitly on the role of external security in the U.S. Civil War. This probably has something to do with the paucity of international relations specialists among the vast legions of scholars who have studied the conflict. It is not as if the question is immaterial or uninteresting; when I first began researching the material for this book and presenting my findings to scholarly audiences, I would regularly hear from American (and American-based) questioners: does your theory have anything to say about our Civil War?

The finer details of the U.S. Civil War have been more than adequately addressed in the voluminous literature devoted to it. Of particular concern to me is first, why the North did not let the South secede, and second why Lincoln changed his preferred policy of dealing with Southern secessionists, from advocating patience and a blockade, to a military strike at Bull Run in the summer of 1861.[220] The escalation to a "militarization" strategy, taking place between April and June of 1861, necessitated both sides raising massive armies—a million men for the unionists, 400,000 for the Confederates—and laid the groundwork for a long, bloody war.[221] In other words, understanding this decision holds great import for understanding why the Civil War developed as it did, or even why a civil war erupted in the first place.

As I argue below, one of the main reasons Northern leaders could not countenance the Confederacy was that they were concerned about the future balance of power on the American continent if their state divided, and were especially wary of an expansionist Britain taking advantage of competition between the Union and an independent Confederacy. Though there were assuredly other factors responsible in Lincoln's refusal to let the south secede, external security was foremost amongst them. Furthermore, when it comes specifically to Lincoln's escalation at Bull Run, recent IR scholarship has shown that its timing was aimed at forestalling British recognition of, and material support to, the Confederacy. The mere threat of third-party support, rather than its delivery, prompted Lincoln to escalate, an interesting application of my theory.

For our purposes, this case is significant because it shows the power of my argument for explaining events and processes in unlikely situations, which in turn can lead to greater confidence in the underlying mechanisms. Strictly speaking, the U.S. Civil War was neither ethno-nationalist in nature nor did it take place in the twentieth century, which goes against the grain of other conflicts studied in this book. However, if external security considerations, including fears of the future balance of power and third-party support behind the secessionists, were operative in an episode that looks superficially different to the others under investigation, we can be more secure that, in general, internal policies are often determined by events and phenomena outside the state. The U.S. Civil War is generally thought to be the product of slavery, political economy, and "state's rights," but the evidence suggests that foreign relations and external security had an important role to play in the crisis.

THE SECESSIONIST CRISIS AND ITS ESCALATION

The United States was less than one hundred years old when it plunged into a secessionist crisis in the second half of the nineteenth century. Unlike all the episodes of secessionism covered in this book, the U.S. Civil War was not strictly ethnically based. Indeed, the United States was probably at its most homogenous, ethnically speaking, on the eve of its Civil War.[222] That said, its similarity to other crises covered lies in its decidedly regionalist nature; it is sometimes hard to tell when region-based grievances end and where ethnic-based grievances begin, given ethnic groups' proclivity to gather within certain territories.[223]

In this particular case, the regional divisions that marked the country were primarily economic, and later, social. The South's was a primarily export-based economy, the Northwest grew and supplied food, and the Eastern and Middle States constituted the country's commercial and manufacturing base.[224] This economic regionalism resulted in a "natural" divergence of interests: the South opposed tariffs, given its reliance on trade, while the North and West supported them. The South was against the use of public funding to expand transportation and communication networks, the landlocked North naturally disagreed. The South did not favor central banking, as opposed to the North, which housed the centers of capital.[225]

Most of all, the people of the North had very different views on slavery than those of the South, and these differences had only been widening since the beginning of the century.[226] As the United States aggressively expanded its territory at a dizzying rate—from 890,000 to 3 million square miles of land, and a sixfold population increase between 1790 and 1850—the question of whether slavery would be expanded to the new territories suddenly brought tension to the fore.[227] Would the United States be a country that had legal slavery or not, and if so, to what geographic extent would it be legal?

The 1860 election brought into sharp relief the different values, interests, and ideologies of the two parts of the country.[228] The Republican candidate for president, Abraham Lincoln, was understood to oppose slavery, the exact issue with which Southern separatism was inextricably bound up. Southern states deemed Lincoln's election the last straw, their collective sentiment captured well by one Georgia editor: "The election of Lincoln is merely the confirmation of a purpose which the South had hoped would be abandoned by the opponents of slavery in the North. It is a declaration that they mean to carry out their aggressive and destructive policy, weakening the institution at every point where it can be assailed either by legislation or by violence, until, in the brutal language of [Senator] Charles Sumner, 'it dies like a poisoned rat in its hole.'"[229]

Southern nationalism did not exist as anything other than opposition to the North—cultural affinity and shared practices notwithstanding—but given the import of the slavery issue, it need not have.[230] The economic implications of slavery and abolition were considerable enough; as one contemporary writer noted, "It was not safe to trust eight hundred million dollars' worth of Negroes in the hands of a power that says we do not own the property, that the title under the Constitution is bad, and under the law of God still worse."[231] The people in slaveholding states were determined to defend slavery and "force the Yankees to recognize not only their rights but also their status as perfectly decent, respectable human beings."[232] Simply put, if slavery was not welcome in the Union, then the Union was not welcome in the South.

When elected, Lincoln claimed that he did not wish to eradicate slavery where it existed, only that he would not permit its expansion, but this did not convince the South, nor did it address the South's biggest grievance, which was the Northern refusal to return fugitive slaves.[233] Southern whites could not fathom a world in which black Americans were free: there were far too many of them to deport, and the idea that they could physically stay in their midst while not being servile was anathema.[234] These differences meant that, functionally speaking, only two out of three goals—peace, union, and abolition—could be reached simultaneously. The South chose slavery over union, when on March 4, the six most southern states voted to secede.[235] A civil war seemed to be in the offing when Southern soldiers fired on and took over Fort Sumter in South Carolina in April. At this secessionist moment, the North had to decide whether it valued peace more than the Union.

THE NORTHERN RESPONSE

Abraham Lincoln had some decisions to make.[236] Lincoln cared, or seemed to care, a great deal more about the union than abolition. In other words, his priority appeared to be maintaining the territorial integrity of the United States, not necessarily fidelity to particular principles. "My paramount objective," he said, "is to save the Union and it is not either to save or to destroy slavery. What I do about slavery and the colored race, I do because I believe it helps save the Union, and what I forbear, I forbear because I do not believe it would help to save the Union."[237] At another point, Lincoln was explicit about his hierarchy of preferences: "My paramount object in this struggle *is* to save the Union, and is *not* either to save or to destroy slavery. If I could save the Union without freeing *any* slave I would do it, and if I could save it by freeing *all* the slaves I would do it; and if I could save it by freeing some and leaving others alone I would also do that."[238]

Indeed, Lincoln's antislavery stance did not extend into warm feelings for American blacks. Lincoln had been a career "colonizationist," which meant that he favored deporting masses of emancipated slaves to other parts of the world because, as he told a delegation of Negroes in 1862, "it is better for us to be separated."[239] His reasoning was that "We have between us a broader difference than exists between almost any other two races. Whether it is right or wrong I need not discuss, but this physical difference is a great disadvantage to us both, as I think your [black] race suffers very greatly, many of them by living among us, while ours suffer from your presence. In a word we suffer on each side. If this is admitted, it affords a reason at least why we should be separated." This was perhaps an unsurprising position for a politician who believed of blacks that "not a single man of your race is made the equal of a single man of ours."[240]

The bottom line is that secession would not be allowed. Lincoln's immediate response to Southern secessionism was marked by caution,[241] employing a wait-and-see policy on how to deal with the crisis in general and the Southern assault on Fort Sumter in South Carolina in particular. Republicans in the North were internally divided on these questions, with four positions taking hold: hardliners wished for a more coercive response from Washington, moderate Republicans emphasized the law-and-order aspects of Southern secessionism, "conciliationists" argued that the North should grant certain concessions so that the forces of disunion would be weakened in the less polarized states of the Upper South, while a nontrivial minority supported peaceful disunion.[242] In the early months of 1861, congressional Republicans mainly supported the conciliatory position, hoping to internally divide the South.[243] Lincoln had to balance firmness and magnanimity; he had to encourage Southern unionism while not providing further fuel for secessionists, all the while keeping his own party united and focused. His main objective in the early stages of the crisis was to play for time.[244]

Lincoln displayed this moderate strain in his inaugural address. He reiterated that he had no intention of threatening slavery in states where it was already legal, that the government did not have the ability to stamp it out even if he personally wanted to, and that his utmost concern was maintaining constitutional rights and laws, such as the return of fugitive slaves, collecting import duties, delivering mail, and defending public property. He claimed that such actions would not represent taking the fight to Southern secessionists, but rather constituted self-defense. He closed memorably: "In *your* hands, my fellow countrymen, and not in *mine*, is the momentous issue of civil war. . . . You can have no conflict, without being yourselves the aggressors, with *you*, and not with *me*, is the solemn question of "Shall it be peace, or a sword?"[245]

Meanwhile, by the end of February, the seceded states had taken over most federal property, had a written constitution, and a government.[246] Lincoln's policy continued to be characterized by patience, believing that if he supplied enough rope to the secessionists, they would hang themselves,[247] summing up his strategy thusly: "The power confided to me will be used to hold, occupy, and possess the property and places belonging to the government, and to collect the duties and imposts; but beyond what may be necessary for these objects, there will be no invasion—no using of force against or among the people anywhere."[248] Indeed, Lincoln continued to be conciliatory, and even softened the stance outlined in the inaugural address.[249] These words, forswearing the use of force, represent Lincoln's initial response to Southern secessionism, characterized by caution and prudence within a law-and-order framework, and form the baseline against which we can judge later deviations from it.

DISALLOWING SECESSION AND ESCALATION: THE BRITISH CONNECTION

Republicans grew increasingly impatient across the North. More crucially, supplies at the captured Fort Sumter were running low, and the more immediate question became whether to evacuate the fort or to attempt supplying it with provisions, almost assuredly baiting an attack.[250] In addition, by March, the first Confederate tariff went into effect, lowering import duties and directly challenging Lincoln's inaugural pledge to "collect the duties and imposts."[251] By late March, onlookers were becoming anxious: when, and what, would Lincoln decide? His military advisers had suggested evacuating the fort, and five of his seven cabinet advisers concurred, including his closest adviser, Secretary of State William Seward.[252] Evacuation was not such an easy call, however, because of the symbolism inherent in abandoning a fort "in the principal city of the most radical secessionist state," South Carolina.[253] As time went on, the division became increasingly partisan.[254]

By early April, Lincoln opted for resupplying the fort, which had predictable consequences: it came under attack, and on April 14, it was abandoned. Many historians consider the attack on the supply expedition to Fort Sumter as the beginning of the Civil War, but this emphasis is probably overstated. The three months following the Fort Sumter attack have been deemed a "phony war," with both sides committed to essentially defensive military strategy, more hold than take. One important development in this period, however, was the formal institution of blockade by Lincoln, on April 16, a policy that had been much discussed.[255]

It is Lincoln's change of heart by late June, however, that really changed the trajectory of the conflict. Now, rather than advocating stalling and delay, Lincoln chose a more aggressive strategy. On June 25 and 29, Lincoln summoned his war council for a pair of meetings, organized to authorize an invasion of the South.[256] This escalation—from a purely defensive strategy resembling policing to a more aggressive militarization—would set the stage for the long, brutal war that was to follow. The question is: what caused it? More generally, why were Lincoln and his advisers against Southern secession?

While there were a number of factors that contributed to the Union disallowing the South's secession, concern about external security is an underappreciated one. Specifically, a divided America would shift the balance of power on the continent toward Britain. Suspicions abounded that the British, given their strategic location in Canada and the Caribbean, would be favorably predisposed to a division of the United States and a reconfiguration of the balance of power on the continent.[257] In Seward's words, "The new confederacy, which in that case Great Britain would have aided into existence, must, like any other new state, seek to expand itself northward, westward, and southward. What part of this continent or of the adjacent islands would be expected to remain in peace?"[258] This eventuality, of an expansionist Confederacy locking horns over territory with the rump Union, would leave only one winner, geopolitically speaking: Britain. As one historian states, "British leaders welcomed the prospect of the permanent division of the vast territory of the United States between two nations" because it would eradicate the threat of American expansionism to Mexican independence and British rule in Canada.[259] Another scholar argues that it was a "popular" belief amongst the American leadership that Britain "would welcome the South into the family of nations as a strategic move designed to divide America and permit England to expand both above and below the republic" while encasing "the Union with a stronger Canada to the north and a Confederate friend to the South."[260] The suspicion was mutual: Britain considered the United States an aggressive, expansionist power and held particular distaste for Seward, "a chauvinistic supporter of Manifest Destiny" and "foremost, an American imperialist," who longed for the annexation British Canada.[261]

Notably, the interpretation that Britain wished for a divided America for its geopolitical purposes was widely shared, with the Russian ambassador to London claiming that "at the bottom of its heart, [Britain] desires the separation of North America into two Republics, which will watch each other jealously and counterbalance one the other. Then England, on terms of peace and commerce with both, would have nothing to fear from either; for she would dominate them, restraining them by their rival ambitions."[262] As one historian notes, "In the earlier years of the war the collapse of the Union seemed at first fight to offer considerable advantages and opportunities to Great Britain," including "the most effective and permanent solution of all Britain's difficulties of defense and diplomacy in America. Palmerston himself had held up the prospect of 'the Swarms [separating] from the Parent Hive' as the one real consolation for an ultimate acquiescence in American expansion."[263] In other words, the Northern leadership was acutely aware of the deleterious consequences of territorial loss for its future security, especially with regard to the future balance of power with Britain, and just as my theory would predict, acted to prevent a change in borders.

Consistent with this theme, there is good reason to believe that when escalating Northern strategy at Bull Run, Lincoln was guided by external factors relating to Britain and its relationship to the Confederacy. In particular, Lincoln and his advisers were concerned with the prospect of European, and especially British, recognition of the Southern separatists, which would strengthen the rebels' resolve and possibly lead down the slippery slope to military aid. Indeed, according to Poast, "Lincoln and his cabinet considered the possibility of British recognition to be *the primary threat* facing the United States with respect to the secession crisis." Furthermore, "key members of Lincoln's cabinet believed and/or received credible information that exercising force against the South could forestall such recognition" while "failure to act might lead the Europeans to perceive *de facto* Southern independence."[264] If this argument is accurate, it suggests that external conditions were not just operative in Lincoln's calculus, but central to it.

To understand why the prospect of British recognition of the Confederacy so concerned Lincoln and advisers, it is necessary to first appreciate British incentives for supporting the South. Southern independence would not just shift the geopolitical balance of power in favor of Britain. The British also stood to gain economically from supporting the Confederacy, mainly due to its reliance on Southern cotton. Under normal conditions, the British, owing to their antislavery stance, could reasonably be expected to support the North over the South, and there was considerable evidence initially that Britain would side overwhelmingly with the forces arrayed against the slave trade—reportedly, Prime Minister Palmerston had read *Uncle Tom's Cabin* three times and was vehemently antislavery.[265] However, Northerners themselves, including Lincoln, diminished the role slavery played in the crisis, so as to not alienate significant numbers of racist Northerners, as well as Unionists in the South and the border states of Maryland, Delaware, Kentucky, and Missouri.[266] This rhetorical strategy— emphasizing the sanctity of the Union and the need for law-and-order, rather than race or slavery as the guiding principles of Northern policy— unwittingly let the British off the hook; no longer did they have to choose between moral and strategic considerations.[267] After all, if the Unionists themselves claimed the crisis was not about slavery, then the British were free to support the South over other principles, such as states' rights,[268] as well as crasser, instrumental reasons.

These instrumental reasons boiled down to one issue: cotton. More than one-sixth of Britain's population relied on the textile industry—"Lancashire depends on South Carolina," in the words of the editors of *The Times*—and over one third of its exports were directly tied to cotton.[269] American cotton first gained a larger share of the European market than Indian cotton in 1796, providing higher yields and proving easier to yarn, and cemented its dominance through the nineteenth century.[270] Southerners were not just aware of British dependence on their cotton, but eager to use it as leverage. This view came to be known as the "King Cotton" thesis and enjoyed widespread acceptance and popularity, including among "operatives, manufacturers, merchants, government agents, prime ministers, all."[271] In the words of South Carolinian James H. Hammond, "Without firing a gun, without drawing a sword, should they make war on us we could bring the world to our feet. The South is perfectly competent to go on, one, two, or even three years without planting a seed of cotton. . . . What would happen if no cotton was furnished for three years? I will not stop to depict what every one can imagine, but this is certain: England would topple headlong and carry the whole civilized world with her, save the South. No, you dare not make war on cotton. No power on earth dares to make war upon it. Cotton is king!"[272] In December 1860, a week before South Carolina declared secession, Texas Senator Louis T. Wigfall agreed, boasting that "I say that cotton is King, and that he waves his scepter not only over these thirty-three States, but over the island of Great Britain and over continental Europe."[273] Part of the South's leverage came from the domestic political economy of both Britain and France, since each had substantial numbers of workers tied up in the textile industry, and these workers were "restless and rebellious and easily persuaded to revolution."[274] More than 80 percent of Britain's cotton supply emanated from the South and by May 1861, the South cut off cotton exports to Britain aside from Southern ports to demonstrate its standing. Luckily for Britain, it had a year's supply in surplus, but the message was sent: "The vital interests of their empire would come into play in about a year's time: Lancashire's cotton mills could not run without cotton."[275]

These geopolitical and economic incentives for Britain to support the South caused Lincoln and his confidantes, particularly Seward, to cast a wary eye across the Atlantic. They were apprehensive about the potential of Britain recognizing the Confederacy, both because it would provide legitimacy to the rebels and because it would open the doors for more explicit, material support, conceivably tipping the material balance in the South's favor.[276] For instance, were the British to recognize the Confederacy, it would gain access to British ports and the right to negotiate military and commercial treaties.

As such, Lincoln and Seward's overarching objectives during the secessionist crisis were to prevent diplomatic recognition of Confederate independence by European powers and to limit any form of European support for the Confederacy, material or otherwise.[277] As Seward wrote to U.S. Minister in Britain, Charles Adams, "The agitator in this bad enterprise [secessionism], justly estimating the influence of the European powers upon even American affairs, do not mistake in supposing that it would derive signal advantage from a recognition by any of those powers, and especially Great Britain. Your task, therefore, apparently so simple and easy, involves the responsibility of preventing the commission of an act by the government of that country which would be fraught with disaster, perhaps ruin, to our own."[278] Seward also vociferously emphasized to diplomatic representatives from other great powers, especially Britain, to not interfere in the crisis, to the point that his warnings were dismissed as "the rantings of a demagogue than as pleas for restraint and vision to preserve world peace."[279] In correspondence to the U.S. minister in London, Seward wrote that "I have never for a moment believed that such a recognition could take place without producing immediately a war between the U.S. and the recognizing power." At another point he warned that "British recognition would be British intervention to create without our own territory a hostile state by overthrowing this Republic itself," adding parenthetically that "when this act of intervention is distinctly performed, we from that hour, shall cease to be friends and become once more, as we have twice before been forced to be, enemies of Great Britain."[280] To the U.S. minister in Paris, he struck a similar tone: "Foreign intervention would obligate us to treat those who yield it as allies of the insurrectionary party and to carry on the war against them as enemies."[281] Regardless of their reception, Seward's ideas, and his message to diplomatic officials in London, were clear: "Every instruction you have received from this department is full of evidence of the fact that the principal danger in the present insurrection which the President has apprehended was that of foreign intervention, aid, or sympathy; and especially of such intervention, aid, or sympathy on the part of the government of Great Britain," adding that "foreign intervention, aid, or sympathy in favor of the insurgents, especially on the part of Great Britain, manifestly could only protract and aggravate the war."[282] Meanwhile, Northern concerns about British support and recognition were matched by Southern obsession with securing it, for the same reasons that it was opposed by the Unionists: it could potentially tip the balance. Historians consider European recognition of Southern independence the "paramount Confederate foreign policy goal," or "the Confederacy's chief objective in foreign affairs," especially during the first two years of the war.[283]

This, then, was the international context in the spring and summer of 1861, with Northern decision makers aware that Britain would sooner or later have to pick a side.[284] Within that period, there were indications that Britain was indeed moving toward recognizing the Confederacy. First, the British pledged neutrality in the conflict, which despite appearances, was not necessarily innocuous behavior: Charles Sumner, chairman of the Senate Foreign Relations Committee, classified the proclamation as "the most hateful act of English history since the time of Charles 2nd."[285] Neutrality so offended the North because it granted coequal belligerent status to the South—as opposed to "rebels" or "insurgents," which is how the North preferred to refer to the Confederate states. As Seward said to Richard Lyons, British minister to the United States, "to us, the rebels are only rebels, and we shall never consent to consider them otherwise. If you wish to recognize their belligerent character, either by addressing an official declaration to us, or by your actions, we shall protest and we shall oppose you."[286] In addition, neutrality, and its attendant belligerent status, bestowed on the Confederacy advantages, including the right of its vessels to confiscate enemy goods, the right of entry to British ports with prizes from privateering, and the right to borrow money and buy material for its armed forces as combatants rather than bandits.[287] Neutrality, the Unionists complained, "awarded stature and credibility to the Confederacy," and was perceived as "the first step in a process leading to recognition of Southern independence."[288] Additionally, the method and timing of the declaration of neutrality—the day of Adams's arrival in England, May 13, and without consultation, as had been previously agreed—was cause for chagrin.[289] As Adams delicately put it after his arrival, "The action taken seemed, at least to my mind, a little more rapid than was absolutely called for by the occasion."[290]

Second, British foreign secretary Russell announced a concert between Britain and France, pointedly without consulting the U.S. government, to arrange for a unified position on the question of neutrality, raising the specter of a joint European intervention in North America by two states that already had considerable stakes on the continent. Indeed, France did not attempt to hide its eagerness to intervene in some way: Napoleon III wished for a stronger foothold in North America, and given the presence of not one but two civil wars on the continent—Mexico was also in the midst of internal conflict, and was more vulnerable to foreign intervention given its indebtedness to European states—the time seemed ripe. France also had more reason to be concerned about the effects of a blockade: it received 93 percent of its cotton from the South, with the corresponding figure for Britain at 80 percent.[291] The announcement of a joint policy did not please Union officials. As Seward put it to Adams on June 19, "When we received official information that an understanding was existing between the British and French governments that they would take one and the same course concerning the insurrection which has occurred in this country, involving the question of recognizing the independence of a revolutionary organization, we instructed you to inform the British government that we had expected from both of those powers a different course of proceeding."[292]

Third, Russell himself had agreed to meet representatives from the Confederacy and hear their case for recognition, albeit in an unofficial capacity, on May 4.[293] This meeting greatly angered Union officials; in a dispatch written by Seward but watered down by Lincoln and finally presented to Russell by U.S. minister in Britain Charles Adams, the British were told that even unofficial contacts with Confederate representatives would be cause for the termination of all diplomatic contact with London.[294] Seward wrote to Adams, noting firmly that "intercourse of any kind with the so-called commissioners is liable to be construed as the recognition of the authority which appointed them. Such intercourse would be none the less hurtful to us for being called unofficial, and it might be even more injurious, because we should have no means of knowing what points might be resolved by it."[295]

It was under these circumstances that Lincoln decided to go on the offensive, abandon his previous policy of patience and caution, and launch an invasion of the South. As Poast argues, for Lincoln and his cabinet, "staving off foreign intervention required taking aggressive measures against Southern forces."[296] The evidence for the claim that Lincoln's escalation was catalyzed by the prospect of British interference is that, first, Lincoln's advisers who supported aggressive measures were cognizant of the threat of foreign recognition and explicitly cited it as a cause for more forthright policy in their communications on the issue. For instance, in April, Attorney General Edward Bates noted in his diary that the Union should choose aggression because the Southern states "warm up their friends and allies, by bold daring, and by the prestige of continued success—while we freeze the spirits of our friends everywhere, by our inaction and the gloomy presage of defeat." The week before the attack on Manassas, he wrote to a friend, and once again, raised the importance of signals sent and received in foreign capitals: "Foreigners do not understand why we should allow a hostile army to remain so long almost in sight of the Capitol, if we were able to drive them off." Similarly, General Scott argued that a more offensive strategy would aid in forestalling recognition of the Southern government abroad.[297]

Second, the historical record shows that the British themselves would have been "impressed" with more aggressive action against the South. After a June 17 meeting with Seward, British minister Lyons wrote a letter to Russell in which he commented on the slow pace of Northern action—"if the advance is to go on the same rate, it will take about half a century to get on to Florida."[298] The particulars of the meeting that led to this letter are suggestive. Given the widespread British belief that the use of force by the Union would command more respect across the Atlantic, and given that this letter was written immediately after meeting Seward, who "no doubt calculates upon the effect which may be produced upon the governments of Europe by the events of the Month," according to Lyons, it is conceivable and perhaps even likely that Seward left the meeting all the more convinced that more aggression would quell the prospect of British recognition.

Third, while we lack direct knowledge of Lincoln's thinking in the run-up to Manassas—primary evidence for Lincoln's thoughts and beliefs is often found in the diaries of John Hay, his private secretary, but between May 12 and August 22, Hay did not write anything because "the nights have been too busy for jottings"[299]—we do have on record his reaction to the consequent defeat at Bull Run. Meeting with Senator Orville Browning after the defeat, Lincoln reported feeling "melancholy" on account of the fact that "they [Britain and France] were determined to have the cotton crop as soon as it matured" and that the British were "now assuming the ground that a nation had no right, whilst a portion of its citizens were in revolt, to close its ports or any of them against foreign Nations." This deep concern over the foreign reaction to the defeat at Bull Run was cause for Lincoln's consternation for at least a year. Thus while we do not have direct evidence connecting foreign intervention and the attack at Manassas in Lincoln's mind, the circumstantial evidence is, at the very least, broadly suggestive that the signals sent to foreign capitals was one of the main reasons for choosing a more aggressive policy vis-à-vis the South.[300] Unfortunately for the Union, their forces were routed at Bull Run—"'Bull's Run' should be known as Yankee's Run," in Palmerston's memorable words. Yet despite the defeat, and further inquiries of the possibilities of formal recognition, the British did not change their position that the South had not yet won independence, and thus recognition would be imprudent.[301]

I do not mean to suggest that the threat of foreign intervention was the *only* factor driving Lincoln and his cabinet to the attack at Manassas. It is to say, however, that the external security implications of Southern secessionism were certainly operative in the decision-making calculus of figures such as Lincoln and Seward at this important juncture. Union officials were concerned about how British and French recognition could further aid the cause of the Confederate independence, an eventuality unacceptable to the Union's future external security due to the intense power competition it would lead to on the continent, and instituted an escalation of Northern policy, with one eye fixedly gazing across the Atlantic. This escalation led, in part, to a serious conflagration that claimed almost a million lives, but would keep the country united.

To the extent that Lincoln and his advisers were concerned about the prospect of a more evenly divided North America, whereby the United States would be one of two or even three equal powers rather than the regional hegemon, my theory can account for Northern opposition to Southern secessionism. Where the U.S. Civil War departs from my theory is that in this case, the host state opted for a harsher response against secessionists to *preempt* foreign support, rather than as a reaction to it. Furthermore, this case also draws into question my insistence (chapter 1) that material support, particularly in the form of arms and training, is more important than financial support and certainly more important than diplomatic or political support. Indeed, this episode demonstrates that under certain conditions, the promise or execution of "mere" diplomatic support can be seen as the first step on a slippery slope that ends in full-blown cooperation and can result in as aggressive a response as any other. This interesting application of my argument in a case of secessionism that was neither strictly ethnic nor in the twentieth century therefore lends it greater credence overall, while also drawing into question the precise role of third-party support.

In this chapter, I have endeavored to considerably broaden the sample of cases examined. I have shown that the lack of external security concerns, both dyadically and regionally, allowed Swedish and Czech leaders to treat Norwegian and Slovak separatism respectively with peaceful concessions that ultimately led to secession in both cases. Conversely, serious concerns about what an independent Palestine would mean for its security have impelled Israel to use coercion against Palestinian nationalists. Even in the nonethnic case of the U.S. Civil War, worries about British aid to Southern secessionists resulting in an independent, expansionist Confederacy forced Union leaders to escalate at a crucial time in 1861.

The reputation argument would expect peaceful concessions in both the Sweden-Norway and Czechoslovakian cases, but for different reasons than mine: those states were both binational, leaving no other potential groups to deter. However, in my investigation, I was able to uncover little evidence of reputational concerns among Swedish or Czech leaders. Moreover, the problem with relying on binationalism is made clear when one considers the Israel-Palestine case and U.S. Civil War, where this argument would expect peace, in complete contradiction to events.

The veto-points argument explains important elements of the Velvet Divorce and Israel-Palestine cases: in the former, concessions to Slovaks were made more credible by the fact that the entire spectrum of the Czech body politic was behind them, while in the latter, Israel's notoriously divided internal politics have meant right-wing parties can stall concessions, especially in the aftermath of Oslo. It is less immediately clear what this argument can do to explain Swedish concessions to Norway and the U.S. Civil War, given that both saw highly centralized decision-making result in opposing reactions: peace in Scandinavia, war in North America.

Conclusion

Security and Separatism in the Contemporary World

The Minsk agreements strain to contain violence in eastern Ukraine between Russia-backed separatists and government forces; Malay-Muslims in southern Thailand continue their armed struggle for independence, often enjoying sanctuary in Malaysia, Chinese leaders sternly warn a novice American president against even hinting at U.S. support for Taiwanese statehood; and against all odds, the Palestinians persist in their fight to win a state. Nationalist movements aimed at independence, and states' often-violent suppression of such efforts, continue to be a regular feature of international politics. Interestingly, not all secessionist demands lead to violence—as evinced by the Velvet Divorce separating the Czech Republic from Slovakia, or the dissolution of the Scandinavian union between Norway and Sweden in 1905. Governments sometimes respond to separatism with negotiations and political concessions, even if they do not grant outright independence, avoiding the untold human suffering of civil war. At other times, they may resort to violence, but calibrate it to relatively low levels. At yet other times, states respond to separatism with genocidal repression.

Two decades after scholars, impelled by the horrors of the dissolution of Yugoslavia, first began devoting systematic attention to secessionist ethnic conflict, I remained deeply curious: what explains separatist violence? Why do some separatist movements encounter a state prepared to concede territory, while others result in them fighting tooth and nail? To address this puzzle, I focused on the state more than the secessionists, since the former's material capabilities, and attendant leeway for action, is significantly wider than the latter's. I have argued that when confronted by an ethnic group seeking independence, a state's response is determined by the external security implications of secessionism.

Specifically, whether a state coerces separatists rests on whether it foresees war after the prospective border change, either against the newly seceded state or existing rivals. In turn, whether a state fears future war depends on the identity relations between it and the seceding ethnic group, which guide its estimate of whether the new state will fight it after independence, as well as war proneness of the regional environment, which helps it assess whether it will face predation from existing states. The possibility of future war worries states because they would face it as a relatively weaker actor; secession would have adversely affected its position in the international balance of power. The balance with respect to the ethnic group would shift against the state because of the military, economic, demographic, and institutional benefits of statehood that would accrue to the separatists. The balance with respect to existing rivals would shift against the state because of its loss of territory and population. Such shifts render secession unpalatable from the state's perspective, impelling it to coerce the separatists. Conversely, a confidence that it will be free from interstate conflict is a necessary condition for the state to adopt concessions, up to and including the granting of full independence. Such sanguinity about its security frees the state from conceptualizing border changes in wary or apocalyptic terms, and opens up the possibility for it dealing with the separatist movement peacefully.

If a state decides that it will use coercion, we are still left with the question of how much violence the state employs. "Coercion," after all, can mean anything from beating protestors with clubs to mass rapes and ethnic cleansing. In my argument, third-party support for the separatists determines the precise level of coercion, for both material and emotional reasons. The transfer of the "technologies of rebellion," especially the provision of military aid, training, and fighters, appreciably changes the capabilities of the separatist movement, forcing the state to escalate in its attempt to defeat it. Moreover, when separatists become tied to external rivals of states, they become susceptible to pathological levels of violence, fueled by a sense of collective betrayal among both leaders and security forces.

External security, then, drives whether, and how much, states coerce separatists. Such an argument stands in direct contrast to existing scholarship on the question of separatist violence, which exclusively focuses on factors within the state, such as its political institutions or demographic profile. In turn, shining this light on the geopolitical implications of secessionism can prove useful to policymakers keen on avoiding, or at least mitigating, the gruesome violence that often accompanies the separation, or attempted separation, of states. Indeed, properly understanding the factors that cause some governments to address secessionist demands on the battlefield, as opposed to the negotiating table, is crucial to peace building. Such an understanding would allow interested parties to pursue strategies designed to keep the peace between ethnic groups in a state, and promote stability more generally.

Policy Implications of an External Security Theory of Separatist Conflict

Although the international community is often reluctant to interfere in civil conflicts[1] because of concerns about political and legal sovereignty,[1] my research suggests that the roots of fighting within countries often lie outside their borders. This implies that the international community can play a significant role in these conflicts by allaying the fears of states facing separatist movements and reassuring them of their security.

For instance, the international community can make the shift in the balance of power attendant with secessionism more palatable to the rump state by providing it defensive guarantees and pledging protection from its military rivals in the future. If the potential for external attack is what truly motivates decisions to react violently against secessionists, ameliorating such fears could translate to less violence and fewer deaths. The international community can tie the promise of security guarantees to good behavior in its dealings with the minority, as part of an explicit quid pro quo. For instance, if the United States had promised Pakistan considerable military aid and a security partnership in 1971 to help it ward off the threat it perceived from India in return for a more measured and less violent policy against the Bengalis, we may never have witnessed the genocide that we did. Of course, counterfactuals are fraught with analytical danger, but the example is meant to be illustrative rather than conclusive: the impulse should be directed toward assuaging the fears of the state experiencing secessionism. Along those lines, a further implication is that as a secessionist conflict brews in a particular country, the international community must restrain that state's geopolitical rivals. These rivals must be encouraged to make explicit and credible guarantees that they will not join forces with the secessionists in any meaningful way, either today or in the near future. This will aid in placating the state and make it less fearful of "encirclement," which often drives the most vicious of responses. It helps the Scots, for instance, that their secessionist moment has arrived at a time of historically unprecedented geopolitical calm for Britain, and that they are not explicitly allied to any of its rivals, such as Russia or China.[2]

My research, then, is highly relevant to policymakers who wish to curtail civil violence. In a nutshell, I suggest that the international community must leverage the externally fueled motivations of central governments repressing secessionists.[3] It also implies that, as with most conflicts, the time to contain the violence is before it actually erupts: by guaranteeing the security of the state in the future, the international community can protect the potential victims of the state in the present. Indeed, diplomacy can often move slowly—too slowly—once a conflict has broken out to do much good in the short term. The Rwandan genocide famously lasted only ten weeks. More perversely, any hint of help from the outside world during a conflict can, rather than help, ramp up the deadly violence a population faces, as chapters 2–5 showed. Outside intervention aimed at reducing violence has to walk a tightrope: it must be targeted at the state's leaders, without giving the impression that it "sides" with the secessionists. Such a fine balance is easier struck before hostilities have commenced.

The overarching lesson of my work is: third-party involvement would be most useful in separatist conflicts if it is (a) early, before hostilities have taken place; (b) made contingent, such that exhortations for better treatment of ethnic minorities goes hand in hand with security (and possibly other) cooperation with the host state, and (c) aimed at dissuading support for the movement by global or regional rivals of the host state.

Unfortunately, it is unlikely policies based on such analysis will be instituted. First and most obviously, states intervening in separatist conflicts have relatively little to gain by expending political, economic, or military capital for humanitarian ends. Conversely, states which intervene for irredentist or opportunistic reasons have plenty to gain: the dismemberment of a rival and possibly the aggrandizement of territory. As such, if intervention does arise in separatist disputes, it is unlikely to be aimed at the safety and security of the minority at risk; rather, it is more likely to be precisely the type of intervention that intensifies violence.

Second, even if the international community could be convinced to intervene on behalf a separatist minority at risk for purely humanitarian reasons, it would be difficult to convince it to promise benefits for, rather than threaten action against, the states poised to coerce the movement. Providing security guarantees or military aid to such states could easily be perceived as being held for ransom, with the state holding a metaphorical gun to its minority's collective head, demanding alliance benefits in return for not shooting. Why reward such behavior? On the other hand, recent research has demonstrated the benefits of outsider powers paying interstate rivals to stop fighting;[4] if the peace between Israel and Egypt is largely held together by the diplomatic equivalent of bribes, it is at least conceivable for such measures to succeed in civil conflicts.

Overall, then, separatist minorities are likely to have their troubles exacerbated, not mitigated, by outside powers. Contemporary South Asia, where half this book's empirical material was drawn from, serves as an example. Two of the disputes discussed in chapters 2 and 3 have heated up recently: Kashmir and Balochistan. Kashmir has been site of widespread mobilization since 2009, reflecting a groundswell of dissatisfaction with the Indian state that, for many locals and observers, recalls the mood in the late 1980s. Tensions escalated further still in the summer of 2016, when Indian security forces killed Burhan Wani, a Hizbul Mujahideen "commander" known more for his social media presence than any military exploits. The resulting rallies and protests have seen the heavy deployment of pellet guns by Indian security forces, killing more than a hundred Kashmiris and blinding over a thousand.[5] Newspapers have been shut down. Kashmir seems primed for exploding, leaving behind the relative two-decade calm brought by India's brutal counterinsurgency from 1991 to 1995. Most damagingly from the perspective of my argument, Pakistan's desire to wrest control of it shows little abating. Pakistan's support of militant groups such as Laskhar-e-Taiba and Jaish-e-Muhammad, as well as incidents of cross-border terrorism in Mumbai in 2008, or Pathankot and Uri in 2016, signals to the Indian state that in Jammu and Kashmir, it is not just facing a separatist movement, but also a long-running interstate conflict. In other words, the toxic mix of a separatist dispute supported by "high" third-party support appears a distinct, and worrying, possibility.

Balochistan, meanwhile, continues to see a simmering low-level war, featuring the Pakistani state's security forces and intelligence agencies against Baloch nationalist groups, such as the BLA. Recent developments are foreboding. The Indian Prime Minister, Narendra Modi, has publicly stated that his country will begin to support the Baloch movement more heavily, marking a significant shift in their relationship (previously, most of the Baloch foreign support emanated from Afghanistan or, some allege, the Soviet Union). An Indian national, which India claims is a retired naval officer but Pakistan alleges is a spy working for India's Research and Analysis Wing (R&AW), was recently arrested in Balochistan. One vivid illustration of India's increasing forthrightness in the province is its granting Brahumdagh Bugti, an exiled leader of a Baloch nationalist organization, a passport and possible asylum. Such increased support spells trouble for Baloch nationalists as well as the Baloch population more generally, at least insofar as the heavy hand of the Pakistani state is concerned. Human rights activists and Baloch leaders might justifiably claim that Pakistan is already quite vicious toward its Baloch citizens. My only point is that it could assuredly get a lot worse—just ask the Bengalis—and indeed will most likely do so, at least if the present trajectory of Baloch-Indian bonhomie continues.

Flaws of an External Security Theory of Separatist Conflict

Few scholars or writers are ever completely satisfied with their work. I am no different: this book and the arguments contained within it suffer from some important flaws. Theoretically, my argument has a perilous dependence on the plausibility of the claim that meaningful concessions, in the form of significant autonomy, will hurt the state because the minority, rather than being satisfied with its gains in self-government, will keep demanding more. A skeptical reader may believe instead that far-reaching reforms could successfully "buy off" the ethnic group to the extent that it never advances further claims. In such a world, my argument that coercion is "rational" in the face of externally threatening secessionists breaks down. Under these circumstances, it would be less costly to transfer meaningful power to the separatists, short of independence, wash one's hands of the problem, and obviate the considerable costs of repression—costs especially relating to popularity and legitimacy in the eyes of the restive ethnic group. While I believe that my claim that minorities will only use autonomy to press their case harder in the future has sound theoretical and empirical basis,[6] I can concede that not all readers will find such a logic compelling.

A second drawback to the argument is that it proposes fears of future war as only a sufficient condition for states violently blocking separatists. Since external security concerns are not a necessary condition for state coercion, there exist other pathways to violence, possibly many of them, which lie outside the bounds of the theory. My argument would be consistent with a separatist movement being treated with violence for reasons other than external security; an observer might find such a consistency dissatisfying. My rejoinder to such concerns would be to point out the cumulative and slow-moving nature of scholarship. I aim to shed light on separatist violence but I cannot, and do not, claim to provide all the answers. Important research before mine has specified certain mechanisms through which we witness separatist violence, and given the significance of the topic, scholars will continue to chart how the outbreak of secessionism leads to death and destruction. My goal is, at best, to be part of this conversation; if future work theorizes separatist violence in ways that can comprehensively account for all or even almost all of its cases, I would be thrilled.

It would be less cause for celebration if my argument was falsified. The most direct evidence that would contradict my argument would be significant concessions granted to separatists by a state in a war-prone region of the world or by a state that has a deep antipathy toward the seceding ethnic group (or both). Given I argue that a rough neighborhood or opposed identity relations are sufficient conditions for coercion, peaceful concessions in the presence of either factor would be an unequivocal falsification of my theory. A minority rising against the state and securing, without a fight, significant autonomy or perhaps independence in regions such as contemporary Asia, Africa, or the Middle East would constitute such falsifying evidence. For example, if the autonomous region of Puntland declared independence from Somalia without inviting a violent response—such as that faced by Somalilanders in their bid to secede from Somalia decades ago—my argument would be flatly contradicted.

Less damaging for the argument in a technical sense, but still cause for concern, would be a secure state, confident in its belief of future invulnerability, disallowing major reforms toward autonomy or independence. Such an occurrence would not technically falsify the theory since I claim only that sanguinity about the future is a necessary, not sufficient, condition for peaceful measures. A state resisting separatism for reasons other than external security is consistent with my argument. Still, it would raise questions for my theory if, for example, Spain continues on its trajectory of denying Catalan independence. As a wealthy country embedded in the most peaceful web of institutions in interstate history—the European Union and NATO—Spain has absolutely no reason to fear a border change: its neighborhood is secure, and its relations with the Catalans, while not cordial, hardly feature the deep divisions that foretell future war. Spanish violence against a Catalan movement aimed at independence would be especially surprising from my perspective. On the other hand, the Spain-Catalan case is an awkward one: it is not clear that Catalonia has even had a secessionist "moment," in that the desire for separatism has been inferred from an election with murky, ambiguous results,[7] a far cry from, say, the Awami League's performance in the 1971 elections. More important, the case is relatively idiosyncratic because Catalonia has been granted so much autonomy previously—thanks to policies in the post-Franco era more consistent with my argument—that there is not much autonomy left to give: there are few viable concessions other than independence.[8] Perhaps if there was still some institutional "slack" left between autonomy and independence, the Spanish state could offer it, and the Catalans could accept—an equilibrium my theory would expect. Absent that slack, which would make the issue "divisible," the situation between the Catalans and the Spanish state seems at an impasse: Catalonia is not satisfied with the Spanish state but also does not seem eager to press its case for full independence, while Spain appears intransigent even if such an unequivocal demand was forthcoming. Regardless, the case is an interesting one for various theories of separatist conflict to contend with.

Extensions of an External Security Theory of Separatist War

How might the arguments contained in this book be extended? The most obvious arena that might be illuminated by my theory is the phenomenon of ideological civil wars. Such civil wars do not feature actors disputing the boundaries of the state, as their secessionist cousins do. Rather, ideological civil wars pit one group or organization against another that disagree intensely about who should be in power in the state, or what direction the state should take—secular versus theocratic or right wing versus left wing, say. The central distinction lies in border changes not being implied in ideological civil wars, while such cartographic adjustments are intrinsic to separatist demands and their ensuing violence. Indeed, that border changes are inherent to separatist civil wars, but not ideological civil wars, is what originally convinced me that there is necessarily a geopolitical component to the former that requires theorizing.

Of course, ideological civil wars do not exist in a geopolitical vacuum either, but I believe the interaction of external concerns and state strategy in ideological civil wars is hazier. From the perspective of a government facing them, the most important difference between ideological and separatist movements is that making significant concessions to the latter necessarily weakens the state, imperiling its future security. By contrast, ideological movements' goals are not zero-sum with the security of the state. It is perfectly plausible for a right-wing government to concede to left-wing mobilization and for the state's material capabilities to remain unaffected, or even increase. As such, if one is chiefly concerned with maintaining the security of the state as a unit in the international relations system, the choice of concessions versus coercion when dealing with ideological movements is not as cut-and-dried as it is in the case of separatist wars.

Things become slightly clearer if one examines the question not from the perspective of "the state" at large, but rather a specific regime. Abandoning the unitary-actor assumption provides an analytical prism through which one can see a closer facsimile of my logic at work in ideological wars. For instance, a right-wing government facing left-wing demands might see concessions in similar, apocalyptic terms that a state sees border changes: their very existence could be threatened.[9] Perhaps conceding to ideological opponents sows the seeds of one's own demise by bestowing on them important resources, à la the commitment problem. What if a left-wing movement takes the inch of concessions I give them as a right-wing government and transforms it into a mile, in a process that ultimately ends with my head on a stake? Such fears are much more likely to be prevalent in authoritarian states, where being in, and then losing, power can be a life-and-death issue. In constitutionally democratic states, by contrast, a secular government, say, is unlikely to consider concessions to a religious movement as threatening its very physical existence.

The upshot is that if one is to gingerly and carefully extend to ideological conflicts my fundamental logic that the fear of the future drives coercion in the present, the extension should be restricted to authoritarian states. For Bashar-al-Assad, concessions to opponents probably do result in a slippery slope ending with his death, while Barack Obama's concessions to congressional Republicans need not be seen in such weighty terms. We should, then, see authoritarian states react "disproportionately" to the demand for ideological reforms, echoing how separatist-wary states behave in my theory.[10]

What about the second leg of my argument, concerning third-party support? The effect of this variable should work in largely similar ways across both separatist and ideological civil wars. Certainly the materialist implications of foreign backing for rebels should be consistent to both types of civil wars: the transfer of "technologies of rebellion" makes the rebel movement stronger, in turn driving up the violence required to defeat it.

However, the "transferability" of the emotional effects of third-party support are more questionable than its materialist implications. There is no doubt that regardless of ethnic or identity attachment, leaders and security forces do not take kindly to insiders seeking and receiving support from the state's rivals. On the surface, then, a left-wing government taking on right-wing rebels should be as offended by third-party support as a state dealing with separatists would. Nevertheless, I maintain that there is a subtle yet seminal difference in how the suspicion of third-party support manifests itself on the ground in war zones and even the halls of power during separatist conflicts. Simply put, there is no ideological equivalent for racism—specifically the racism that conflates domestic citizens with foreigners based on ascriptive characteristics. Racism allows for leaders and security forces to see particular populations, say Christian Armenians or Kashmiri Muslims, as congenitally tied to neighboring or regional states, fueling the view that "they are all the same"—a belief that often results in gruesome violence. It is harder, though not impossible, to generate such essentialist beliefs in ideological conflicts. Note that this does not necessarily imply the expectation that separatist civil wars will feature more brutal violence than ideological ones more generally.[11] A right-wing government may well commit horrific violence against a left-wing movement, as dictators in Latin America did throughout the Cold War, but for distinct reasons than "betrayed" states in my theory. I claim only that if third-party support is forthcoming in either type of war, it is likely to result in more extreme brutality in a separatist war than in an ideological one.

In addition to ideological civil wars, my argument can be extended to the issue of state-minority relations more generally. As other scholars have pointed out, groups deemed an "internal enemy" in a larger fight against external forces are often vulnerable to state repression.[12] Recent events even in ostensibly liberal democracies, from Brexit to the election of Donald Trump, to say nothing of the fate of sectarian minorities in places such as Syria, have demonstrated the latent and actual dangers posed to ethnic minorities in a time of global tensions. When states convince themselves that they are in the midst of a civilizational fight to the death, as several states have in the aftermath of 9/11, large groups of their citizens caught on "the wrong side" of those battles are uniquely vulnerable. It is revealing, for instance, that even the putatively progressive candidate in the U.S. election, Hillary Clinton, only considered two roles for American Muslims in her public rhetoric: possible terrorism suspects or potential informants against terrorism suspects. Groups that are "securitized" in this way can become potential targets for state coercion. From the perspective of my argument, it would not be surprising to see Western states take even more stringent measures against their Muslim populations in the coming decade, especially given the congealment of an us-against-them view of Islam and Muslims in the West.

Directions for Future Research

I hope that writing this book opens up several avenues for further inquiry on separatist conflict, civil war, and ethno-national violence. First, theories of secessionist violence explain the phenomenon with reference to state-level variables, such as national demography, institutions, or security threats. What such a lens occludes is the consideration of microlevel processes, such as why one neighborhood may suffer more violence than another in the same city, or why rebel commanders in similar villages with similar backgrounds may behave differently. While civil war research more generally has moved in asking such microlevel questions, scholarship specifically focused on separatist violence could benefit from such attention.

Second, future research could examine the importance of what I call "ethnic hostages." All states and geographic regions contain ethnically mixed populations. Often, two states (or two regions within a state) will each host groups that the other feels some attachment to or responsibility for. For example, Slovakia may care deeply about the fate of ethnic Slovaks in Hungary, while a Hungarian leader could evince a similar concern with her coethnics in Slovakia. Research for this book has convinced me that such enclaves play an underappreciated role in secessionist conflict, especially if they are similarly sized. Primarily, they seem to serve a deterrence function, similar to nuclear weapons: I will refrain from victimizing your people in my country if you do the same with my people in yours. Such ethnic hostages can therefore help keep the peace between regions and states during crises. The corollary is that if such a "balance of ethnic hostages" is threatened, say by large-scale migration in one of the regions, conflict may become more likely. Carefully and precisely charting the systematic effects of ethnic hostages, before and during secessionist conflict, should be of interest to scholars of separatism and ethno-national politics more generally.

Third, and building off my perspective that "basic" IR principles such as the balance of power and the commitment problem need to be imported into studies of separatism, I would be curious to learn about the alliance strategies of separatists in ethnically heterogeneous states. To what extent, and under what circumstances, should one expect coordination, cooperation, or competition between different ethnic communities demanding independence from the same state? The long tradition of alliance politics has recently made its way into the study of civil war more generally;[13] a further step along these lines would be to examine patterns of alliance making by groups in multiethnic states facing the same "enemy": the central government.

Fourth, and most ambitiously, it would be a unique achievement if a scholar could aggregate various levels of analysis into a comprehensive explanation of ethno-nationalist violence. At present, studies of ethnic

223

violence exist, broadly speaking, at three levels: communal and local vio-lence, civil war, and interstate war. The explanatory variables emphasized by these families of theories depends on the corresponding arena: scholars of communal violence focus on electoral incentives or the relative abun-dance of civic organizations;[14] civil war researchers highlight state-level variables, such as its physical or political geography, institutions, or demo-graphic profile;[15] and scholars working on interstate violence point to the importance of macrohistorical ideologies, such as nationalism.[16] Is there a common process at play across these arenas? Or is it a bridge too far for any one theory to account for ethno-nationalist violence in such varied con-texts? Perhaps it is, but enterprising scholars should attempt to do so regardless, given the potential analytical payoff.

Notes

Introduction

1. Sisson and Rose 1990.
2. Pavkovic and Radan 2007, 73–78.
3. PRIO Armed Conflict Data (Gleditsch et al. 2002).
4. Walter 2009, 1.
5. According to PRIO, territorial civil wars have accounted for 1,575 conflict-years between 1946 and 2005.
6. Fearon 2004.
7. Kaufmann 1996.
8. Walter 1997; Fearon 2004.
9. According to PRIO, there have been ninety-five territorial and ninety-two ideological civil wars.
10. Walter 2009, 1.
11. Pierson 2004, 89.
12. Following standard definitions of secessionism, such as Horowitz (2000).
13. Horowitz 2000, 231–32; Cunningham 2014, 70–72.
14. Lustick et al. 2004, Grigoryan 2015, Brancati 2006.
15. I am immensely grateful to Bridget Coggins (2011, 2014) for providing me her data on secessionist movements. I made three main adjustments to this data. First, Coggins's data begins in 1931, but I used only post-1946 movements. This is because data on violent ethnic conflict, for which I used Ethnic Armed Conflict dataset (Wimmer, Cederman, and Min 2009) is only available for that period. Second, I culled nationalist movements against imperial rule. For theoretical reasons, I do not believe secessionist movements in modern nation-states should be conflated with anticolonial movements. Any movement that was geographically cut off from its target by a substantial body of water, as was the case for African and Asian movements against British, French, Portuguese, and Dutch rule, was deleted. With geographic contiguity in mind, I included the dissolution of the Soviet Union, which some scholars (but not me) consider an "empire." Third, I added nine cases not included in the Coggins data but part of the EAC data: Mali-MPA (1990–94), Nigeria-Biafra (1967–70), Ethiopia-Ogaden I (1975–83), Ethiopia-Ogaden II (1996–2005), Ethiopia-Afar (1996), Iran-Kurds I (1946), Iran-Azerbaijan (1946), Indonesia-South Moluccas (1950), and Macedonia-UCK (2001).

16. See Hale 2008, Hechter 1992, Horowitz 2000, Jenne 2007, Siroky 2009, Sorens 2008, Sorens 2012, and Wood 1981.

17. Gourevitch 1978, Rogowski 1987, and Midford 1993.

18. Gilpin 1983.

19. Fearon 1995, Copeland 2000, Powell 2006.

20. Fearon and Laitin 2003, Kalyvas 2006, Walter 1997, and Staniland 2012.

21. Weinstein 2007.

22. Staniland 2014.

23. Pearlman 2011, Krause 2014, Christia 2013, Seymour 2014.

24. Weinstein 2007, 6.

25. Valentino 2004 and Downes 2007.

26. Ron 2003.

27. Davenport 2007.

28. Walter 2009, Toft 2003.

29. Walter 2009, 20–21.

30. Walter (2009, 88) finds that "reputation building is not just a significant factor in government decision-making, it is also a substantively important one, but Toft (2003, 43), espousing the same argument, attains different results: a positive but insignificant relationship.

31. Toft 2002–3.

32. Walter (2009, 25) attempts to ameliorate the internal variation problem by arguing that the reputation argument can indeed account for variation within states by focusing on the element of time: even though ethnic profiles do not change over time, later movements will see less violence than earlier ones, because governments have more of a reputation to create earlier. Notwithstanding the dubious logic of this claim—why would a state, which practiced violence in an earlier time period, use less violence when faced with another secessionist movement, when clearly its bid to create a "harsh" reputation failed?—the empirical record is simply at odds with her argument. Of the nineteen states which saw varied levels of violence against secessionist movements, only four (United Kingdom, Spain, Azerbaijan, and Philippines) were more violent against earlier rather than later movements, according to the Ethnic Armed Conflict dataset. The remaining fifteen states were either more violent against later secessionists, or faced secessionist movements during similar time periods—a possibility Walter does not consider.

33. Cunningham 2014, 38.

34. Ibid., 83.

35. Ibid. This move is reflective of a broader trend to analyze rebel movements' internal structures and cohesion. See Pearlman (2011), Staniland (2014), and Krause (2014).

36. Cunningham 2011, Cunningham 2013.

37. Cunningham 2014, 82, 92, 122.

38. Ibid., 37.

39. Spruyt (2005) shows that a high number of veto points within imperial metropoles made concessions to anticolonial nationalists less likely, consistent with Cunningham, but he does not argue, as she does, that a low number of veto points also make concessions unlikely.

40. As opposed to all the other reasons a group might distrust a state's offer of concessions.

41. Not least because Cunningham (2014) does not probe the conditional effects of "veto factions" at low, mean, and high levels of veto factions on the likelihood of either "concessions" or "institutional concessions."

42. Griffiths 2015.

43. On such conflicts, see Spruyt 2005, Lawrence 2013, MacDonald 2013.

44. For example, see Balcells 2010, Ahmad 2015, Lyall, Blair, and Imai 2013, Shesterinina 2016. For a notable exception, see Kalyvas and Balcells 2010.

45. Mearsheimer 2001.

46. IR scholars, e.g., Vasquez (1993) generally consider territory as something to be fought "over," but in this case territory plays a more subtle role, since the state is not fighting "for" the territory per se.

47. The literature on these questions in general is massive. Some influential works on nationalism include Anderson (1983), Gellner (1983), Greenfeld (1993), Hobsbawm (1983, 2012), and Smith (1986). On ethnic conflict, the classic work remains Horowitz (2000). On nationalism and war, see Posen (1993b), Van Evera (1994), Cederman et al. (2011), and Wimmer (2012).

48. Mylonas 2012.

49. Bulutgil 2008.

50. Kalyvas and Balcells 2010.

51. On such decisions, see Saideman (1997).

52. Jenne 2015, 32–36.

53. Regan 2002; Balch-Lindsay, Enterline, and Joyce 2008.

54. See Kuperman 2008, Bloom 1999, Jenne 2007, and Siroky 2009.

55. Fazal 2007, Atzili 2011

56. Horowitz 2000, 272.

57. Coggins 2011 and Coggins 2014.

58. Defined as those conflicts that (a) were fought within states over territory, that is, secessionist conflicts, and (b) reached "Level 2" intensity according to PRIO.

59. Heraclides 1990, 348–50.

60. Which is often either an overstated concern or a fig leaf for other interests. See Krasner (1999).

61. On the importance of large bodies of water in international politics, see Mearsheimer (2001).

62. The dissolution of the Soviet Union is a unique case in the study of secessionism, evinced by even the ethnic core of the state—the Russian nation—seeking to "secede" from it. See Beissinger (2002).

63. Gerring 2007, 40–58.

64. Ibid., 131; Van Evera 1997, 84; George and Bennett 2004, 151.

65. Gerring 2007, 131–33.

66. George and Bennett 2004, 166–67.

67. Ibid., 156–60.

68. Mahoney 2003, 360–63. See also George and Bennett (2004), 207–17.

69. George and Bennett 2004, 211.

70. Gerring 2007, 88–90 and Van Evera 1997, 78.

71. For the Balkans, see, for example, Siroky (2009). For the Caucasus, see Toft (2003).

72. Gerring 2007, 91–93.

73. Ibid., 97–101; and Van Evera 1997, 82.

74. See Staniland 2012.

75. Van Evera 1997, 79.

76. Gerring 2007, 115–16.

77. Ibid., 101–02.

78. Ibid., 104.

79. George and Bennet 2004, 23.

80. Primarily from the National Archives (College Park, Maryland), the Foreign Relations of the United States (FRUS) volumes, and the Foreign Office Files for India, Pakistan and Afghanistan, 1947–80.

81. Archives at the Library of Congress, Washington, DC.

1. An External Security Theory of Secessionist Conflict

1. On this point, see Downes (2007) and Valentino (2004).

2. Downes 2007, Valentino 2004.

3. Kalyvas and Balcells 2010.

4. See Hale 2008, Hechter 1992, Horowitz 2000, Jenne 2007, Siroky 2009, Sorens 2008, Sorens 2012, and Wood 1981.

5. Horowitz 2000, 231–32; Cunningham 2014, 70–72.

6. Arreguín-Toft 2001.

7. Moravcsik 1998, 22–23.

8. Wilkinson 2006.

9. Toft 2003, Walter 2009, Cunningham 2014.

10. Lyons 2009, 168. This generosity was down to Eritrean rebels helping the ruling party's ascent to power in a long and brutal civil war. See Lorton 2000, 101–2.

11. Negash 1997, 175–77; and Tekle 1994.

12. Abbink 2003, 409.

13. Zegeye and Tegegn 2007, 14.

14. Lorton 2000, 103–5.

15. Natsios 2012, 215–18; and LeRiche and Arnold 2012, 188–212.

16. Cunningham 2014, 3–4.

17. For a challenge of the anarchy assumption, see Lake (2009), Clark (2009), Donnelly (2009), and Butt (2013). Mearsheimer 2001, 32–33. For an important critique of the overemphasized role that the idea of fear occupies in some branches of IR theory, see Brooks (1997), especially 447–50. For a more general and an extremely cogent critique of this pessimistic view of interstate relations, see Wendt (1992) and Wendt (1999).

18. Mearsheimer 2001, 55–75. See also Waltz 1979, 192.

19. Tilly 1985 and Tilly 1992.

20. Ibid.

21. Olson 1993.

22. See, inter alia, Laitin 1985 and Posner 2005.

23. Gellner 1983.

24. Hirschman 1969, 13.

25. Ibid., 14.

26. Gilpin 2001.

27. Gowa and Mansfield 1993.

28. Abbott and Snidal 1998.

29. This clever analogy is from Coggins (2011).

30. Bull 1977, 13.

31. A similar dynamic is observed with externally imposed sanctions. Pape (1997) argues that one of the reasons economic sanctions are ineffective is that targeted regimes deflect the costs of those sanctions onto domestic rivals and enemies, presumably including ethnic rivals.

32. Both Mearsheimer (2001) and Waltz (1979) make the point in their discussions of material power.

33. Quoted in Reynolds (2009). Emphasis added.

34. Toft 2003.

35. Jana 2011, 115.

36. Mearsheimer 2001.

37. Ibid., 57.

38. National Material Capabilities dataset, from the Correlates of War. Re. IR scholarly works, e.g., Mearsheimer 2001.

39. Singer, Bremer, and Stuckey 1972; Singer 1987.

40. Vasquez and Henehan 2001.

41. See, inter alia, Toft 2003, Kahler 2006, Goddard 2010, Shelef 2010.

42. Huth 1996, 114.

43. Mearsheimer 2001.

44. The discussion of the commitment problem is drawn from Fearon (1995) and Powell (2006).

45. Grigoryan 2015.

46. Brancati 2006.

47. Elkins and Sides 2007.

48. Though coercion also has long-term costs in such models. See Lustick et al. 2004.

49. For an alternative model of ethnic war as a commitment problem, where the inability to commit explains minority group's secessionist demands rather than the state's response to them, see Fearon (1994).

50. Brubaker 1996, 80–81.

51. There is a vast literature on the state's promotion of particular national myths. Inter alia, see Podeh 2002, Wang 2008, VanSledright 2008, Brand 2014, Guichard 2010.

52. On civic and ethnic nationalism, see Greenfeld (1992) and Brubaker (1992).

53. Posner 2005, Wilkinson 2006.

54. Christia 2013.

55. Glaser 2010, 35–36.

56. Hale 2008, 48.

57. Ibid., 75.

58. Kramer 1992, 4.

59. On signaling intentions in IR, see Yarhi-Milo (2014) and Kertzer (2016).

60. Seward to Adams, April 10, 1861 (FRUS).

61. Butt 2013, 591.

62. Freilich 2012, 12.

63. Separatist movements from Coggins's (2011, 2014) dataset that did not result in a war, as defined by either PRIO or the Ethnic Armed Conflict dataset: UK-Scotland, France-Brittany, France-Basques, France-Corsica, France-Savoy, Spain-Catalans, Italy-South Tyrol, Italy-Sardinia, Italy-Padania. Re. the Pacific, Australia-Papua New Guinea, New Zealand-Maori, Vanuatu-Tafea, Vanuatu-Vemeranans, Soloman Islands-Guadacanal.

64. The Kurds against each of Iran, Iraq, and Turkey. India's conflicts in the Northeast (Nagaland, Mizoram, Tripura, Assam) and Northwest (Kashmir and Punjab), Pakistan (Bengalis), Sri Lanka (Tamils), and Bangladesh (Chittagong Hill).

65. Indonesia (Aceh, East Timor), Philippines (Mindanao), and most commonly, Myanmar (Karens, Mons, Arakenese, Kachins, Shans). The violent dissolution of Yugoslavia, featuring Serbs, Croats, Bosnians, Albanians, and Slovenians; Georgia (South Ossetia, Abkhazia), Azerbaijan (Nagoro-Karabakh).

66. Nigeria (Biafra), Ethiopia (Eritreans, Oromo, Somali, Ogaden, Afar), Sudan (Southerners). One must be careful in not overstating trends in the large-n data without more sophisticated statistical analysis. More important, the bulk of the empirical support for my argument follows in the historical chapters. However, it is heartening for the theory that it is not obviously falsified by the geographic distribution of separatist conflict. For instance, if states in peaceful regions tended to use coercive policies, or more damagingly, if war-prone regions such as the Middle East and South Asia consistently saw states adopt accommodationist stances, one would have significant cause for concern. That is evidently not the case.

67. Kalyvas and Balcells 2010.

68. See Mylonas (2012), Bulutgil (2008), and Grigoryan (2010) on how alliances with geopolitical rivals of the state can spell trouble for ethnic groups.

69. Weiner 1971's "Macedonian syndrome."

70. Horowitz 2000, 281–85.

71. Moore and Davis 1998, Saideman 1997.

72. Mylonas 2012, 41–42.

73. Kalyvas and Balcells 2010.

74. Downes 2007 and Valentino 2004.

75. Kaufman 2001, 3.

76. See the discussion by Wendt (1999, 215) on whether "states are people too."

77. Mercer 2014.

78. Petersen 2002, 19, 37; Kaufman 2001, 27–28.

79. Petersen 2002, 40–68.

80. Elangovan and Shapiro 1998, 548. See also Joskowicz-Jabloner and Leiser 2013, 1799.

81. Rovner 2011.

82. Salehyan 2009, 26–27; ibid., 29. Emphasis in original.

83. Ibid., 38–39.

84. Ibid., 37.
85. Kalyvas and Balcells 2010
86. Cunningham 2014, 72–74.
87. See Cunningham 2011.
88. Staniland 2012.

2. Pakistan's Genocide in Bengal and Limited War in Balochistan, 1971–1977

1. The third chapter in Fair (2014) is titled "Born an Insecure State."
2. Jalal 1995, 22–23.
3. Pakistan got the "short end of the stick in terms of the division of fixed assets," notes Fair (2014, 56).
4. Talbot 2009, 95.
5. Ibid., 96; and Fair 2014, 65.
6. Talbot 2009, 124.
7. Lieven 2011, 62.
8. Jones 2002, 110.
9. Ibid., 110.
10. Ibid., 110–11; Cohen 2004, 206.
11. Butt 2013.
12. Gerring 2007, 97–101; Van Evera 1997, 82.
13. Gerring 2007, 131; Van Evera 1997, 84; George and Bennett 2004, 151.
14. Van Evera 1997, 86–87.
15. Bass 2013, 21.
16. Jones 2002, 152.
17. Ayres 2004, 45.
18. Jones 2002, 152.
19. "Let me make it very clear to you that the State Language of Pakistan is going to be Urdu and no other language. Anyone who tries to mislead you is really the enemy of Pakistan. Without one State language, no nation can remain tied up solidly together and function . . . therefore, so far as the State language is concerned, Pakistan's language shall be Urdu." Quoted from Ayres (2004, 43–44). Original speech available in Mahomed Ali Jinnah, *Quaid-i-Azam Mahomed Ali Jinnah: Speeches as Governor-General of Pakistan 1947–48* (Karachi: Pakistan Publications, 1976), 82–86.
20. Jones 2002, 154–55. See also Sisson and Rose 1990, 9–12.
21. Jones 2002, 156–57.
22. http://www.defencejournal.com/2002/dec/demons.htm.
23. Jones 2002, 157–58.
24. Baxter 1971, 207. On the respective social and political backgrounds of Bhutto and Mujib, see Raghavan (2013, 21–22).
25. The theme of exploitation was one Mujib strongly emphasized in his election campaign in both wings of the country. See *Dawn* reports: "Jagirdars, capitalists will not be elected: Mujib urges W. Pakistanis to make efforts," 07/05/70; "90 lakh jobless in East Pakistan: Mujib denounces 'exploiters,'" 09/01/70; "AL to realise 6-point plan at all cost: It will end long chapter of oppression, says Mujib," 09/21/70; "Past regimes exploited Bengal, says Mujib: 'Elections to decide people's fate for years to come,'" 10/10/70; "'Awami League deserves overwhelming majority': Mujib warns people against 'exploiters and vested interests,'" 10/13/70; "If elected AL will end exploitation, says Mujib: W. Wing people urged to rise against exploiters," 11/1/70.
26. Sisson and Rose 1990, 30–31. These results reflected a growing regionalization of Pakistan's politics. See Raghavan 2013, 28.
27. Bass 2013, 25.
28. "Bhutto calls on Yahya: 'Useful talks' on vital problems of country," *Dawn*, 12/29/70.

29. "NA to be convened at the earliest, says Mujib," *Dawn*, 01/14/71; "Yahya satisfied with useful talks with Mujib: Matters relating to NA session also discussed," *Dawn*, 01/15/71.

30. "Yahya and Bhutto have long talks: Generals Hamid & Peerzada join in briefly," *Dawn* 01/18/71; "Bhutto to meet Mujib shortly, Yahya discloses: 'Top national leaders must cooperate': Useful exchange of views with PPP chief," *Dawn*, 01/19/71.

31. "Mujib-Bhutto talks end: search for accord to go on," *Dawn*, 01/30/15. Multiple sources attest to Awami League disgust with Bhutto's focus on ministries for the PPP during these talks.

32. Blood, Confidential telegram 371, December 1970. Interestingly, this very stance is itself strong evidence against the persistent belief that Mujib was always a secessionist; his strident demands to exercise power in Pakistan, as late as March 1971, should in some way be seen as an indication he did not want to leave it.

33. Notably, other parties based in the West did not consider Bhutto their representative despite his attempts to cast himself as such, and decried his extreme tactics. See *Dawn* reports: "Azam asks Bhutto to take cue from Sheikh Mujib," 12/30/70; "NAP MNAs to attend NA session, says Wali: 'Constitution-making should be above party politics,'" 02/18/71; "Presence of all parties in NA essential: CML willing to play full part, says party statement," 02/24/71; "Convention ML decides to take part in NA session," 02/28/71; "Ahle Sunnat to attend NA session: Earlier decision reversed," 02/28/71; "Bhutto's 'threatening attitude' criticized: Reactions to postponement of N.A. session," 03/04/71; "Transfer power to AL now: Only solution of crisis, says Asghar," 03/05/71; "Mujib has right to rule, says Nur Khan," 03/07/71; "Azam asks Bhutto to explain his latest stand," 03/08/71; and, especially, "Leaders want immediate calling of Assembly session," 03/05/71; "People demand NA session," 03/06/71; "Many leaders support Mujib's four demands: Bhutto's intransigence held responsible for crisis," 03/09/71; "NA minority groups back AL's four-point demand: Plea for interim governments at Centre and Provinces," 03/14/71; "Shock expressed over Bhutto's demand: Transfer of power to 'two majority parties,'" 03/15/71; and "Early transfer of power urged," 03/15/71. See also Ahmed (1979, 214).

34. Jones 2002, 163. As early as December 21, Awami League leaders felt compelled to publicly contradict Bhutto's claim that Sindh and Punjab were "bastions of power" and thus the constitution required PPP input. "AL competent to make constitution alone: Tajuddin repudiates Bhutto's contention: No 'bastions of power' after establishment of democracy," *Dawn*, 12/22/70.

35. Ahmed 1979, 211. See Bhutto's making dexterous legal and political objections to Mujib's proposals in Bhutto (1971, 45–46).

36. In his book on the 1971 war, Bhutto wrote that "in essence, the Six Point formula was meant to strike at the roots of our nationhood. Initially it would have created two Pakistans, and later might well have brought five independent States into being." He also criticized Mujib for "unleashing hatred against West Pakistan" and "blam[ing] West Pakistan for everything" and claimed, without any discernible hint of self-awareness, that Mujib's "language and methods were of fascism" (Bhutto 1971, 13–14). Also see Sisson and Rose 1990, 59–60.

37. Wolpert 1993, 145.

38. Ahmed 1979, 206.

39. In multiple telegrams, American and British diplomatic sources attested to Yahya's ex-ante desire to transfer power to civilians.

40. Jones 2002, 165.

41. Sisson and Rose 1990, 88–89. See also Raghavan 2013, 36–40.

42. Mujib was informed of the decision by Admiral S. M. Ahsan, a man sympathetic to the Bengali leader.

43. Laporte 1972, 100.

44. Wolpert 1993, 148.

45. Sisson and Rose 1990, 90.

46. Rahman 1972, 94.

47. Laporte 1972, 101.

48. Bhutto 1971, 41.
49. Williams 1972, 59.
50. Sisson and Rose 1990, 132.
51. "Political activity banned: Awami League is outlawed," *Dawn*, 01/27/71.
52. Jones 2002, 146–47.
53. Sisson and Rose 1990, 132.
54. Haqqani 2005, 71.
55. Jones 2002, 168.
56. Haqqani 2005, 73.
57. Bass 2013, 53.
58. Sisson and Rose 1990, 222.
59. Nawaz 2008, 258; Haqqani 2005, 62–63; Wolpert 1993, 135.
60. Choudhury 1993, 187; Haqqani 2005, 51; Sisson and Rose 1990, 222.
61. "Mujib wants peace with neighbours: Kashmir, Farakka issues to be settled with India amicably," *Dawn*, 01/04/71.
62. Secret letter by J. D. Hennings to I.J.M. Sutherland, Feb 26, 1971, DO 133/201.
63. Confidential telegram A-0002 by the Consul-In-Charge Andrew Killgore January 7, 1970.
64. Telegram Dacca 02586 by US Consul Archer Blood, December 1970.
65. Ahmed 1979, 219.
66. Murshid 1971, 12–13.
67. Quoted in Devji 2013, 97.
68. Jalal 1994, 241
69. Devji 2013, 5.
70. Hechter 2000, chapter 4; Brubaker 1996, 79–80.
71. Weber 1976, chapter 10; Posen 1993b; Hobsbawm 1983.
72. Fair 2014, 69.
73. Cohen 2004, 67–68. As Ayub himself put it in a *Foreign Affairs* essay in 1960, Pakistani state-builders faced a challenge: "Prior to 1947, our nationalism was based more on an idea than on any territorial definition. Till then, ideologically we were Muslims; territorially we happened to be Indians; and parochially we were a conglomeration of at least eleven smaller, provincial loyalties. But when suddenly Pakistan emerged as a reality, we who had got together from every nook and corner of the vast sub-continent of India were faced with the task of transforming all our traditional, territorial and parochial loyalties into one great loyalty for the new state of Pakistan." Pakistan's diversity called "for a new and bold experiment with political and administrative science to weave unity out of diversity. The situation is often difficult but not baffling, for a common ideology provides a positive base for cohesion. The firmness of this base is strong or weak accordingly as that ideology is understood and practiced rightly or wrongly." Khan (1960, 548–59).
74. Fair 2014, 154, 278.
75. Ayres 2004, 51.
76. Bass 2013, 81.
77. Khan 1967, 189.
78. Bhutto 1971, 17; and Williams 1972, 44.
79. Williams 1972, 77.
80. Jones 2002, 170.
81. Wolpert 1993, 156. Bass (2013) writes an interesting history of the war, organized around this famous telegram.
82. Bass 2013, 72.
83. Ibid. See also Confidential telegram Dacca 01010 by Blood, March 31, 1971, confidential telegram Dacca 01037 by Bell, April 1, 1971.
84. Confidential telegram Dacca 01037 by Bell, April 1, 1971.
85. Hamoodur Rehman Commission report 2000, 510; see also Bass 2013, 82–83.
86. BBC Urdu: Hindu ko khatam kar do. http://www.bbc.co.uk/urdu/interactivity/specials/1143_16_december/page8.shtml. My translation.

87. Salik 1977, 72–73. Among all the books written by military officials serving in the war, Salik's is perhaps the least biased and most honest.
88. Ali 2010, 57–58. See also Bass 2013, 53–54.
89. Telegram Dacca 01338, April 16, 1971; Telegram Dacca 01797 by Blood, May 20, 1971.
90. Telegram Dacca 01745 by Parr, May 17, 1971.
91. Confidential telegram Dacca 01722 by Blood, May 14, 1971.
92. Telegram Dacca 02187 by Carle, June 17, 1971.
93. Nasr 1994, 168–69.
94. Ibid., 66–67.
95. Laporte 1972n26.
96. Confidential telegram Dacca 01193 by Blood, April 8, 1971.
97. Airgram A-103 by Farland, "Conversations with West Paks and Bengalis," June 4, 1971.
98. Telegram Karach 01710 by Luppi, August 24, 1971.
99. Confidential telegram Dacca 01193 by Blood, April 8, 1971.
100. Confidential telegram Islama 04007 2/2 by Farland, April 29, 1971.
101. Confidential telegram Islama 04655 by Farland, May 15, 1971.
102. Confidential telegram Dacca 01722 by Blood, May 14, 1971.
103. Intelligence memorandum 73 No. 2074/71, Directorate of Intelligence, October 12, 1971, "The Situation in East Pakistan."
104. Memorandum, Office of National Estimates, September 22, 1971, "The Indo-Pakistani Crisis: Six Months Later."
105. Intelligence memorandum 81, Office of National Estimates, May 28, 1971, "Indo-Pakistani Tensions."
106. Article attached to Airgram A-871 from US Embassy in London, June 16, 1971.
107. BBC Urdu: Sonar Bangla sey taaruf. http://www.bbc.co.uk/urdu/interactivity/spe cials/1143_16_december/index.shtml. My translation.
108. As Blood said of disentangling the government's anti-Indian/Hindu propagandistic position from genuine anti-Indian/Hindu beliefs held by soldiers, it was an "already complex issue . . . clouded further." Dacca 01193, April 8, 1971.
109. Confidential telegram Islamabad 050825Z, FCO 37/904. Similarly, see Confidential letter from D. F. Duncan, British High Commission in Islamabad, May 19, 1971, DO 133/203 and Confidential telegram Islama 03180 by Farland, April 7, 1971.
110. See selected *Dawn* reports from the first two months of the war: "Armed Indians enter E. Wing: adequate steps taken," 04/02/71; "Infiltration by armed Indians an act of war: leaders slate interference in Pakistan's internal affairs," 04/02/71; "'Relief' camps dole out arms: Military vehicles for Indian infiltrators," 04/03/71; "'Consequences will be serious': India warned by Pakistan again," 04/03/71; "Indian arms convoy destroyed: Fresh infiltrations reported," 04/04/71; "Arms smuggling from India into E. Wing: Foreign newspapers expose Delhi's doings, motive," 04/04/71; "Indian troops moving covertly into E. Wing," 04/06/71; "Armed infiltrators being effectively dealt with: Miscreants isolated, rejected by people of E. Wing," 04/06/71; "India preparing to invade E. Wing: Unusual military activity along international border," 04/08/71; "Pakistan warns India: Infiltration, gun running must stop," 04/09/71; "People helping Army in checking infiltrators," 04/11/71; "2 companies of Indian BSF wiped out: Captured soldiers give details of Delhi buildup," 04/12/71; "Confrontation on the border: Aggressive Indian advance to frontier," 04/13/71; "Arms captured from Indian infiltrators," 04/15/71; "Armed forces out to destroy infiltrators: Tikka warns citizens not give shelter to miscreants," 04/19/71; "Pakistan's strong protest against Indian intrusion: Border post between Comilla and Brahmanbaria attacked," 04/20/71; "More arms depots set up in Tripura: Frantic Indian bid to help infiltrators sent into E. Wing," 04/20/71; "Armed interference by India condemned: Delhi advised to abide by wise counsels of world," 04/23/71; "Indian arms, ammunition seized in Rajshahi: Responsible witnesses give account of enemy activities," 04/27/71; "India mobilizing more infiltrators: 10,000 ex-servicemen to aid insurgents," 04/29/71; "Arms supplies from India for insurgents," 05/01/71; "India steps up aid to agents in E. Wing," 05/02/71; "Indian bid for foreign interference: aid-to-refugees plan politically motivated, not humanitarian," 05/05/71; "Bangla Desh Guerillas: Training Camps in India,"

(05/08/71); "India to increase assistance to E. Wing secessionists," 05/10/71; "Wireless set seized from infiltrators: organized resistance liquidated by Army," 05/10/71; "Armed incursions by India in Jessore sector," 05/12/71; "Indian military moves: W. Bengal border cleared," (05/13/71); "War threat by Mrs Gandhi: Refugee bogey raised as pretext," 05/20/71; "Captured deserter admits Indian help to rebels: People handed over ex-2nd Lieutenant to Army," 05/24/71; "Systematic Indian confrontation aims at undoing Pakistan," 05/26/71; "Unique war moves under glare of publicity: Lok Sabha told of Indian Army 'alert': tension reports," 05/29/71; "India's diabolical plot unveiled: Delhi wanted to cripple and enslave East Pakistan," 05/31/71.

111. Arif 2001, 119.

112. Niazi 1998, 39

113. Ibid. 33.

114. Ibid., 41–45.

115. Telegram from the Embassy in Pakistan to the Department of State, April 6, 1971.

116. Niazi 1998, 46. Emphasis added.

117. Telegram 936, April 8, 1971, DO 133/201.

118. Confidential telegram Delhi 1358, April 8, 1971, FCO 37/904.

119. Confidential telegram Calcut 00470 by Gordon, March 27, 1971; secret telegram from I.J.M Sutherland, April 14, 1971, FCO 37/904; Confidential telegram from James, FCO 37/904, April 6, 1971; confidential telegram Delhi 080950Z, FCO 37/904, April 8, 1971.

120. "Charges of Indian military support to opposition forces in post-March 25 period visibly have more substance" than those alleging collusion before March, according to Telegram Islama 08049, August 8, 1971.

121. Confidential telegram Delhi 151015Z, April 15, 1971, FCO 37/905.

122. Confidential telegram Delhi 221115Z, April 22, 1971, FCO 37/905.

123. Confidential telegram Calcutta 071039Z, May 7, 1971, FCO 37/905.

124. Secret telegram Calcut 00744 by Gordon, April 27, 1971.

125. Confidential letter from Major General J. H. Penrose, British High Commission Delhi, May 12, 1971, FCO 37/905; confidential telegram Calcutta 211300Z, May 21, 1971, FCO 37/905.

126. Confidential telegram Calcut 00750 by Gordon, April 28, 1971.

127. Rashiduzzaman 1972, 196.

128. J. D. Hennings to I.J.M. Sutherland, July 23, 1971, FCO 37/919 and A. J. Collins to G. L. Bullard, September 21, 1971, FCO 37/920.

129. Eleanor R. Lane to South Asian Department, July 23, 1971, FCO 37/919.

130. Eleanor R. Lane, August 25, 1971, FCO 37/919; Intelligence note, Bureau of Intelligence and Research, April 26, 1971, "India and 'Bangla Desh'"

131. Central Intelligence Bulletin No.42, Directorate of Intelligence, July 22, 1971.

132. Confidential telegram Islama 04007 by Farland, April 29, 1971.

133. For example, see Telegram Dacca 03200 by Spivack, August 13, 1971.

134. Telegram Dacca 02733 by Carle, July 20, 1971. Pakistani authorities admitted to the policy of collective punishment. See Telegram Dacca 02495, July 5, 1971. For a description of such reprisal attacks, see Telegram 04123, September 30, 1971.

135. Telegram Islama 09795 by Farland, September 27, 1971.

136. Record of conversation between British permanent undersecretary of state and Indian high commissioner, April 19, 1971, FCO 37/905.

137. Central Intelligence Bulletin No. 42, Directorate of Intelligence, July 22, 1971, "Pakistan."

138. For example, see Confidential telegram Islama 02277 by Sober, March 15, 1971.

139. Confidential telegram Delhi 051000Z, FCO 37/904.

140. Letter from the Pakistani Ambassador to Secretary of State Rogers, March 31 1971.

141. For example, see Telegram Islama 06012, June 16, 1971.

142. Telegram Dacca 02733 by Carle, July 20, 1971.

143. Confidential telegram Dacca 01052 by Blood, April 2, 1971.

144. Telegram Dacca 04895 by Spivack, November 11, 1971.

145. Kalyvas 2006, 138–50.

146. Confidential letter from the British High Commission in Dhaka, July 27, 1971, https://pbs.twimg.com/media/CKboH2iUcAEIv46.png.

147. Confidential telegram 331, May 21, 1971, DO 133/203.

148. For example, see Confidential telegram 331, May 21, 1971, FCO 37/905; Confidential telegram 1349, May 27, 1971, FCO 37/905; Confidential telegram 361, May 31, 1971, FCO 37/905; Confidential telegram 1413, June 3, 1971, FCO 37/905; Confidential letter from F.S. Miles, British Deputy High Commissioner, May 27, 1971, DO 133/203; Confidential telegram 1477, June 10, 1971, FCO 37/905.

149. Laporte 1972, 103.

150. Kumar 1975. See also Bass (2013 chapter 3). Indeed, the early days of the crisis saw speculation that "Awami League appeals for Indian help have so far only related to medicines, ammunition, and walky-talky sets. The supply of such items across the long stretches of the unguarded frontier might of course be somewhat less risky and more feasible for the Indian authorities if they decide to help at all." P. J. Fowler to J. D. Hennings, April 2, 1971, DO 133/201.

151. As one British diplomat cabled in March, 1971, "Ashok Ray, Head of the Pakistan Division of the MEA [Ministry of External Affairs], has for example told me on two occasions that it is part of the Indian calculation that if Pakistan divides or if Rahman gains control of East Pakistan's revenue, Pakistan will not be in a position to support an army of more than six divisions. He has also said that India would welcome this because of the consequences which would follow as the threat from Pakistan against Kashmir diminished." W. K. Slatcher to J. A. Birch, March 19, 1971, DO 133/201. Similarly, an American diplomat noted in secret telegram Delhi 301315Z, March 30, 1971, that "the Indians would prefer [an independent Bangladesh] quickly. The result would be the emergence of an independent East Bengal, which the Indians believe they could live with and contain . . . [independence] would also offer the advantage that an independent West Pakistan deprived of the resources of East Pakistan would no longer be able to pose a credible threat against Kashmir."

152. http://www.defencejournal.com/2002/dec/demons.htm.

153. Jones 2002, 135.

154. Marri 1974, 299.

155. Khan 2009, 1072.

156. Quoted in Harrison (1981, 25).

157. Makran, Kharan and Lasbela were the others (Jones 2002, 132).

158. Independent princely states were quickly incorporated into either India or Pakistan, sometimes by force. The most famous instance was Kashmir, whose incorporation into the Indian Union is still cause for considerable controversy and dispute today.

159. Jones 2002, 132.

160. Hussain 2003, 35.

161. Pak Institute for Peace Studies 2008, 47–48.

162. Ahmad 1992, 149–54.

163. Talbot 2009, 225.

164. Ibid., 224; and Jones 2002, 133.

165. Jones 2002, 133.

166. Some interviewees, such as Rashed Rahman, suggest the number of Nauroz's men executed was as high as nine. M.M.A. Talpur claimed the number was seven. Also, Dunne 2006, 32–33; and Bansal 2006.

167. The antecedent organization of the NAP was the Pakistan National Party, a coalition of leftist and ethnic parties based in West Pakistan. See Hussain (2003, 38).

168. Pak Institute for Peace Studies 2008, 49.

169. Lindholm 1977, 62.

170. Ahmad 1992, 181.

171. Sober, confidential telegram 4632, May 26, 1971, FCO 37/1140. Telegram Islama 03904, May 3, 1972, also ominously noted that "numerous problems in province-center relations remain to be ironed out, some of which have potential for serious trouble."

172. Ahmad 1992, 182.

173. Wolpert 1993, 211; Ali Dayan Hasan, who has "spoken extensively" to Bugti during the month they spent together in 2001, told me that Bugti admitted to "destroying" the Baloch nationalist movement in the 1970s. Hasan described Bugti colorfully as a "historical turncoat" and "a toady, a lackey, ass-licker of the state." Rashed Rahman told me that Bugti had predictable, parochial concerns: he wanted to be governor of the province, but the constitutional accord Bhutto had signed with the NAP gave the provincial governments the power to appoint governor, and thus Bugti spent a good part of 1972 in Bhutto's ear, telling him of a "big rebellion brewing" in the province. Bugti himself claimed publicly that "I, as a Baluch, felt that the NAP was embarked upon a path that could only mean the ultimate destruction of the Baluch and that it had to be stopped. NAP leadership had discredited itself in its ability to give Baluchistan good Government. Discrediting Baluch leadership would ultimately mean the end of the Baluch." Speech at Pakistan Army Staff College, Quetta, November 23, 1973, reported in U.S. State Department Aigram A-105 from the U.S. Consul General, Karachi, November 29, 1973.

174. Wolpert 1993, 211.

175. Talbot 2009, 225–26.

176. "Mengal's warning against fomenting trouble in provinces," *Dawn*, 01/14/73; "NAP Executive blames vested interests for Lasbela fighting," *Dawn*, 01/28/73.

177. "Bizenjo says Qayyum instigating armed rebellion in Lasbela," *Dawn*, 01/27/73. See also Mengal's similar rendition to British officials in February 1973, contained in J. R. Venning, confidential letter "Lasbela Affair," February 15, 1973, FCO 37/1336 and to American officials in March, contained in Airgram A-18 from the U.S. Consul General in Karachi, March 14, 1973.

178. "The situation in Lasbela," *Dawn*, 02/03/73.

179. "Centre sending troops to Baluchistan to restore law and order," *Dawn*, 01/31/73.

180. Baloch nationalists such as M.M.A. Talpur categorically told me that the jam of Lasbela, one of Bhutto's "handpicked people," created the initial unrest in Balochistan. Rashed Rahman agreed with this sentiment, noting that "from day one, there was an attempt to sabotage the Balochistan government," and that "some sardars with Bhutto, like the Jam of Lasbela" created a rebellion which the Baloch government could only deal with by raising a *lashkar* (tribal fighting force). Shehryar Mazari stuck to this line too: the jam of Lasbela—"with the establishment" he told me—instigated the uprising, for which Mengal raised a levy, which Bhutto used an excuse to send in troops.

181. J. R. Paterson, confidential telegram "Troubles in Baluchistan," January 31, 1973, FCO 37/1336.

182. Jones 2002, 133.

183. Intelligence Note RNAN-9 Prepared in the Bureau of Intelligence and Research, Washington, February 15, 1973; Telegram 1606 from the Embassy in Pakistan to the Department of State, February 24, 1973.

184. M.M.A. Talpur told me that the entire Iraqi arms incident was "a whole show, on media" and Rashed Rahman told me that Bhutto was "the author of, or complicit in, the plan to have arms shipped to the Iraqi embassy" and that there was "no evidence ever produced for Bhutto's position" on the question.

185. Intelligence Note RNAN-9 Prepared in the Bureau of Intelligence and Research, Washington, February 15, 1973, and Telegram 1389 from the Embassy in Pakistan to the Department of State, February 16, 1973.

186. Mazari 1999, 309.

187. Khan 2009, 1076; and Dunne 2006, 35–36.

188. Interviews with Hamid Hussain and Mohammad Taqi.

189. Ahmad 1992, 185; Talbot 2009, 226.

190. Wolpert 1993, 217, 230.

191. Jones 2002, 134.

192. Dunne 2006, 36–38; and Harrison 1981, 37.

193. Mazari 1999, 301.

194. Harrison 1981, 38–39; and Dunne 2006, 38.

195. Jones 2002, 135.

196. Ahmad 2000, 185.

197. See, for example, Mazari 1999, 305; Nawaz 2008, 332–35; Talbot 2009, 224.

198. Nawaz 2008, 333.

199. Valentino 2004, Schirmer 1998, McGill 1989, Collazo-Davila 1980.

200. "Federal Constituted Presented," "Wali demands national debate," *Dawn*, 01/01/73; "Wali Khan for more powers to Senate, less to premier," *Dawn*, 01/02/73.

201. "Opposition slated for backing out of accord," *Dawn*, 01/03/73; "A Document of Trust," *Dawn* editorial, 01/06/73; interview with Rashed Rahman.

202. "If accord is broken, PPP will give its own constitution," *Dawn*, 01/04/73; "PPP constitution not acceptable: Wali accuses ruling party of flouting mandate," *Dawn*, 01/08/73; "Any backing out of constitutional accord unjustified: Rashid on PPP mandate," *Dawn*, 01/15/73; "No moral or legal force in Wali Khan's stand: Pirzada recalls his consent to Accord," *Dawn*, 01/19/73; "Ajmal Khattak denies backing accord: Says Bizenjo, Arbab did not consult Wali," *Dawn*, 01/20/73.

203. "Wali accepts PPP offer of talks on Constitution," *Dawn*, 01/21/73; "Bhutto holds talks with Wali, Bizenjo" *Dawn*, 1/29/73; "NAP rejects certain provisions of draft Constitution but keeps door open for further negotiations," *Dawn*, 01/28/73; "Pakistan must get a democratic constitution at any cost, says Bhutto," *Dawn*, 01/31/73.

204. "Wali accuses PPP of diversions from Constitution-making," *Dawn*, 02/24/73.

205. "Centre sending troops to Baluchistan to restore law and order," *Dawn*, 01/31/73; "Pakistan must get a democratic constitution at any cost, says Bhutto," *Dawn*, 01/31/73; "Constitutional deadlock may end, says Bizenjo" *Dawn*, 01/31/73.

206. "Bhutto's speech in Sibi: Constitution assured by March 23 or April 21 at latest," *Dawn*, 03/01/73; "Wali urges mutual trust, consensus on Constitution," *Dawn*, 03/04/73; "Wali, Kasuri, Mufti criticise draft Constitution in NA," *Dawn*, 03/06/73; "New conference on constitutional accord proposed," *Dawn*, 03/06/73.

207. "Bhutto removes both NAP governors and Mengal's govt," *Dawn*, 02/16/73; and "NA begins today task of framing a constitution," *Dawn*, 02/17/73.

208. J. L. Pumphrey, confidential telegram 1896, August 17, 1973, FCO 37/1336.

209. Airgram A-32 from U.S. Consul General Karachi, May 3, 1972.

210. Airgram A-135 from U.S. Embassy, August 22, 1972. Khair Bakhsh Marri, the president of the Balochistan NAP, and Sardar Ataullah Mengal, the then chief minister, reportedly had the strongest reservations. See Telegram Karach 02192, November 4, 1972.

211. Telegram 011054Z from Sober, March 1, 1973.

212. Telegram 201127Z from Sober, March 1973. From the same month and source, see also Telegram 061213Z from Sober, March 1973, especially paragraph 5.

213. Pumphrey, Telegram 3736, December 8, 1972, FCO 37/1139.

214. Research Study RNAS-15 Prepared in the Bureau of Intelligence and Research, Washington, July 17, 1973.

215. Telegram 3585 from the Embassy in Pakistan to the Department of State, May 3, 1973.

216. Proceedings from Islamic Republic of Pakistan v. Abdul Wali Khan, PLD 1976 Supreme Court 57.

217. Interestingly, as one of my interviewees emphasized, the *pukka* left—that of the student unions and urban labor, especially in Karachi—did not support the Baloch nationalists, primarily out of discomfort with the notion of allying with tribal chieftains who exploited the peasantry. But the London Group was composed of affluent Punjabis, left-leaning though they may have been, that saw the conflict more in terms of anti-Bhuttoism than pro-Baloch. Interviews with Ali Dayan Hasan, Ahmed Rashid, and Rashed Rahman.

218. Interview with MMA Talpur.

219. Interview with Shehryar Mazari.

220. Anonymous Mazari family member.

221. Translated by Saniya Masood, research assistant at the Lahore University of Management Sciences.

222. Niazi 1987.

223. Rasheed 2012.

224. Raza 1997.

225. He recounts stories of meeting local tribal chiefs from the Marri tribe alone and armed with only a pistol—"my behavior was reckless," he writes with a strange sense of pride—and working on flood relief in 1976, but little else. See Musharraf 2008, 158–59.

226. Talbot 2009, 226.

227. Telegram Karach 00692, May 3, 1973.

228. Airgram E.O. 11652 from Amconsul Peshawar, May 18, 1973. See also C. R. Budd from the British Embassy in Islamabad, May 3, 1973, FCO 37/1336, Airgram A-003 from Peshawar, March 16, 1973, and Mazari 1999, 304.

229. Ramsbotham, confidential telegram 336, April 2, 1972, FCO 37/1140. Indeed, as early as February 1972, the shah was "very worried about the future of Pakistan" and it "was very much in Iran's interest that Pakistan should hold together and become viable." R.A. Burrows, confidential telegram February 8, 1972, FCO 37/1140.

230. Telegram 071048Z from Sober, May 7, 1973.

231. "Shah due in Larkana today: Talks on matters of bilateral interest," *Dawn*, 01/15/73; "Shahanshah in Larkana," *Dawn*, 01/18/73.

232. Telegram Islama 00469, January 17, 1973.

233. South Asia Department, secret note on "Baluchistan: The Present Situation," February 22, 1973, FCO 37/1336.

234. "Shahanshah is satisfied with his talks here," *Dawn*, 01/24/73.

235. Feldman 1974, 136–37.

236. Telegram 130455Z from Hekc, March 13, 1973.

237. "Teheran gives fraternal welcome to President," *Dawn*, 05/11/73; "Iran not to recognise BD before Pakistan," *Dawn*, 05/12/73.

238. "Summit talks successful," *Dawn*, 05/12/73; "Tangible results of Shah, Bhutto talks forecast," *Dawn*, 05/14/73.

239. "We not only look upon you as the Head of State of a friendly, brotherly, and allied country to which we are bound by common ties of religion. But we also have the highest regards for Your Excellency personally as a statesman who under extremely difficult and exceptional circumstances has completely dedicated himself to serving his nation . . . from the very start of your assumption of this responsibility you have had to face such difficulties as rarely beset by statesman. Your Excellency has confronted all these difficulties with fortitude, faith, and with an unflagging spirit, and you have always been mindful of your vital responsibilities towards your people and history, which developed upon you when you accepted the Presidency." Quoted from "Shah and Bhutto reaffirm everlasting ties," *Dawn*, 05/12/73.

240. "Shah's warning: No bid to harm Pakistan will be tolerated," *Dawn*, 05/13/73; "Defence cooperation pledged: Iran, Pakistan joint communique," *Dawn*, 05/15/73.

241. "Shahanshah to visit Pakistan," *Dawn*, 05/15/73.

242. Telegram 160750Z by Hekc, May 16, 1973.

243. Secret telegram from British embassy in Delhi, FOB 762, August 31, 1973, Confidential telegram from British embassy in Islamabad, FOB 280345Z, August 1973, Telegram 150850Z from U.S. Consul in Karachi, August 15, 1973.

244. Telegram Tehran 08238, November 21, 1973.

245. J. R. Paterson, confidential letter on "Baluchistan," June 13, 1973, FCO 37/1336.

246. Ahmad 1992, 184; Telegram Karach 01626, August 6, 1974.

247. Interview with Asad Munir.

248. Interview with S. P. Shahid.

249. Interview with Hamid Hussain and S. P. Shahid.

250. Interview with Hamid Hussain.

251. Raman 2007, 21.

252. Jones 2002, 134–35.

253. Ahmad 1992, 178.

254. Interview with Hamid Hussain.

255. Interview with M.M.A. Talpur and with Asad Munir. Interestingly, Rashed Rahman provocatively claimed in an interview that the Soviets did in fact offer support to the movement, but its asking price in terms of acquiescence was too high; accepting this aid would be "exchanging one set of masters for another." However, most historical and interview sources lay the lack of support at the feet of the Soviets, not the rebels.

256. Intelligence note, "Pakistan: Bhutto smites the NAP," Bureau of Intelligence and Research, February 16, 1973. See also Memorandum by Deputy Secretary of State Kenneth Rush, July 17, 1973.

257. Interviews with Ahmed Rashid, Rashed Rahman.

258. Jones 2002, 134.

259. Haqqani 2005, 170. See also Fair 2014, 116.

260. Interview with Shehryar Mazari.

261. Interview with Hamid Hussain.

262. Interview with Asad Munir.

263. Interview with Mohammad Taqi.

264. Interview with Shehryar Mazari.

265. Interviews with Hamid Hussain and with anonymous military officer. Interview also with Asad Munir.

266. Telegram 051241Z from the U.S. embassy in Islamabad, March 1973, noted that "according to our best information, Afghan forces remain substantially where they were prior to recent developments." This state of affairs did not change throughout the conflict, probably because of internal upheaval in Afghanistan.

267. Interview with S. P. Shahid.

268. J. R. Paterson, confidential telegram on "Foreign Arms in Baluchistan," January 9, 1973, FCO 37/1336.

269. Telegram 110541Z by Sober, April 11, 1973; Telegram Islama 01816, March 2, 1973; Telegram Islama 08632, October 4, 1973.

270. Telegram 011030Z by Tiger, March 1, 1973.

271. Wolpert 1993, 217.

272. Interviews with Hamid Hussain, Mohammad Taqi, and Asad Munir.

273. Interview with Ali Dayan Hasan and Asad Munir; Talbot 2009, 225.

274. Valentino 2004, 207.

275. Schirmer 1998, 16–17.

276. McGill 1989, 12; and Collazo-Davila 1980, 115–16.

277. Schirmer 1998, 36; McGill 1989, 13; Valentino 2004, 207.

278. P. D. McEntee, Confidential telegram, September 24, 1973, FCO 37/1336.

279. See Valentino 2004 and Downes 2007 on how increased military threats usually see more brutal responses.

280. Interview with S.P. Shahid.

281. Hamid Hussain.

282. Interview with S. P. Shahid.

283. Walter 2009, 29.

284. George and Bennett 2004, 207–17.

285. Bhutto may have been a civilian but his democratic credentials were not overwhelming. See Wolpert 1993.

286. Rashiduzzaman 1972, 191.

287. Haqqani 2005, 73.

288. Nawaz 2008.

289. Lieven 2011, 59.

290. Indeed, as Fair (2014) shows, how *little* Pakistan's military learns strategic lessons is itself a puzzle.

291. Interview with Hamid Hussain.

292. Wolpert 1993, 203.

293. Khan 2009, 1075.

3. India's Strategies against Separatism in Assam, Punjab, and Kashmir, 1984–1994

1. In Coggins's (2011, 2014) dataset, only Myanmar and Indonesia come close to India's level of secessionism.
2. Garver 2002, 11; ibid., 14.
3. Nayar and Paul 2002, 115.
4. Ibid., 133.
5. Garver 2002, 16.
6. Nayar and Paul 2002, 118.
7. Ibid., 132–35.
8. Cohen 2004, 27–28, 53; Mistry 2004, 74.
9. Nayar and Paul 2002, 135.
10. Thomas 1986, 11.
11. Wilkinson 2015, 127–31.
12. Thomas 1986, 12–13.
13. Ibid., 19.
14. See, inter alia, Mudiam 1994, 16 and Parekh 1991, 35.
15. Mudiam 1994, 16.
16. Tanham 1992, 24; Thomas 1986, 57.
17. "Borders can be soft if there is no hostility, says Indira," *Dawn*, 03/10/73.
18. Lacina 2009, 998–1000; Upadhyay 2009, 35.
19. Baruah 2005. Bhaumik 2009 explicitly questions this phrasing: "It is unfair, however, to signpost this remote periphery as a region of 'durable disorder.'" See Bhaumik 2009, 88.
20. Lacina 2009, 1000.
21. Upadhyay 2009, 29.
22. Ibid., 41.
23. Gopalakrishnan 1995, 62.
24. Interview with Sanjoy Hazarika.
25. For example, see Sahadevan 2003; Dasgupta 1988, 146.
26. Sahni and George 2001, 298; Dasgupta 1988, 157.
27. Dasgupta 1988, 157; and Bhaumik 2009, 115–16.
28. Baruah 1994, 868.
29. Upadhyay 2009, 42.
30. Dasgupta 1988, 159.
31. Bhaumik 2009, 115.
32. Baruah 1986, 1187.
33. Ibid., 1189–90.
34. Sahadevan 2003, 406; Dasgupta 1997, 352; Dasgupta 1988, 161.
35. Baruah 1999, 121.
36. Barpujari 1998, 57.
37. See quote by S. L. Shakdher, India's chief election officer, in Baruah 1999, 120.
38. Bhaumik 2009, 117–18.
39. Barpujari 1998, 59–60.
40. Dasgupta 1988, 160.
41. Baruah 1986n11.
42. Ibid., 1193–98.
43. Barpujari 1998, 61–67; Baruah 1986, 1198–99; Dasgupta 1988, 162.
44. "Peace fragile in Assam a year after carnage," *New York Times*, 02/26/84.
45. "Fresh move on Assam finalized," *Times of India*, 01/07/1985; "Assam leaders to get invitation soon," *Times of India* 01/07/1985; "Assam talks resume," *Times of India*, 02/01/1985.
46. The agitators wanted the state assembly dissolved, Rajiv didn't. "Assam problem near solution," *Times of India*, 06/01/1985.
47. "Optimism on Assam," *Times of India*, 08/03/1985; "Assam solution at hand: PM," *Times of India*, 08/13/1985.

48. "Major setback to Assam talks," *Times of India*, 08/15/1985; "Accord signed on Assam," *Times of India*, 08/16/1985.

49. The text of the entire accord is available in appendix C of Barpujari 1998.

50. "Gandhi seen near success in reaching accord in Assam," *Washington Post*, 08/13/85.

51. Interview with Sanjoy Hazarika.

52. "Gandhi cools another hot spot with Assam pact," *Los Angeles Times*, 08/16/85; "Another success for Rajiv," *Christian Science Monitor*, 08/19/85.

53. "Assam accord negotiated by Gandhi," *Washington Post*, 08/16/85.

54. "In Assam's pastoral setting, blind hatred thrives," *New York Times*, 12/06/85; "Unnecessary misgivings," *Assam Tribune*, 09/21/1985; "PM's visit," *Assam Tribune*, 08/12/1985; "Leaders welcome accord," *Assam Tribune*, 08/17/1985; "AASU leaders express happiness over accord," *Assam Tribune*, 08/18/1985; "Assam accord a Magna Carta for peace, says Assam Minister," *Assam Tribune*, 08/31/1985.

55. "Unprecedented ovation to movement leaders," *Assam Tribune*, 08/22/1985.

56. "Assam agitationists form new party," *Times of India*, 10/14/1985; Baruah 1994, 871; Dasgupta 1988, 165.

57. "Assam said to plan to deport Bangladeshis," *New York Times*, 12/21/85.

58. "A leader of anti-immigrant radicals takes office in Assam," *New York Times*, 12/25/85.

59. Jana 2011, 115.

60. "AGP disillusioning its supporters," *Times of India*, 05/01/1987.

61. Dasgupta 1997, 354; Barpujari 1998, 74. "Assam party starts off shakily," *Times of India*, 10/19/1985; "Major shake-up in Assam," *Times of India*, 12/26/1985. Also see Lacina 2009; and Sahni and George 2001.

62. Quoted in Barpujari 1998, 74; "Turbulence in Assam," *Times of India*, 07/03/1987; "Centre worried about Bodo agitation," *Assam Tribune*, 05/13/1989; "Assam 'identity crisis' gains momentum," *Times of India*, 03/17/1988; "Centre not meddling in Assam: PM," *Times of India*, 09/19/1989; "Assam seeks more security forces," *Times of India*, 03/13/1989; "Centre to solve Bodo problem soon: PM," *Assam Tribune*, 06/23/1989.

63. Interview with Sanjoy Hazarika; Das 2003, 62–63; Barpujari 1998, 75; "Mahanta stress on Assam accord," *Times of India*, 02/05/1986; "Centre neglecting Assam accord," *Times of India*, 04/06/1987; "India's Assam state demanding ban on migration," *New York Times*, 09/13/87. "Centre's attitude worries Assam," *Times of India*, 10/15/1987; "'Assam being forced to confront Centre,'" *Times of India*, 09/20/1988.

64. "Political tremors rocking Assam," *Times of India*, 08/15/1988; interview with Kishalay Bhattacharjee.

65. "Assam and the ULFA: Posing a complex challenge," *Times of India*, 05/26/1990.

66. Interview with Sudir Bhaumik.

67. "ULFA stepping up welfare activities," *Assam Tribune*, 12/22/1989.

68. "Assam extremists biding time," *Times of India*, 03/11/1987.

69. Bhaumik 2009, 119–20.

70. "Tea factories shut after threats by militants," *New York Times*, 11/25/90; "Northeast India state challenged by student agitators and rivals," *New York Times*, 12/20/1989.

71. "Rebels hold sway over rural Assam," *Times of India*, 12/23/1989; "ULFA fear grips Assam districts," *Times of India*, 04/29/1990.

72. "Insurgency in Assam," *Times of India*, 11/17/1990.

73. "Curb secessionism in Assam, govt. told," *Times of India* 02/12/1990; "BJP's concern over situation in Assam," *Assam Tribune*, 03/21/1990; "Choices in Assam," *Times of India*, 03/27/1990; "Mufti urges effective steps against ULFA," *Assam Tribune*, 01/25/1990; "AGP govt will have to check ULFA activities—Sahay," *Assam Tribune*, 07/06/1990; "PM assures all help to Assam govt," *Assam Tribune* 04/06/1990.

74. Interview with Rajeev Bhattacharyya.

75. "VP stresses removal of regional imbalances," *Assam Tribune*,01/06/1990; "Rousing welcome to VP: Oil royalty raised by Rs. 100 per tonne, refinery to be set up at Numaligarh," *Assam Tribune*, 01/03/1990; "VP announces Assam package," *Times of India* 01/03/1990; "Govt.

will honour Assam accord: PM," *Times of India*, 01/04/1990; "Time-frame for Assam accord," *Times of India*, 01/25/1990; "Promises for Assam," *Times of India*, 01/05/1990; "V.P.'s visit dispels Assam's mistrust," *Times of India*, 01/07/1990; "A package for Assam," *Assam Tribune*, 01/05/1990.

76. "Strategy to curb growing influence of ULFA," *Assam Tribune*, 05/18/1990.

77. "Centre's concern at ULFA's threat to tea planters," *Assam Tribune*, 05/04/1990; "'Tea industry facing ULFA threat,'" *Assam Tribune*, 07/02/1990; "ULFA's warning to businessmen," *Assam Tribune*, 11/13/1990; "Action plan to contain ULFA activities," *Assam Tribune*, 08/02/1990; "Special Delhi meet on Assam," *Assam Tribune*, 09/06/1990; "Crucial Delhi meet in Assam tomorrow," *Assam Tribune*, 11/14/1990.

78. Interview with anonymous Indian journalist A.

79. Bhaumik 2009, 119–20.

80. "President's rule in Assam: State declared disturbed area," *Assam Tribune*, 11/29/1990; "President's rule in Assam: Army hunt on for ULFA rebels," *Times of India*, 11/29/1990.

81. "Central rule only option: PM," *Assam Tribune*, 11/30/1990.

82. "India arms rights rebels in Assam," *New York Times*, 11/29/90.

83. "The President's rule," *Assam Tribune*, 11/30/1990; "Fear, uncertainty in Upper Assam," *Assam Tribune*, 11/30/1990; "Women protest army atrocities," *Assam Tribune*, 12/04/1990; "Army atrocities condemned," *Assam Tribune*, 12/06/1990; Baruah 1994, 874.

84. "Raids continue, 25 more ULFA men nabbed," *Assam Tribune*, 12/02/1990; "11 more ULFA men nabbed by army," *Assam Tribune*, 12/03/1990; "678 alleged extremists held so far," *Assam Tribune*, 12/15/1990; "1300 suspected ULFA activists held so far," *Assam Tribune*, 01/02/1991; "2365 ULFA suspects apprehended so far," *Assam Tribune*, 02/12/1991; "One more ULFA camp found in Charaipung," *Assam Tribune*, 12/08/1990; "ULFA training camp inside Digboi forest," *Assam Tribune*, 12/14/1990

85. "Troops pull out of Assam," *Times of India* 03/07/199; "ULFA announces ceasefire," *Assam Tribune*, 03/03/1991.

86. "Assam separatists terrorizing tea planters," *New York Times*, 02/14/91.

87. Interview with Rajeev Bhattacharyya; "Insurgents in India's Northeast calls for peace talks," *New York Times*, 02/20/91.

88. "Govt. for polls in Punjab and Assam," *Times of India*, 04/12/1991; "Govt decides to hold polls in Assam: EC to announce dates," *Assam Tribune*, 04/12/1991.

89. "'Operation Bajrang' suspended," *Assam Tribune*, 04/20/1991; "Cong gets absolute majority in Assam: AGP poor second," *Assam Tribune*, 06/20/1991; "Saikia returning tomorrow," *Assam Tribune*, 06/27/1991.

90. "Over the brink," *Assam Tribune*, 09/10/1991; "ULFA violence a serious challenge: CM," *Assam Tribune*, 08/01/1991.

91. "Army action begins," *Assam Tribune*, 09/15/1991; "Army crackdown on ULFA in nine districts," *Assam Tribune*, 09/16/1991.

92. "CM to discuss ULFA issue with PM today," *Assam Tribune*, 09/25/1991; "CM reviews law & order with Army Chief," *Assam Tribune*, 02/05/1992; "Indirect contact made with ULFA chairman: CM," *Assam Tribune*, 11/26/1991; "CM going tomorrow to Delhi for crucial talks," *Assam Tribune*, 12/20/1991; "Talks with ULFA soon: Saikia," *Assam Tribune*, 12/27/1991; "Secret ULFA talks: CM leaves for Delhi today," *Assam Tribune*, 01/06/1992; "Saikia meets PM with ULFA mediator," *Assam Tribune*, 1/08/1992.

93. "Rebel group ends uprising in India," *New York Times*, 12/18/91; "Prospects in Assam," *Times of India*, 01/03/1992.

94. "ULFA announces total indefinite ceasefire," *Assam Tribune*, 12/18/1991; "Next step in Assam," *Assam Tribune*, 12/22/1991.

95. "'Cracks in ULFA revealed,'" *Assam Tribune*, 09/29/1991.

96. "Many ULFA men willing to surrender: CM," *Assam Tribune*, 10/26/1991; "237 ULFA suspects surrender," *Assam Tribune*, 11/17/1991; "One shot dead, 30 ultras surrender," *Assam Tribune*, 11/19/1991; "26 ULFA activists surrender," *Assam Tribune*, 12/5/1991; "132 ULFA suspects surrender," *Assam Tribune*, 12/29/1991; "3 ULFA leaders for cessation of hostilities," *Assam Tribune*, 1/10/1992; "ULFA surrendering in a big way—Chavan," *Assam Tribune*,

04/30/1992; "'No ULFA member has surrendered," *Assam Tribune*, 12/10/1991; "Arabinda, Anup declare: No division in ULFA cadres," *Assam Tribune*, 1/22/1992.

97. "Split in ULFA near complete," *Assam Tribune*, 03/30/1992.

98. "Army out in Assam," *Times of India*, 04/02/1992.

99. "PM ready for talks with Assam ultras," *Times of India*, 01/09/1991; "PM favours talks with militants in Assam," *Assam Tribune*, 01/09/1991; "Hope for Govt-ULFA talks," *Assam Tribune*, 01/25/1991; "ULFA hails efforts for talks," *Assam Tribune*, 02/03/1991; "Centre eager to hold talks with ULFA—Sahay," *Assam Tribune*, 03/02/1991; "'Enough scope for talks with ULFA,'" *Assam Tribune*, 03/07/1991; "CM's appeal to ULFA: Hold talks, eschew violence," *Assam Tribune*, 11/1/1991; "'Delhi, Dispur keen on holding talks with ULFA,'" *Assam Tribune*, 11/23/1991; "Uncertainty in Assam," *Times of India*, 04/02/1992.

100. "Delhi's package," *Assam Tribune*, 10/26/1991; "Centre will give all help to Assam—Dr. Singh," *Assam Tribune*, 03/23/1992.

101. On the selectiveness of coercion, see "Army action resumed in selected areas," *Assam Tribune*, 04/02/1992; "Selective operations will continue," *Assam Tribune*, 05/12/1992; "Rajkhowa rules out talks," *Assam Tribune*, 06/19/1992; "Govt to launch 'limited action' against ULFA," *Assam Tribune*, 06/26/1992. On talks with moderates, see "Pro-talks faction holds parley with CM," *Assam Tribune*, 04/01/1992; "Pro-talks faction to surrender arms," *Assam Tribune*, 04/02/1992; "Govt holding talks with ULFA factions," *Assam Tribune* 06/12/1992; "90 pc ULFA militants favour talks: CM," *Assam Tribune*, 06/23/1992.

102. Dasgupta 1988, 164.

103. On Rajiv Gandhi's "problem-solving" reputation in his early days, see Nugent 1990, chapter 6.

104. Interviews with Sudir Bhaumik and Brigadier (retired) Ranjit Barthakur.

105. "Minefield of uncertainties: the Assam accord and after," *Times of India*, 08/20/1985.

106. Interview with Sudir Bhaumik.

107. "ULFA, a formidable force in Assam," *Times of India*, 12/27/1990.

108. Interviews with Mirza Zulfiqar Rahman and Sanjoy Hazarika.

109. Interview with Mirza Zulfiqar Rahman. See also Bhaumik 2009, 153–56.

110. Bhaumik 2009, 153–56, quote from 163.

111. Interview with Sanjoy Hazarika.

112. Interview with former security official.

113. Interviews with Kishalay Bhattacharjee, Mirza Zulfiqar Rahman, Nitin Gokhale.

114. Interviews with Ranjit Barthakur and Sudir Bhaumik. See also Bhat 2009.

115. Interviews with Nitin Gokhale and Sanjoy Hazarika.

116. "Unlike in the two northern states of Punjab and Kashmir, terrorist groups in Assam have neither been outlawed nor are they under attack by security forces." See "Secessionism thrives in Assam," *Times of India*, 11/25/1990.

117. "Assam's travails," *Times of India*, 04/14/1990.

118. Interview with Mirza Zulfiqar Rahman.

119. Interview with Nithin Gokhale.

120. Interview with Mirza Zulfiqar Rahman.

121. Interview with Monirul Hussain.

122. Interview with Kishalay Bhattacharjee.

123. Wallace 1986, 364.

124. Kohli 1990, 355–58.

125. Shani 2008, 46–48.

126. Ibid., 48–50. Several interviewees, including Hartosh Bal, emphasized that when militancy came to the state, it was led by either poor Jat Sikh peasants or Mazhabi Sikhs (Dalit converts).

127. Pettigrew 1995, 4–5.

128. Nayar and Singh 1984, 47.

129. Singh 1987, 1272–74; Kohli 1997, 336.

130. This discussion is based on Kohli 1990, Brass 1988, and Nayar and Singh 1984.

131. Nayar and Singh 1984, 25.

132. Sethi 1984, 157.
133. Singh 1984, 9–10. See also Singh 2002, 52–53.
134. Brass 1988, 185.
135. Interview with Vipul Mugdal.
136. Interview with Hartosh Bal. For an academic source, see Brass 1988, 179–80.
137. Wilkinson 2006. See also Brass 2003.
138. Though a slightly biased account generally, Dhillon 2006 contains good discussions about Longowal and his role in negotiations.
139. Gill 2001, 28.
140. See Fair and Ganguly 2008.
141. Quoted in Nayar and Singh 1984, 92.
142. Ibid., 96.
143. Kapur 1986, 229.
144. Interview with Hartosh Bal.
145. Gill 2001, 30.
146. Aurora 1985.
147. Interview with Satish Jacob.
148. Interview with Julio Ribeiro.
149. Interview with Kanwar Sandhu.
150. "Punjab raid: unanswered questions," *New York Times*, 06/19/84.
151. Nayar and Singh 1984, 107.
152. http://www.caravanmagazine.in/reportage/sins-commission.
153. Kapur 1986, 236–37.
154. "Anandpur resolution unacceptable: PM," *Chandigarh Tribune*, 12/2/84; "Separatists will be crushed: PM," *Chandigarh Tribune*, 12/12/84.
155. Quoted in Nugent 1990, 91.
156. "Gandhi appoints panel on Punjab separatism," *New York Times*, 01/06/85.
157. Wallace 1986, 377.
158. Kohli 1990, 364–65. For a contesting view, see Dhillon 2006, who terms the accord "phony."
159. Brass 1988, 210.
160. Kapur 1986, 238.
161. Kohli 1990, 365–68.
162. Nugent 1990, 96.
163. "Punjab: end of nightmare," *Times of India*, 07/26/85; "Punjab Hindu party chief supports pact," *Times of India*, 08/12/85; "Centre, Akali Dal sign agreement: Chandigarh goes to Punjab," *Times of India*, 07/25/85.
164. "Blueprint for peace," *Chandigarh Tribune*, 07/26/1985.
165. "Normalcy in Punjab soon: Arjun," *Times of India*, 08/03/85.
166. "Punjab near solution," *Times of India*, 06/14/85; "PM is optimistic of Punjab solution," *Times of India*, 07/08/85.
167. Kohli 1990, 364–67; Brass 1988, 206–10.
168. Nugent 1990, 97. Interviewees, such as Sanjoy Hazarika, also emphasized this aspect of Rajiv being a "problem solver."
169. "Foreign forces at work: PM calls for vigilance," *Chandigarh Tribune*, 08/05/84; "The 'foreign' factor," *Chandigarh Tribune* editorial, 10/06/84.
170. "India talks of C.I.A. role in unrest," *New York Times*, 06/16/84.
171. "Indian official accuses Pakistan of training Sikh guerillas," *Washington Post*, 06/14/84.
172. "Punjab tension," *Christian Science Monitor*, 05/07/84.
173. "Pakistan arming terrorists," *Chandigarh Tribune*, 07/15/85.
174. "India talks of C.I.A. role in unrest," *New York Times*, 06/16/84.
175. "Army sure of Pakistani hand," *Chandigarh Tribune*, 07/26/84.
176. Interview with Kanwar Sandhu.
177. Nugent 1990, 99.
178. "S.I. shot dead in Amritsar," *Chandigarh Tribune*, 07/28/85.

179. "A sellout, says 'united' Dal," *Chandigarh Tribune*, 07/26/85.

180. "Exchange of fire in temple complex," *Chandigarh Tribune*, 07/31/85.

181. "Bid to disturb Dal (L) meeting," *Chandigarh Tribune*, 08/17/85.

182. "Akali bid to close ranks," *Chandigarh Tribune*, 08/11/85. See also "Sant to select Dal nominees: Badal, Tohra stay away," *Chandigarh Tribune*, 08/20/85.

183. "Badal, Tohra back Longowal," *Chandigarh Tribune*, 08/21/85; "Tearful farewell to Longowal," *Chandigarh Tribune*, 08/22/85.

184. "Crime against peace," *Chandigarh Tribune*, 08/22/85.

185. "Advani assails Punjab pact," *Times of India*, 09/23/85; "Save Punjab pact, PM urged," *Times of India*, 03/07/86; "Punjab eager to seal border," *Times of India*, 02/27/86; "Punjab accord alive: Tripathi," *Times of India*, 06/24/86.

186. "Akalis head for two-thirds majority in Punjab," *Times of India*, 09/27/85.

187. Interview with Vipul Mugdal.

188. "The trap in Punjab," *Times of India*, 02/20/86.

189. "Barnala's dilemma," *Chandigarh Tribune*, 02/11/87.

190. "The Punjab logjam," *Times of India*, 10/21/1986; "Action in Punjab," *Times of India*, 05/15/1987; "PM invites Barnala for talks," *Chandigarh Tribune*, 01/14/87; "An expedient, not a cure," *Chandigarh Tribune*, 05/13/87.

191. "Outrage in Punjab," *Times of India*, 12/2/1986.

192. "Impose President's rule in Punjab: Advani," *Times of India*, 01/12/1987; "PM vacillating on Punjab: Vajpayee," *Times of India*, 01/12/1987; "Thackeray for emergency in Punjab," *Times of India*, 02/04/1987; "'PM solely responsible for Punjab situation,'" *Times of India*, 01/14/1987.

193. "Central intervention in Punjab imminent," *Times of India*, 05/11/1987; "President's rule in Punjab, assembly suspended," *Times of India*, 05/12/1987.

194. "Sweeping powers for Punjab govt.," *Times of India*, 12/5/1986.

195. "No compromise with terrorism: PM address CPP(I)," *Chandigarh Tribune*, 07/13/87; "No leniency in Punjab: PM," *Times of India*, 06/08/87.

196. See editorial, "Firmness on Punjab," *Times of India*, 06/09/1987.

197. "Major offensive in Punjab launched," *Times of India*, 05/30/87.

198. "Punjab terrorists butcher 76," *Times of India*, 07/08/1987.

199. "Police in thick of battle: Ribeiro," *Chandigarh Tribune*, 09/03/87.

200. Interview with Julio Ribeiro.

201. http://www.satp.org/satporgtp/publication/faultlines/volume1/Fault1-kpstext.htm.

202. Swami 2004, 166; http://www.satp.org/satporgtp/publication/faultlines/volume1/Fault1-kpstext.htm; Human Rights Watch 1994, 11.

203. http://www.satp.org/satporgtp/publication/faultlines/volume19/Article1.htm.

204. Ibid.

205. Chima 2010, 220; Fair 2009, 110.

206. Human Rights Watch 1994, quote from 16; quoted in Chima 2010, 220.

207. Gayer 2009, 242.

208. Ibid., 243–44; Interview with Laurent Gayer.

209. Swami 2007, 147; 149.

210. Swami 2004, 149, 151. See also Gill (2001).

211. Interview with Ajay Sahni.

212. Swami 2004, 156. For a conflicting view, asserting Pakistani support in the form of military aid and training as early as 1994, see Raman 2007, 92, 138.

213. Swami 2007, 148–49.

214. Interview with K. P. S. Gill.

215. http://www.satp.org/satporgtp/publication/faultlines/volume1/Fault1-kpstext.htm.

216. Interview with Prakash Singh.

217. "Special training for Punjab cops," *Times of India*, 06/17/86; Interview with Hartosh Bal.

218. Interviews with Shekhar Gupta and Ajay Sahni.

219. Interview with Kanwar Sandhu.

220. http://www.satp.org/satporgtp/publication/faultlines/volume19/Article1.htm.

221. Pearlman 2011, 14. See also Krause 2014, 83; Pearlman 2011, 18.

222. Wilkinson 2015, 44–50.

223. Ibid., 151.

224. Interview with anonymous Indian journalist B.

225. Interview with Hartosh Bal.

226. South Asian Terrorist Portal data on Punjab. See http://www.satp.org/satporgtp/countries/india/states/punjab/data_sheets/annual_casualties.htm. See also Swami 2004.

227. Swami 2004, 151–56.

228. Behera 2006, 74.

229. Jones 2008, 4; Das 2001, 27.

230. See Bose 2003, chapter 2.

231. Widmalm 1997, 71.

232. Das 2001, 37–38.

233. Behera 2006, 31–37.

234. Ibid., 40; Widmalm 1997, 72–73.

235. Malik 2002, 146–49.

236. Schofield 1996, 221.

237. Das 2001, 42; Schofield 1996, 224–25.

238. Schofield 1996, 225.

239. Ibid., 226–27; Widmalm 1997, 81–91.

240. Das 2001, 47.

241. Bose 2003, 102.

242. Widmalm 1997, 91–96.

243. Ganguly 1996, 83–99.

244. Widmalm 1997, 99.

245. Ganguly 1996, 105.

246. Quoted in Widmalm 1997, 100.

247. Singh 1995, 122.

248. Jones 2008, 10.

249. Interview with Yusuf Jameel.

250. "India barring foreign journalists from turbulent Kashmir," *New York Times*, 02/18/90.

251. Das 2001, 70; Jones 2008, 11; Bose 2003, 113; Behera 2006, 149; Bose 2007, 237; "India's growing peril: Kashmir and Punjab separatism," *New York Times*, 04/17/90; "Separatist violence boils in Kashmir," *Christian Science Monitor*, 05/02/90.

252. Bloeria 2000, 159; Jagmohan 1991, 523.

253. Singh 1995, 128–29.

254. Das 2001, 70.

255. Ganguly 1996, 76; V. 4.0 of Correlates of War dataset: Singer, Bremer, and Stuckey 1972, 19–48.

256. Bose 2007, 231.

257. Das 2001, 71, Jones 2008, 11.

258. Schofield 1996, 250.

259. Bose 2003, 112. Emphasis in original.

260. See, for example, "11 Kashmir cities get curfew to counter militants," *New York Times*, 01/06/90; "Remove curfew," *Kashmir Times*, 10/01/90; "Indian troops told to shoot Kashmir's curfew violators," *New York Times*, 03/31/90.

261. "Indian troops told to shoot Kashmir's curfew violators," *New York Times*, 03/31/90, Bose 2003, 113–14. Peer (2010) is a journalistic book on the Kashmir conflict and contains a first-person account of these crackdowns (see 49–54).

262. Bose 2003, 114.

263. Singh 1995, 132–33.

264. Bose 2003, 109.

265. Singh 1995, 139.

266. Schofield 2000, 153; Singh 1995, 154–59.

267. Human Rights Watch 1991, 25. See also Human Rights Watch 1993, 37–39, and Amnesty International 1995.

268. Human Rights Watch 1991, 31, 37, 40.

269. "Bleeding Kashmir," *US News and World Report*, 11/19/90, 52; "Kashmiris describe India resorting to arson in rebel war," *Washington Post*, 11/16/90; "India moves against Kashmir rebels," *New York Times*, 04/07/91.

270. Bose 2003, 111.

271. "Support widens for firm measures to curb terrorism in Kashmir," *Kashmir Times*, 03/21/90; "RS debates 'grave' Kashmir situation," *Kashmir Times*, 03/15/90. See also "Lok Sabha voices concern at Pak aid to terrorism in Kashmir, PM warns of swift, decisive action," *Kashmir Times*, 03/14/90.

272. "Controversial governor of Kashmir resigns," *New York Times*, 05/26/90; "New Kashmir governor to maintain crackdown," *Washington Post*, 05/27/90.

273. "India says Pakistan is stirring up Kashmir unrest," *New York Times*, 02/01/90.

274. Ganguly 1996, 79–80.

275. Quoted in Das 2001, 31–58.

276. Ganguly 1996, 80–82; Behera 2006, 74–78.

277. Widmalm 1997, 72.

278. Das 2001, 49.

279. Widmalm 1997, 109; Schofield 1996, 235–36; Bose 2003, 126–27; Singh 1995, 138; Staniland 2014, 72; Joshi 1999, 38.

280. Interview with anonymous Indian journalist B.

281. Behera 2006, 81–82; Jones 2008, 7–9; Sahni 1999, 399.

282. Joshi 1999, 46–47.

283. Staniland 2014.

284. On the differences between JKLF and HM, and Pakistan's differing treatment of them, see Bose 2007, 232–43; Jones 2008, 9–10; Das 2001, 50–51; Bose 2003, 129–33; Devdas 2007, 206–7; Sahni 1999, 399–405.

285. Interviews with Sumir Kaul and Ishfaq-ul-Hassan.

286. Interview with Manoj Joshi.

287. "Proxy war in Kashmir: Need for a security belt," *Times of India*, 05/15/90, 12.

288. Devadas 2007, 216–17.

289. "500 Pak-trained terrorists in Kashmir valley," *Times of India*, 02/11/90, 6; "Correct approach to policing in Kashmir," *Times of India*, 02/06/90, 12.

290. Jagmohan 1991, 345, 355, 373.

291. Ibid., 404.

292. Bloeria 2000, 118.

293. Ibid., 128–29.

294. Ibid., 131, 149.

295. "Rethinking among militants: Governor," *Kashmir Times*, 10/05/90.

296. Dulat 2015, 66.

297. Schofield 1996, 235–36.

298. Bose 2003, 112–13.

299. Bloeria 2000, 158–59.

300. Quoted in Schofield 1996, 248.

301. Governor Jagmohan, when prodded to adopt a softer line and help local craftsmen and laborers to sell their goods outside the state, is reported to have furiously replied that he would not give money to Pakistanis. See Singh 1995, 145.

302. "BSF's delicate task in Kashmir," *Times of India*, 11/25/92, 11.

303. Bose 2007, 237.

304. Das 2001, 47.

305. Bose 2003, 112–13.

306. Bose, Mohan, Navlakha, and Banerjee 1990, 650.

307. Interviews with Shujaat Bukhari and Zafar Meraj.

308. Interviews with anonymous Kashmiri journalist and with Basharat Peer.

309. Interview with Samar Halarnkar.

310. Interview with Sankarshan Thakur.

311. Interview with anonymous former security official.

312. "BJP for clear signals on Kashmir: Advani ridicules talks of political initiative, assembly revival," *Kashmir Times*, 04/02/90; "BJP wants right signals to Pak against misadventure in Kashmir," *Kashmir Times*, 04/07/90; "BJP national executive meet: NF Govt criticized for 'soft policies' on Kashmir, Punjab," 04/09/70; "BJP calls for 'bullet for bullet' approach in Kashmir," *Kashmir Times*, 05/03/90; and "BJP wants Saxena to get tough with militants," *Kashmir Times*, 06/07/90; "BJP warns centre against initiating political process in Kashmir," *Kashmir Times*, 03/14/90.

313. "Fresh measures evolved to check infiltration in J&K, Punjab," *Kashmir Times*, 03/10/90; "Strict vigilance on borders following Pak intrusions," *Kashmir Times*, 02/19/90; "Control line violation in J&K will be punished: Gen Sharma," *Kashmir Times*, 01/31/90; "Pak troops in forward areas," *Kashmir Times*, 04/14/90; "Indo-Pak border to be sealed," *Kashmir Times*, 05/07/90; "Pak army troops fire on Indian army officers in Poonch," *Kashmir Times*, 05/20/90; "Heavy shelling by Pak troops in Kupwara sector," *Kashmir Times*, 08/21/90; "DG BSF says: Pak still pushing in militants," *Kashmir Times*, 11/08/90.

314. "'Difficult time ahead,'" *Kashmir Times*, 06/22/90; "Pak desperate about pushing 6,000 militants into Valley," *Kashmir Times*, 07/16/90; "Over 3,000 militants in POK may attempt to cross into Valley," *Kashmir Times*, 09/21/90

315. "A delicate task," *Kashmir Times*, 05/28/90.

316. Interview with anonymous former Congress Party official.

317. Interview with Dileep Padgoankar.

318. Interview with Rahul Pandita.

319. "Kashmir violence reignites India-Pakistan tensions," *Los Angeles Times*, 02/11/90.

320. "PM: Pak will pay price," *Kashmir Times*, 04/11/90. See also "PM warns Pak against subversion," *Kashmir Times*, 04/23/90.

321. "PM: no compromise with secessionists," *Kashmir Times*, 04/12/90. See also "Secessionists will be stamped out: PM," *Kashmir Times*, 08/16/90.

322. "Uproar in parliament: Kashmir action not excessive," *Kashmir Times*, 05/23/90.

323. "PM for strong measures in J&K, Punjab," *Kashmir Times*, 12/15/90.

324. "Kashmir dispute is souring India-Pakistan ties," *New York Times*, 01/31/90.

325. "Indian crackdown in Kashmir helps fuel separatist cause; militants, troops skirmish daily in city," *Washington Post*, 05/06/90.

326. Interview with anonymous former Congress Party official; "Mufti: no slackness in dealing with militants," *Kashmir Times*, 04/07/90.

327. "Mufti warns Pak against aiding, abetting terrorism in Kashmir," *Kashmir Times*, 05/13/90; "Mufti warns Pak, asks 'misguided' youths to lay down arms," *Kashmir Times*, 06/18/90.

328. "Farooq for iron hand policy, radical solution in Kashmir," *Kashmir Times*, 12/13/90. The previous year, he had promised to "raze Srinagar" if compelled to by Pakistan's war in the state. See "Trouble in Kashmir," *Far Eastern Economic Review*, 05/18/89.

329. Interview with retired colonel Vivek Chaddha.

330. Interview with retired lieutenant general H. S. Panag.

331. "Ultra-sophisticated arms to be used in Kashmir, Punjab," *Kashmir Times*, 06/07/90.

332. "Long haul in Kashmir," *Times of India*, 07/07/90, 10.

333. "Kashmir militants' mood subdued," *Times of India*, 04/24/90, 11.

334. "Sheer politicking," *Kashmir Times*, 03/07/90.

335. "Probe into excesses," *Kashmir Times*, 10/06/90; "As Srinagar burns," *Kashmir Times*, 10/11/90. See also "Caught in crossfire," *Kashmir Times*, 10/15/90.

336. "First things first," *Kashmir Times*, 02/02/90.

337. "Remove confusion," *Kashmir Times*, 03/26/90. See a similar position espoused in "A breakthrough," *Kashmir Times*, 03/24/90.

338. "J&K comes under President's rule," *Kashmir Times*, 07/19/90.
339. Cunningham 2014, 72–74.
340. Interview with anonymous former security official.
341. Bhaumik 1996, 42. Raman (2007, 7–8) claims Pakistani training of Naga rebels began in 1956.
342. Bhaumik 2009, 16, 97, 158.
343. For example, see Raman 2007, 34–37.
344. Ganguly 1996n3.

4. The Ottoman Empire's Escalation from Reforms to the Armenian Genocide, 1908–1915

1. Van Evera 1997, 79.
2. George and Bennett 2004, 166–67.
3. Lewy 2005.
4. Hovannisian 2007, 3–17. For an excellent critique of the contested and often biased historiography of the genocide, see Dyer (1976). As he points out, it is difficult for unbiased students of the conflict to understand what happened, caught between alleged Turkish "falsifiers" and Armenian "deceivers." Suny (2011) is also a worthwhile account on the historiography of the Armenian genocide. Because of the deep politicization associated with it, the Armenian genocide can be fraught with peril for scholars. Gingeras (2009) describes the process by which he came to decide on the subject of his dissertation in his preface: "Friends and colleagues with years of experience in Ottoman studies warned me that I was essentially contemplating professional suicide . . . there were the political consequences to consider. A dissertation dealing with Kurds, Armenians, or other taboo subjects in Turkey was bound to bring troubles down around me. No matter what I did, I was told, someone would be very unhappy with my work. Someone, be it a member of the Turkish government, members of the Armenian diaspora, or other Ottoman scholars, would eat me alive for having challenged, upheld, or ignored some aspect of Eastern Anatolia's recent history. In short, the advice I had was: don't do it. Drop it. Don't kill your career before it begins." He settled on aspects related to western Anatolia instead.
5. For reasons I am unable to gather, such books are often published in English by the University of Utah press.
6. For example, Gunter (2011, 2) exhorts those "who presently support anti-Turkish positions" to "realize that the unfortunate events so often described as 'genocide' would be best seen otherwise."
7. As Orwell famously warned, language and rhetoric are often the plains on which such battles are fought; writers such as Güclü (2010, 51 and 97) do not even concede the use of the word *deportation*, instead using the more anodyne "relocation." Alternatively, massacres are described as "energetic measures."
8. See, for example, Güclü (2012, 44–45).
9. Gunter 2011, 8. Elsewhere he writes, "Both the Armenians and Turks suffered horribly at each other's hands. Neither had a monopoly on total innocence or evil. Both, however, continue to maintain grossly exaggerated positions highly favorable to themselves and react negatively to contrary suggestions with vehement self-righteousness" (16).
10. Somakian 1995, 1–3.
11. Ibid.
12. Somakian 1995, 4. Toft (2003) describes the importance of demographic factors—particularly population concentration—to the process of political mobilization along ethnic lines. For an example of Turkish-based historiography that dismisses Armenian claims of atrocities based on allegedly skewed demographic figures, see Güclü (2010, 33) and Gunter (2011, 22).
13. Naimark 2001, 19.
14. Dadrian 1995, 45–47.
15. Güclü 2010, 36.
16. Dadrian 1995, 31.

17. Bloxham 2003, 147.
18. Valentino 2004, 158.
19. Somakian 1995, 5–9.
20. Dadrian 1995, 35.
21. Bodger 1984, 76. On the conditions under which states will support ethnic affiliates across borders, see Saideman (1997).
22. Bodger 1984, 76–77.
23. Sohrabi 2011, 73.
24. Ibid., 72–78, quote on 72.
25. Kayali 1997, 41.
26. Kirakossian 1992, 63.
27. Turfan 2000, 133 and 144.
28. Kirakossian 1992, 59.
29. Zürcher 1984, 8–15.
30. Göçek 2011, 63. The era was referred to as such because the Young Turks were restoring the constitution of 1876, in effect for two years only.
31. On the rise of nationalism in the press during the Young Turk era, see Arai (1992).
32. Naimark 2001, 24.
33. Kirakossian 1992, 71–72.
34. Bloxham 2005, 49.
35. Rae 2002, 140; and Dadrian 1999, 69. Notwithstanding a flier for the Armenian Revolutionary Federation, or the Dashnaks, which claimed that it would "fight until its last drop of blood for the liberation of the fatherland." See Bloxham 2005, 50.
36. Kayali 1997, 43–44.
37. Ibid., 1997, 51.
38. Melson 1987, 69.
39. Melson 1992, 155–56; and Ahmad 1969, 27. See also Turfan 2000, 151. It should be noted, however, that despite being in alliance with the Young Turks, there were very few Armenians in the movement itself. See Zürcher 1984, 22.
40. Ahmad 1969, 9.
41. Turfan 2000, 145.
42. Üngör 2011, 28.
43. Somakian 1995, 38; Kirakossian 1992, 89; Suny 2015, 156. Quote from Morgenthau 1918, 195.
44. Quoted in Kirakossian 1992, 107. See also Suny 2015, 158–60.
45. Quoted in Kirakossian 1992, 90–91.
46. Kaligian 2009, 13; and Rae 2002, 148.
47. Suny 2015, 155–57.
48. Aydin 2013, 51; Ünal 1996, 36–37. While Ünal bizarrely put these conciliatory efforts down to the Ottoman Empire's "fundamental" hatred of European powers, much more likely is that at the time, the revolutionary and often Western-based Young Turks genuinely desired, and believed in, cooperative relations with Europe.
49. Kayali 1997, 82.
50. Morgenthau 1918, 194.
51. In a similar vein, Mylonas (2012) discusses "accommodationist" versus "assimilationist" policies.
52. Rae 2002, 137.
53. Üngör 2011, 30.
54. Kirakossian 1992, 80.
55. Üngör 2011, 25–27.
56. Akçam 2004, 62–67.
57. Üngör 2011, 42.
58. Melson 1987, 72.
59. Ahmad 1969, 153.
60. Üngör 2011, 43. See also Melson 1987, 71.

61. Melson 1992, 153–61; Rae 2002, 152; and Ahmad 1969, 152–54.
62. Mann 2005, 129.
63. Hovanissian 1987, 26.
64. Balakian 2003, 165. For more on Gökalp and the new Turkish nationalism, see Üngör (2011, 33–36).
65. Bloxham 2005, 59.
66. Melson 1992, 161–62. See also Davison 1948, 481.
67. Somakian 1995, 39.
68. Balakian 2003, 162.
69. Gingeras 2009, 39.
70. Ibid., 38. Indeed, there is evidence that such motifs revolving around territorial loss and abandonment have survived to the contemporary Turkish state. See Göçek 2011, 41.
71. Balakian 2003, 159. See also Bloxham 2005, 59–60. There is a fourth point to be made about the losses in the Balkan wars, and that is that the Young Turks' families were overrepresented among refugees from the conflicts. The Young Turks generally originated from Salonika and Pristina, now under Greek and Serbian rule respectively. Young Turk leaders such as Talaat, Renda, and Cavit became refugees along with their families, and this doubtless played a role in their radicalization. See Üngör 2011, 45–46.
72. Üngör 2011, 50.
73. Morgenthau 1918, 198.
74. McCarthy 2001, 95–96.
75. Kirakossian 1992, 77.
76. Quoted in Kirakossian 1992, 95.
77. Akçam 2012, 139; Gingeras 2009, 37–38; and Balakian 2003, 159–60.
78. Bloxham 2003, 146. Erickson 2001, 15–17. Given these facts, the Ottoman Empire performed adequately in the Great War, especially when one considers its substandard equipment, training, and development. See Macfie 1998, 128–60.
79. Somakian 1995, 46–48.
80. Bloxham 2005, 54.
81. Bodger 1984, 90–95.
82. Davison 1948, 486–88.
83. Quoted from Somakian 1995, 58.
84. Davison 1948.
85. Bloxham 2003, 150–51.
86. Somakian 1995, 59.
87. In fact, the long-term trend in this regard was clear, as Ottoman sovereignty had been chipped away beginning with the externally imposed Islahat Fermani of 1856, a program of reform concerning human rights and public policy, and continuing through the postwar settlement after 1878 (see Aras and Caha 2000, 31). Emblematic of this larger trend were the so-called Capitulations, or contracts between the Ottomans and foreign powers concerning foreign nationals. These contracts, which began in the sixteenth century under Suleyman I, were privileges the Ottoman government granted non-Ottoman subjects when they were traveling or living on Ottoman soil. These were cause for great resentment and were done away with on the eve of the Great War; Foreign Minister Halil claimed that Turkey had finally freed itself from the "tutelage of the great powers." See Ahmad 2000; Akçam 2006, 78–81; and Balakian 2003, 171.
88. Quoted in Akçam 2006, 118.
89. Quoted in Kirakossian 1992, 98.
90. Somakian 1995, 58–59.
91. Bodger 1984, 96.
92. Dadrian 1995, 44–45.
93. Kirakossian 1992, 96.
94. Dadrian 1995, 192–93. See also Akçam 2006, 119.
95. Quoted in Balakian 2003, 161. As he notes in a comment on the editorial, "In the Turkish mind, the struggle to keep the Balkans was never far from the Armenian Question."

96. Akçam 2004, 87.

97. Bloxham 2003, 150–51.

98. Mylonas 2012, 9. See also Kirakossian 1992, 104.

99. Gingeras 2009, 42.

100. The only sliver of possibility of cooperation between the two groups was itself security based. The Young Turks offered the Armenian community autonomy if it resolved to support it in the war—on both the Turkish and Russian sides of the border. The Ottoman Armenians refused, arguing that Russian Armenians could not be expected to fight for the Ottomans. See Mann 2005, 134–35.

101. Quoted in Reynolds 2009, 165. Emphasis added.

102. Ibid., 165.

103. Ibid., 166–67

104. Suny 2015, 285.

105. On the massacres under the sultan between 1894 and 1896, see Dadrian (1995) and Melson (1992, chapter 2).

106. See, for example, Suny 2015.

107. Armenian historians often use U.S. Ambassador Morgenthau's memoirs as supporting evidence for their claims that the Turks were simply racist and were looking for an opportunity to exterminate the Armenian people. Certainly Morgenthau was better placed than most to make observations on Ottoman policy. But it bears noting that Ambassador Morgenthau was hardly the most impartial of observers. Indeed, those who have read his memoirs could scarcely walk away from them without feeling that Morgenthau was, simply put, a racist man. To wit, this is how he characterized the Turks as a people: "Essentially the Turk is a bully and a coward; he is brave as a lion when things are going his way, but cringing, abject, and nerveless when reverses are overwhelming him. And now that the fortunes of war were apparently favouring the empire, I began to see an entirely new Turk unfolding before my eyes. The hesitating and fearful Ottoman, feeling his way cautiously amid the mazes of European diplomacy, and seeking opportunities to find an advantage for himself in the divided counsels of the European powers, gave place to an understanding, almost dashing figure, proud and assertive, determined to live his own life and absolutely contemptuous of his Christian foes. I was really witnessing a remarkable development in race psychology—an almost classical instance of reversion to type. . . . We must realize that the basic fact underlying the Turkish mentality is its utter contempt for all other races. A fairly insane pride is the element that largely explains this strange human species. . . .

They were lacking in what we may call the fundamentals of a civilized community. They had no alphabet and no art of writing; no books, no poets, no art, and no architecture; they built no cities and they established no lasting state. . . . They were simply wild and marauding horsemen, whose one conception of tribal success was to pounce upon people who were more civilized than themselves and plunder them." Citing testimony from such racists is common practice for scholars making the case that the Turks had always longed for genocide. For another example, see Dadrian (1999, 70), where we are expected to trust the word of an observer who claims that "the Turk is extremely jealous of the Armenian, jealous of his mental superiority, of his thrift, and business enterprise. He has, therefore, resorted to oppression."

108. Dyer 1976, 99. There are concerns about "blaming the victim" when writing about issues such as genocide, particularly since explanations that use the war and the threatening environment are often conflated with the so-called provocation thesis, which essentially claims that the Armenians had it coming. The former does not imply the latter. See Melson 1992, 159.

109. McCarthy 2001, 97. It should be noted that there was nothing inevitable about Turkey's choice of allies in the war. Senior members of the CUP sent feelers to both Britain and France in the lead up to the war. See Üngör 2011, 55–56.

110. Bodger 1984, 97.

111. Akçam 2006, 112. Indeed, just before the war began, the Ottomans attempted to rid themselves of the various reform plans instituted from without altogether. The Dutch inspector general appointed to head the reform plan was delayed in beginning his duties because of the

"critical situation in which the world then found itself"; he was asked to return to his country shortly thereafter. See Akçam 2006, 119.

112. Balakian 2003, 173.
113. Kirakossian 1992, 113.
114. Telegrams quoted in Akçam (2012, 139–41).
115. Ibid., 142.
116. Lewy 2005, 91.
117. Gunter 2011, 6–7; Gingeras 2009, 42.
118. McCarthy 2001, 106. This was no exaggeration by Turkish sources. United States ambassador Morgenthau also believed the true number of armed Armenians fighting, or preparing to fight, on behalf of the Russians was about twenty-five thousand. See Lewy 2005, 92.
119. Quoted in Shaw and Shaw 1977, 314–15.
120. Quoted in Holquist 2011, 154.
121. Bloxham 2005, 72–73.
122. Bloxham 2003, 164.
123. Cable 1915–02–02-DE-001.
124. Suny 2015, 222.
125. Balakian 2003, 172.
126. Naimark 2001, 27. See also Lewy 2005, 91.
127. Akçam 2006, 141.
128. Balakian 2003, 163–67.
129. Bloxham 2003, 154–55; and Mann 2005, 140.
130. Bloxham 2003, 141.
131. Göçek 2011, 89.
132. Balakian 2003, 175–76.
133. For a general study of forced migration and security in international politics, see Greenhill (2010).
134. Hartunian 1986, 64.
135. Melson 1992, 142–44. Suny (2015, 247) also ascribes a central role to Bahaeddin Sakir.
136. Ahmad 1969, 159.
137. Quoted in Kirakossian 1992, 118.
138. Quoted in Naimark 2001, 29.
139. Morgenthau 1918, 236.
140. Ibid., 237–39.
141. Quoted in Akçam 2012, 134–35.
142. Morgenthau 1918, 230.
143. Ibid., 231.
144. Ibid., 228–29.
145. Lewy 2005, 101.
146. That was not the only time Ambassador Morgenthau heard prescient analysis of how the genocide would unfold. At the beginning of the war—before Turkey had even formally entered—Morgenthau told German ambassador Wangenheim that the Turks would massacre the Armenians in Anatolia. Wangenheim replied, "So long as England does not attack Canakkale or some other Turkish port there is nothing to fear. Otherwise, nothing can be guaranteed." Here, too, advance warning was being given on the association between the external threat and internal decision-making in the Ottoman Empire. See Akçam 2006, 126–27.
147. Bloxham 2003, 143 and 152.
148. Valentino 2004, 163. See also Bloxham 2005, 66–67; and Mann 2005, 141.
149. Üngör 2011, 59.
150. While Enver did scapegoat the Armenian community for the loss in the Caucasus, he also bizarrely sought to separately thank them for their service. In a letter sent on February 26, Enver wrote to the Armenian patriarchate and requested that the patriarch send his message of "pleasure and thanks to the Armenian Nation, which was known to represent an example of complete loyalty to the Ottoman Government." German consular officials corroborated this account, which on the surface, makes very little sense. See Akçam 2006, 143.

151. Reynolds 2011, 134.
152. Balakian 2003, 200
153. Lewy 2005, 102; Mann 2005, 141.
154. Bloxham 2003, 164.
155. Rogan 2015, 159.
156. Reynolds 2011, 135.
157. Akçam 2012, 157.
158. Gingeras 2009, 41.
159. Reynolds 2011, 135.
160. McMeekin 2015, 234.
161. Üngör 2011, 61.
162. Suny 2011, 243–44.
163. McMeekin 2015, 235–36.
164. Ibid., 236–37.
165. Erickson 2013, 161–62.
166. Suny 2015, 232.
167. Erickson 2013, 169.
168. Ibid., 169–71.
169. Ibid., 179–80.
170. McMeekin 2015, 225.
171. Erickson 2013, 189.
172. McCarthy 2001, 107; and Morgenthau 1918, 202. See also Üngör 2011, 66–71.
173. McMeekin 2015, 227–28.
174. Balakian 2003, 197.
175. Bloxham 2003, 156–57.
176. Balakian 2003, 202.
177. On the development of the conflict in Van, see Balakian (2003, 205–7)
178. Lewy 2005, 96–99.
179. Quoted in Lewy 2005, 103.
180. Cable 1915–05–08-DE-001.
181. Reynolds 2011, 147.
182. Rogan 2015, 171–72.
183. Bloxham 2003.
184. Akçam 2006, 146–47.
185. Bloxham 2003, 169–71.
186. Ibid., 173–74. See also Akçam 2012, 179–80.
187. Macfie 1998, 132.
188. Morgenthau 1918, 243.
189. Bloxham 2003, 180–82.
190. Gingeras 2009, 44.
191. Bloxham 2005, 83–90.
192. About 15 percent of deportees survived deportation (see Naimark 2001, 34). An account of Turkish history overly sympathetic to the state does not assign responsibility for the deaths during the forced marches and deportations to the Ottoman state. "Specific instructions were issued for the army to protect the Armenians against nomadic attacks and to provide them with sufficient food and other supplies to meet their needs during the march and after they were settled. Warnings were sent to the Ottoman military commanders to make certain that neither the Kurds nor any other Muslims used the situation to gain vengeance for the long years of Armenian terrorism. The Armenians were to be protected and cared for until they returned to their homes after their war" (see Shaw and Shaw 1977, 315). It would be an understatement to suggest that this view is not the dominant one held by neutral historians.
193. Bloxham 2003, 168–69, quote drawn from 169.
194. Macfie 1998, 133; Reynolds 2011, 149–50.
195. Suny 2015, 283.
196. Cable 1915–12–18-DE-001.

197. Valentino 2004, 163.
198. Lewy 2005, 98.
199. Holquist 2011, 151.
200. Bloxham 2005, 68.
201. Kirakossian 1992, 112.
202. Inter alia, see work by Bloxham and Melson.
203. Gunter 2011, 20–21.
204. Dyer 1976, 106–7.
205. Gingeras 2009, 43.
206. Ibid., 42.
207. Mann 2005, 141.
208. Bloxham 2005, 62.
209. Ibid., 66.
210. For examples of the weakness of such "evidence," see Dadrian (1999, 96–99, 128–29). Such scholars go as far as to say the regime entered the Great War only as an excuse to annihilate the Armenians in their midst (see Dadrian 1999, 125).
211. Akçam 2012, 128.
212. Mann 2005, 112.
213. Akçam 2012, 137.

5. Peaceful and Violent Separatism in North America, Europe, and the Middle East, 1861–1993

1. Van Evera 1997, 86–87.
2. Coggins 2011, 2014.
3. Gerring 2007, 101–2.
4. Indeed, recent datasets on secessionism such as Coggins (2011, 2014) include both the first and second intifadas. For a discussion on the term *secession* as it applies to Israel-Palestine, see Lustick 1993, 22–25.
5. Ron 2003, 131; Kimmerling and Migdal 2003, 241.
6. Younis 2000, 3.
7. Butt 2013.
8. Though there was an increasing tendency to define them as Palestinian nationals, Arabs in Palestine would also subscribe to religious, Arab, local, and clan-based identities. See Khalidi 1997, 19.
9. Pearlman 2011, 27; and Khalidi 1997, 20.
10. Khalidi 2006, 33–36; and Pearlman 2011, 28.
11. Pearlman 2011, 35–39; and Khalidi 2006, 21–30.
12. Khalidi 2006, 120–22.
13. Pearlman 2011, 56.
14. Pearlman 2011, 56–58; Khalidi 2006, 131.
15. Khalidi 2006, 1–8.
16. Grinberg 2010, 30.
17. Khalidi 2006, 124, 191–92.
18. Pearlman 2011, 62–66; and Khalidi 2006, 136.
19. Lustick 1993, 353; see (7–27) for a synopsis of the ideological debates within Israel's body politic on the annexation of the West Bank.
20. Quoted in Bregman 2014, xxxviii.
21. Rubin 1994, 24–44.
22. Cobban 1984, 94–95, 119–20; Kimmerling and Migdal 2003, 259–73.
23. Morris 1999, 394, claims that "the Arabs' success in springing this strategic surprise" was, from the perspective of military history a feat on par with Hitler's invasion of Russia and the Japanese attack on Pearl Harbor.
24. Schiff and Ya'ari 1989, 45–46; Kimmerling and Migdal 2003, 327–28.
25. Morris 1999, 561–63; Younis 2000, 163; Grinberg 2010, 34.

26. Kimmerling and Migdal 2003, 286–96.
27. Morris 1999, 565–68.
28. Ibid., 573.
29. Younis 2000, 162.
30. Morris 1999, 574.
31. Ibid., 575–76.
32. Sayigh 1989, 248.
33. Morris 1999, 580–81; and Azoulay and Ophir 2013, 74.
34. The section on the Israeli response to the first intifada is drawn from Morris 1999, 586–94; Ron 2003, 154; Schiff and Ya'ari 1989, 145–50; and Azoulay and Ophir 2013, 76–78.
35. Petrelli 2013, 668.
36. Ron 2003, 147–48.
37. Pearlman 2011, 124.
38. Interview with anonymous Palestinian academic A.
39. Interview with Afif Safieh.
40. Pearlman 2011, 128.
41. Interviews with Nimrod Goren, Ori Nir, Yael Patir.
42. Interview with Ilai Saltzman.
43. Kimmerling and Migdal 2003, 361.
44. Shlaim 2001, 507.
45. Ibid., 502–3.
46. Khalidi 2006, 184.
47. Shlaim 2001, 504. See also Grinberg 2010, 44.
48. Freilich 2012, 12.
49. Butt 2013.
50. Interview with Danny Rubenstein.
51. Interview with Amos Harel.
52. Netanyahu 1993, 187.
53. Younis 2000, 8–9.
54. http://www.newyorker.com/magazine/2013/01/21/the-party-faithful?currentPage=all.
55. Barnett 1999, 19.
56. Thomas 2011, 123.
57. Ibid., 125. Emphasis in original.
58. "Israeli-PLO talks snagged on security," *Christian Science Monitor*, 10/26/1993.
59. "When it comes to talking peace with the Palestinians, Israel's army is in charge," *Christian Science Monitor*, 02/25/1994.
60. "Bibi scoffs at Sharon power bid," *Forward*, 06/03/1994.
61. "Israel's new premier drags his foot on peace," *Christian Science Monitor*, 07/29/1996.
62. "A poor and mangled peace," *Financial Times*, 10/04/1996.
63. Slater 2001, 178.
64. Shlaim 2001, 566–67.
65. Ibid., 524; and Azoulay and Ophir 2013, 83–84.
66. Shlaim 2001, 528, 546.
67. This section on demilitarization is the product of interviews with Yonatan Touval, Chaim Levinson, Gadi Baltiansky, Toby Greene, Ilan Baruch.
68. Morris 2009, 136–39. Palestinians and left-wing Israelis both scoffed at the notion of Barak's concessions, pointing out that we know remarkably little about the precise details of the offer, and that there has been a concerted effort at myth making within Barak's government, both for domestic and international reasons, to exaggerate his generosity at Camp David. Pressman (2003, 15) argues that "the Israeli offer was unprecedented, but it was neither as generous not as complete as Israel has since suggested," especially concerning the contiguity of the Palestinian state in the West Bank, sovereignty in East Jerusalem, and the right of return. Rather, the Palestinian version of events, according to Pressman "is much closer to the

evidentiary record of articles, interviews, and documents produced by participants in the negotiations, journalists, and other analysts" (6). For similar criticism of Barak's so-called generosity, see Slater 2001, 179–88.

69. Interviews with Mohammad Daraghmeh, Wafa Amr. A second reason pointed out by some interviewees was Arafat's concerns about the civil-military balance, given a history of coups in the region, and the Palestinian military being a competing center of power within a prospective Palestinian state.

70. Interviews with Afif Safieh, anonymous PLO official, anonymous Palestinian academic B.

71. Interview with Sam Bahour.

72. Interview with anonymous Palestinian academic A.

73. On path dependence, see Mahoney 2000 and Pierson 2000.

74. Interview with Ori Nir.

75. Interview with Ehud Eiran.

76. Morris 2009, 165.

77. Interview with Ori Nir.

78. Interview with Danny Rubenstein.

79. http://en.idi.org.il/media/3930815/Peace_Index_February_2015-Eng.pdf.

80. http://en.idi.org.il/media/599212/Peace%20Index-October-trans.pdf.

81. Interview with Afif Safieh.

82. Ron 2003, 118–25; Newman 2005, 204.

83. Newman 2005, 205.

84. Shlaim 2001, 548–49.

85. Morris 2009, 162–63.

86. The most recent iteration of the peace process, led by U.S. secretary of state John Kerry, also fell apart due to Prime Minister Netanyahu's inability to concede to a settlement freeze. See http://www.newrepublic.com/article/118751/how-israel-palestine-peace-deal-died.

87. http://www.newyorker.com/magazine/2013/01/21/the-party-faithful?currentPage=all.

88. Pundak 2001, 35.

89. Interviews with anonymous Palestinian academic B, anonymous former Palestinian Authority official, Mohammad Daraghmeh, and Gadi Baltiansky. Ilai Saltzman said that while delaying discussions of final status issues was a mistake, it was an "inevitable" one; things had to move slowly given the lack of trust between the parties.

90. Khalidi 2006, 158.

91. Interview with Afif Safieh.

92. Freilich 2012, 61.

93. Azoulay and Ophir 2013, 127.

94. Grinberg 2010, 172, 155.

95. Ibid., 160.

96. Morris 2009, 151.

97. Grinberg 2010, 160.

98. Ibid., 163.

99. Brym and Andersen 2011, 492.

100. Schulze 2001, 227–28.

101. Interviews with Ehud Eiran, Yael Patir.

102. Interviews with Amos Harel and an anonymous Israeli academic.

103. Interview with Nimrod Goren.

104. Interview with Wafa Amr. Sharon's rise to power following the second intifada was not coincidental. As Ehud Eiran put it, "The first intifada helped the left, the second destroyed the left."

105. Ron 2003, 198–99, and interview with Ehud Eiran.

106. Pearlman 2011, 151–52.

107. Ibid., chapter 6.

108. Pape 2005, 48.

109. Kramer 1992, 2.

110. Bookman 1994, 175; Ulč 1996, 331.

111. Kramer 1992, 2–3.

112. Ulč 1996, 332.

113. Ibid., 332.

114. Ibid., 333–34.

115. Kramer 1992, 6.

116. Interview with Jeffrey Simon.

117. Ulč 1996, 337–38.

118. Ibid., 338.

119. Bookman 1994, 178.

120. Wolchik 1995, 228.

121. Ibid.

122. Ulč 1996, 341.

123. Interview with Darina Malová.

124. "Czechs, Slovaks split in elections; outcome could hasten country's breakup," *Washington Post*, 06/07/1992; "Czechoslovakia vote sets up sticky summer," *Los Angeles Times*, 06/07/1992; "Czechs and Slovaks reconsider the federation," *Financial Times*, 06/08/1992

125. "Slovak vote fuels move toward new nationhood," *Christian Science Monitor*, 06/08/1992.

126. Kraus 2000, 213.

127. Interviews with anonymous U.S. State Department official, Grigorij Meseznikov, and Zora Bútorová.

128. Interviews with Kevin Deegan-Krause and Grigorij Meseznikov.

129. "Prospect of split worries Slovaks," *Edmonton Journal*, 06/28/1992.

130. Wolchik 1995, 239–40. Given the tepid support for full-blown secession among the respective publics, *The Economist* magazine noted that the divorce was "happening by accident." Quoted in Wolchik 1995, 230.

131. Interviews with Zora Bútorová and Grigorij Meseznikov.

132. Interview with anonymous U.S. diplomatic official.

133. Interviews with Ted Russell and Martin Bútora.

134. Interview with Kevin Deegan-Krause and Darina Malová.

135. Kramer 1992, 13–14.

136. Hilde 1999, 647.

137. Interview with Jeffrey Simon.

138. Rupnik 1995, 272.

139. Kraus 2000, 202.

140. Interviews with Darina Malová, David Cowles, Grigorij Meseznikov, Jan Eichler, Michael Kraus, Zora Bútorová, Tim Haughton, and Martin Bútora.

141. Interview with Michael Kraus.

142. Interview with Jeffrey Simon.

143. Interview with Ondřej Ditrych.

144. Interview with Mills Kelly.

145. "Ethnic Hungarians in Slovakia hasten to protect rights," *Christian Science Monitor*, 09/03/1992; "Hungary: Harsh words," *The Economist*, 10/31/1992.

146. Interview with Sharon Wolchik.

147. Interview with Jan Eichler.

148. "Sorting out foreign ties, minority needs," *Christian Science Monitor*, 12/24/1992.

149. Interview with anonymous U.S. diplomatic official and with Ondřej Ditrych.

150. Simon 1993, 1–6.

151. Interestingly, Klaus would go on to become a Euroskeptic. According to Tim Haughton, this was because while European integration until Maastricht was about markets, Klaus found the EU's involvement in social policy less acceptable. Similarly, Petr Kopecky told me of Klaus's opposition to the euro currency, which he saw as a loss of national sovereignty.

152. Interview with Rick Zednick and Mills Kelly.

NOTES TO PAGES 191–194

153. Interview with Ondřej Ditrych.
154. Interview with Jeffrey Simon and Chris Donnelly.
155. Interviews with Jeffrey Simon, Chris Donnelly, and Petr Kopecky.
156. Interview with Jeffrey Simon.
157. Interview with Ted Russell.
158. Bookman 1994, 179.
159. Kramer 1992, 23.
160. Simon 1993, 7–9.
161. "Czechoslovakia: Blue Velvet," *The Economist*, 10/10/1992.
162. Bookman 1994, 183. Contemporary media reports affirmed that the split spelled greater trouble for Slovaks' prospects than the Czechs'. See inter alia, "For Slovaks, cost of split with Czechs will be high," *Christian Science Monitor*, 06/24/1992.
163. Interview with Jeffrey Simon.
164. "Czechs and Slovaks divide up assets on brink of separation," *New York Times*, 12/11/1992.
165. Interview with Chris Donnelly.
166. Wolchik 1995, 230–31.
167. "Czechs and Slovaks," *Washington Post*, 06/09/1992.
168. Interviews with Darina Malová, Grigorij Meseznikov, Zora Bútorová, and Martin Bútora.
169. Interview with Mills Kelly.
170. Kramer 1992, 4.
171. "Slovaks yearn to speak for themselves—Independence Movement Shakes Czechoslovak Unity," *Wall Street Journal*, 05/22/1992.
172. "The Velvet Dissolution—Elections to decide unity of country," *The Guardian*, 06/05/1992.
173. Several people commented on the cordiality of relations between the two since 1993, and many, including Zora Bútorová and Grigorij Meseznikov, credited the 1993 split for allowing such bonhomie. The typical argument put to me was that by going their separate ways, the Slovaks were forced to stand on their own, without the ability to blame the Czechs for their problems. Conversely, the split precluded the patronizing big brother–little brother attitude the Czechs often embodied in their dealings with the Slovaks. As such, the two ethnic groups enjoy better relations with each other today than what would have been possible had they remained united. As Tim Haughton told me, the situation is analogous to two brothers fighting over the top bunk or the remote: once they each get their own room, the squabbling disappears.
174. As Lipson 1984 argued, when push comes to shove for states, security concerns tend to trump economic ones.
175. Ulč 1996, 346.
176. Kramer 1992, 27.
177. Ulč 1996, 341; "Czechoslovakia: Velvet Divorce?" *The Economist*, 06/13/1992.
178. Ironically, one of the major factors behind Mečiar being turned out of power in the 1998 was the discontent among the Slovak body politic and society at being excluded from European institutions like the EU when all its neighbors were invited.
179. "A velvet divorce, but a rough road to single life: The Czech and Slovak republics will face different challenges after separation," *Financial Times*, 06/22/1992.
180. Rupnik 1995, 274–76. Interestingly, there was a brief concern among some Czech politicians that splitting would slow, not hasten, admission to European institutions, which gave them pause. See "The world from . . . Czechoslovakia," *Christian Science Monitor*, 06/17/1992.
181. Interview with Jeffrey Simon.
182. Interview with Chris Donnelly.
183. Interviews with Rick Zednick and Kevin Deegan-Krause. Notably, Havel's persistent calls for a referendum during the summer of 1992 were ignored by Mečiar and Klaus, because each knew the result of such a referendum would make a split problematic. See "Check, O Slovakia," *The Economist*, 06/27/1992.

184. Interview with Mills Kelly.
185. Interviews with Kevin Deegan-Krause, Chris Donnelly, and anonymous U.S. diplomatic official.
186. Interview with Kevin Deegan-Krause.
187. Interview with author.
188. Interview with Michael Kraus. Despite this relatively "clean" break, certain towns and villages still represented "anomalies" if not "territorial disputes" that had to be resolved. See "Borderline case," *The Guardian*, 10/20/1992.
189. Interview with Michael Kraus.
190. For example, see Young (1994). On the other hand, some scholars note their hesitance to call the dissolution of the Norway-Sweden union a case of "real" secession, "since the ties between the political entities involved were very loose at the outset." See Dion (1996, 270).
191. Parent 2006, 214–17.
192. Scott 1988, 327.
193. Parent 2006, 218–19.
194. Scott 1988, 327–28.
195. Pahre 2001, 147.
196. Young 1994, 777.
197. Parent 2006, 226.
198. Lindgren 1959, 62–63.
199. Barton 2003, 72.
200. Scott 1988, 328.
201. Lindgren 1959, 62–70; and Derry 1973, 147–52.
202. Derry 1973, 152.
203. Barton 2003, 75.
204. Parent 2006, 224.
205. Barton 2003, 75.
206. Nansen 1905, 83.
207. Derry 1973, 160–62.
208. Barton 2003, 78.
209. Quoted in Scott 1988, 330.
210. Barton 2003, 78–82.
211. Young 1994, 786. Interestingly, a professor at Uppsala University published in early 1905 a series of articles that laid out the conditions for the dissolution of the union; his plans included the razing of the frontier forts and the establishment of a neutral zone on the border (see Scott 1988, 330).
212. Parent 2006, 227.
213. Ibid., 221–22.
214. See Elgström 2000, especially chapter 4.
215. Derry 1973, 164–65.
216. Lindgren 1959, 144.
217. "Moving along to agreement: Norway will destroy all new fortifications," *Los Angeles Times*, 09/19/1905.
218. Lindgren 1959, 76, 132–35; Parent 2006, 224, 232; Barton 2003, 81; Derry 1973, 153, 158.
219. Such as the *Journal of the Civil War Era*.
220. Poast 2014, 1.
221. Ibid., 1.
222. Potter 2011, 8.
223. Toft 2003.
224. Potter 2011, 9.
225. Ibid., 32.
226. Ibid., 38.
227. Ibid., 7, 48–49; Foreman 2000, chapter 1.
228. Potter 2011, 447.

229. Quoted in Craven 1965, 60.
230. Potter 2011, 456–69.
231. Quoted in Craven 1965, 61.
232. Potter 2011, 478.
233. Craven 1965, 62.
234. Ibid., 73–75.
235. Mahin 2000, 7.
236. The focus on Lincoln is hardly misplaced, since, according to historians, "The final decision regarding compromise lay in the hands of one party, and ultimately of just one man: Abraham Lincoln." See McClintock 2008, 164.
237. Quoted in Potter 1965, 90.
238. Jones 1999, 92.
239. Potter 2011, 36.
240. Jones 1999, 91.
241. McClintock 2008, 134.
242. Ibid., 138–50.
243. Ibid., 165–66.
244. Ibid., 170–71; see also Potter 1965, 98–103.
245. Ibid., 172–73.
246. Ibid., 185.
247. Ibid., 195–96, 205.
248. Poast 2014, 7–10, quote on 7.
249. McClintock 2008, 206.
250. Ibid., 212–15.
251. Ibid., 216–17.
252. Ibid., 225.
253. Ibid., 226.
254. Ibid.
255. Mahin 2000, 44–45.
256. Poast 2014, 11.
257. Jones 1992, 10–11.
258. Seward to Adams, April 10, 1861, Foreign Relations of the United States
259. Mahin 2000, 23–24.
260. Jones 1992, 20; Jones 1999, 85.
261. Campbell 2003, 30.
262. Quoted in Ferris 1976, 36.
263. Bourne 1967, 252–53.
264. Ferris 1976, 24, emphasis in original; ibid., 2–3.
265. Foreman 2000, 23–27.
266. Jones 1992, 15–16.
267. Mahin 2000, 30–31.
268. Jones 1992, 34.
269. Ferris 1976, 34.
270. Owsley 2008, 2–3; Jones 2010, 12.
271. Owsley 2008, 12.
272. Quoted in Owsley 2008, 16.
273. Quoted in Jones 2010, 12.
274. Ibid., 15.
275. Jones 1992, 45.
276. Poast 2014, 29.
277. Mahin 2000, 12.
278. Seward to Adams, April 1, 1861 (FRUS).
279. Ferris 1976, 15. Ferris goes on to add that "after more than a generation of dealing with Americans who were coarse, bellicose, and often maladroit, Englishmen were inclined to be

supercilious and irritable about infringements by their trans-Atlantic cousins upon what they fancied as their rights and interests."

280. Ferris 1976, 22–23.

281. Quoted in Mahin 2000, 13–14.

282. Seward to Adams, June 3, 1861 (FRUS).

283. Mahin 2000, 17–22, quote on 17; Jones 2010, 11.

284. Jones 1992, 26.

285. Quoted in Poast 2014, 31.

286. Quoted in Ferris 1976, 46.

287. Jones 2010, 44.

288. Jones 1992, 29.

289. Ibid., 51.

290. Ferris 1976, 43.

291. Ibid., 72–74. Indeed, French enthusiasm for intervention, if anything, worked against British desires to intervene, given British concerns that a stronger foothold in North America would allow Napoleon III, considered unpredictable and opportunistic, to pursue adventurous schemes elsewhere (see Jones 2010, 24).

292. Seward to Adams, June 19, 1861 (FRUS).

293. Mahin 2000, 46.

294. Ibid., 49.

295. Seward to Adams, May 21, 1861 (FRUS)

296. Poast 2014, 34.

297. Ibid., 34–35.

298. Ibid., 36.

299. John Hay, diary entry, August 22 (see Dennett 1939).

300. Furthermore, the direction of events in the midst, rather than just the beginning, of the civil war also point to the centrality of concerns over British involvement. For instance, Lincoln's famous and well-chronicled choice of emancipation was in large part a way to ward off the prospect of British intervention, which he felt was around the corner for ostensibly humanitarian reasons, given the increasingly costly toll the war was taking (see Jones 1999, chapters 3–4). Ironically, the decision-making on the other side of the conflict at this exact time was also partly motivated by external considerations; Lee's strike at Antietam was aimed at showing the British and French the Confederacy was a viable entity. I thank Robert Art for this point.

301. Jones 1992, 57–59.

Conclusion

1. Which is often either an overstated concern or a fig leaf for other interests. See Krasner 1999.

2. Goddard (2010, 223) and Cox (1997, 682–86) discuss how the collapse of the Soviet Union led Irish Republicans to believe that England would no longer consider the prospect of an independent Ireland a threat, opening up the possibility of peace in Northern Ireland in the 1990s.

3. Jenne (2015) similarly argues that stabilizing regional conflicts is the key to peacefully resolving domestic disputes.

4. Arena and Pechenkina 2016.

5. https://thewire.in/114376/tensions-rise-as-centre-orders-more-pellet-guns-for-kashmir/.

6. Grigoryan 2015, Brancati 2006, Elkins and Sides 2007. For a nuanced position on this issue, see Bakke 2015.

7. https://www.ft.com/content/0fa5b3b4-766b-11e6-b60a-de4532d5ea35.

8. https://www.economist.com/blogs/charlemagne/2014/09/catalonias-referendum.

9. Walter 1997.

10. It is worth reiterating that theoretically, I expect democratic states to be no less (or no more, depending on one's point of view) violent than autocratic states when dealing with separatist movements—reflected in the experiences of India and Israel, to name two examples.

11. Although, as it so happens, separatist wars do last longer and are more intense than ideological civil wars.

12. Mylonas 2012, Bulutgil 2008.

13. Christia 2013.

14. Wilkinson 2006, Posner 2005, Varshney 2002.

15. Toft 2003, Ron 2003, Cunningham 2014, Walter 2009.

16. Wimmer 2002, Cederman et al. 2011.

References

Abbink, Jon. 2003. "Ethiopia-Eritrea: Proxy Wars and Prospects of Peace in the Horn of Africa." *Journal of Contemporary African Studies* 21, no. 3: 407–426.

Abbott, Kenneth W., and Duncan Snidal. 1998. "Why States Act through Formal International Organizations." *Journal of Conflict Resolution* 42, no. 1: 3–32.

Acemoglu, Daron, and James Robinson. 2012. *Why Nations Fail: The Origins of Power, Prosperity, and Poverty*. New York: Crown.

Ahmad, Aisha. 2015. "The Security Bazaar: Business Interests and Islamist Power in Civil War Somalia." *International Security* 39, no. 3: 89–117.

Ahmad, Feroz. 1969. *The Young Turks: The Committee of Union and Progress in Turkish Politics, 1908–1914*. Oxford: Oxford University Press.

———. 2000. "Ottoman Perceptions of the Capitulations 1800–1914." *Journal of Islamic Studies* 11, no. 1: 1–20.

Ahmad, Syed Iqbal. 1992. *Balochistan: Its Strategic Importance*. Karachi: Royal Book.

Ahmed, Moudud. 1979. *Bangladesh: Constitutional Quest for Autonomy*. Dhaka: University Press.

Akçam, Taner. 2004. *From Empire to Republic: Turkish Nationalism and the Armenian Genocide*. New York: Zed Books.

———. 2006. *A Shameful Act: The Armenian Genocide and the Question of Turkish Responsibility*. New York: Metropolitan Books.

———. 2012. *The Young Turks' Crime against Humanity: The Armenian Genocide and Ethnic Cleansing in the Ottoman Empire*. Princeton: Princeton University Press.

Ali, S. Mahmud. 2010. *Understanding Bangladesh*. New York: Columbia University Press.

Amnesty International. 1995. "India: Torture and Deaths in Custody in Jammu and Kashmir."

Anderson, Benedict. 1983. *Imagined Communities: Reflections on the Origin and Spread of Nationalism*. London: Verso.

Arai, Masami. 1992. *Turkish Nationalism in the Young Turk Era*. Leiden, Netherlands: E. J. Brill.

Aras, Bulent, and Omer Caha. 2000. "Fethullah Gulen and his Liberal 'Turkish Islam' Movement." *Middle East Review of International Affairs* 4, no. 4: 30–42.

Arif, Khalid M. 2001. *Khaki Shadows: Pakistan, 1947–1997*. Karachi: Oxford University Press.

Arreguín-Toft, Ivan. 2001. "How the Weak Win Wars: A Theory of Asymmetric Conflict." *International Security* 26, no. 1: 93–128.

Atzili, Boaz. 2011. *Good Fences, Bad Neighbors: Border Fixity and International Conflict*. Chicago: University of Chicago Press.

Aurora, J. S. 1985. "If Khalistan Comes, the Sikhs Will Be the Losers." Interview in *Punjab: The Fatal Miscalculation*, edited by Patwant Singh and Harji Malik. New Delhi: Crescent Printing.

Aydin, Cemil. 2013. "Japanese Pan-Asianism through the Mirror of Pan-Islamism." In *Tumultuous Decade: Empire, Society, and Diplomacy in 1930s Japan*, edited by I. Masato Kimura and Tosh Minohara. Toronto: University of Toronto Press.

Ayres, Alyssa. 2004. "Speaking Like a State: Nationalism, Language, and the Case of Pakistan." Ph.D. diss., University of Chicago.

Azoulay, Ariella, and Adi Ophir. 2013. *The One-State Condition: Occupation and Democracy in Israel/Palestine*. Stanford: Stanford University Press.

Bakke, Kristin M. 2015. *Decentralization and Intrastate Struggles: Chechnya, Punjab, and Quebec*. New York: Cambridge University Press.

Balakian, Peter. 2003. *The Burning Tigris: The Armenian Genocide and America's Response*. New York: Harper Collins.

Balcells, Laia. 2010. "Rivalry and Revenge: Violence against Civilians in Conventional Civil Wars." *International Studies Quarterly* 54, no. 2: 291–313.

Balch-Lindsay, Dylan, Andrew J. Enterline, and Kyle A. Joyce. 2008. "Third Party Intervention and the Civil War Process." *Journal of Peace Research* 45, no. 3: 345–363.

Bansal, Alok. 2006. "Balochistan: Continuing Violence and Its Implications." *Strategic Analysis* 30, no. 1: 46–63.

Barnett, Michael. 1999. "Culture, Strategy and Foreign Policy Change: Israel's Road to Oslo." *European Journal of International Relations* 5, no. 1: 5–36.

Barpujari, H. K. 1998. *North-East India: Problems, Policies and Prospects*. Guwahati, India: Spectrum Publications.

Barton, H. Arnold. 2003. *Sweden and Visions of Norway: Politics and Culture, 1814–1905*. Carbondale: Southern Illinois University Press.

Baruah, Sanjib. 1986. "Immigration, Ethnic Conflict, and Political Turmoil—Assam, 1979–1985." *Asian Survey* 26, no. 11: 1184–1206.

——. 1994. "The State and Separatist Militancy in Assam: Winning a Battle and Losing the War?" *Asian Survey* 34, no. 10: 863–877.

——. 1999. *India against Itself: Assam and the Politics of Nationality*. Philadelphia: University of Pennsylvania Press.

——. 2005. *Durable Disorder: Understanding the Politics of Northeast India*. New Delhi: Oxford University Press.

Bass, Gary J. 2013. *The Blood Telegram: Nixon, Kissinger, and a Forgotten Genocide*. Knopf: New York.

Baxter, Craig. 1971. "Pakistan Votes—1970." *Asian Survey* 11, no. 3: 197–218.

Behera, Navnita C. 2006. *Demystifying Kashmir*. Washington DC: Brookings Institution Press.

Beissinger, Mark R. 2002. *Nationalist Mobilization and the Collapse of the Soviet State*. New York: Cambridge University Press.

Bhat, Anil. 2009. *Assam Terrorism and the Demographic Challenge*. New Delhi: Center for Land Warfare Studies.

Bhaumik, Subir. 1996. *Insurgent Crossfire: North-East India*. New Delhi: Lancer.

——. 2009. *Troubled Periphery: Crisis of India's North East*. New Delhi: Sage.

Bhutto, Zulfiqar A. 1971. *The Great Tragedy*. Karachi: Pakistan People's Party.

——. 1973. *Politics of the People: A Collection of Articles, Statements, and Speeches*. Rawalpindi: Pakistan Publications.

Billmyer, John R. 2011. "The IDF: Tactical Success-Strategic Failure, SOD, the Second Intifada and Beyond." School of Advanced Military Studies, United States Army Command and General Staff College, Leavenworth, KS.

Bloeria, Sudhir S. 2000. *Pakistan's Insurgency vs India's Security: Tackling Militancy in Kashmir*. New Delhi: Manas.

Bloom, Mia M. 1999. "Failures of Intervention: The Unintended Consequences of Mixed Messages and the Exacerbation of Ethnic Conflict." Ph.D. diss., Columbia University.

Bloom, William. 1993. *Personal Identity, National Identity, and International Relations*. Cambridge: Cambridge University Press.

Bloxham, Donald. 2003. "The Armenian Genocide of 1915–1916: Cumulative Radicalization and the Development of a Destruction Policy." *Past and Present* 181, no. 1: 141–191.

——. 2005. *The Great Game of Genocide: Imperialism, Nationalism, and the Destruction of the Ottoman Armenians*. New York: Oxford University Press.

Bodger, Alan. 1984. "Russia and the End of the Ottoman Empire." In *The Great Powers and the End of the Ottoman Empire*, edited by Marian Kent. London: George Allen & Unwin.

Bookman, Milica Z. 1994. "War and Peace: The Divergent Breakups of Yugoslavia and Czechoslovakia." *Journal of Peace Research* 31, no. 2: 175–187.

Bose, Sumantra. 2003. *Kashmir: Roots of Conflict, Paths to Peace*. Cambridge, MA: Harvard University Press.

——. 2007. "The JKLF and JKHM: The Kashmir Insurgents." In *Terror, Insurgency, and the State: Ending Protracted Conflicts*, edited by Marianne Heiberg, Brendan O'Leary, and John Tirman. Philadelphia: University of Pennsylvania Press.

Bose, Tapan, Dinesh Mohan, Gautam Navlakha, and Sumanta Banerjee. 1990. "India's Kashmir War." *Economic and Political Weekly* 25, no. 13.

Bourne, Kenneth. 1967. *Britain and the Balance of Power in North America 1815–1908*. Berkeley: University of California Press.

Brancati, Dawn. 2006. "Decentralization: Fueling the Fire or Dampening the Flames of Ethnic Conflict and Secessionism." *International Organization* 60, no. 3: 651–685.

Brand, Laurie. 2014. *Official Stories: Politics and National Narratives in Egypt and Algeria*. Stanford: Stanford University Press.

Brass, Paul R. 1988. "The Punjab Crisis and the Unity of India." In *India's Democracy: An Analysis of Changing State-Society Relations*, edited by Atul Kohli. Princeton: Princeton University Press.

——. 2003. *The Production of Hindu-Muslim Violence in Contemporary India*. Seattle: University of Washington Press.

Bregman, Ahron. 2014. *Cursed Victory: A History of Israel and the Occupied Territories*. London: Allen Lane.

Brooks, Stephen G. 1997. "Dueling Realisms." *International Organization* 51, no. 3: 445–477.

Brubaker, Rogers. 1992. *Citizenship and Nationhood in France and Germany*. Cambridge: Harvard University Press.

——. 1996. *Nationalism Reframed: Nationhood and the National Question in the New Europe*. New York: Cambridge University Press.

Brym, Robert J., and Robert Andersen. 2011. "Rational Choice and the Political Bases of Changing Israeli Counterinsurgency Strategy." *British Journal of Sociology* 62, no. 3: 482–503.

Bull, Hedley. 1977. *The Anarchical Society: A Study of Order in World Politics*. New York: Columbia University Press.

Bulutgil, Zeynep. 2008. "Territorial Conflict and Ethnic Cleansing." Ph.D. diss., University of Chicago.

Butt, Ahsan I. 2013. "Anarchy and Hierarchy in International Relations: Explaining South America's War-Prone Decade, 1932–1941." *International Organization* 67, no. 3: 575–607.

Campbell, Duncan A. 2003. *English Public Opinion and the American Civil War*. Woodbridge, UK: Boydell Press.

Cederman, Lars-Erik, T. Camber Warren, and Didier Sornette. 2011. "Testing Clausewitz: Nationalism, Mass Mobilization, and the Severity of War." *International Organization* 65, no. 4: 605–638.

Chenoweth, Erica, and Adria Lawrence, eds. 2010. *Rethinking Violence: States and Non-State Actors in Conflict*. Cambridge: MIT Press.

Chima, Jugdep S. 2010. *The Sikh Separatist Insurgency in India: Political Leadership and Ethnonationalist Movements*. New Delhi: Sage Publications.

Choudhury, G. W. 1993. *The Last Days of United Pakistan*. New York: Oxford University Press.

Christia, Fotini. 2013. *Alliance Formation in Civil Wars*. New York: Cambridge University Press.

Clark, Ian. 2009. "Towards an English School Theory of Hegemony." *European Journal of International Relations* 15, no. 2: 203–28

Cobban, Helena. 1984. *The Palestinian Liberation Organization: People, Power and Politics*. New York: Cambridge University Press.

Coggins, Bridgett. 2011. "Friends in High Places: International Politics and the Emergence of States from Secessionism." *International Organization* 65, no. 3: 433–467.

——. 2014. *Power Politics and State Formation in the Twentieth Century: The Dynamics of Recognition*. New York: Cambridge University Press.

Cohen, Stephen P. 2004. *The Idea of Pakistan*. Washington DC: Brookings Institution Press.

Collazo-Davila, Vincente. 1980. "The Guatemalan Insurrection." In *Insurgency in the Modern World*, edited by Bard E. O'Neill. Boulder, CO: Westview Press.

Connor, Walker. 1972. "Nation-Building or Nation-Destroying?" *World Politics*, 24, no. 3: 319–355.

Cox, Michael. 1997. "Bringing in the 'International': The IRA Ceasefire and the End of the Cold War." *International Affairs* 73, no. 4: 671–693.

Craven, Avery O. 1965. "Why the Southern States Seceded." In *The Crisis of the Union 1860–1861*, edited by George H. Knoles. Baton Rouge: Louisiana State University Press.

Crawford, Timothy W., and Alan J. Kuperman, eds. 2006. *Gambling on Humanitarian Intervention: Moral Hazard, Rebellion, and Civil War*. Oxon, UK: Routledge.

Cunningham, Kathleen G. 2011. "Divide and Conquer or Divide and Concede: How Do States Respond to Internally Divided Separatists?" *American Political Science Review* 105, no. 2: 275–297.

——. 2013. "Actor Fragmentation and Civil War Bargaining: How Internal Divisions Generate Civil Conflict." *American Journal of Political Science* 57, no. 3: 659–672.

——. 2014. *Inside the Politics of Self-Determination*. New York: Oxford University Press.

Dadrian, Vahakn N. 1995. *The History of the Armenian Genocide: Ethnic Conflict from the Balkans to Anatolia to the Caucasus*. New York: Berghahn Books.

——. 1999. *Warrant for Genocide: Key Elements of Turk-Armenian Conflict*. New Brunswick, NJ: Transaction Publishers.

Das, Samir K. 2003. *Ethnicity, Nation, and Security: Essays on Northeastern India*. New Delhi: South Asian Publishers.

Das, Suranjan. 2001. *Kashmir and Sindh: Nation-Building Ethnicity and Regional Politics in South Asia*. London: Anthem Press.

Dasgupta, Jyotirindra. 1988. "Ethnicity, Democracy, and Development in India: Assam in a General Perspective." In *India's Democracy: An Analysis of Changing State-Society Relations*, edited by Atul Kohli. Princeton: Princeton University Press.

——. 1997. "Community, Authenticity, and Autonomy: Insurgence and Institutional Development in India's Northeast." *Journal of Asian Studies* 56, no. 2: 345–370.

Davenport, Christian. 2007. *State Repression and the Domestic Democratic Peace*. Cambridge: Cambridge University Press.

Davison, Roderic H. 1948. "The Armenian Crisis, 1912–1914." *American Historical Review* 53, no. 3: 481–505.

Dennett, Tyler. 1939. *Lincoln and the Civil War in the Diaries and Letters of John Hay*. New York: Dodd, Mead.

Derry, T. K. 1973. *A History of Modern Norway: 1814–1972*. Oxford: Oxford University Press.

Devadas, David. 2007. *In Search of a Future: The Story of Kashmir*. New Delhi: Penguin.

Devji, Faisal. 2013. *Muslim Zion: Pakistan as a Political Idea*. Cambridge, MA: Harvard University Press.

Dhillon, Kirpal. 2006. *Identity and Survival: Sikh Militancy in India, 1978–1993*. London: Penguin Books.

Dion, Stephane. 1996. "Why is Secession Difficult in Well-Established Democracies? Lessons from Quebec." *British Journal of Political Science* 26, no. 2: 269–283.

Donnelly, Jack. 2009. "Rethinking Political Structures: From 'Ordering Principles' to 'Vertical Differentiation'—and Beyond." *International Theory* 1, no. 1: 49–86.

Downes, Alexander B. 2007. *Targeting Civilians in War*. Ithaca: Cornell University Press.

Dulat, A. S., with Aditya Sinha. 2015. *Kashmir: The Vajpayee Years*. Noida, Uttar Pradesh: Harper Collins.

Dunne, Justin S. 2006. "Crisis in Baluchistan: A Historical Analysis of the Baluch Nationalist Movement in Pakistan." Master's thesis, Naval Postgraduate School.

Dyer, Gwynne. 1976. "Turkish 'Falsifiers' and Armenian 'Deceivers': Historiography and the Armenian Massacres." *Middle Eastern Studies* 12, no. 1: 99–107.

Elangovan, A. R., and Debra L. Shapiro. 1998. "Betrayal of Trust in Organizations." *Academy of Management Review* 23, no. 3: 547–566.

Elgström, Ole. 2000. *Images and Strategies for Autonomy: Explaining Swedish Security Policy Strategies in the 19th Century*. Dordrecht, Netherlands: Kluwer Academic.

Elkins, Zachary, and John Sides. 2007. "Can Institutions Build Unity in Multiethnic States?" *American Political Science Review* 101, no. 4: 693–708.

Erickson, Edward J. 2001. *Ordered to Die: A History of the Ottoman Army in the First World War*. Westport, CT: Greenwood Press.

——. 2013. *Ottomans and Armenians: A Study in Counterinsurgency*. New York: Palgrave MacMillan.

Fair, C. Christine. 2014. *Fighting to the End: The Pakistan Army's Way of War*. New York: Oxford University Press.

Fair, C. Christine, and Sumit Ganguly. 2008. *Treading on Hallowed Ground: Counterinsurgency Operations in Sacred Spaces*. New York: Oxford University Press.

Fazal, Tanisha M. 2007. *State Death: The Politics and Geography of Conquest, Occupation, and Annexation*. Princeton: Princeton University Press.

Fearon, James D. 1994. "Ethnic War as a Commitment Problem." Paper presented at the Annual Meeting of the American Political Science Association, New York, August 30–September 2.

——. 1995. "Rationalist Explanations for War." *International Organization* 49, no. 3: 379–414.

——. 2004. "Why Do Some Civil Wars Last So Much Longer than Others?" *Journal of Peace Research* 41, no. 3: 275–301.

Fearon, James D., and David D. Laitin. 2003. "Ethnicity, Insurgency, and Civil War." *American Political Science Review* 97, no. 1: 75–90.

Feldman, Herbert. 1974. "Pakistan—1973." *Asian Survey* 14, no. 2: 136–142.

Ferris, Norman B. 1976. *Desperate Diplomacy: William H. Seward's Foreign Policy, 1861*. Knoxville: University of Tennessee Press.

Foreman, Amanda. 2000. *A World on Fire: Britain's Crucial Role in the American Civil War*. New York: Random House.

Freilich, Charles D. 2012. *Zion's Dilemmas: How Israel Makes National Security Policy*. Ithaca: Cornell University Press.

Ganguly, Sumit. 1996. "Explaining the Kashmir Insurgency: Political Mobilization and Institutional Decay." *International Security* 21, no. 2: 76–107.

Garver, John W. 2002. *Protracted Contest: Sino-Indian Rivalry in the Twentieth Century*. Seattle: University of Washington Press.

Gayer, Laurent. 2009. "The Khalistan Militias: Servants and Users of the State." In *Armed Militias of South Asia: Fundamentalists, Maoists, and Separatists*, edited by Laurent Gayer and Christophe Jaffrelot. New York: Columbia University Press.

Gellner, Ernest. 1983. *Nations and Nationalism*. Ithaca: Cornell University Press.

George, Alexander L., and Andrew Bennett. 2004. *Case Studies and Theory Development in the Social Sciences*. Cambridge: MIT Press.

Gerring, John. 2007. *Case-Study Research: Principles and Practices*. New York: Cambridge University Press.

Gill, K. P. S. 2001. "Endgame in Punjab: 1988–93." In *Terror and Containment Perspectives of India's Internal Security*, edited by K. P. S. Gill and Ajai Sahni. New Delhi: Gyan.

Gilpin, Robert. 1983. *War and Change in World Politics*. New York: Cambridge University Press.

——. 2001. *Global Political Economy: Understanding the International Economic Order*. Princeton: Princeton University Press.

Gingeras, Ryan. 2009. *Sorrowful Shores: Violence, Ethnicity, and the End of the Ottoman Empire, 1912–1923*. Oxford: Oxford University Press.

Glaser, Charles L. 1997. "The Security Dilemma Revisited." *World Politics* 50, no. 1: 171–201.

——. 2010. *Rational Theory of International Politics*. Princeton: Princeton University Press.

Gleditsch, Nils P., Peter Wallenstein, Mikael Eriksson, Margareta Sollenberg, and Håvard Strand. 2002. "Armed Conflict 1946–2001: A New Dataset." *Journal of Peace Research* 39, no. 5: 615–637.

Göçek, Fatma M. 2011. *The Transformation of Turkey: Redefining State and Society from the Ottoman Empire to the Modern Era*. New York: I. B. Tauris.

Goddard, Stacie E. 2010. *Indivisible Territory and the Politics of Legitimacy: Jerusalem and Northern Island*. New York: Cambridge University Press.

Gopalakrishnan, R. 1995. *North-East India: From a Geographical Expression to Regional Accommodation*. New Delhi: Har-Anand.

Gourevitch, Peter. 1978. "The Second Image Reversed: International Influences on Domestic Politics." *International Organization* 32, no. 4: 881–912.

Government of Pakistan. 1974. *White Paper on Baluchistan*. Rawalpindi: Government of Pakistan.

Gowa, Joanne, and Edward D. Mansfield. 1993. "Power Politics and International Trade." *American Political Science Review* 87, no. 2: 408–420.

Greenfeld, Liah. 1993. *Nationalism: Five Roads to Modernity*. Cambridge, MA: Harvard University Press.

Greenhill, Kelly M. 2010. *Weapons of Mass Migration: Forced Displacement, Coercion, and Foreign Policy*. Ithaca: Cornell University Press.

Griffiths, Ryan D. 2015. "Between Dissolution and Blood: How Administrative Lines and Categories Shape Secessionist Outcomes." *International Organization* 69, no. 3: 731–751.

Grigoryan, Arman. 2010. "Third-Party Intervention and the Escalation of State-Minority Conflicts." *International Studies Quarterly* 54, no. 4: 1143–1174.

——. 2015. "Concessions or Coercion? How Governments Respond to Restive Ethnic Minorities." *International Security* 39, no. 4: 170–207.

271

Grinberg, Lev L. 2010. *Politics and Violence in Israel/Palestine: Democracy versus Military Rule.* New York: Routledge.

Güclü, Yücel. 2010. *Armenians and the Allies in Cilicia, 1914–1923.* Salt Lake City: University of Utah Press.

———. 2012. *The Holocaust and the Armenian Case in Comparative Perspective.* Lanham, MD: University Press of America.

Guichard, Sylvie. 2010. *The Construction of History and Nationalism in India: Textbooks, Controversies and Politics.* New York: Routledge.

Gunter, Michael M. 2011. *Armenian History and the Question of Genocide.* New York: Palgrave MacMillan.

Gust, Wolfgang, ed. 2014. *The Armenian Genocide: Evidence from the German Foreign Office Archives, 1915–1916.* New York: Berghahn.

Hale, Henry E. 2008. *The Foundations of Ethnic Politics: Separatism of States and Nations in Eurasia and the World.* New York: Cambridge University Press.

Hall, Rodney B. 1999. *National Collective Identity: Social Constructs and International Systems.* New York: Columbia University Press.

Hamoodur Rehman Commission of Inquiry into the 1971 War. 2000. *The Report of the Hamoodur Rahman Commission of Inquiry into the 1971 War: As Declassified by the Government of Pakistan.* Lahore: Vanguard.

Haqqani, Husain. 2005. *Pakistan: Between Mosque and Military.* Washington: Carnegie Endowment for International Peace.

Hastings, Adrian. 1997. *The Construction of Nationhood: Ethnicity, Religion, and Nationalism.* Cambridge: Cambridge University Press.

Harrison, Selig S. 1981. *In Afghanistan's Shadow: Baluch Nationalism and Soviet Temptations.* New York: Carnegie Endowment for International Peace.

Hartunian, Abraham H. 1986. *Neither to Laugh nor to Weep: A Memoir of the Armenian Genocide.* Cambridge: Armenian Heritage Press.

Hechter, Michael. 1992. "The Dynamics of Secession." *Acta Sociologica* 35, no. 4: 267–283.

———. 2000. *Containing Nationalism.* New York: Oxford University Press.

Heraclides, Alexis. 1990. "Secessionist Minorities and External Involvement." *International Organization* 44, no. 3: 341–378.

Hilde, Paal S. 1999. "Slovak Nationalism and the Break-up of Czechoslovakia." *Europe-Asia Studies* 51, no. 4: 647–665.

Hirschman, Albert O. 1969. *National Power and the Structure of Foreign Trade.* Berkeley: University of California Press.

Hobsbawm, Eric. 1983. "Mass-Producing Traditions: Europe, 1870–1914." In *The Invention of Tradition,* edited by Eric Hobsbawm and Terence Ranger. New York: Cambridge University Press.

———. 2012. *Nations and Nationalism since 1780.* New York: Cambridge University Press.

Holquist, Peter. 2011. "The Politics and Practice of the Russian Occupation of Armenia, 1915–February 1917." In *A Question of Genocide: Armenians and Turks at the End of the Ottoman Empire,* edited by Ronald G. Suny, Fatma M. Göçek, and Norman M. Naimark. Oxford: Oxford University Press.

Horowitz, Donald L. 2000. *Ethnic Groups in Conflict.* Berkeley: University of California Press.

Hovannisian, Richard G. 1987. "The Historical Dimensions of the Armenian Question, 1878–1923." In *The Armenian Genocide in Perspective*, edited by Richard Hovannisian. New Brunswick, NJ: Transaction Publishers.

——. 2007. "The Armenian Genocide: Wartime Radicalization or Premeditated Continuum." In *The Armenian Genocide: Cultural and Ethical Legacies*, edited by Richard Hovannisian. New Brunswick, NJ: Transaction Publishers.

Human Rights Watch. 1991. "Human Rights in India: Kashmir Under Siege."

——. 1993. "The Human Rights Crisis in Kashmir: A Pattern of Impunity."

——. 1994. "Dead Silence: The Legacy of Human Rights Abuses in Punjab."

Hussain, Arif. 2003. "Ethno-Nationalism and Modernising Project in Post-Colonial Societies: The Case of Baloch Nationalism in Pakistan (1947–1977)." Master's thesis, University of Dalarna.

Hussain, Asaf. 1976. "Ethnicity, National Identity, and Praetorianism: The Case of Pakistan." *Asian Survey* 16, no. 10: 918–930.

Huth, Paul K. 1996. *Standing Your Ground: Territorial Disputes and International Conflict*. Ann Arbor: University of Michigan Press.

Jagmohan, Shri. 1991. *My Frozen Turbulence in Kashmir*. New Delhi: Allied Publishers.

Jahan, Rounaq. 1973. "Bangladesh in 1972: Nation Building in a New State." *Asian Survey* 13, no. 2: 199–210.

Jalal, Ayesha. 1994. *The Sole Spokesman: Jinnah, the Muslim League, and the Demand for Pakistan*. Cambridge: Cambridge University Press.

——. 1995. *Democracy and Authoritarianism in South Asia: A Comparative and Historical Perspective*. Cambridge: Cambridge University Press.

Jana, Arun K. 2011. "Development and Democratic Decentralization: Assam under Asom Gana Parishad Led Government (1996–2001)." In *Development and Disorder: The Crises of Governance in the Northeast and East of India*, edited by Maya Ghosh and Arun K. Jana. New Delhi: South Asian Publishers.

Jenne, Erin K. 2007. *Ethnic Bargaining: The Paradox of Minority Empowerment*. Ithaca: Cornell University Press.

——. 2015. *Nested Security: Lessons in Conflict Management from the League of Nations and the European Union*. Ithaca: Cornell University Press.

Jones, Howard. 1992. *Union in Peril: The Crisis over British Intervention in the Civil War*. Lincoln: University of Nebraska Press.

——. 1999. *Abraham Lincoln and a New Birth of Freedom: The Union and Slavery in the Diplomacy of the Civil War*. Lincoln: University of Nebraska Press.

——. 2010. *Blue and Gray Diplomacy: A History of Union and Confederate Foreign Relations*. Chapel Hill: University of North Carolina Press.

Jones, Owen B. 2002. *Pakistan: Eye of the Storm*. New Haven: Yale University Press.

Jones, Simon. 2008. "India, Pakistan, and Counterinsurgency Operations in Jammu and Kashmir." *Small Wars and Insurgencies* 19, no. 1: 1–22.

Joshi, Manoj. 1999. *The Lost Rebellion: Kashmir in the Nineties*. New Delhi: Penguin Books.

Joskowicz-Jabloner, Lisa, and David Leiser. 2013. "Varieties of Trust-Betrayal: Emotion and Relief Patterns in Different Domains." *Journal of Applied Social Psychology* 43, no. 9: 1799–1813.

Kahler, Miles. 2006. "Territoriality and Conflict in an Era of Globalization." In *Territorality and Conflict in an Era of Globalization*, edited by Miles Kahler and Barbara F. Walter. New York: Cambridge University Press.

Kaligian, Dikran M. 2009. *Armenian Organization and Ideology under Ottoman Rule, 1908–1914*. New Brunswick, NJ: Transaction Publishers.

Kalyvas, Stathis N. 2006. *The Logic of Violence in Civil War*. Cambridge: Cambridge University Press.

Kalyvas, Stathis, and Laia Balcells. 2010. "International System and Technologies of Rebellion: How the End of the Cold War Shaped Internal Conflict." *American Political Science Review* 104, no. 3: 415–429.

Kapur, Rajiv A. 1986. *Sikh Separatism: The Politics of Faith*. London: Allen and Unwin.

Kaufman, Stuart J. 2001. *Modern Hatreds: The Symbolic Politics of Ethnic War*. Ithaca: Cornell University Press.

Kaufmann, Chaim. 1996. "Possible and Impossible Solutions to Ethnic Civil Wars." *International Security* 20, no. 4: 136–175.

Kayali, Hasan. 1997. *Arabs and Young Turks: Ottomanism, Arabism, and Islamism in the Ottoman Empire, 1908–1918*. Berkeley: University of California Press.

Kertzer, Joshua D. 2016. *Resolve in International Politics*. Princeton: Princeton University Press.

Khalidi, Rashid. 1997. *Palestinian Identity: The Construction of Modern National Consciousness*. New York: Columbia University Press.

——. 2006. *The Iron Cage: The Story of the Palestinian Struggle for Statehood*. Boston: Beacon Press.

Khan, Adeel. 2009. "Renewed Ethnonationalist Insurgency in Balochistan, Pakistan: The Militarized State and Continuing Economic Deprivation." *Asian Survey* 49, no. 6: 1071–1091.

Khan, Ayub. 1960. "Pakistan Perspective." *Foreign Affairs* (July issue).

——. 1967. *Friends not Masters: A Political Autobiography*. New York: Oxford University Press.

Khan, Yasmin. 2007. *The Great Partition: The Making of India and Pakistan*. New Haven: Yale University Press.

Kimmerling, Baruch, and Joel S. Migdal. 2003. *The Palestinian People: A History*. Cambridge, MA: Harvard University Press.

Kirakossian, John S. 1992. *The Armenian Genocide: The Young Turks before the Judgment of History*. Madison, CT: Sphinx Press.

Kohli, Atul. 1990. *Democracy and Discontent: India's Growing Crisis of Governability*. Cambridge: Cambridge University Press.

——. 1997. "Can Democracies Accommodate Ethnic Nationalism? Rise and Decline of Self-Determination Movements in India." *Journal of Asian Studies* 56, no. 2: 325–344.

Kramer, Mark. 1992. "The Czech-Slovak Rupture and European Security." Discussion paper for the Security for Europe Project, Center for Foreign Policy Development.

Krasner, Stephen D. 1999. *Sovereignty: Organized Hypocrisy*. Stanford: Stanford University Press.

Kraus, Michael. 2000. "The End of Czechoslovakia: International Forces and Factors." *Irreconcilable Differences? Explaining Czechoslovakia's Dissolution*, edited by Michael Kraus and Alliston Stanger. Lanham, MD: Rowman & Littlefield.

Krause, Peter. 2014. "The Structure of Success: How the Internal Distribution of Power Drives Armed Group Behavior and National Movement Effectiveness." *International Security* 38, no. 3: 72–117.

Kumar, Satish. 1975. "The Evolution of India's Policy towards Bangladesh in 1971." *Asian Survey* 15, no. 6: 488–498.

Kuperman, Alan J. 2008. "The Moral Hazard of Humanitarian Intervention: Lessons from the Balkans." *International Studies Quarterly* 52, no. 1: 49–80.

Lacina, Bethany. 2009. "The Problem of Political Stability in Northeast India: Local Ethnic Autocracy and the Rule of Law." *Asian Survey* 49, no. 6: 998–1020.

Laitin, David D. 1985. "Hegemony and Religious Conflict: British Imperial Control and Political Cleavages in Yorubaland." In *Bringing the State Back In*, edited by Peter B. Evans, Dietrich Rueschemeyer, and Theda Skocpol. Cambridge: Cambridge University Press.

Lake, David A. 2009. *Hierarchy in International Relations*. Ithaca: Cornell University Press.

Lake, David A., and Donald Rothchild. 1998. "Spreading Fear: The Genesis of Transnational Ethnic Conflict." In *The International Spread of Ethnic Conflict: Fear, Diffusion, and Escalation*, edited by David A. Lake and Donald Rothchild. Princeton: Princeton University Press.

Laporte, Robert, Jr. 1972. "Pakistan in 1971: The Disintegration of a Nation." *Asian Survey* 12, no. 2: 97–108.

Lawrence, Adria. 2013. *Imperial Rule and the Politics of Nationalism: Anti-Colonial Protest in the French Empire*. New York: Cambridge University Press.

LeRiche, Matthew, and Matthew Arnold. 2012. *South Sudan: From Revolution to Independence*. London: Hurst.

Lewy, Guenter. 2005. *The Armenian Massacres in Ottoman Turkey: A Disputed Genocide*. Salt Lake City: University of Utah Press.

Lieven, Anatol. 2011. *Pakistan: A Hard Country*. New York: Public Affairs.

Lijphart, Arend. 1968. *The Politics of Accommodation: Pluralism and Democracy in the Netherlands*. Berkeley: University of California Press.

Lindgren, Raymond E. 1959. *Norway-Sweden: Union, Disunion, and Scandinavian Integration*. Princeton: Princeton University Press.

Lindholm, Charles. 1977. "The Segmentary Lineage System: Its Applicability to Pakistan's Political Structure." In *Pakistan's Western Borderlands: The Transformation of a Political Order*, edited by Ainslee T. Embree. Durham, NC: Carolina Academic Press.

Lipson, Charles. 1984. "International Cooperation in Economic and Security Affairs." *World Politics* 37, no. 1: 1–23.

Lorton, Fiona. 2000. "The Ethiopia-Eritrea Conflict: A Fragile Peace." *African Security Review* 9, no. 4: 101–111.

Lustick, Ian S. 1993. *Unsettled States, Disputed Lands: Britain and Ireland, France and Algeria, Israel and the West Bank-Gaza*. Ithaca: Cornell University Press.

Lustick, Ian S., Dan Miodownik, and Roy J. Eidelson. 2004. "Secessionism in Multicultural States: Does Sharing Power Prevent or Encourage It?" *American Political Science Review* 98, no. 2: 209–229.

Lyall, Jason, Graeme Blair, and Kosuke Imai. 2013. "Explaining Support for Combatants During Wartime: A Survey Experiment in Afghanistan." *American Political Science Review* 107, no. 4: 679–705.

Lyall, Jason, and Isaiah Wilson III. 2009. "Rage against the Machines: Explaining Outcomes in Counterinsurgency Wars." *International Organization* 63, no. 1: 67–106.

Lyons, Terrence. 2009. "The Ethiopia-Eritrea Conflict and the Search for Peace in the Horn of Africa." *Review of African Political Economy* 36: 167–180.

MacDonald, Paul K. 2013. "'Retribution Must Succeed Rebellion': The Colonial Origins of Counterinsurgency Failure." *International Organization* 67, no. 2: 253–286.

Macfie, A. L. 1998. *The End of the Ottoman Empire 1908–1923*. New York: Longman.

Mahadevan, Prem. 2007. "Counter Terrorism in the Indian Punjab: Assessing the 'Cat' System." *Faultlines* 18: 19–54.

Mahin, Dean B. 2000. *One War at a Time: The International Dimensions of the American Civil War*. Washington, DC: Brassey's.

Mahmood, Cynthia K. 1989. "Sikh Rebellion and the Hindu Concept of Order." *Asian Survey* 29, no. 3: 326–340.

Mahoney, James. 2000. "Path Dependence in Historical Sociology." *Theory and Society* 29, no. 4: 507–548.

——. 2003. "Strategies of Causal Assessment in Comparative Historical Analysis." In *Comparative Historical Analysis in the Social Sciences*, edited by James Mahoney and Dietrich Rueschemeyer. New York: Cambridge University Press.

Malik, Iffat. 2002. *Kashmir: Ethnic Conflict, International Dispute*. Oxford: Oxford University Press.

Malka, Amos. 2008. "Israel and Asymmetrical Deterrence." *Comparative Strategy* 27, no. 1: 1–19.

Mann, Michael. 2005. *The Dark Side of Democracy: Explaining Ethnic Cleansing*. New York: Cambridge University Press.

Marri, Mir Khuda Bakhsh. 1974. *Searchlights on Baloches and Balochistan*. Karachi: Royal Book.

Mayall, James. 1990. *Nationalism and International Society*. Cambridge: Cambridge University Press.

Mazari, Sherbaz Khan. 1999. *A Journey to Disillusionment*. New York: Oxford University Press.

McCarthy, Justin. 2001. *The Ottoman Peoples and the End of Empire*. New York: Oxford University Press.

McClintock, Russell. 2008. *Lincoln and the Decision for War: The Northern Response to Secession*. Chapel Hill: University of North Carolina Press.

McGill, William D., II. 1989. "The Guatemalan Counterinsurgency Strategy." Study Project, U.S. Army War College, Carlisle Barracks, PA.

McLeod, W. H. 1989. *The Sikhs: History, Religion, and Society*. New York: Columbia University Press.

McMeekin, Sean. 2015. *The Ottoman Endgame: War, Revolution, and the Making of the Modern Middle East, 1908–1923*. New York: Penguin.

Mearsheimer, John J. 2001. *The Tragedy of Great Power Politics*. New York: W. W. Norton.

——. 2011. "Kissing Cousins: Nationalism and Realism." Paper presented at Yale Workshop on International Relations. Available at http://irworkshop.sites.yale.edu/sites/default/files/Mearsheimer_IRW.PDF.

Mehta, Suketu. 2005. *Maximum City: Bombay Lost and Found*. New York: Random House.

Melson, Robert. 1987. "Provocation or Nationalism: A Critical Inquiry into the Armenians Genocide of 1915." In *The Armenian Genocide in Perspective*, edited by Richard Hovannisian. New Brunswick, NJ: Transaction.

——. 1992. *Revolution and Genocide: On the Origins of the Armenian Genocide and the Holocaust*. Chicago: University of Chicago Press.

Mercer, Jonathan. 2014. "Feeling Like a State: Social Emotion and Identity." *International Theory* 6, no. 3: 515–535.

Midford, Paul. 1993. "International Trade and Domestic Politics: Improving on Rogowski's Model of Political Alignments." *International Organization* 47, no. 4: 535–564.

Mistry, Dinshaw. 2004. "A Theoretical and Empirical Assessment of India as an Emerging World Power." *India Review* 3, no. 1: 64–87.

Mitzen, Jennifer. 2006. "Ontological Security in World Politics: State Identity and the Security Dilemma." *European Journal of International Relations* 12, no. 3: 341–370.

Moore, Barrington. 1993. *Social Origins of Dictatorship and Democracy: Lord and Peasant in the Making of the Modern World*. Boston: Beacon Press.

Moore, Will H., and David R. Davis. 1998. "Transnational Ethnic Ties and Foreign Policy." In *The International Spread of Ethnic Conflict: Fear, Diffusion, and Escalation*, edited by David A. Lake and Donald Rothchild. Princeton: Princeton University Press.

Moravcsik, Andrew. 1998. *The Choice for Europe: Social Purpose and State Power from Messina to Maastricht*. Ithaca: Cornell University Press.

Morgenthau, Henry. 1918; reprint 2003. *Ambassador Morgenthau's Story*. Garden City, NY: Doubleday, Page.

Morris, Benny. 1999. *Righteous Victims: A History of the Zionist-Arab Conflict, 1881–2001*. New York: Vintage Books.

——. 2009. *One State, Two States: Resolving the Israel/Palestine Conflict*. New Haven: Yale University Press.

Mudiam, Pirthvi R. 1994. *India and the Middle East*. New York: I. B. Tauris.

Murshid, Abul K. M. 1971. "Sheikh Mujibur Rahman and Pakistan Deal." *Daily News* (Kuwait). Available at http://profilebengal.com/mnnews/page122.html.

Murty, T. S. 1983. *Assam, the Difficult Years: A Study of Political Developments in 1979–83*. New Delhi: Himalayan Books.

Musharraf, Pervez. 2008. *In the Line of Fire: A Memoir*. New York: Simon and Schuster.

Mylonas, Harris. 2012. *The Politics of Nation-Building: Making Co-Nationals, Refugees, and Minorities*. New York: Cambridge University Press.

Naimark, Norman M. 2001. *Fires of Hatred: Ethnic Cleansing in Twentieth-Century Europe*. Cambridge, MA: Harvard University Press.

Nansen, Fridtjof. 1905. *Norway and the Union with Sweden*. New York: MacMillan.

Nasr, Seyyed Vali Reza. 1994. *The Vanguard of the Islamic Revolution: The Jama'at-i-Islami of Pakistan*. Berkeley: University of California Press.

Natsios, Andrew. 2012. *Sudan, South Sudan, and Darfur: What Everyone Needs to Know*. New York: Oxford University Press.

Nawaz, Shuja. 2008. *Crossed Swords: Pakistan, Its Army, and the Wars Within*. Oxford: Oxford University Press.

Nayar, Baldev R., and T. V. Paul. 2002. *India in the World Order: Searching for Major Power Status*. New York: Cambridge University Press.

Nayar, Kuldip, and Khushwant Singh. 1984. *Tragedy of Punjab: Operation Bluestar and After.* New Delhi: Vision Books.

Negash, Tekeste. 1997. *Eritrea and Ethiopia: The Federal Experience.* New Brunswick, NJ: Transaction Publishers.

Netanyahu, Benjamin. 1993. *A Place among the Nations: Israel and the World.* New York: Bantam Press.

Newman, David. 2005. "From Hitnachalut to Hitnatkut: The Impact of Gush Emunim and the Settlement Movement on Israeli Politics and Society." *Israel Studies* 10, no. 3: 192–224.

Niazi, Amir Abdullah K. 1998. *The Betrayal of East Pakistan.* Karachi: Oxford University Press.

Niazi, Kausar. 1987. *Aur Line Cut Gai.* Lahore: Jang Publishers.

Nugent, Nicholas. 1990. *Rajiv Gandhi: Son of a Dynasty.* London: BBC Books.

Olson, Mancur. 1993. "Dictatorship, Democracy, and Development." *American Political Science Review* 87, no. 3: 567–576.

Owsley, Frank L., Sr. 2008. *King Cotton Diplomacy: Foreign Relations of the Confederate States of America.* Tuscaloosa: University of Alabama Press.

Pahre, Robert. 2001. "Divided Government and International Cooperation in Austria-Hungary, Sweden-Norway, and the European Union." *European Union Politics* 2, no. 2: 131–162.

Pak Institute for Peace Studies. 2008. *Balochistan: Conflicts and Players: A Research Study.* Islamabad: Pak Institute for Peace Studies.

Pape, Robert. 1997. "Why Economic Sanctions Do Not Work." *International Security* 22, no. 2: 90–136.

———. 2005. *Dying to Win: The Strategic Logic of Suicide Terrorism.* New York: Random House.

Parekh, Bhikhu. 1991. "Nehru and the National Philosophy of India." *Economic and Political Weekly* 26, nos. 1–2: 35–48.

Parent, Joseph M. 2006. "E Pluribus Unum: Political Unification and Political Realism." Ph.D. diss., Columbia University.

———. 2011. *Uniting States: Voluntary Union in World Politics.* New York: Oxford University Press.

Pavkovic, Aleksandar, and Peter Radan. 2007. *Creating New States: Theory and Practice of Secession.* Burlington, VT: Ashgate.

Pearlman, Wendy. 2011. *Violence, Nonviolence, and the Palestinian National Movement.* New York: Cambridge University Press.

Peer, Basharat. *Curfewed Night: One Kashmiri Journalist's Frontline Account of Life, Love, and War in His Homeland.* New York: Simon and Schuster.

Petersen, Roger D. 2002. *Understanding Ethnic Violence: Fear, Hatred, and Resentment in Twentieth-Century Eastern Europe.* Cambridge: Cambridge University Press.

Petrelli, Niccolò. 2013. "Deterring Insurgents: Culture, Adaptation, and the Evolution of Israeli Counterinsurgency, 1987–2005." *Journal of Strategic Studies* 36, no. 5: 666–691.

Pettigrew, Joyce J. M. 1995. *The Sikhs of the Punjab: Unheard Voices of State and Guerilla Violence.* London: Zed Books.

Pierson, Paul. 2000. "Increasing Returns, Path Dependence, and the Study of Politics." *American Political Science Review* 94, no. 2: 251–267.

———. 2004. *Politics in Time: History, Institutions, and Social Analysis*. Princeton: Princeton University Press.

Poast, Paul. 2014. "Lincoln's Gamble: How the Southern Secession Crisis Became the American Civil War." Unpublished manuscript, Rutgers University.

Podeh, Elie. 2002. *The Arab-Israeli Conflict in Israeli History Textbooks, 1948–2000*. Westport, CT: Greenwood.

Posen, Barry R. 1993a. "The Security Dilemma and Ethnic Conflict." In *Ethnic Conflict and International Security*, edited by Michael E. Brown. Princeton: Princeton University Press.

———. 1993b. "Nationalism, the Mass Army, and Military Power." *International Security* 18, no. 2: 80–124.

Posner, Daniel N. 2005. *Institutions and Ethnic Politics in Africa*. Cambridge: Cambridge University Press.

Potter, David M. 1965. "Why the Republicans Rejected Both Compromise and Secession." In *The Crisis of the Union 1860–1861*, edited by George H. Knoles. Baton Rouge: Louisiana State University Press.

———. 2011. *The Impending Crisis: America before the Civil War, 1848–1861*. New York: Harper Perennial.

Powell, Robert. 2006. "War as a Commitment Problem." *International Organization* 60, no. 1: 169–203.

Pressman, Jeremy. 2003. "The Second Intifada: Background and Causes of the Israel-Palestinian Conflict." *Journal of Conflict Studies* 23, no. 2.

———. 2003. "Visions in Collision: What Happened at Camp David and Taba?" *International Security* 28, no. 2: 5–43.

Pundak, Ron. 2001. "From Oslo to Taba: What Went Wrong?" *Survival* 43, no. 3: 31–45.

Rae, Heather. 2002. *State Identities and the Homogenisation of Peoples*. Cambridge: Cambridge University Press.

Raghavan, Srinath. 2013. *1971: A Global History of the Creation of Bangladesh*. Cambridge, MA: Harvard University Press.

Rahman, Sheikh Mujibur. 1972. *Bangladesh, My Bangladesh: Selected Speeches and Statements, October 28, 1970, to March 26, 1971*. New Delhi: Orient Longman.

Rahman, Tariq. 1997. "The Urdu-English Controversy in Pakistan." *Modern Asian Studies* 31, no. 1: 177–207.

Raman, B. 2007. *The Kaoboys of R&AW: Down Memory Lane*. New Delhi: Lancer.

Rasheed, Rao. 2012. *Jo Meine Dekha*. Lahore: Jumhoori Publications.

Rashiduzzaman, M. 1972. "Leadership, Organization, Strategies, and Tactics of the Bangla Desh Movement." *Asian Survey* 12, no. 3: 185–200.

Raza, Rafi. 1997. *Zulfikar Ali Bhutto and Pakistan 1967–1977*. Karachi: Oxford University Press.

Regan, Patrick M. 2002. "Third-party Interventions and the Duration of Intrastate Conflicts." *Journal of Conflict Resolution* 46, no. 1: 55–73.

Reynolds, Michael A. 2009. "Buffers, not Brethren: Young Turk Military Policy in the First World War and the Myth of Panturanism." *Past and Present* 203, no. 1: 137–179.

———. 2011. *Shattering Empires: The Clash and the Collapse of the Ottoman and Russian Empires 1908–1918*. New York: Cambridge University Press.

Rogowski, Ronald. 1987. "Political Cleavages and Changing Exposure to Trade." *American Political Science Review* 81, no. 4: 1121–1137.

Ron, James. 2003. *Frontiers and Ghettos: State Violence in Serbia and Israel*. Berkeley: University of California Press.

Rosato, Sebastian. 2003. "The Flawed Logic of Democratic Peace Theory." *American Political Science Review* 97, no. 4: 585–602.

Rovner, Joshua. 2011. *Fixing the Facts: National Security and the Politics of Intelligence*. Ithaca: Cornell University Press.

Rubin, Barry. 1994. *Revolution until Victory? The Politics and History of the PLO*. Cambridge, MA: Harvard University Press.

Rupnik, Jacques. 1995. "The International Context." In *The End of Czechoslovakia*, edited by Jiří Musil. Budapest: Central European University Press.

Sahadevan, P. 2003. "Ending Ethnic War: The South Asian Experience." *International Negotiation* 8, no. 2: 403–440.

Sahni, Ajai, and J. George. 2001. "Security and Development in India's Northeast: An Alternative Perspective." In *Terror and Containment Perspectives of India's Internal Security*, edited by K. P. S. Gill and Ajai Sahni. New Delhi: Gyan.

Sahni, Sati. 1999. *Kashmir Underground*. New Delhi: Har-Anand.

Saideman, Stephen M. 1997. "Explaining the International Relations of Secessionist Conflicts: Vulnerability versus Ethnic Ties." *International Organization* 51, no. 4: 721–753.

——. 1998. "Is Pandora's Box Half Empty or Half Full? The Limited Virulence of Secessionism and the Domestic Sources of Disintegration." In *The International Spread of Ethnic Conflict: Fear, Diffusion, and Escalation*, edited by David A. Lake and Donald Rothchild. Princeton: Princeton University Press.

Salehyan, Idean. 2009. *Rebels without Borders: Transnational Insurgencies in World Politics*. Ithaca: Cornell University Press.

Salik, Siddiq. 1977. *Witness to Surrender*. Karachi: Oxford University Press.

Sayigh, Yezid. 1989. "Struggle Within, Struggle Without: The Transformation of PLO Politics since 1982." *International Affairs* 65, no. 2: 247–271.

Schiff, Zeev, and Ehud Ya'ari. 1989. *Intifada: The Palestinian Uprising—Israel's Third Front*. New York: Simon and Schuster.

Schirmer, Jennifer G. 1998. *The Guatemalan Military Project: A Violence Called Democracy*. Philadelphia: University of Pennsylvania Press.

Schofield, Victoria. 1996. *Kashmir in the Crossfire*. New York: I. B. Tauris.

——. 2000. *Kashmir in Conflict: India, Pakistan and the Unfinished War*. New York: I.B. Tauris.

Schulze, Kirsten E. 2001. "Camp David and the *Al-Aqsa Intifada*: An Assessment of the State of the Israel-Palestinian Peace Process, July–December 2000." *Studies in Conflict and Terrorism* 24, no. 3: 215–233.

Scott, Franklin D. 1988. *Sweden: The Nation's History*. Carbondale: Southern Illinois University Press.

Sethi, Sunil. 1984. "The Great Divide." In *The Punjab Story*, edited by Amarjit Kaur et al. New Delhi: Roli Books International.

Seton-Watson, Hugh. 1977. *Nations and States: An Enquiry into the Origins of Nations and the Politics of Nationalism*. Boulder, CO: Westview Press.

Seymour, Lee JM. 2014. "Why Factions Switch Sides in Civil Wars: Rivalry, Patronage, and Realignment in Sudan." *International Security* 39, no. 2: 92–131.

Shani, Giorgio. 2008. *Sikh Nationalism and Identity in a Global Age*. New York: Routledge.

Shaw, Stanford J. and Ezel K. Shaw. 1977. *History of the Ottoman Empire and Modern Turkey:* Vol. 2. *Reform, Revolution, and Republic: The Rise of Modern Turkey, 1808–1975*. New York: Cambridge University Press.

Shelef, Nadav G. 2010. *Evolving Nationalism: Homeland, Identity, and Religion in Israel, 1925–2005*. Ithaca: Cornell University Press.

Shesterinina, Anastasia. 2016. "Collective Threat Framing and Mobilization in Civil War." *American Political Science Review* 110, no. 3: 411–427.

Shlaim, Avi. 2001. *The Iron Wall: Israel and the Arab World*. New York: W. W. Norton.

Simon, Jeffrey. 1993. "Czechoslvakia's 'Velvet Divorce,' Visegrad Cohesion, and European Fault Lines." McNair Paper 23, Institute for National Strategic Studies, National Defense University.

Singer, David J., Stuart Bremer, and John Stuckey. 1972. "Capability Distribution, Uncertainty, and Major Power War, 1820–1965." In *Peace, War, and Numbers*, edited by Bruce Russert. Beverly Hills: Sage. Dataset version 4.0 available from http://www.correlatesofwar.org/COW2%20Data/Capabilities/NMC_v4_0.csv.

Singh, Birinder P. 2002. *Violence as Political Discourse*. Shimla: Indian Institute of Advanced Study.

Singh, Gurharpal. 1987. "Understanding the 'Punjab Problem.'" *Asian Survey* 27, no. 12: 1268–1277.

Singh, Khushwant. 1984. "Genesis of the Hindu-Sikh Divide." In *The Punjab Story*, edited by Amarjit Kaur et al. New Delhi: Roli Books.

Singh, Tavleen. 1995. *Kashmir: A Tragedy of Errors*. New Delhi: Viking.

Siroky, David S. 2009. "Secession and Survival: Nations, States, and Violent Conflict." Ph.D. diss., Duke University.

Sisson, Richard, and Leo. E. Rose. 1990. *War and Secession: Pakistan, India, and the Creation of Bangladesh*. Berkeley: University of California Press.

Slater, Jerome. 2001. "What Went Wrong? The Collapse of the Israeli-Palestinian Peace Process." *Political Science Quarterly* 116, no. 2: 171–199.

Smith, Anthony D. 1986. *The Ethnic Origins of Nations*. Cambridge: Blackwell.

Smith, Lahra. 2013. *Making Citizens in Africa: Ethnicity, Gender, and National Identity in Ethiopia*. New York: Cambridge University Press.

Snyder, Jack, and Karen Ballentine. 1996. "Nationalism and the Marketplace of Ideas." *International Security* 21, no. 2: 5–40.

Sohrabi, Nader. 2011. *Revolution and Constitutionalism in the Ottoman Empire and Iran*. New York: Cambridge University Press.

Somakian, Manoug J. 1995. *Empires in Conflict: Armenia and the Great Powers, 1895–1920*. London: Tauris.

Sorens, Jason. 2008. "Regionalists against Secession: The Political Economy of Territory in Advanced Democracies." *Nationalism and Ethnic Politics* 14 no. 3: 325–360.

——. 2012. *Secessionism: Identity, Interest, and Strategy*. Montreal: McGill University Press.

Spruyt, Hendrik. 2005. *Ending Empire: Contested Sovereignty and Territorial Partition*. Ithaca: Cornell University Press.

Staniland, Paul. 2012. "States, Insurgents, and Wartime Political Orders." *Perspectives on Politics* 10, no. 2: 243–264.

———. 2014. *Networks of Rebellion: Explaining Insurgent Cohesion and Collapse*. Ithaca: Cornell University Press.

Suny, Ronald G. 2011. "Writing Genocide: The Fate of the Ottoman Armenians." In *A Question of Genocide: Armenians and Turks at the End of the Ottoman Empire*, edited by Ronald G. Suny, Fatma M. Göçek, and Norman M. Naimark. Oxford: Oxford University Press.

———. 2015. *"They Can Live in the Desert but Nowhere Else": A History of the Armenian Genocide*. Princeton: Princeton University Press.

Swami, Praveen. 2004. "Failed Threats and Flawed Fences: India's Military Responses to Pakistan's Proxy War." *India Review* 3, no. 2: 147–170.

———. 2007. *India, Pakistan, and the Secret Jihad*. New York: Routledge.

Talbot, Ian. 2009. *Pakistan: A Modern History*. New York: Palgrave Macmillan.

———. 2010. "Pakistan and Sikh Nationalism: State Policy and Private Perceptions." *Sikh Formations: Religion, Culture, Theory* 6, no. 1: 63–76.

Tanham, George K. 1992. "Indian Strategic Thought: An Interpretive Essay." RAND Corporation.

Tekle, Amare. 1994. "The Basis of Eritrean-Ethiopian Cooperation." In *Eritrea and Ethiopia: From Conflict to Cooperation*, edited by Amare Tekle. Lawrenceville, NJ: Red Sea Press.

Thomas, Baylis. 2011. *The Dark Side of Zionism: Israel's Quest for Security through Dominance*. New York: Rowman & Littlefield.

Thomas, R.G.C. 1986. *Indian Security Policy*. Princeton: Princeton University Press.

Tilly, Charles. 1985. "War Making and State Making as Organized Crime." In *Bringing the State Back In*, edited by Peter B. Evans, Dietrich Rueschemeyer, and Theda Skocpol. Cambridge: Cambridge University Press.

———. 1992. *Coercion, Capital, and European States, AD 990–1992*. Malden, MA: Blackwell.

Toft, Monica D. 2002–3. "Indivisible Territory, Geographic Concentration, and Ethnic War." *Security Studies* 12, no. 2: 82–119.

———. 2003. *The Geography of Ethnic Violence: Identity, Interests, and the Indivisibility of Territory*. Princeton: Princeton University Press.

Turfan, M. Naim. 2000. *Rise of the Young Turks: Politics, the Military and Ottoman Collapse*. New York: I. B. Tauris.

Ulč, Otto. 1996. "Czechoslovakia's Velvet Divorce." *East European Quarterly* 20, no. 3: 331–352.

Ünal, Hasan. 1996. "Young Turk Assessments of International Politics." *Middle Eastern Studies* 32, no. 2: 30–44.

Üngör, Uğur U. 2011. *The Making of Modern Turkey: Nation and State in Eastern Anatolia, 1913–1950*. Oxford: Oxford University Press.

Upadhyay, Archana. 2009. *India's Fragile Borderlands: The Dynamics of Terrorism in North East India*. New York: I. B. Tauris.

Valentino, Benjamin A. 2004. *Final Solutions: Mass Killing and Genocide in the 20th Century*. Ithaca: Cornell University Press.

Van Evera, Stephen. 1994. "Hypotheses on Nationalism and War." *International Security* 18, no. 4: 5–39.

———. 1997. *Guide to Methods for Students of Political Science*. Ithaca: Cornell University Press.

VanSledright, Bruce. 2008. "Narratives of Nation-State, Historical Knowledge, and School History Education." *Review of Research in Education* 32: 109–146.

Varshney, Ashutosh. 2002. *Ethnic Conflict and Civic Life: Hindus and Muslims in India*. New Haven: Yale University Press.

Vasquez, John A. 1993. *The War Puzzle*. New York: Cambridge University Press.

Vasquez, John A., and Marie T. Henehan. 2001. "Territorial Disputes and the Probability of War." *Journal of Peace Research* 38, no. 2: 123–138.

Wallace, Paul. 1986. "The Sikhs as a 'Minority' in a Sikh Majority State in India." *Asian Survey* 26, no. 3: 363–377.

Walt, Stephen M. 1987. *The Origins of Alliances*. Ithaca: Cornell University Press.

Walter, Barbara F. 1997. "The Critical Barrier to Civil War Settlement." *International Organization* 51, no. 3: 335–364.

——. 2009. *Reputation and Civil War: Why Separatist Conflicts Are So Violent*. Cambridge: Cambridge University Press.

Waltz, Kenneth N. 1979. *Theory of International Politics*. Boston: McGraw-Hill.

Wang, Zheng. 2008. "National Humiliation, History Education, and the Politics of Historical Memory: Patriotic Education Campaign in China." *International Studies Quarterly* 52, no. 4: 783–806.

Weber, Eugen. 1976. *Peasants into Frenchmen: The Modernization of Rural France, 1870–1914*. Stanford: Stanford University Press.

Weiner, Myron. 1971. "The Macedonian Syndrome: An Historical Model of International Relations and Political Development." *World Politics* 23, no. 4: 665–683.

Weingast, Barry R. 1995. "Constructing Trust: The Political and Economic Roots of Ethnic and Regional Conflict." Unpublished manuscript, Stanford University.

Weinstein, Jeremy M. 2007. *Inside Rebellion: The Politics of Insurgent Violence*. Cambridge: Cambridge University Press.

Wendt, Alexander. 1992. "Anarchy Is What States Make of It: The Social Construction of Power Politics." *International Organization* 46, no. 2: 391–425.

——. 1999. *Social Theory of International Politics*. Cambridge: Cambridge University Press.

Wheeler, Richard S. 1976. "Pakistan in 1975: The Hydra of Opposition." *Asian Survey* 16, no. 2: 111–118.

Widmalm, Sten. 1997. "Democracy and Violent Separatism in India: Kashmir in a Comparative Perspective." Ph.D. diss., Uppsala University.

Wilkinson, Steven I. 2006. *Votes and Violence: Electoral Competition and Ethnic Riots in India*. Cambridge: Cambridge University Press.

——. 2015. *Army and Nation: The Military and Indian Democracy since Independence*. Cambridge, MA: Harvard University Press.

Williams, L. F. Rushbrook. 1972. *The East Pakistan Tragedy*. London: Tom Stacey.

Wimmer, Andreas. 2002. *Nationalist Exclusion and Ethnic Conflict: Shadows of Modernity*. Cambridge: Cambridge University Press.

——. 2012. *Waves of War: Nationalism, State Formation, and Ethnic Exclusion in the Modern World*. New York: Cambridge University Press.

Wimmer, Andreas, Lars-Erik Cederman, and Brian Min. 2009. "Ethnic Politics and Armed Conflict: A Configurational Analysis of a New Global Dataset." *American Sociological Review* 74, no. 2: 316–337.

Wolchik, Sharon L. 1995. "The Politics of Transition and the Break-Up of Czecho-slovakia." In *The End of Czechoslovakia*, edited by Jiří Musil. Budapest: Central European University Press.

Wolpert, Stanley. 1993. *Zulfi Bhutto of Pakistan: His Life and Times*. New York: Oxford University Press.

Wood, John R. 1981. "Secession: A Comparative Analytical Framework." *Canadian Journal of Political Science* 14, no. 1: 107–134.

Yarhi-Milo, Keren. 2014. *Knowing the Adversary: Leaders, Intelligence, and Assessment of Intentions in International Relations*. Princeton: Princeton University Press.

Young, Robert A. 1994. "How do Peaceful Secessions Happen?" *Canadian Journal of Political Science* 27, no. 4: 773–792.

Younis, Mona N. 2000. *Liberation and Democratization: The South African and Pales-tinian National Movements*. Minneapolis: University of Minnesota Press.

Zegeye, Abebe, and Melakou Tegegn. 2007. "The Ethiopia-Eritrea Conflict: A Crit-ical Observation." Occasional Paper 54, Institute for Global Dialogue.

Zürcher, Erik J. 1984. *The Unionist Factor: The Role of the Committee of Union and Prog-ress in the Turkish National Movement 1905–1926*. Leiden, Netherlands: E. J. Brill.

Index

Page numbers in italics refer to figures and tables.

CPSIA information can be obtained
at www.ICGtesting.com
Printed in the USA
BVOW09*0130061017
496686BV00002B/4/P